Social and educational research in action:
a book of readings

Edited by
M. J. Wilson
at the Open University

Published by
Longman in association with
The Open University Press

Longman Group Limited
Longman House
Burnt Mill, Harlow
Essex CM20 2JE, England
Associated companies throughout the world

*Published in the United States of America
by Longman Inc., New York*

First published 1979
Second impression 1983
Third impression 1986

Library of British Cataloging in Publication Data

Social and educational research in action.
  1. Social science research – Addresses, essays,
  lecturers
  300'7'2   H62   78–40770

  ISBN 0–582–29004–X

Produced by Longman Group (FE) Ltd
Printed in Hong Kong

Contents

Section 4 Data collection and codification

Section 5 Data analysis

Acknowledgements

This reader has been prepared in connection with the Open University course *Research Methods in Education and the Social Sciences*. Many members of the course team, both from the Open University and from other universities, have suggested articles for inclusion in this book, only some of which I have been able to use here because of shortage of space. To all my colleagues I owe thanks for their help, much of which has come from our discussions during the preparation of the course which have done a great deal to improve my knowledge of the social sciences. I am particularly grateful to the following for assistance: John Bynner, Peter Coxhead, Martin Bulmer, Albert Pilliner, Martin Hammersley, Paul Atkinson, Jeff Evans, Fred Lockwood, A. N. Oppenheim, Desmond Nuttall, Jim Davis, Bob Peacock, Cathie Marsh, and Keith Stribley.

My thanks to Martin Ferns of the Open University for help in editing the articles, to Elizabeth Joseph who has borne the burden of typing my manuscripts, and to Glen McDougall for valuable advice throughout the preparation of this book.

Michael Wilson
Faculty of Social Sciences
The Open University

article 'The Fate of Idealism in Medical School' from *American Sociological Review* Vol 23, February 1958, pp. 50–56; the author, Mr. W. Baldamus for his unpublished discussion paper *Alienation, Anomie and Industrial Accidents*; Basic Books Inc., for 'Self and Identity in the Context of Deviance: The Case of Criminal Abortion' by Donald W. Ball, in *Theoretical Perspectives on Deviance,* edited by Robert A. Scott and Jack D. Douglas © 1972 by Robert A. Scott and Jack D. Douglas, Basic Books Inc., Publishers, New York; David and Charles Ltd., for an extract from 'National Wealth and Infant Mortality' from *Patterns in Human Geography* by D. Smith; the author, Mr. B. Hedges for his unpublished paper *Sampling Minority Groups;* Heinemann Educational Books Ltd., for the article 'An Index of Educational Deprivation' by A. Little and C. Mabey from *Social Indicators and Social Policy* edited by A. Shonfield and S. Shaw; Her Majesty's Stationery Office for an extract from *Children and their Primary Schools* pp. 50–68 Vol 1, a report of the Central Advisory Council for Education, from *Educational Priority Areas* pp. vii–xi, 3–30 Vol 1 edited by A. H. Halsey, reproduced with the permission of the Controller of Her Majesty's Stationery Office; Manchester University Press and the author, Mr. R. Nash for the article 'Pupils' Expectations for their Teachers' in *Research in Education* No. 12; New Science Publications for an extract from the article 'What is a Bad School' by H. Acland in *New Society* September 9th, 1971, and the article 'Does Parent Involvement Matter?' by H. Acland in *New Society* September 16th, 1971, first appeared in New Society, London, the weekly review of the Social Sciences; The Open University for an unpublished paper *The Importance of Politics* by F. Castles and R. D. McKinlay; Routledge and Kegan Paul Ltd., for the article 'Problems of Sociological Fieldwork: a review of the methodology of Hightown Grammar' by C. Lacey from *The Organisation and Impact of Social Research* edited by M. Shipman; Routledge and Kegan Paul Ltd., and Humanities Press Inc., for 'Some Sociological Perspectives on Plowden' by B. Bernstein and B. Davies for *Perspectives on Plowden* edited by R. Peters, and 'Justice and the Comprehensive Idea' from *Social Class and the Comprehensive School* by J. Ford.

General introduction

The purpose of this book is to show the social sciences in the process of contributing to our knowledge of significant social problems. The social sciences in action have a variety of contributions to make since they are capable of answering very limited questions fairly exactly or broad questions rather inexactly. If the general reader wishes to know, for example, how much faith he can put on the latest opinion poll that the Conservatives lead Labour by 5 percentage points, the answer is straightforward – he can have little faith in its accuracy because the sampling error will be nearly as big as the difference between the parties.

If, however, you want to know what policy reforms will achieve absolute equality of educational opportunity then our answers become disconcertingly tentative and hedged about with qualifications. The truth is that most social science lacks the successful predictive power of the natural sciences because we do not have theories capable of explaining social events with a small margin of error.

What social science can do, at the least, is clarify the relations between social means and social ends; between policy proposals and policy aims. This is more of a virtue than at first might appear since to say what will *not* work or what will have undesirable and unintended effects is a large addition to social knowledge. Section 1 of this reader contains extracts of the debate which followed the report of the Plowden Committee and the results of the policies which it recommended. You will see that the debate revolves around the means which will attain the goal of equal educational opportunity for our children.

The first benefit of the Plowden research is one that is easily overlooked. It identified the problem of the low attainment and failure to reach potential of children from poor homes. Social science has largely taken over the definition of social problems, so much so that Sir Keith Joseph when Secretary of State in the Department of Health and Social Security could use the language of sociology in his famous speech on the 'Cycle of deprivation' or the continuation of poverty in an affluent society. It is social science which now tells us how to define a social problem.

A second benefit of the Plowden research illustrates how social science refines our understanding of social processes by testing policies. A test of a policy which seeks to change the condition or state of a group (such as educationally deprived children) is also a test of the theory or explanation which underlies that policy and which tries to account for the observed condition of a group. In the Plowden case, the policy of positive discrimination consisted of identifying the schools in which low-achieving children were concentrated and then putting extra educational resources into those schools so as to raise performance levels. This policy has been shown, by research, not to work; or not to work very effectively. The failure to compensate educationally handicapped children by purely educational means forces social science to rethink its explanations and to attempt new solutions to problems. The readings in Section 1 show how far sociology has gone in refining the problems of under-achievement at school.

The title of this book – *Research in Action* – has a double significance. The first aspect of the research reports chosen for this reader is that they should point to the connection between social research and social policy. The most clear-cut example of this is the Plowden case study in Section 1. The Ford and Lacey readings have strong implications for schooling in comprehensive schools, the Little and Mabey reading in Section 4 demonstrates the problems and success of translating a definite policy objective into social practice. Equally interesting are the Baldamus and Castles readings, although they are on the face of it much further away from social policy than the readings cited above. However, they have a feature in common; they both identify an hitherto unknown problem and lay the groundwork for work which might well result in recommending political policies in the future. This is especially true of Baldamus since the enormous rise in industrial accidents from the early 1960s on (the new level has been sustained in the 1970s) was noted at the time by government circles but dismissed as relatively unimportant.

The second aspect of the research reports is that they are meant to show social scientists at work. The activities which go under the rubric of 'social science research' are very varied. They range from the sustained and cumulative attack on a series of related problems (as in the Plowden example) to careful methodological exploration of technical problems in the conduct of research, e.g. the Hedges article on the sampling of minority groups. Methodological studies are very valuable to other social scientists and thus indirectly to the sort of research which attracts public attention.

The division of the book into sections corresponds to the division of research into phases of defining the research problem and exploring hypotheses; the design of research; the collection of data and its codification; and the analysis of data. Although these phases can be recognised, in principle, for a lot of social science research it must be borne in mind that the authors whose work is reprinted here were originally writing for other purposes rather than to illustrate a book on social research methods. Thus, most of the articles cover more than one phase of research, some like Castles' and McKinlay's cover all the phases noted above. The main points about research methods which the sections illustrate are as follows:

Section 1: *The Plowden case study* is mainly concerned with the *evaluation* of a body of research. Evaluation is the attempt to judge the implications of research, having regard to the various findings and the methods which were used to reach them and the conclusions which authors have drawn from their own work. The Plowden case study also serves the purpose of pointing up the dialectic of social change and social research and how the two inform each other continuously.

Section 2: *Formulating the problem* is mainly concerned with the differences in the way in which a social scientist will define a research problem and how the lay world's conception of what is a problem is unrefined by social science standards and usually not susceptible to systematic research. This phase of research can be very exploratory (Baldamus) or an attempt to formalise incoherent propositions (as in the Ford reading) so that research can proceed on a sound basis.

Section 3: *The design of research* covers issues of the selection of particular methods for problems in such a way that the interpretation of the empirical results of the research activity should be as clear-cut as possible. The four readings represented here show the importance of design issues in the evaluation of research reports, partly by their numbers but mainly because they represent different traditions of methods; the experimental (Baumrind and Milgram), the survey (Hedges), and the ethnographic (Ball and Lacey). There are common issues of the methodology of design cutting across the research traditions; these concern the answers to such questions as: Is another interpretation of the author's results equally plausible? Can these findings be replicated by another investigator?

Section 4: *Data collection and codification* illustrates the choices which researchers make when, having defined their research problem and chosen a research design, they have to enter the field to collect data. The choice of methods of data collection is wide but only two are shown here: observation (Nash) and the use of survey questionnaires and administrative records (Little and Mabey). The use of unstructured interviewing is also illustrated by Becker and Geer in Section 5 and a form of participant observation by Ball in Section 3.

Section 5: *Data analysis.* The form of analysis depends both on the nature of the data which have been collected (e.g. field notes in Becker and Geer's case, and official statistics which stem from a variant of the survey in Castles' case) and the sort of conclusions which the author wishes to draw. This may be the test of an hypothesis in the classical way (Castles and McKinlay) or the interpretation of extensive interview notes as in Becker and Geer. In both cases there are rules to be observed before we are able to say that the conclusions follow from the analysis, although the rules for the testing of hypotheses which are quantitatively tested are different from the rules which cover the interpretation of qualitative fieldwork.

The Open University's approach to a course on social research methods has been to recognise the diversity of traditions and methods which can be found in the social sciences. We see three traditions which are represented in this book (as well as in the related Open University course) and we have chosen the readings so as to reveal this diversity. The Survey (e.g. the Plowden National Survey in Section 1) which uses a fixed schedule of standard questions over a relatively large sample of respondents has a strongly developed methodology in the social science literature. Its chief advantages are its ability to use representative samples for research and its usefulness for quantitative analysis which allows precise hypotheses to be tested or models to be built in which the connections between variables may have numerical estimates put upon them. The Survey seems to offer us a way of building fairly precise models of the social world, but it has disadvantages too. One is that it is difficult to determine cause and effect in survey analysis because the information about the variables is collected at the same point in time. We need to know what variable is prior in time to other variables before we can assign causes and effects, although the idea of cause is more demanding than temporal priority.

The experiment directly manipulates causes or experimental treatments and can thus determine cause and effect under laboratory conditions. The problems of the experiment are that it is difficult to translate findings from laboratory conditions to the real world where many more variables than the few allowed to operate in a controlled experiment will also influence the effect under study.

The Survey is more 'realistic' than the experiment in generalising findings to the world of multiple causes (the social world); on the other hand, the experiment is less prone to certain errors when we make causal inferences.

The third tradition or style of research methods is the most internally diverse and it is also the one which is most difficult to find a name for. This is the 'interpretive' style of research which uses more informal methods such as participant observation or unstructured interviews (not conducted according to a fixed schedule of questions). Its origins lie in social anthropology where the anthropologist would use a variety of observational methods or naturalistic interviews to collect his or her data. The early aim of this style in anthropology was the careful description of self-contained cultures, and this naturalistic method has been used to study shop-floor workers, street gangs, medical students, as well as many others. We have chosen to portray one of the interpretive methods in research in this course – the ethnographic method. Ball's observation of an abortion clinic is the most sustained example in this book of this style of research.

It is often charged against the ethnographic method that it lacks the replicability of other social science research, since the use of the method is rather subjective and a complete reporting of methods is usually impossible so that differences between one investigation and another of the same phenomena could be attributable either to a real difference or to some difference in the methods of study which cannot be documented. This charge is often exaggerated, but none the less the persistence and even growth of this method in modern social science research shows that it has strong advantages which the other two styles lack. The first of these advantages is that in skilled hands ethnographic research is less reactive than surveys and certainly than experiments. Reactivity is the phenomenon that the study of social phenomena can change the behaviour being studied, so that the results of research may be an artefact rather than the 'real thing'. The second advantage is that this method is naturalistic in form. It lends itself to describing the world as the social actors in it see it themselves. Since any investigation of individuals is a social act, a highly structured method of data collection such as the structured interview runs the risk of misunderstanding the meaning or actors' words or the significance of what they do. Careful, unobtrusive, observation (as with Ball) allows the context of action in real settings to be captured better than by answers to survey questions.

Each style represents a trade-off between the advantages it has and the penalties of its weaknesses. Until methods are invented which alter this calculus we can expect to see the persistence of several styles of research in social science for the foreseeable future.

Some readings in this reader are preceded by a preface which supplies the context of related research to that reported in the reading. This is done because the substance of the investigation needs to be understood before a judgement can be made on the worth of the results and the methods employed. The introductions also direct the reader to the style of methods which a particular author uses and point out the special advantages and losses which that author seems to have incurred in the choice of methods of investigation.

Section 1

Plowden Commission on English primary education

Preface to Section 1

The Plowden Committee was appointed in 1964 'to consider primary education in all its aspects, and the transition to secondary education' (Plowden 1967, Vol. I, p. i). The report in 1967 argued for, among other less important recommendations, the concepts of positive discrimination in favour of disadvantaged children, of community schools, and of Educational Priority schools. Positive discrimination meant that extra resources should go to raise the educational provision of the low-achieving child who was found disproportionately in Educational Priority Areas where poor housing was allied to low social class and a general disregard of education and the opportunities which it could bring. The idea of Educational Priority Areas rapidly became a euphemism for run-down neighbourhoods with high proportions of immigrants or poor whites, often (but not exclusively) in the decaying housing of the inner cities.

The Plowden formula for remedial action appeared to rest on the research results which the Committee commissioned at the beginning of its investigations. The most important piece of research which Plowden used was the National Survey of Primary School Children (Plowden 1967, Vol. 2, App. 3–7). The results of this survey were thought to enable the Committee to realise its investigative objective: 'to disentangle some of the principal influences that shape the educational opportunities of children and to assess and compare their importance' (Plowden 1967, Vol. 1, Ch. 5, para. 131). But whether the National Survey did give unequivocal answers to this question and, leaving this aspect aside of evaluating a major and difficult research report, whether a clear and justifiable link between 'facts' and policy recommendations was made by Plowden has been the subject of much debate.

Plowden worked with a multiple-cause theory of educational attainment in which the aspirations of parents, the educational level of parents, the economic and cultural resources of the home, and the quality and organisation of the school combined in some manner to 'produce' the effect of a particular level of attainment by pupils. The debate on the evaluation of the National Survey conclusions revolves around two central issues:

1. Do the results of the Survey allow us to 'weigh', i.e. to assess and compare, the relative strengths of the causes producing pupils' attainments? How are the multiple causes organised in a model which explains differences in attainments?

2. How is the explanation represented by the National Survey's causal model to be translated into policy changes? On policy recommendations, we can specifically ask if the recommendation of Educational Priority schools will raise the level of the poorest schools in the country to that of the best, as Plowden wished? We should also ask that even if Educational Priority works as a policy will it then equalise educational opportunity for all children? What do we mean by equality of educational opportunity anyway?

These two sets of questions are related. One cannot simply evaluate research results by pointing to the 'facts' which are self-evident. Interpretation of results involves questions of judgement as much as purely technical questions to do with the use of statistical analysis, which where advanced techniques are used are debatable in any event.

Let us first consider the results of the National Survey in the light of the first set of questions. The Survey was based on a sample of 1,349 children in 173 primary schools in England. The sample was selected so as to be representative of school size, of type of primary school, and of the range of individual pupil characteristics. The data were collected by individual interviews with each child's mother and by questionnaires directed to the schools to elicit information on school organisation and teachers' qualifications. The third element in the data-collection procedures was the administering, in the classroom, of a reading comprehension test to all pupils in the sample. The child's reading comprehension score, together with teachers' rankings of the child in terms of his or her ability relative to others in the class, become the dependent variable in the analysis. That is, a model was eventually constructed which related the causes (or independent variables) to an effect – measured by the child's score. The analysis rested, then, on accounting for differences between children's scores on this measure of attainment in terms of the causal model.

There were 120 variables in the analysis. This complexity was reduced by grouping the variables into sets and a model was constructed which placed these sets of variables in a causal order (a causal model). A technique known as multiple regression analysis was used to estimate the 'weight' which should be placed on each causal arrow in the model. A simplified version of the model showing the major variable groups and their relative influences or weight is given on p. 4. The definitions of the variable-groups (denoted by the circles in the diagram) can only be given in terms of the specific indicators which make up the variable-groups. 'Parents' education' is measured by the educational level achieved by the father and mother. 'Other family background variables' includes the father's social class position. 'State of school' includes such variables as school organisation and staffing. This group also included assessments of the school's quality, such as 'average teaching competence', for example. This judgement was made by the schools' inspectors but it can hardly be said to be objective in the same way that school staffing ratios are.

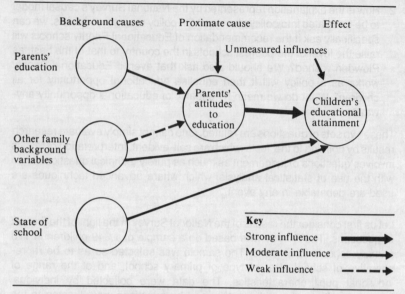

Plowden causal model showing major influences on children's educational attainment. (*Source*: adapted from Bynner 1978)

'Parental attitudes to education' is composed of variables such as 'parents' aspirations' (for the child), 'responsibility and initiative taken by parents over the child's education', 'paternal interest and support', and 'literacy of the home' – this last was measured by the number of books in the home at the interview. To interpret a causal model like this we must know something of the way in which it is constructed. First of all, the grouping of the variables into sets is done by a technique of factor analysis which uses the intercorrelations between individual variables. In the Plowden case this was done for parental attitudes to education but not for the other groups. The implication of this technique's results is that (for example) 'parental interest and support' is strongly related to 'literacy of the home' and both can be seen as indicators or manifestations of an underlying factor, thus justifying their being grouped together.

Secondly, the ordering of the variables into background causes, proximate or immediate causes, is done on the basis of the meaning of the variables themselves. There is no exact technique for arranging the order of the causes in such a model; it rests on what seems reasonable having regard to the nature of the variables. Clearly, the level of education achieved by the parents will be determined before they marry and have children (usually) and thus it is possible that 'parents' education' *may* be a cause of 'parents' attitudes to their child's education' or of their 'child's educational attainment', but the reverse order is not plausible. One variable *may* be the cause of another, we reason. To show that it is the case we have to show that the two variables covary systematically. That is, the values of the variables are correlated. As one variable rises in value over a sample, the other variable also tends to rise in value (or to fall, as long as the covariation is systematic). This alone is not sufficient since it may be the effect of a third variable which is causing one variable to fluctuate. This problem is overcome, in multiple regression analysis, by finding the correlation holding between two variables *when the effect of all other variables is held constant.*

Correlation can be expressed as the proportion of the variance (or more loosely, the variability of a set of scores, such as attainment scores, around their mean) which is accounted for or explained by another variable. Taking the Plowden model, the variable whose variance is to be explained is the dependent variable of child's attainment. We have *three* groups of variables which can independently make a contribution to explaining the variance of child's attainment – hence the term *multiple*, rather than simple, regression.

These three groups of variables represent a further simplification of the causal model depicted in the diagram. Family background variables and parents' education are combined to give a variable group of home circumstances (note that both of these variable groups are in the same causal position in the diagram). The other two variable groups are state of school and parents' attitudes to education. When the variance in the attainment scores (based on the averages for each school – in a between-schools analysis or comparison) was divided by the multiple regression analysis among the three sets of causes or variable groups, the results were:

Home Circumstances accounted for 20 per cent of the variance in Attainment.
State of School accounted for 17 per cent of the variance in Attainment.
Parental Attitudes accounted for 28 per cent of the variance in Attainment.
Variance in Attainment which was unexplained was 35 per cent.
(*Source*: Plowden 1967, Vol. 1, Table 1, p. 33)

Plowden concluded two things from these results; (*a*) Parental attitudes are more important as a determinant of attainment than is child's home circumstances which, in turn, is more important than the variables of state of school.*
(*b*) Parental attitudes are a more immediate cause of differences in attainment and, moreover, they are relatively autonomous for 75 per cent of the variance in parental attitudes was unexplained by home circumstances (including father's social class and parents' education). Therefore, argued the Plowden Report, to improve school attainment we should operate directly on parental attitudes. We could, for example, try directly to raise the levels of knowledge and interest by parents in the school and their children's work by improved teacher-parent contact and cooperation.

Now this is an attractive formula because it is cheap and because it implies that educational disadvantage may be remedied by purely educational means. If poor attainment were a product of poverty and low social class then rather more radical alterations to society are called for if one wishes to achieve

---

*This same order of importance for the variable groups was found when the analysis was conducted for the whole sample of pupils – the within-schools analysis.

the aim that equality of opportunity be established. This is one of the points on which Bernstein and Davies (Reading No. 4) attack the Plowden Report – on the separation as autonomous variables of social class and parental attitudes. Why, they ask, define attitudes as independently variable of social class? A narrow view of social class – classified by occupation – is misleading since it neglects the cultural aspect of class.

Bernstein and Davies give as a telling example of their criticism the way in which the father's interest and support for the child's career in primary school rises steadily through the social class order. They point out that the father's role is defined by the culture of specific classes; in the lower social classes, fathers are not expected to play a part in the upbringing of young children. Thus, what is seen as a matter of parental attitudes specific to particular families may simply be yet another facet of the pervasive phenomena of class differences, which Plowden obscures by firstly relying on a rather crude classification of class (that of the Registrar-General's) and secondly, by arbitrarily grouping parental attitudes separately from social class.

Halsey (in Reading No. 5) also casts doubt on the prescription that low educational achievement may be remedied by educational compensation in priority areas. There is a paradox in Plowden's recommendations for direct educational compensation since as Halsey puts it, their '. . . analysis of low educational standards in EPAs points to causes outside the school in the neighbourhood structure of life and therefore calls for a widely based pro-gramme of social reform alongside positive discrimination in education' (Halsey 1972b). Plowden limited itself (unsurprisingly) to educational recom-mendations, even though the objective criteria which they list for the designation of priority areas and schools contained six out of eight criteria which are not based on the schools or the pupils' school performance (Plowden 1967, Vol. 1, para. 153). Halsey (Reading No. 5) in his review of American experience of compensatory education concludes that their experience (which is more extensive both in finance and time than the British one) is similar to Plowden's: in attempting to solve the educational problem, the Americans 'were forced to go further and further outside the educational system, as the ramifications of the initial problem were uncovered' (Halsey 1972c, p. 88).

The problem identified by Plowden in the British context and by Coleman in the United States (Coleman 1966) as a significant proportion of children underachieving in school becomes a question of the correct diagnosis and the effective remedies to apply in the light of that diagnosis. Can we effectively compensate these children through the formal channels of schooling, or should we attempt to operate earlier in the causal chain by attacking the poverty, both cultural and financial, of their families? If we decide on the latter then we need a theory of the causes of poverty which will allow us to choose the right weapons for the attack.

The debate about the remedies for low attainment at school is, then, also a debate about the reasons for the continuation of poverty in the now affluent West, with the recognition by both left and right in politics that poverty is both cultural and financial. To observers such as Sir Keith Joseph the continuation of poverty today can only be explained by the personal characteristics of the poor, of which low cultural resources are but one of their personal inadequacies. The remedy if one holds this theory is to upgrade family resources so that in the field of education, for example, the parents' capacity to raise their child's potential is increased.

The Educational Priority programme (directed by Halsey) tried compensation programmes in deprived areas, but with inconclusive results. We cannot tell if the lack of conclusive evidence in the action-research programmes is due to the unrigorous design of much of the research or to the fact that new educational programmes cannot compensate for the social and cultural handicaps of the homes of deprived children. Action research is a form of field experiment. These experiments required a firm knowledge of the starting point of the pupils and a measurable 'effect' such as reading comprehension so that the change in the attainment of the children which is due to the experimental treatment can be assessed. Furthermore, an experiment requires that other variables which might cause the effect are controlled so that only the effect due to the experimentally induced treatment is measured. It appears from Halsey (Reading No. 5) that these conditions could not be observed for a number of practical and political reasons.

The success of such programmes would be a confirmation of the cultural deprivation theory of poverty, at least in so far as it concerns educational attainment. American experience with direct educational compensation programmes has shown in some cases that measurable and sustained improvements in children's abilities can be produced, but the conditions seem to be that intensive work with the mothers is required and it needs sustaining over a long period (Halsey, Reading No. 5).

In contrast to the theory which holds that poverty is learnt in the form of personality characteristics which are transmitted from one generation to the next, an alternative theory is that poverty is simply the result of certain specific features created by the legal, political, and institutional structure of society. Poverty in this analysis is the direct result of single parents, the unemployed, the aged, or of large families – to give the major examples. The cure here is to supplement incomes of individuals in these categories. If that is done then the 'culture of poverty' will disappear, and the children of such parents will in time be indistinguishable in their average attainments from other children.

Halsey believes that a combination of the two sorts of policies, based as they are on the two theories, will be necessary if we are to achieve the social goal of equality of opportunity. He is sympathetic to Coleman's redefinition of equality of opportunity to mean equality of outcome so that children from lower-working-class families or from black groups are represented in the higher levels of education in strict proportion to their numbers in the population. The implications here are that the bias towards the children of the upper social classes acquiring a disproportionate number of the upper occupations will also disappear since education now largely determines future occupation. Such a society will be very different from the one which we have today.

The relationship between the Plowden analysis and Plowden's policy recommendations is shown to be a tenuous one in the light of this discussion and of the evidence from Britain and the USA which shows that direct educational compensation programmes have at best only a limited effect. But would the Plowden policy of Educational Priority have worked in its own terms? Would it have concentrated extra resources on the deprived children, in other words? Acland (Readings 2 and 3) thinks not for the simple reason that there are nearly as many low-achieving children to be found outside Educational Priority schools as there are inside them, and this is asserted on the basis of a reworking of Plowden's own National Survey. The policy, whether or not it would have achieved the effect for the children it touched, would be inefficient.

On balance, then, the Plowden Report and its recommendations (now over ten years old) are deficient. The deficiency is partly in the analysis but more strongly in the way in which the policy proposals are remarkably tame and ineffectual. However, the Plowden Report does have the great merit of starting a course of research which has helped greatly to clarify our understanding of poverty and its relationship to educational performance, and in so doing has made clearer the possible means which we need to employ if we wish to eradicate educational inequality.

References

Acland, H. (1971a) 'What is a bad school?', *New Society*, 9 Sept., pp. 450–53.
– (1971b) 'Does parent involvement matter', *New Society*, 16 Sept., pp. 507–10.
Halsey, A. H. (1972a) 'Preface' to *Educational Priority*, Vol. 1, London: HMSO.
– (1972b) *op. cit.*, Ch. 1.
– (1972c) *op. cit.*, Ch. 2.
Bernstein, B. and Davies, B. (1972) 'Some sociological comments on Plowden', in R. S. Peters (ed.) *Perspectives on Plowden*, London: Routledge & Kegan Paul.
Bynner, J. (1978) *The Evaluation of Research*, Block 1, Part 2, DE304 *Research Methods in Education and the Social Sciences*, The Open University.
Coleman, J. S. (1966) *Equality of Educational Opportunity*, Washington D. C. US Government Printing Office.
Plowden (1967) *Children and Their Primary Schools: A Report of the Central Advisory Council for Education (England)*, London: HMSO. Vol. 1, Report; Vol. 2, Appendices.

Educational priority areas

Plowden Report

131. [Earlier in the Report] we tried to disentangle some of the principal influences that shape the educational opportunities of children, and to assess and compare their importance. The task of abstracting them and measuring the impact made by each when 'all other things are equal' is the continuing concern of research workers. But policy makers and administrators must act in a world where other things never are equal; this, too, is the world in which the children grow up, where everything influences everything else, where nothing succeeds like success and nothing fails like failure. The outlook and aspirations of their own parents; the opportunities and handicaps of the neighbourhood in which they live; the skill of their teachers and the resources of the schools they go to; their genetic inheritance; and other factors still unmeasured or unknown surround the children with a seamless web of circumstance.

132. In a neighbourhood where the jobs people do and the status they hold owe little to their education it is natural for children as they grow older to regard school as a brief prelude to work rather than an avenue to future opportunities. Some of these neighbourhoods have for generations been starved of new schools, new houses and new investments of every kind. Everyone knows this; but for year after year priority has been given to the new towns and new suburbs, because if new schools do not keep pace with the new houses some children will be unable to go to school at all. The continually rising proportion of children staying on at school beyond the minimum age has led some authorities to build secondary schools and postpone the rebuilding of older primary schools. Not surprisingly, many teachers are unwilling to work in a neighbourhood where the schools are old, where housing of the sort they want is unobtainable, and where education does not attain the standards they expect for their own children. From some neighbourhoods, urban and rural, there has been a continuing outflow of the more successful young people. The loss of their enterprise and skill makes things worse for those left behind. Thus the vicious circle may turn from generation to generation and the schools play a central

From *Children and their Primary Schools: A Report of the Central Advisory Council for Education (England)*, London: HMSO, 1967, Ch. 5, pp. 50–68, paras. 131–77.

part in the process, both causing and suffering cumulative deprivation.

133. We have ourselves seen schools caught in such vicious circles and read accounts of many more. They are quite untypical of schools in the rest of the country. We noted the grim approaches; incessant traffic noise in narrow streets; parked vehicles hemming in the pavement; rubbish dumps on waste land nearby; the absence of green playing spaces on or near the school sites; tiny playgrounds; gaunt looking buildings; often poor decorative conditions inside; narrow passages; dark rooms; unheated and cramped cloakrooms; unroofed outside lavatories; tiny staff rooms; inadequate storage space with consequent restriction on teaching materials and therefore methods; inadequate space for movement and P.E.; meals in classrooms; art on desks; music only to the discomfort of others in an echoing building; non-soundproof partitions between classes; lack of smaller rooms for group work; lack of spare room for tuition of small groups; insufficient display space; attractive books kept unseen in cupboards for lack of space to lay them out; no privacy for parents waiting to see the head; sometimes the head and his secretary sharing the same room; and, sometimes all around, the ingrained grime of generations.

134. We heard from local education authorities of growing difficulty in replacing heads with successors of similar calibre. It is becoming particularly hard to find good heads of infant or deputy heads of junior schools. We are not surprised to hear of the rapid turnover of staff, of vacancies sometimes unfilled or filled with a succession of temporary and supply teachers of one kind or another. Probationary teachers are trained by heads to meet the needs of their schools but then pass on to others where strains are not so great. Many teachers able to do a decent job in an ordinary school are defeated by these conditions. Some become dispirited by long journeys to decaying buildings to see each morning children among whom some seem to have learned only how not to learn. Heads rely on the faithful, devoted and hard working regulars. There may be one or two in any school, or they may be as many as half the staff, who have so much to do in keeping the school running that they are sometimes too tired even to enjoy their own holidays.

135. We saw admission registers whose pages of new names with so many rapid crossings out told their own story of a migratory population. In one school 111 out of 150 pupils were recent newcomers. We heard heads explain, as they looked down the lines, that many of those who had gone were good pupils, while a high proportion of those who had been long in the school came from crowded, down-at-heel homes.

The educational needs of deprived areas

136. What these deprived areas need most are perfectly normal, good primary schools alive with experience from which children of all

kinds can benefit. What we say elsewhere about primary school work generally applies equally to these difficult areas. The best schools already there show that it is absurd to say, as one used to hear, 'it may be all very well in a nice suburb, but it won't work here'. But, of course, there are special and additional demands on teachers who work in deprived areas with deprived children. They meet special challenges. Teachers must be constantly aware that ideas, values and relationships within the school may conflict with those of the home, and that the world assumed by teachers and school books may be unreal to the children. There will have to be constant communication between parents and the schools if the aims of the schools are to be fully understood. The child from a really impoverished background may well have had a normal, satisfactory emotional life. What he often lacks is the opportunity to develop intellectual interests. This shows in his poor command of language. It is not, however, with vocabulary that teaching can begin. The primary school must first supply experiences and establish relationships which enable children to discriminate, to reason and to express themselves. Placing such children in the right stance for further learning is a very skilled operation. But those who have done remedial work will be aware of the astonishing rapidity of the progress which can be achieved, particularly in extending vocabulary, once children's curiosity is released. The thrust to learn seems to be latent in every child, at least within a very wide range of normality. But however good the opportunities, some children may not be able to take advantage of them. Failure may have taken away from them their urge to learn.

137. A teacher cannot and should not give the deep, personal love that each child needs from his parents. There are ways he can help:

(*a*) He can relieve children of responsibility without dominating them in a way which prevents them from developing independence. Deprived children may have been forced into premature responsibility. They are often given the care of younger children and are free to roam, to go to bed or to stay up, to eat when and where they can. This produces what is often a spurious maturity. Confidence can be encouraged by tasks which are fully within their capacity. A measure of irresponsibility has to be allowed for: it will pretty certainly come later, and in a less acceptable form, if not permitted at the proper time.

(*b*) A teacher can do much by listening and trying to understand the context of the questions the children ask. It will be much easier if he knows the child's family and the neighbourhood surrounding his home.

(*c*) Children in deprived neighbourhoods are often backward. There is a risk that an inexperienced teacher will think there is not time for anything but the three Rs if the child is not to be handicapped throughout his life. This is quite wrong. These children need time for play and imaginative and expressive work and may suffer later if they do not get it at school.

(*d*) Teachers need to use books which make sense to the children they teach. They will often have to search hard for material which is suitable for downtown children.

(*e*) Record-keeping is especially necessary for teachers in schools in deprived neighbourhoods. There is so much coming and going by families that a child's progress may depend very much on the amount and quality of information that can be sent with him from school to school.

Hope for the future

138. In our cities there are whole districts which have been scarcely touched by the advances made in more fortunate places. Yet such conditions have been overcome and striking progress has been achieved where sufficiently determined and comprehensive attack has been made on the problem. In the most deprived areas, one of H.M. Inspectors reported, 'Some heads approach magnificence, but they cannot do everything . . . The demands on them as welfare agents are never ending.' Many children with parents in the least skilled jobs do outstandingly well in school. The educational aspirations of parents and the support and encouragement given to children in some of the poorest neighbourhoods are impressive. Over half of the unskilled workers in our National Survey (Plowden Report, Vol. 2, App. 3, Table 26) want their children to be given homework to do after school hours; over half want their children to stay at school beyond the minimum leaving age (Table 27). One-third of them hoped their children would go to a grammar school or one with similar opportunities (Table 28). The educational aspirations of unskilled workers for their children have risen year by year. It has been stressed[1] to us that the range of ability in all social classes is so wide that there is a great reservoir of unrealised potential in families dependent on the least skilled and lowest paid work. A larger part of the housing programme than ever before is to be devoted to rebuilding and renewing obsolete and decaying neighbourhoods. The opportunity must be seized to rebuild the schools as well as the houses, and to see that both schools and houses serve families from every social class. It will be possible to make some progress in reducing the size of classes in primary schools in these areas as well as elsewhere. Colleges of education which have taken a special interest in deprived areas report that their students respond in an encouraging fashion to the challenge of working in these neighbourhoods. Most important of all, there is a growing awareness in the nation at large, greatly stimulated, we believe, by our predecessors' Reports, of the complex social handicaps afflicting such areas and the need for a more radical assault on their

problems. These are the strengths on which we can build. How can they be brought to bear?

139. We propose a nation-wide scheme for helping those schools and neighbourhoods in which children are most severely handicapped. This policy will have an influence over the whole educational system, and it colours all the subsequent recommendations in our Report. It must not be put into practice simply by robbing more fortunate areas of all the opportunities for progress to which they have been looking forward; it can only succeed if a larger share of the nation's resources is devoted to education. So far-reaching a set of proposals must be firmly rooted in educational grounds, yet the arguments for them inevitably extend beyond this field into many other branches of the nation's affairs. Before explaining these proposals we give a brief outline of the reasoning which led us to make them.

Educational assumptions and policies

140. Our study of these problems compelled us to consider the process of economic and social development and the contribution made to it by the schools. Industrial development in many respects is the motor of social progress. We recognise that there are limits to the resources that can be mobilised for education and the primary schools. But it does not necessarily follow, as many have assumed, that the fruits of economic growth, together with the present pattern of public services, will in time give every child increasing opportunities of contributing to the nation's progress. It does not follow that education, because its development depends in the long run on the growth of the economy, must therefore follow in its wake, rather than contribute to the promotion of growth. Nor does it follow that a 'fair' or 'efficient' distribution of educational resources is one that provides a reasonably equal supply of teachers, classrooms, and other essentials to each school child in each area. Nor does it follow that the government's responsibility for promoting progress within the limits permitted by these resources must be confined to encouraging development in the most capable areas, spreading word of their progress to others, and pressing on the rearguard of the laggard or less fortunate whenever opportunity permits. Though many of these assumptions are already being questioned or abandoned, our own proposals are unlikely to convince those who still accept them, and we must, therefore, challenge each in turn.

141. During the Second World War there was a considerable improvement in the living conditions which bear most directly upon children in deprived groups and areas. In spite of this there has not been any appreciable narrowing of the gap between the least well off and the rest of the population. This is most obvious among children, particularly those in large families. 'It is . . . clear that, on average, the

larger families in all classes, and also those containing adolescents and children, constitute the most vulnerable groups nutritionally'.[2,3] Signs of rickets have recently been reported again from the slums of Glasgow; mortality among children during the first year of life has fallen sharply since 1950, but the difference between social classes remains great.[4] Much the same goes for stillbirth rates which, in different social classes 'despite a dramatic wartime fall, were as far apart in 1950 as in 1939'. Meanwhile 'class differentials in perinatal mortality are as resistant to change as those of infant mortality. The results of the (Perinatal Mortality) Survey suggest, indeed, that the gap may be increasing rather than narrowing'.[5] The Milner Holland Committee's study of housing conditions in London covered a period in which this country probably achieved a faster rate of economic growth than it has ever experienced before, and an area in which conditions are generally better and improving faster than elsewhere. But it showed that progress has been most rapid in those parts of the town where conditions were already best. In less fortunate neighbourhoods there has been less improvement and in some respects an appreciable deterioration. Families with low incomes and several young children were among those who suffered most.[6]

142. If the fruits of growth are left to accumulate within the framework of present policies and provisions, there is no assurance that the living conditions which handicap educationally deprived children will automatically improve – still less that the gap between these conditions and those of more fortunate children will be narrowed.

143. The contribution made by education to economic development poses complicated questions, upon which systematic research has only recently begun, and we cannot present firm conclusions about it. Comparisons with other countries – all of them more recently industrialised than Britain but all now at a similar stage of economic development – suggest that we have not done enough to provide the educational background necessary to support an economy which needs fewer and fewer unskilled workers and increasing numbers of skilled and adaptable people. One example can be drawn from a pioneer piece of research in comparative educational achievements. This compares mathematical skills at several stages of secondary education.[7] It shows that in the early stages England was distinguished from other countries not by the average standard attained (which was closely similar to the average for the other countries compared) but by the scatter of its results. English children achieved more than their share of the best results, and more of the worst results. Our educational system, originally moulded by the impress of Victorian economic and social requirements, may not yet have been fully adapted to present needs. In the deprived areas with which this reading is concerned too many children leave school as soon as they are allowed to with no desire to carry their education further and without the knowledge to fit them for

a job more intellectually demanding than their father's or their grandfather's. Yet they face a future in which they must expect during their working life to have to change their job, to learn new skills, to adapt themselves to new economic conditions and to form new human relationships. They will suffer, and so will the economy; both needlessly. It should not be assumed that even the ablest children can surmount every handicap. They may suffer as much as any from adverse conditions.

144. If the schools are to play their part in resolving and forestalling these problems much of the action required must be taken at the secondary and higher stages of the system. But this action cannot be fully effective if it does not touch the primary schools. Recent research has shown how early in the lives of children the selective processes begin to operate.[8] There are primary schools from which scarcely any children ever take a secondary school course which leads them to 'O' level in GCE. Children of good potential ability enter them, but the doors to educational opportunity have already closed against them when their schooling has scarcely begun. Reforming zeal and expenditure directed to later stages of education will be wasted unless early handicaps can be reduced.

145. The schools unaided cannot provide all the opportunities their pupils deserve, or create the labour force this country needs. Industry, and the authorities responsible for housing, planning, employment and other services must also play their part. But, from the earliest stages of education, the schools enlarge or restrict the contribution their pupils can make to the life of the nation. Money spent on education is an investment which helps to determine the scope for future economic and social development.

146. Our argument thus far can be briefly summarised. As things are at the moment there is no reason why the educational handicaps of the most deprived children should disappear. Although standards will rise, inequalities will persist and the potential of many children will never be realised. The range of achievement amongst English children is wide, and the standards attained by the most and the least successful begin to diverge very early. Steps should be taken to improve the educational chances and the attainments of the least well placed, and to bring them up to the levels that prevail generally. This will call for a new distribution of educational resources.

The distribution of resources

147. The principle that certain local authorities (but not districts within local authorities) should receive special help from the rest of the community is already recognised. At the national level the government takes needs into account when distributing grants to local authorities for educational and other purposes. The basic grant consists of so much

per head of population plus so much for each child under fifteen years of age. The supplementary grants allow for:

the number of children under five;
the number of people over 65;
school children in excess of a prescribed proportion;
density;
sparsity;
declining population; and
Metropolitan Areas.

There is also a formula that increases the grant paid to authorities with lower rateable values and reduces it for wealthier ones. The same principle of district priorities applies to educational building programmes. The needs of districts with a growing population come first; the next buildings to be sanctioned must be for the purpose of making good the deficiencies of existing schools. This principle can also be seen at work in the distribution of teachers. Local education authorities with an exceptionally high proportion of immigrant children may apply for an addition to their quota of teachers.

148. Redistribution of resources within local authority areas has been less marked. 'Equality' has an appealing ring, 'discrimination' has not. It is simpler and easier, for example, to defend staff–pupil ratios that are roughly the same in each school than to explain why they should be better in some and to decide which are to be the favoured. Even so, more and more local authorities do discriminate. They look with a more generous eye on schools whose 'social need' is greatest, as reckoned by the free dinner list, by the proportion of children who do not speak English at home, or (which may be an even better guide) by the opinion of experienced teachers and administrators. These schools may be allowed an extra teacher or more non-teaching help, or a slightly bigger ration of 'consumable stocks'.

149. These are no more than a tentative beginning. The formulae for allocating grants are designed to equalise the financial resources of poorer and wealthier authorities. But equality is not enough. The formulae do not distinguish between the districts within authorities' areas in which children and schools are most severely handicapped. These districts need more spending on them, and government and local authorities between them must provide the funds. Permission is required before the money can be spent on what is most needed – additional teachers and better buildings. The authority's quota must be raised before extra teachers can be engaged, and additions to the building programme must be sanctioned by the Department of Education. Even if this happens the battle is not over. Some authorities whose need for teachers is great find it impossible to recruit for deprived schools the teachers to whom they are entitled. The vicious circle continues.

150. A study of the educational expenditure of 83 county boroughs has been made for us by Mr B. P. Davies[9] (see Plowden Report, Vol. 2, App. 14). He compared the way money was spent with the evidence about the needs of each borough. He found no link between the amount spent on primary schools and their pupils and the social character of the area they served. In general, deprived areas were neither more nor less likely than others to get a bigger share of the total expenditure. A large proportion of expenditure was devoted to the salaries of teachers, whose distribution is subject to quota rules, and to the provision of those essential services which give little scope for variation. Other services, on which an education authority has great scope for independent decision, often tended to have more spent on them in those boroughs where the needs appeared to be less urgent. There are signs of this in the expenditure on nursery schools, and (less clearly) on child guidance. The same applied to school meals where parental preferences exert an influence. More striking, perhaps, was the persistence of these patterns. The boroughs in which expenditure was generally low were much the same in 1960–61 as they were in 1950–51.

Educational priority areas

151. The many teachers who do so well in face of adversity cannot manage without cost to themselves. They carry the burdens of parents, probation officers and welfare officers on top of their classroom duties. It is time the nation came to their aid. The principle, already accepted, that special need calls for special help, should be given a new cutting edge. We ask for 'positive discrimination' in favour of such schools and the children in them, going well beyond an attempt to equalise resources. Schools in deprived areas should be given priority in many respects. The first step must be to raise the schools with low standards to the national average; the second, quite deliberately to make them better. The justification is that the homes and neighbourhoods from which many of their children come provide little support and stimulus for learning. The schools must supply a compensating environment. The attempts so far made within the educational system to do this have not been sufficiently generous or sustained, because the handicaps imposed by the environment have not been explicitly and sufficiently allowed for. They should be.

152. The proposition that good schools should make up for a poor environment is far from new. It derives from the notion that there should be equality of opportunity for all, but recognises that children in some districts will only get the same opportunity as those who live elsewhere if they have unequally generous treatment. It was accepted before the First World War that some children could not be effectively taught until they had been properly fed. Hence free meals were pro-

vided. Today their need is for enriched intellectual nourishment. Planned and positive discrimination in favour of deprived areas could bring about an advance in the education of children in the 1970s as great as the advance in their nutrition to which school meals and milk contributed so much.

153. Every authority where deprivation is found should be asked to adopt 'positive discrimination' within its own area, and to report from time to time on the progress made. Some authorities contain schools or even one school of this kind where deprivation is so serious that they need special help. Most of these schools and areas are already well known to teachers, administrators, local inspectors and H.M. Inspectors. Local knowledge will not be sufficient to justify decisions which are bound on occasion to be controversial. Objective criteria for the selection of 'educational priority schools and areas' will be needed to identify those schools which need special help and to determine how much assistance should be given by the government. Our National Survey showed the prime importance of parental attitudes, and it might be thought that a measure of these attitudes could be devised. But the data for the selection of priority schools and areas must be readily available, without additional surveys, and in any event the validity of answers given by parents with the education of their children at stake might fairly be questioned. The criteria required must identify those places where educational handicaps are reinforced by social handicaps. Some of the main criteria which could be used in an assessment of deprivation are given below. They are not placed in order of importance, nor is any formula suggested by which they should be combined. They may require further study. The criteria are:

(*a*) *Occupation*. The National Census can report on occupations within quite small areas, and, for particular schools, the data can be supplemented without too much difficulty. The analyses would show the proportions of unskilled and semi-skilled manual workers.

(*b*) *Size of Families*. The larger the family, the more likely are the children to be in poverty. Wages are no larger for a married man with young children than they are for a single man with none. Family size is still associated with social class, and men with four or more children tend to be amongst the lowest wage earners. Family size also correlates with the results of intelligence tests – the larger the family, the lower the scores of the children. The children are liable to suffer from a double handicap, both genetic and environmental – the latter because, it is suggested, they have less encouragement and stimulus from parents who have more children amongst whom to divide their attention. Those earning the lowest wages often make up their incomes by working longer hours. Often, too, their wives have less time and energy to devote to their children. Family size likewise correlates with nutrition, with physical growth and with overcrowding, and is therefore an apt indicator (when allowance is made for the age structure of the local population, and particularly the number of mothers of child bearing age) of the poor home conditions for which schools should compensate. The National Census, supplemented by the schools' censuses made by the education authorities, would provide the information required.

(c) *Supplements in Cash or Kind from the State* are of various kinds. Where the parents are needy, children are allowed school meals free. The proportions so benefiting vary greatly from school to school, and afford a reasonably good guide to relative need. The procedures laid down are designed to give free meals according to scales similar to those used by the Ministry of Social Security. Another criterion of the same type is the number of families depending on National Assistance, or its future equivalent, in a particular locality. The weakness of these criteria taken by themselves is that some people do not know their rights or are unwilling to seek them.

(d) *Overcrowding and Sharing of Houses* should certainly be included amongst the criteria. It will identify families in cramped accommodation in central and run-down areas of our cities. It is a less sure guide than some others because it may miss the educational needs of some housing estates and other areas which can also be severe.

(e) *Poor Attendance and Truancy* are a pointer to home conditions, and to what Burt long ago singled out as a determinant of school progress, the 'efficiency of the mother'. Truancy is also related to delinquency. The National Survey showed that 4 per cent of the children in the sample were absent, on their teachers' assessment, for unsatisfactory reasons. (Plowden Report, Vol. 2, App. 5, para. 27).

(f) *Proportions of Retarded, Disturbed or Handicapped Pupils* in ordinary schools. These vary from authority to authority according to the special schools available and the policies governing their use. But, everywhere, the proportions tend to be highest in deprived districts. It is accepted that special schools need additional staff, and the same advantages should be extended to normal schools with many pupils of a similar kind.

(g) *Incomplete Families* where one or other of the parents is dead, or not living at home for whatever reason, are often unable to provide a satisfactory upbringing for their children without special help.

(h) *Children Unable to Speak English* need much extra attention if they are to find their feet in England. This is already recognised in arranging teachers' quotas, but should also be used as a general criterion.

154. All authorities would be asked to consider which of their schools should qualify, to rank them according to criteria such as those

we have listed, and to submit supporting data. Advice would also be available from HM Inspectors of Schools. In this way the Department of Education and Science would have full information both about the social and the educational needs of the schools and areas. Many of the criteria would be closely correlated. With experience the data required could be simplified so as to ease administration; but meanwhile, a wide variety of criteria should be employed. The schools near the bottom of the resulting rankings would be entitled to priority. We envisage a formal procedure enabling the Secretary of State for Education and Science to designate particular schools or groups of schools as priority schools or areas. Those so designated would qualify for the favourable treatment described later in this chapter. Local education authorities would submit regular reports on these schools to the Secretary of State for the purpose of determining what progress was being made, how long their designation should continue, which aspects of the programme were proving most effective, and what further steps should be taken.

Special groups

155. However good the information secured, and however extensive the experience gained in using it, the administration of this policy would always call for wise judgement and careful interpretation. An infallible formula cannot be devised. Severe deprivation can be found among particular groups which are unlikely to be singled out by such criteria. Canal boat families are an example. Another are the gypsies whose plight is described in Appendix 12 (see Plowden Report, Vol. 2).They are probably the most severely deprived children in the country. Most of them do not even go to school, and the potential abilities of those who do are stunted. They tend to be excluded by their way of life and their lack of education from entering normal occupations and confined to others that compel continual travelling. Thus, unless action is taken to arrest the cycle, their children will in turn suffer educational deprivations which will become increasingly severe in their effects as general standards of education rise. The age distribution of this group bears a telling resemblance to that of England in 1841 and so does their education or lack of it. The numbers of gypsy children are small – those of compulsory school age probably amounting in total to less than four thousand. But they are increasing, and in the next 20 years their numbers are likely to double. In their own interests and in the nation's, they merit help of the kind we recommend. Yet the criteria listed in paragraph 153 would not select them. They move too frequently to be accurately recorded in census data, they are too seldom in school to appear in figures (of free school meals, for instance) derived from the school population, and the districts in which they are found, particularly the rural areas

surrounding the South-eastern and West Midland conurbations, are unlikely to contain many educational priority areas.

156. Another group of children which would not be identified by the suggested criteria are from Army and Air Force families in areas with large service populations. There is evidence of serious backwardness among them and of high turnover of pupils and teachers.

157. The case of the gypsies illustrates another aspect of the policies required in educational priority areas. Improved education alone cannot solve the problems of these children. Simultaneous action is needed by the authorities responsible for employment, industrial training, housing and planning. There will be similar, though less extreme, needs for co-ordinated action on behalf of other groups deserving priority. The experience of those engaged in the 'war on poverty' in the United States gives warning of the disappointments which sometimes follow from attempts to improve the education of the poorest which are not coupled to an effective attack on unemployment. Where there are plans for new centres of economic growth in the less prosperous regions, extra resources for education should be temporarily concentrated in areas where the whole pace of development is likely to be increased. In such places, joint operations of this kind could before long go far to eliminate educational deprivation.

More teachers

158. Once educational priority areas have been selected, the next step must be to give them the help they need. Each authority would be asked not only to say which schools had been selected, and why, but also what it proposed by way of remedy. The most important thing is to bring more experienced and successful teachers into these areas and to support them by a generous number of teachers' aides. Until there are more teachers all round, the possibility for increasing their numbers in these schools will, of course, be limited. But a beginning could be made, and the right framework created for the future. To start with, quotas should be raised for authorities with educational priority areas. But the schools in greatest need often cannot recruit their full complement at present, and to increase it, if that were all, would do nothing but cause irritation. Additional incentives are needed. We therefore recommend that there should be extra allowances for teachers and head teachers serving in schools in difficult areas. In many ways their work is already more arduous than their colleagues'. They will in future be expected to assume yet further responsibilities, not only in making contact with parents but also in arranging activities for their children outside the normal limits of the school day, and in collaborating with other local social services. Teachers in such schools deserve extra recognition and reward, and to give it to them would be

one way of achieving something even more important, greater fairness between one child and another. The government has already reached the same conclusion in its search for means of recruiting doctors to the less popular areas; financial incentives are being offered to those who are willing to work in them. Salary incentives, of course, present difficulties for the professions concerned, but we believe that the teachers, who understand better than most the urgency of the need, will be prepared to accept the remedies their medical colleagues are already adopting.

159. The Dame Jean Roberts Committee on Measures to Secure a More Equitable Distribution of Teachers in Scotland studied these problems independently and we were unaware that they had reached similar conclusions until our own Report was nearly completed. They call in their Report[10] for the designation of individual schools in which the scarcity of teachers is particularly severe, and for the payment of an additional £100 a year to all teachers serving in these schools. Our scheme differs from the Scottish plan in one important respect. The criteria we recommend are all social, not educational, so that priority schools and areas will not lose their privileged status, whether they have enough teachers or not, until the social conditions improve. As we understand the Scottish proposals, designation as a school of temporary shortage is to be subject to annual review and the additions to salaries will be paid only during the time when the school is so designated.

160. There is an important distinction between 'mobile' teachers, often young and sometimes still unmarried, and the 'immobile', who are more often married. Many authorities have succeeded in attracting back to work women teachers who had resigned after marriage, and the more who return the better. But the schools to which they go are often those near their own homes, and therefore in middle-class neighbourhoods not in the queue for priority. Each woman who returns could release an additional mobile teacher for priority areas, but that will not be achieved unless more carefully drawn distinctions can be made between the mobile and immobile, and the quotas to be applied to each. The principle underlying these arrangements should be that authorities must employ every immobile teacher in their areas before drawing on mobile teachers who may be available for the priority areas. The administrative difficulties of such an arrangement are considerable, but while teachers remain so scarce every effort should be made to overcome them.

161. There are two obvious problems about this scheme which should be mentioned. The first is the risk that, while the black areas may become white, the neighbouring grey areas may be turned black by an exodus of teachers attracted by salary incentives. But the fact that the priority areas will seldom, if ever, cover a whole authority will be a safeguard. They will usually consist of much smaller districts, some containing one or two schools only, within the territory of an

authority and the authority can exercise considerable control over the recruitment and deployment of its teachers and ensure that a balance is maintained between the claims of all its schools, good and bad. The second concerns our proposals for different rules for the employment of mobile and immobile teachers. The Department of Education and Science does not know where the immobile live, especially if they left teaching some years ago. This information might be collected by local education authorities. This should form the basis of information for the Department, who should modify its quota arrangements to take into account the varying resources of immobile teachers in each area.

162. Priority areas are not the kind of place where teachers normally live. Yet those whose homes are near their pupils' can often do a better job than those who travel great distances. They belong to the same community; they can understand their background better. What is more, the creation of vast one-class districts from which all professional people are excluded is bad in itself. Sustained efforts ought to be made to diversify the social composition of the priority areas. Many professional workers feel the need to start buying a house early in their careers because mortgage terms may be more favourable, and because once they own a house it is easier for them to secure another one if they move elsewhere. Their needs should be recognised by the housing and planning authorities. There should be a mixture of houses for renting, for owner-occupation, and for co-ownership, and cost-rent schemes run by housing associations. As our enquiries showed, many authorities can, and some do, provide housing for teachers and others whose claims derive not from the urgency of their housing needs but from the contribution they make to the community which provides the houses. The housing needs of families in badly overcrowded places are likely to be more urgent than those of teachers; but their children will not get the education they deserve if teachers are systematically excluded from the locality. The Dame Jean Roberts Committee urges, and we agree, that local education authorities 'should be allowed greater freedom than at present to purchase, and if necessary to adapt, houses to let to teachers willing to serve at shortage points. Expenditure incurred on the purchase and adaptation of such houses should not be regarded as a charge on an authority's capital investment allocation for school building' (p. 25). We agree with this. It does not follow that any help with housing would entitle teachers to subsidies designed for tenants with lower incomes. The Dame Jean Roberts Committee recommended also that there should be travel allowances for teachers working in difficult areas at a distance from their homes. We recommend that local authorities consider this.

Colleges of education

163. Teachers in training also have a part to play. In our visit to the

United States we were much struck by the value of linking teacher-training establishments with schools in deprived areas. In some cities young teachers are attracted to such places and helped to settle down there by the appointment of special consultants who regularly visit new teachers in schools where the conditions are difficult, support them in their work, and are available on call to give advice. On a smaller scale, the benefits of such links can already be seen in England. We urge that colleges should be asked to establish wherever possible a continuing link with schools in priority areas. Students should be sent to them for a part of their teaching practice. We also hope that in many of these areas a generously equipped teachers' centre can be set up for the in-service training of teachers already working there, partly staffed by the affiliated college of education and partly by local inspectors, HM inspectors and experienced local teachers and heads. The improved staffing ratio we recommend should make an in-service training pro-gramme possible. Longer courses to equip teachers for work in the priority areas could be run from such centres and in colleges of education, and be recognised for purposes of Burnham allowances. Over the years this work would help to build up a body of knowledge about the best ways of teaching children in socially deprived neighbourhoods. Co-operation for research purposes with university departments and with colleges of education would also enable the successes, and failures, of the whole venture to be properly assessed.

Buildings

164. The shortage of buildings is going to be as acute as the shortage of teachers. New building is committed for several years ahead to keep pace with the birth-rate and the rise in the school-leaving age. There will not be much to spare for the priority areas in the immediate future. Our criteria should be given great weight when determining which of the schools with old and out-of-date buildings is to be replaced first. It would also help if the element in the total building programme reserved for minor works were increased specially for the benefit of these areas. Schools in the greatest plight could be given preference, for the improvement of lavatories and wash places, and for mod-ifications to classrooms. They also should be frequently redecorated. There is urgent need for decent staff rooms to replace those ones thought good enough 60 years ago, if indeed there were any at all. In making estimates of the costs involved we have assumed that an average of £5,000 should be spent on each of these schools. Some will need more; others will need very little. What goes into the building is likewise important. The need for extra 'consumable stocks' has already been mentioned. Additional books and audio-visual equipment of various kinds, including television sets and tape-recorders, would be particularly valuable in these schools.

Nursery education

165. We [believe] that part-time attendance at a nursery school is desirable for most children. It is even more so for children in socially deprived neighbourhoods. They need above all the verbal stimulus, the opportunities for constructive play, a more richly differentiated environment and the access to medical care that good nursery schools can provide. It will be many years before they are generally available. The building of new nursery schools and extensions to existing schools should start in priority areas and spread outwards. As a minimum we suggest that all children aged four to five who live in the areas should have the opportunity of part-time attendance and that perhaps 50 per cent should have full-time places (although their need for a gradual introduction is the same as that of all other children).

Other priorities

166. The development of social work carried out in conjunction with the schools [. . .] should [also] be concentrated first in the priority areas.

167. It might be thought that our proposal for community schools, made in the previous chapter, would be hardest to implement in these districts. But in many of them the demand for centres for activities outside the home of various kinds is keen, as the existence of university settlements and similar bodies shows. It will take special skill to seize these opportunities and use them for educational purposes. But the gains that could be made in mutual understanding between teachers and parents through the work of a well-run community school in a priority area make the scheme well worth trying.

First steps

168. Local education authorities which have a number of priority schools will not be able to embark on a policy of positive discrimination until they know what help they can get from the central government. The nation's supply of the principal resources required – teachers and school buildings – is known and committed, several years in advance, often to other parts of the educational system. We must, therefore, think in terms of an immediate programme, on which a start can be made without waiting for additional resources of major changes in existing plans, and after that a longer term programme to follow.

169. The principles on which we have based the immediate programme are as follows:

(i) A start should be made as quickly as possible by giving priority to the schools which by our criteria contain the 10 per cent of most deprived children. Starting at 2 per cent in the first year this percentage should be reached within five years. The additional budget for these areas should not engross the entire increase in educational resources available for the whole country, year by year. There must be a margin permitting some improvement in the schools serving the rest of the population.

(ii) The programme should begin as quickly as possible at varying dates for different elements in the system (teachers' aides, for example, may be available sooner than an over-all increase in the school building programme).

170. During a period to start in 1968 and to reach its peak in 1972 the following steps should be taken in educational priority areas (or in individual priority schools):

(i) The staffing ratio should be improved so that no class need exceed 30.

(ii) Additions to salary of £120 (as are given to teachers of handicapped children or those with other special responsibilities) should be available at a rate of one for every teacher in the priority areas. But it would be open to local education authorities to award these increases according to any plan approved by the Department of Education and Science as being likely to improve education in the designated schools. The additional resources should be used flexibly; for example, an allowance might be allocated to a remedial teacher specialising in helping these schools, or allowances might be withheld and become payable only after a brief qualifying period. They would not, of course, be paid to staff working mainly in other schools. These arrangements will require an amendment of the Burnham Report.

(iii) Teachers' aides should be provided to help teachers [. . .] at the [. . .] ratio of one aide for every two classes in infant and junior schools.

(iv) Those educational priority schools with poor buildings should be allocated, within the first five years, a minor building project. The average costs between all priority schools might be £5,000 though some will need little or no new building.

(v) The full provision for nursery education should be introduced for children aged four and five. [. . .] A higher proportion than in the rest of the country will attend full-time (up to 50 per cent).

(vi) Research should be set on foot to determine which of these measures has the most positive effect as a basis for planning the longer term programme.

(vii) We estimate [. . .] that by 1972/73 the educational priority areas will add £11 million to the total current costs of the maintained primary schools. It is clear therefore that the total of Exchequer grants to local authorities will have to be increased to take account of this. It is not for us to plan the mechanism for the distribution of these grants. A new specific grant for authorities containing priority areas may be required, on the lines of the proposed grant to authorities with large numbers of Commonwealth immigrants; or the formula for the distribution of the new rate support grant might be modified.

A continuing policy

171. The longer term programme will call for additional resources, over and above those at present allocated to education. Our proposals are not intended to be a once-for-all expedient. The lead in the ratio of teachers to pupils which the priority areas should have attained by 1972 must be maintained. It is suggested they should be restricted to an arbitrary figure of 10 per cent of the population initially, in order to provide a serious test of the effectiveness of different elements of priority within the resources that can be found without depriving the rest of the country of scope for improvement. It will be much longer before reliable conclusions can be reached about the outcome, but already by 1972 it should be easier to decide how far and in what way to extend the programme. The need may well be shown to go beyond 10 per cent of children. The Council's last report estimated that just under a fifth of modern school pupils were in 'problem areas', very similar to what we describe as educational priority areas.[11]

172. The arguments for this policy are general, and apply to whole districts that have been educationally handicapped for years. They are not confined to primary schools and apply to secondary schools as well. But a start should, in our view, be made in primary schools. They have long had less than their share of new building and their classes have always been larger. Since they draw their pupils from smaller catchment areas they feel the full impact of social conditions in their immediate neighbourhood, whereas rather more secondary schools can draw from a mixture of neighbourhoods, with the more fortunate offsetting the less.

Conclusion

173. Positive discrimination accords with experience and thinking in many other countries, and in other spheres of social policy. It calls both for some redistribution of the resources devoted to education and, just as much, for an increase in their total volume. It must not be interpreted simply as a gloss upon the recommendations which follow in later chapters. This would not only be a misunderstanding of the scheme; it would destroy all hope of its success. For it would be unreasonable and self-defeating – economically, professionally and politically – to try to do justice by the most deprived children by using only resources that can be diverted from more fortunate areas. We have argued that the gap between the educational opportunities of the

most and least fortunate children should be closed, for economic and social reasons alike. It cannot be done, unless extra effort, extra skill and extra resources are devoted to the task.

Recommendations

174.

(i) As a matter of national policy, 'positive discrimination' should favour schools in neighbourhoods where children are most severely handicapped by home conditions. The programme should be phased to make schools in the most deprived areas as good as the best in the country. For this, it may be necessary that their greater claim on resources should be maintained.

(ii) A start should be made as soon as possible by giving priority to the most severely deprived pupils, starting with 2 per cent of the pupils and building up to 10 per cent over five years. The purpose of the short-term programme would be partly to discover which measures best compensate for educational deprivation. In the longer term, the programme may be expanded to cover a larger proportion of the population.

(iii) Every local education authority having schools in which children's educational handicaps are reinforced by social deprivation should be asked to adopt the measures suggested below and to report from time to time on the progress made. Local authorities should be encouraged to select schools within their areas for special attention even though they are not eligible for extra help from national resources.

(iv) A wide variety of criteria should be employed initially. Experience will show which of these criteria are most useful.

(v) Authorities should be asked to say which of their schools should receive extra help from national resources. The Department of Education should formally designate those schools and areas in most need as educational priority areas. Priority areas and the progress made in them should be reappraised regularly by local education authorities and the Department of Education and Science.

(vi) Authorities and the Department of Education and Science should ensure that the needs of other educationally deprived groups, such as gypsies, which will not be picked out by the general criteria laid down, are not overlooked.

Steps to be taken: 1968 to 1972

175.

(i) Measures should be taken to improve the ratio of teachers to children in educational priority areas to a point at which no class in these areas exceeds 30. Additions to salary amounting in total to £120 for every teacher in the priority areas should be paid. It should be open to authorities to award increases according to any plan approved by the Department of Education and Science as being likely to improve education in these areas.

(ii) Teachers' aides should be provided in the priority schools at a ratio of one to every two infant and junior classes.

(iii) In building programmes, priority should be given to these areas for the replacement or improvement of schools with old or out of date premises. The element of the total school building programme reserved for minor works should be increased specifically for their benefit. Approximately £5,000 should be allocated for minor works in each school.

(iv) Extra books and equipment should be given for schools in priority areas.

(v) The expansion of nursery education should begin in the priority areas.

176.

(i) The Department of Education and Science should modify its quota arrangements so that they take into account the varying resources of immobile teachers available in each area. Authorities with large numbers of qualified married women willing to teach but unable to work in other areas should gradually be persuaded to employ all of them before drawing on mobile teachers who might be available for priority areas.

(ii) Colleges of education should, wherever possible, establish a continuing link with priority schools. Students should do part of their teaching practice in these schools.

(iii) Teachers' centres should be set up for in-service training. They might run longer courses with the co-operation of local colleges of education. Such courses might be recognised for salary purposes.

(iv) The development of social work in conjunction with schools should begin in priority areas and be more heavily concentrated there subsequently.

(v) Community schools should be tried out first in priority areas.

177.

(i) Sustained efforts should be made to diversify the social composition of the districts where priority schools are so that teachers and others who make an essential contribution to the life and public services of the neighbourhood are not excluded from them. Co-ordinated action will be necessary on the part of authorities responsible for employment, industrial training, housing and town planning if educational deprivation is to be rapidly reduced.

(ii) Research should be started to discover which of the developments in educational priority areas have the most constructive effects, so as to assist in planning the longer term programme to follow.

(iii) Exchequer grants to local authorities with educational priority areas should be increased and the necessary changes in the grant-making system made.

References

1. Professor S. Wiseman. Oral evidence to Council.
2. National Food Survey, 1963.
3. R. Lambert, *Nutrition in Britain 1950—1960,* London: G. Bell, 1964.
4. G. C. Arneil and J. C. Crosbie, 'Infantile rickets returns to Glasgow', *Lancet* (1963), **2,** 423. Quoted in T. Arie, 'Class and disease', *New Society,* 27 Jan. 1966.
5. R. Illsley and J. C. Kincaid, 'Social correlation of perinatal mortality', in N. R. Butler and D. G. Bonham, *Perinatal Mortality,* Edinburgh: Livingstone, 1963, p. 271.
6. Milner Holland Report, *Report of the Committee on Housing in Greater London,* Cmnd 2605, 1965.
7. T. Husen (ed.) *A Comparative Study of Outcomes of Mathematical Instruction in Twelve Countries,* Stockholm: Almquist and Hicksell (forthcoming). T. Husen *Attainment: The Implications for Primary Education,* Stockholm: Almquist and Hicksell, 1967.
8. For example, J. W. B. Douglas, *Home and School,* MacGibbon and Kee, 1964. The same data forms the basis of arguments in Robbins Report, Vol. II.
9. B. Davies, *Relative Inequality and Interrelationships Between Standards of Provisions of Primary, Secondary and Other Forms of Education and Socio-Economic Factors Affecting Education Performance* (to be published).
10. *Report of the Dame Jean Roberts Committee on Measures to Secure a More Equitable Distribution of Teachers in Scotland,* HMSO, 1966.
11. *Half Our Future,* HMSO, 1963, para. 31.

2

What is a 'bad' school?

H. Acland

Weary education reformers are suitably cynical about the life-expectancy and effectiveness of government reports. But the Plowden report on *Children and their Primary Schools* is now four years old and its message is not just a matter for discussion – it is also a guide to practice. Particularly over 'compensatory education', the effect of the report is obvious. In this and a subsequent article, I want to discuss two specific aspects of these policies: the education priority area pro-gramme and the scheme designed to increase parent participation in schools.

My discussion is prompted by, but not limited to, a reanalysis of the national survey data collected at the committee's request. I undertook this reanalysis in the belief that the same data could be interpreted in a number of different ways. In some cases, differences would arise because of apparent errors in the original analysis. More often my own analysis would be no more or less reasonable than any other. The point I wished to establish was that preconceptions had an influence on the conduct and conclusions of research.

This first article will be concerned with Plowden's EPA policy, and more specifically with the action taken by the Department of Education, at the national level, to carry out the Plowden report's recommendations. Briefly, this has consisted of a special building programme for EPA areas started in 1967; an alteration of teacher distribution quotas in favour of these schools; a £75 salary increase for the teachers, and an increase in the number of nursery school places.

The EPA idea is now familiar. The areas are selected by using a number of social indicators, such as overcrowding of the social class level of the neighbourhood. These schools are then given special allowances of resources and personnel. The assumption is that the target population will be concentrated in the schools identified by these criteria. But to what extent is this assumption true? Suppose we define the target population in terms of academic performance, and call the group scoring in the lowest 10 per cent range the under-

From *New Society*, 9 Sept. 1971, pp. 450–53.

achievers. My reanalysis indicates that a surprisingly small proportion of this group is to be found in EPA schools.

In Fig. 2.1 [. . .], A, B and C are three fictitious schools. The lines under each letter represent the range of attainment scores for each school. The bulk of the pupils will be concentrated towards the middle of the range with relatively few at the extremes. Of the two alternatives, the one on the left shows a situation where schools are markedly different from one another so far as attainment is concerned. School B obviously contains almost all the slower children. This would justify the EPA assumption.

But my own analysis of the Plowden data indicates that the situation is more accurately represented by the right-hand alternative, where all three schools have a much more similar share of students at all ability levels. This contradicts the EPA policy assumption that the 'bad' schools contain all or most of the bad pupils. Equally, the 'good' schools do not contain most of the good pupils.

Assuming we decide to define disadvantage in terms of achievement – a question that I shall discuss below – a second type of difficulty arises in the EPA policy. If, as is the case, there is a somewhat loose relationship between the indices of priority schools and the average achievement of pupils, we would not expect to find that there are large concentrations of under-achievers in these schools. To explore this, I used the Plowden survey data to select from among its 173 schools those which had EPA characteristics. Would the proportion of under-achieving pupils in these schools be substantially greater than for the sample as a whole?

My method of selecting EPA schools was based on the eight criteria suggested by Plowden as the relevant dimensions for assessing the quality of the school neighbourhood. Schools were chosen as priority schools if they had scores in the lowest 10 per cent on two out of five of the indicators (social class, family size, incomplete families, parents from abroad, too few bedrooms). Defining under-achievement as a score in the lowest 10 per cent of the test-score range, I found that for the special EPA pupils only one-fifth or less were under-achievers, compared with one-tenth for the whole sample. (The method of selecting students, and the form of analysis used, is described in greater detail in a mimeographed paper, which I can make available on request.) In other words, there is *some* concentration of 'slower' children in the EPA schools. But the difference is not educationally exceptional.

Admittedly, my estimates are based on a sample of primary schools, and on a small number of pupils selected from within these schools, but if the evidence is reasonably accurate, it requires a familiar preconception to be revised – that where there is one social problem (in this case, bad schools) there will also be another (underachieving pupils). Possibly our preconceptions have been formed by a characteristic common to social reformers, a preoccupation with the 'obvious' indi-

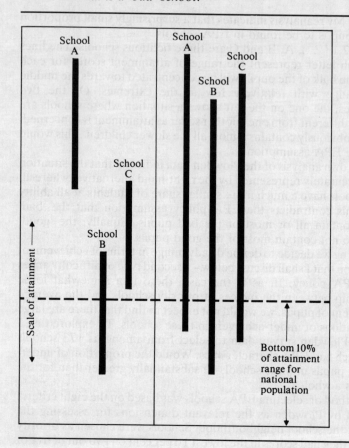

Fig. 2.1 The alternative representations of the distribution of attainment in schools.

cators of deprivation, the dilapidated school buildings and the squalor of homes. Would it not be reasonable to look at the even more obvious indicator of need, the academic performance of children?

The Plowden committee took a much more general view of deprivation. The deprived child was not simply one who did badly at school; he was one who suffered from many forms of social disadvantage in home and neighbourhood. Loose definitions of this kind seem to lead to loosely defined programmes for 'compensation'. Instead of concentrating on the narrow issue of school achievement, the aim became to improve the child's 'self-concept', to develop his understanding of the community he lives in; or, even more generally, to use the school as a forum where the community itself can realise its identity. Relatively diffuse aims such as these are typical of the EPA demonstration projects.

We should realise that there are pitfalls in this approach. First, imprecisely defined programmes tend to evaporate, leaving little behind. Second, there are real dangers in offering substantially different curricula to the clever and the slow children. Teaching an EPA child about the way his local government works may put him even further behind in the conventional scholastic race. This leads me on to the one basic reason for taking the narrower approach to the problem of compensation.

Even in the distant future of comprehensives, a child's academic achievement will be important in determining his educational career. The decision to stay on at school, and more especially the decision to take exams, will be directly influenced by his academic performance. There are good reasons for thinking that the number of years completed at school, and the number of exams passed, are fundamental in shaping occupational careers. Unless we decide to do something drastic to change the criterion of success in schools, it seems fairest to approach compensation in the spirit of *traditional* academic standards.

The second question, then, is whether the alterations made to the schools in EPA areas are likely to affect the children's performance. Despite all the problems and inadequacies of the research evidence, the indication is that they will not.

Before I look at this conclusion in greater detail, I would like to consider one fundamental problem. Was the EPA programme ever intended to raise achievement scores? If the Plowden committee did reject the goal of improving attainment, this was not made clear. The nearest indication is that the programme *was* designed to this end: 'Steps should be taken to improve the educational chances and the attainments of the least well placed . . .' But no doubt EPAS do more than that. Anne Corbett suggested ('Are educational priority areas working?' *New Society* 13 November 1969) that Plowden was 'never very specific about the motivations for an EPA policy. It is said that, once the members had agreed on the policy, the committee did not want to shatter the consensus by disagreeing on its reasoning.'

Now to the research evidence, starting with the Plowden report itself. A detailed examination of the committee's survey findings yields no support for the view that altering class size, providing more in-service training for teachers, increasing the stability of the school's staff, having qualified teachers or improving the quality of the books, is going to make an appreciable impact on attainment. Not only that, but the HM inspectors' assessments – either of the school's overall quality, or the quality of the head teacher – are not closely related to the average ability-level of students in those schools. True, the researchers claim that the quality of the class teachers makes a difference. But, as we shall see, the interpretation of this finding is obscure.

Other research evidence reinforces the view that differences between schools are not impressively related to differences in student performance. The Coleman report, *Inequality in Education*

Opportunity, published in the United States in 1965 – in many ways the counterpart of the Plowden survey – produced little evidence in favour of the view that school quality had a consistent or considerable relationship with attainment. Several re-workings of the Coleman data have failed to alter this conclusion. Even more enlightening is the outcome of the More Effective Schools programme, started in 1964 and still running in New York. Like EPAS, this programme operates on poverty area schools and, like EPAS, it works by improving pupil/teacher ratios, using teachers' aides and making substantial improvements in the schools' facilities. Though there are some minor squabbles about the evaluation of the programme's success, the consensus is that the schools in the programme did not raise achievement significantly, *despite* an average per pupil expenditure of £527 each year – roughly twice the regular amount.

Obviously these findings, like many social science findings, are not beyond reproach. But are criticisms severe enough to allow us to overlook the evidence?

Let me mention briefly three problems about the evidence. First, the measures of the school environment are often the wrong ones. Indeed, many people believe that we shall never be able to classify schools on the really important dimensions. Second, we tend to overlook the cumulative effects of schooling. Third, though we have been able to define some associations – for example, that between teacher quality and student performance – we cannot assume that the first causes the second, even though this is what we want to believe. It may be that the better teachers are assigned to the better students, so that the observed association is better interpreted in the opposite way to our expectations.

One more point can be added, though, which suggests that, even if we find the research evidence disheartening, we can still believe that schools could make a difference to performance. In the nature of survey research, our conclusions must be limited to the range of observations we made in the first place. For example, evidence collected from British schools on the effects of a teacher's salary on his students' performance will tell us something about the effect of altering salary levels, within the range of £1,000 to £2,500. But we cannot extrapolate beyond this range to prophesy what would happen if we quadrupled teachers' incomes. If this view of the research had been taken seriously by Plowden, we might have expected to find radical proposals for changing schools. If what we knew didn't work, what we didn't know might. But all the EPA measures are modest and unexceptional, well within the bounds of conventional school practice.

So far I have pointed out my reasons for thinking the EPA programme would reach only a small proportion of the under-achievers and why I am doubtful about the effect of the alterations to EPA schools. But there are some compliments to be paid, too.

The EPA programme is, after all, the first large-scale and deliberate attempt to redress the position of the under-achieving group. Admittedly, local authorities had been giving privileged treatment to slum schools for a long time, but the EPA programme was the first national initiative that gave formal recognition to the problem. As a demonstration of government intent, and as a matter of social justice, the programme should no doubt be retained.

Another reason for retaining at least part of the programme is that it meets teachers' demands that special recognition be given to those who work in difficult circumstances. At least teacher recruitment should be a less persistent burden on the head teachers' energy in these schools. It also seems obvious that the teachers themselves will be happier, but unless they are in agreement with the official demarcations between EPA and non-EPA schools, it is likely that teachers falling just outside the areas will feel hard done by. The overall effect may then be negative. However, there is much circumstantial evidence that teachers' morale is boosted by prog-rammes like these. This should surprise no one, nor does it come as a surprise to find that though teachers are happier they do not respond by making basic changes in their teaching methods. Those who have been watching the outcome of the More Effective Schools programme think that the failure of teachers to alter the way they teach may have caused the programme's failure to raise achievement.

Bearing in mind, then, these reasons in favour of at least keeping EPAS, we can still look at alternative ways of spending our money and energy. Here, I shall consider new ways in which these compensatory funds could be delivered to under-achieving children, paying little attention to the content of such programmes.

My reanalysis suggests that we should adopt some scheme for identifying disadvantaged *individuals* rather than disadvantaged *schools*. There are three ways this might be done. First, as an extreme solution, might it be possible to separate under-achieving children in special schools, diverting *all* compensatory funds to those schools alone? The potential advantage of this scheme is that, once one had selected the children, one could be sure that effort and money were being concentrated on the right group. School administrators have a built-in tendency to favour the good students, even when the resources they control are intended for the disadvantaged. Also, when funds and resources are severely limited, the temptation is to spread them thinly rather than concentrate them on a particular group. Both these difficulties would be circumvented by putting disadvantaged children in one school.

On the other hand, the difficulties with this scheme far outweigh this single advantage. It would involve a complicated screening procedure. The problem of arranging for the transportation of children would be tremendous, especially in rural areas. More serious still, the separation of children would emphasise, if not actually create, a powerful sense of shame and humiliation. Finally, there is some support for the view that the composition of the pupil body has an independent influence on pupil achievement. We could not suppose that to be at a school with pupils of similar background and ability would tell in favour of the disadvantaged child.

The second way is one that would work within the existing school set-up. Instead of selecting priority schools, why not select the children from the lower streams of *all* schools and concentrate resources on them alone? The advantage of this alternative is that it is administratively much more straightforward than the first. It is even more feasible than the EPA programme, which requires the use of a complicated, and ultimately rather arbitrary selection procedure. But its main attraction is that we would locate roughly 80 per cent to 90 per cent of the children scoring in the lowest 10 per cent range of achievement tests. The remedy would follow Plowden's scheme for resource allocation, but here it would be the *lower stream* teachers who would get more money, the *lower stream* that would get better books. The resources would be allocated within schools and not between them.

Naturally, this alternative has its problems, too. Not all primary schools are streamed, at least in the earlier years. We would have to evolve special strategies for both schools which were too small to have a viable streaming arrangement and for schools which were genuinely unstreamed, the programme would condone the practice of streaming – an aspect of school organisation that may have an independent influence on attainment. And even though I take the view that the distribution of ability differences lies mainly *within* schools, there is *some* segregation of ability between schools. Some schools have greater proportions of disadvantaged children than others, even though Plowden was mistaken about the extent of this. Given that schools arrange streams so that each contains a similar proportion of the year group, we would expect that students in the high stream in a school with a low average ability would be placed in a lower stream if they were transplanted to a school with a higher average ability. This means of delivering compensatory funds would therefore not reach a number of students in schools with below-average achievement.

The third way is administratively much more complicated. But it avoids some of the problems raised by the first and second suggestions. Could compensatory funds be divided between schools on the basis of the proportion of under-achieving children within each school? Were this possible, we would get round the fact that under-achievers are concentrated in certain schools by giving the money in relation to existing segregation by ability. Implicit in this suggestion is some nationally defined level of under-achievement – say, one standard deviation below the national mean.

A series of national surveys of reading ability (see Plowden's App. 7) provide us with a good background for making such a judgement. But the actual administration of nation-wide testing would clearly pose a formidable administrative problem, and be expensive, too.

The sum each school was to receive would be fixed, but would not be given to the school until a suitable proposal had been submitted by the school demonstrating how the money was going to be spent. This would require an organised system for evaluating proposals; a local authority panel would be needed to assess, pass, or recommend changes in these proposals and this in turn would assume a set of criteria for determining what constitutes an acceptable proposal.

I would suggest very elementary criteria. First, that the school's proposal be written and approved by a group including some representative of the parents' interests. Second, that the proposal should be designed to improve basic cognitive skills – reading, writing and arithmetic – so that there would be a safeguard against diverting funds to the construction of gymnasia or the redecorating of the staffroom. Third, the proposal should convince the panel that the under-achieving group in the school would get the advantages of the funds.

Within these limits, anything would be allowed; indeed, experimentation would be encouraged. I believe that no body of experts can yet prescribe the correct formula for raising achievement levels and this makes me think that the best effect a compensatory programme can have is to allow head teachers a little extra elbowroom to try out innovations which their standard budgets restrict them from attempting.

3

Does parent involvement matter?

H. Acland

[In my article 'What is a "bad" school?'] I put forward reasons for thinking that the educational priority area policy would not alter children's attainment in school. One of the reasons for my pessimism was that the programme would not reach a significantly large proportion of the under-achieving children. I then looked at some other ways of delivering compensatory funds to the children in need.

My other reason for thinking that the EPA policy would not alter achievement levels is [. . .] that the school characteristics that would be changed in EPA schools by Plowden's priorities are not impressively related to student performance. This leaves open the question of what would constitute a better programme. In discussing one alternative way of delivering compensatory funds, I got as far as suggesting that it ought to be the head teachers who decided, within broad limits, how the money should be spent. In other words, I dodged the problem of prescribing specific programmes for compensation. I now want to come back to that problem in a discussion of how achievement might be improved by increasing the interaction between the child's home and his school.

What does it mean – to increase interaction between home and school? What rationale leads us to think it will improve performance? In their book, *Learning Begins at Home,* Michael Young and Patrick McGeeney described the 'syllogism of parental participation' in these terms: 'A rise in the level of parental encouragement augments their children's performance in school. Teachers, by involving parents in the school, bring about a rise in the level of parental encouragement. Teachers, by involving parents in the school, augment the children's performance.'

To give this statement flesh, let us see what it is that schools will do to involve parents. The Plowden committee – of which Michael Young was, of course, a member – recommended a regular system for meeting parents before the child entered the school, private talks with parents twice a year, open days, booklets on education and school choice for

From *New Society,* 16 Sept. 1971, pp. 507–10.

distribution to parents, reports once a year, and encouraging parents to use the school out of hours.

Young and McGeeney's research sought to measure the effects of making such changes in a school. They persuaded the headmaster to make a variety of changes in the school they had selected for experimental treatment. He sent a letter to all parents, meetings were held at the beginning of term for teachers and parents, private talks and four general meetings on educational topics were arranged. In addition, home visits were made for parents who had not come to the meetings. Ten homes were visited out of about 200 households where neither parent had attended. This was some indication that there were real problems in getting the cooperation of both staff and parents. Nevertheless, the changes that Young and McGeeney achieved went as far as anything that Plowden recommended.

I want to emphasise the proposed reforms in the schools are relatively minor. They did not require extensive reorganisation and did not need specialised personnel. Furthermore, the objective of the programme does not extend beyond the fairly simple matter of keeping parents better informed about their child's education.

The justification for parent participation programmes is based on our knowledge of the relationship between social class and achievement, but it also caught on for economic and administrative reasons. Unlike EPA recommendations for smaller classes, better buildings and larger teacher salaries (which are all extremely expensive), the parent participation scheme was cheap. Not only that, it could be run with the minimum of government intervention and effort. If we take Plowden literally, the extent of this intervention was to be the publication of a booklet 'containing examples of good practice in parent-teacher relations', which was to be produced by the Department of Education.

But the explicit justification for the policy was the research evidence from the national survey, which 'pointed to the influence upon performance of parental attitudes. *It follows* that one of the essentials for educational advance is a closer partnership between the two parties to every child's education' (my italics). The first question I want to raise is about the interpretation of the research evidence. The quotation from the survey makes it clear that parents' attitudes were seen as the most important determinants of the child's achievement, but it makes some difference to know just what these 'attitudes' were.

It appears that the researchers assumed that the attitudes were measures of the parents' level of cooperation with the school and of the degree of encouragement they gave their child: 'Before the inquiry it was plain . . . that *parental encouragement and support* would take the child some way. What the inquiry has shown is that "some way" can be interpreted as "a long way", and the variation in *parental encouragement and support* has much greater effect than either the variation in home circumstances or the variation in schools.' . . . 'If the least *cooperative* parents rose to the level of the most cooperative, the effect would be much larger than if the worst schools rose to the level of the best or the least prosperous parents to the level of the most prosperous' (my italics).

I think that this interpretation is not strictly accurate. A close inspection of the printed results shows that the most consistent and significant attitudes in Plowden's analysis were parental aspirations (defined, for example, by whether or not the parent hoped the child would go to grammar school) and parental literacy, measured by their reading habits and the number of books they possessed. It is arguable that these are surrogate measures of parental cooperation and encouragement. But the point must be emphasised that the variables that were most significant in the analysis were not direct measures of either of these attributes.

In my reanalysis of the same data, I have examined the importance of variables that ostensibly *do* measure the level of parental involvement with the school (measured by how often they were in contact with it), parents' attitudes to the school (whether they feel teachers welcome them or not, for example), as well as the parents' level of encouragement and support given to their child, as defined by the help a child gets with homework or whether the mother reports that she has time to spend with the child (to take two measures used). My conclusion is that these variables are substantially less important than the traditional measures of social class and income.

For example, the correlation between a measure of parents' socio-economic status and the child's performance is up to four times as large as the correlation between a measure of parental encouragement and performance. Evidence of this kind bears only obliquely on the problem policy-makers face – what to do to improve attainment levels.

It would be much more satisfying to know what happens to children's performance when we actually alter the level of parental involvement in schools. All the EPA demonstration projects are working in this direction even though there are big differences in approach. But it is almost certain that when the evaluations are in we will not be able to judge if the parent participation schemes were effective or not, simply because the projects have not been designed with a view to rigorous analysis that could decide the matter.

The evidence we need must be based on students' tested performance before we institute a parent participation programme, and then again at some point after that programme has been set up. Would the gains in this case be greater than those of students in another school where no such programme had been established?

Unfortunately, little work of this kind has been done, and almost none of it in England. Young and McGeeney's study is the lone exception and the results of their work certainly cannot be advanced to make strong claims about parent participation.

In the United States rather more research has been done in this area and, typically, the attitude to evaluation has been tough-minded. Merle Karnes's pre-school programme, run at the University of Illinois, makes a comparison between two groups of students. The first group had one year of pre-school education only; the second group, however, not only attended the pre-school, but had the advantage of receiving help from their parents. Their mothers attended a weekly session at school so as to learn about the objectives of the pre-school programme and to develop materials and methods to use at home. The mothers were rewarded for attending and participation was high. Parents who failed to attend were followed up each week with home visits. The outcome was discouraging; children whose parents took part in the programme did not score higher than the other children by the time they were in first grade (age six to seven).

But not all studies have been unfavourable. In Flint, Michigan, Mildred Smith's programme concentrated exclusively on the possibility of raising achievement through the parents. For twelve months, children in the programme were given a daily homework assignment. The parents' chief responsibility was to provide a quiet time and a helpful atmosphere in which this work could be done. Teachers then kept a public record of children who completed each day's task – a strong incentive for the children to study. Parents were also taught how to help their children to read, to listen to them and to read to them.

Materials for use in the home were supplied and, in addition to the day-to-day reading materials that the child himself needed, a dictionary was given to each household and a file box for word cards. In a more general way, 'parents were made to realise that their attitudes and values greatly influenced those of their children'. Between pre-test and post-test the expected gain in test score was five months, but the control group gained only 2.7 months and the experimental group 5.4 months – showing a clear superiority for the children who had received special treatment.

Conflicting results of this kind are an occupational hazard. Were there real differences between programmes or can we only say that the outcome is unpredictable? In most research of this kind the number of subjects involved is usually very small anyway. My guess is that there are four features of parent involvement programmes, some or all of which must be present for them to work.

1. The fact that mothers cannot, or do not want to, attend training sessions and keep appointments must be taken into account. Some compensation for inconvenience or lost working time must be used.
2. Personnel must be appointed whose main responsibility is to work with the parents, and who are trained to do so.
3. Contacts with parents should be weekly, in order to maintain continuity. This implies a high staffing ratio.

4. The objectives and methods should be specific, rather than general. It is clear that programmes differ markedly in the degree of specificity in this matter. For example, contrast one which aimed 'to provide for parent involvement which will enhance conditions of learning for . . . children by developing pupil-parent-teacher activities related to the instructional component, and using parents as resource persons and aides', with another which emphasised 'verbal communication and vocabulary development' and where one of the parents of the enrolled children attended the child's class for one day each week, attended parents' meetings and joined the class for study trips.

These features add up to a sophisticated and expensive undertaking far beyond the limits of parent participation as we currently understand it. The most extensive work of this kind has been undertaken at the Demonstration and Research Centre for Early Education (DARCEE), under the direction of Susan Gray at George Peabody College. I shall describe parts of Susan Gray's first and second projects – although there are 20 or more which have stemmed from these initial studies.

The basis of her programmes is a pre-school treatment which takes place at DARCEE itself, in which parents of the children taking part are incorporated in a variety of ways. I shall concentrate entirely on the various programmes run for the parents.

Children in the first programme went to pre-school for ten weeks during the summer months. During that time, parents were kept informed about the aims and methods of the pre-school programme by specially appointed home visitors. In addition, the home visitors suggested things the mother might do in response to the child's own reaction to pre-school, while the children themselves were encouraged to tell the mother what they had been doing at school. The home visitors were specially qualified elementary school teachers whose main responsibility was to the 20 parents assigned to them.

Following the summer programme, from September through to the end of May, the home visitors made weekly visits to the mothers. Their purpose was to make the parents more effective for the education of their children, although they did much else besides – advising mothers about nutrition, or informing them about opportunities for jobs, housing and adult education.

The visitors developed the confidence and skill of parents by acting out situations in which the mother could imagine she was interacting with the child. They provided children's books and magazines and they persuaded the mother to join a library and to go through the process of checking a book out for the child.

The programme was run for one experimental group of 19 children for a period of three years, so the children went to three summer schools; and for another experimental group for two years, the children attending two summer schools. Immediately after the intervention, both these groups outscored the control groups by between 12 and 16 IQ points. The children were followed through school and although the differences between experimental and control groups decreased over time (to between 2 and 12 points) by the age of 10 to 11 the programme effect was still quite visible.

The second DARCEE study looked at the effects of intervention on the younger brothers and sisters of the children who participated in the first programme. Would it make an impact on the younger children's attainment by improving the general educational atmosphere of the home? Again, the basis of the programme was a special training experience for the child. But this time there were three experimental groups designed so as to isolate the effects of home intervention from pre-school intervention.

For the first group, both mothers and children were involved at the training centre, the child attending five days a week and the mother one. This influence was reinforced by home visits along the lines of Susan Gray's first project. In the second group only the child was involved – by attending the training programme – and this time no attempt was made to involve the parents. The third group had the converse treatment. There was no child training programme but the home visitor set-up was carried through. The fourth group was a matched control which received no treatment of any kind. Once again, the results were favourable: the younger brothers and sisters of the first and third groups scored higher than those of the other groups, suggesting that the home contact element is a crucial one for the scheme's success.

But again the project is highly specialised and complicated. Mothers were paid to attend the training centre where, to begin with, they worked at helping to run the programme. While they were there they could observe, through one-way windows, their children being taught the special programme. This helped them understand more about how their child learned and how teachers reinforced the children's efforts. The mothers were also trained to be better teachers themselves while they were at the centre, eventually being introduced to the formal instruction sessions as assistants. Altogether, every care was taken to use the mothers to best advantage.

I would say then that involving parents in the child's education *can* be a good way to raise achievement levels. This is no mean conclusion. Undoubtedly, we will need many more DARCEE studies before we can prescribe compensatory programmes with any confidence, but at some point we ought to be able to describe the 'parent involvement package' needed.

However, the scale on which these programmes must be run to be successful is quite different from that envisaged by Plowden or the EPA demonstration projects. There is no evidence that the British programmes will make an appreciable impact on achievement. To give some idea of the cost of thorough-going parent involvement projects, Susan Gray estimates that her home visitor programme costs around £170 per child per year. Beside this, Plowden's scheme appears to be little more than a public relations exercise between school and home.

Parent participation is not, of course, seen merely as a means to boost test scores by its protagonists. Perhaps the greater part of its appeal is that it does something more general for the community, increasing its awareness of the school and establishing a sense of coherence in the area as a whole. This is usually described in a vague and imprecise way since, after all, it is a non-measurable property we are discussing. But although these vague concepts are generally regarded as beyond the scope of research, there is generally reason to think that general changes do occur.

The More Effective Schools programmes [...] improved community relations beyond the basic development of favourable attitudes to the school. S. M. Miller has reported that parents change as a result of the Gray-type intervention: they find new jobs, go back to school to educate themselves and become involved in community activities from bowling leagues to church and school councils. No doubt the EPA projects will accumulate a great deal more evidence of this kind.

However worthy these ends, it still seems to me that the programmes do nothing to alter the fundamental relationship between home and school. The potential for the parents to make choices or decisions about their child's education is not increased, nor would the schools be in any way more accountable to those who use them than they are now. The essence of parent participation is that parents come to school, learn about the way the school operates and through doing this become more effective so far as their children's education is concerned. It is clear that parents are there to understand and accept; they are not there to represent their own position if this conflicts with that of the school. There is not room here to discuss the transfer of power from teachers to parents, I merely want to point out that involvement programmes as they are now being run do nothing to expand parents' freedom to make choices, though they may appear to be making schools more responsive to parents.

I should add that parents already have the theoretical ability to choose between schools. But, in practice, parents, especially poor parents, cannot afford to send children to distant schools, and except in towns where the population density is high enough, there is no possibility of having alternatives. Even where a parent could choose between schools, the inadequate one is hardly threatened by parents withdrawing support providing the number of school places is in line with the number of school-age children in the district. Education is monopolised.

We should not, then, have unrealistic expectations of EPA programmes or schemes to improve school–home relations. That has been my main point, last week and this. It is likely that the EPA programme will do a lot to make teachers' lives easier, and it is certainly a worthwhile start to correcting the unfair allocation of educational resources. Equally, the parent participation programmes in all their various forms will likely make parents a great deal happier about their children's education. But what neither of these will do is alter the fact that schools do not at present function to improve the position of the disadvantaged.

4

Some sociological comments on Plowden

B. Bernstein and B. Davies

Introduction

Now that the once fashionable pastime of 'waiting for Plowden' has given way to the rapidly institutionalized sport of baiting it, it may well be most useful to ask first, in general terms, what sort of critique of its content is liable to prove most useful. Given the breadth of the Council's terms of reference – to enquire into 'primary education in all its aspects' (Plowden, 1967, Vol. 1, p. 1) – what can reasonably be expected of the Report is that firstly, it should recognize the social dimensions of its problems, secondly, that it should recognize existing work already in the field and thirdly, that it should exhibit a willingness to look at evidence without implicit preference for certain forms of explanation over others. The Report, like previous reports of the Central Advisory Council, sets out to encompass descriptively a huge field of practice in schools. On the strength of its findings, arrived at in the light of current evidence, it recommends numerous changes. The twin necessities of describing and recommending without offending seem to have induced in the Report a lack of analytic rigour not conducive to good sociological explanation, the essential character of which is to 'look behind' the publicly acknowledged reasons for our arrangements (see Berger, 1966, Burns, 1967). To be quite explicit, the Report [. . .] regularly leaps from value to fact in respect of all of its central themes. It can be shown to be committed to a particular horticultural view of child nature and development (Plowden, 1967, Vol. 1, Part II *passim*) and to a particular view of the teacher, school and curriculum which this commitment logically entails. In general terms, this view comes very close to the semi-official ideology of primary education in this country, the most systematic exposition of which may be found in many colleges of education. Even if the manifest intentions for reform in Plowden come to nothing, therefore, its possible latent function as official reinforcement (better still, *martyred* official reinforcement) for such views must be brought out and the views exposed to examination.

From R. Peters (ed.) *Perspectives on Plowden,* London: Routledge & Kegan Paul, 1972. Ch. 4, pp. 55–83.

A constructive sociological critique will, then, have two sides to it. It will look at any explicit models of the child, home, school, teacher or curriculum in the Report or make explicit those which are implicit. It will also examine what the Report does with existing sociological evidence and the light shed by its own evidence. The Report acknowledges that divisions in description and analysis of the various facets of primary education are somewhat inconvenient. For the sake of brevity and coherence we shall nevertheless look at the child, homes and parents, teachers and schools in sequence. This paper is not so much a critique of Plowden, but rather an attempt to add a sociological perspective to the discussion of pupils, teachers and the primary school.

The child

The model of the child in the Report is essentially biological. The child's growth is regarded as best viewed as passing through a series of stages behaviourally, intellectually and emotionally. The child's successive problems and ultimate maturity are presented as basically developmental. There is an implicit but marked playing down of age and age-grouping as sources of identity and interests (Plowden, 1967, Vol. 1, p. 10, para. 20). The overwhelming characteristic of children insisted upon in chapters one and two is their individual difference. Childhood is seen essentially as a series of ends in itself, change within it from one phase to another being marked by critical periods of maximum learning – sensitivity and readiness. The existence of such periods is demonstrated by examples from animal psychology and ethology. They are assumed to be the case for humans, despite the statement that 'we do not know to what extent such periods occur in the development of children' (para. 28). There is a tendency to equate the development of behaviour with the development of cognitive behaviour (paras. 42–52) to which the growth of language is seen as vital (para. 54). The views of Piaget and Inhelder are quoted in respect of cognitive and Luria and Bernstein in respect of linguistic development. Emotional developments, like the intellectual, 'follow a regular sequence' (para. 65), while social development moves crucially through stages (para. 72). In all of these respects, development is viewed as the product of an interaction of nature and nurture, with a possibility of the environment being inadequate, the child becoming deprived and individual differences becoming heightened. For example, lack of consistency in general and early maternal absence in particular are noted as important contributory factors capable of disturbing emotional development (para. 70). Even more particularly, going to school for the first time may lead to a major crisis for the child in respect of emotional and learning difficulties if mother encourages over-dependency at this time (para. 71).

In general, this is a view of 'the child' from one perspective. 'Stages' figure in explanation to the exclusion of sub-cultural differences. There is a lack of a sufficient grasp of the varieties in family background. How such variation can lead to different degrees of preparedness of the child is not systematically brought out, despite the evidence of the surveys. A notion of the very different orders of role relationships into which children may be socialized before school-going, would give a much wider perspective on the potential significance of that event. Apart from a brief observation in chapter ten, upon the propriety of parents having some say in the 'readiness' of their child for school, the Report has nothing to say, other than that which is noted above, on the matter. While systematic research in this field is relatively recent, it is known that different children arrive at school with thoroughly different initial orientations toward it and their role as pupil: that they come with differential capabilities for role-playing and for meeting the requirements of the school situation. The tendency to espouse an 'undifferentiated' view of the child at school-going age is not Plowden's alone. (See Parsons, 1961.) These differences arise, not so much from a biological basis or relatively unique psychological characteristics of parents, but from differences in the social background of families which are related in turn to differences in language use, values and forms of social control.

Work has been done in recent years by the London Institute of Education Sociological Research Unit upon a range of issues bearing upon the relationship between the home and the primary school. The pre-school child is largely dependent for his ideas of the school on what his mother tells him about it or how she interprets the experience of his brothers and sisters to him. Evidence suggests a strong relationship between social class and the extent of the mother's preparation of her child for school. In a total sample of over three hundred families, working-class mothers have been shown to make minimal preparation, while nearly half of the middle-class mothers mention three or more ways in which they prepare the child. [. . .] Bernstein has drawn attention to the importance of the differential awareness of mothers to the educational functions of play and toys and suggests that

Working-class children often have to learn at school what is part of the experience of the middle-class child. Some middle-class mothers understand, even if they do not always approve, the classroom world of the infant school. Many working-class mothers are at a loss to see what it all means. For a child of these mothers, school is one thing and his life outside school a very different thing. For many middle-class children, the home and the school are in step; for working-class children this is not the case. This continuity and discontinuity affects the extent to which the child can benefit from school and benefit cannot be measured only by grades and examinations (Bernstein, 1967).

Many children from both middle- and working-class backgrounds are, in different ways, inadequately prepared for school.

Plowden also ignores the cultural shaping and expression of biological sex-differences, an omission which may again be related to its narrowly psychologistic view of the child. On this particular point, Blyth notes that the cultural expression of sex-differences in behaviour in middle childhood cut across class differences, while he suggests that peer group relationships exhibit interesting differences between classes. In general, he suggests 'that the cultural component in the characteristic behaviour of children in the middle years is much greater than has often been realized' (Blyth, 1965, Vol. II, pp. 11–12), and in this respect, his strictures upon the 1931 Report (pp. 4, 5) may be extended to include Plowden.

It is this sort of failure to get clear the social significance of age that leads the Report to an inconsistent stand upon the relationship between developmental and chronological age and their bearing upon the ages of transfer. Despite the vital importance attached to developmental age (para. 75), the Report concludes that children are better with friends in their own age-group unless there is clear evidence to the contrary. The sort of 'clear evidence' that is seen as potentially admissible might relate, for instance, to the advisibility of transferring early maturing girls from the top of the middle school before the normal age of transfer (para. 377). At a more general level, the new suggested ages of transfer from first and middle schools, at eight and twelve respectively, are justified in terms of a number of criteria of a developmental and cognitive order. On a particular issue of age-mixing, the Report fails to decide upon the advisibility of vertical (or 'family') groupings in the infants school (paras. 799–804). It does come down quite firmly in favour, though, of separate first and middle schools on pedagogic grounds (para. 426).

What is never really made clear is any recognition of the positive importance of age-status to young children.

In changing the ages of entering and leaving schools, the Report is in fact redefining the notion of childhood. Blyth, who was aware that Plowden was considering this matter when he produced his study, points out some of the possible effects of such a change for both children and schools. For example, at the top end of the middle school, he believes that the change proposed may 'have the effect of reducing the girl's predominance in the good pupil role' (Blyth, 1965, p. 189). As referred to above, the Report is willing to see some of this same category of girls singled out for early promotion to secondary education. Yet this willingness to countenance extreme variability in the treatment of children has to be contrasted with the rigid notion adopted by the Report upon the need for separate first and middle schools. The unacknowledged reason for their proposed separateness could be adjudged more important than those officially avowed. That is to say, that 'children, like adults, enjoy and are stimulated by novelty and change. The first day at school, the transfer to the "big school" are landmarks in the process of growing up.' Children hang on to 'the myth that "going up" must mean going to something better' (para. 427). In other words, that passing from one important age-category to another is both eased and stamped-in by the ritual of changing school, by the physical removal of the child from the context of his old status to that of the new.

In broad terms, the Report would have enabled us to see much more clearly the inter-relationships between the biological and cultural components of childhood if it had examined the recent changes which have taken place in the structure of the family and processes of socialization. It is a loss that it did not discern the importance of this sort of analysis from Crowther, which placed the development of the education of 15–18-year-old pupils in the perspective of relevant social, economic and demographic changes.

Homes and parents

It is held as an important truth in the Report that 'the child's physique, personality and capacity to learn develop as a result of a continuous interaction between his environmental and genetical inheritance' (para. 75). Parents are thus important as providers of 'genetical inheritance' and of probably the most significant part of the child's environment. While genetic factors are unalterable, 'environmental factors are, or ought to be, largely within our control'.

From the whole orientation of the Report, it is clear that the assumption behind its views of homes and parents is that they can be altered and controlled. It is recognized that children grow up in different environmental backgrounds, in different socio-economic groups with their more or less 'adverse circumstances' providing conditions which affect body-size, the age of puberty, standards of nutrition, family size and intelligence (paras. 33–38). However, although these facts are important for education 'in the light that they throw on progress, or lack of it, made towards equalizing even the simple circumstances of life between different classes', it is maintained that 'socio-economic classes are heterogeneous and artificial, and it is not so much the family's occupation or income that is operative here as its attitudes and traditions of child care, its child-centredness, its whole cultural outlook'. At the same time, 'the educational disadvantage of being born the child of an unskilled worker is both financial and psychological' (para. 85).

It has been necessary to quote at length at this point in order to establish what the Report has to say in general terms about class differences. Let it be said immediately that any index of social class is bound to be relatively 'heterogeneous and artificial'. Nevertheless, the operational measures refer to real behaviour. Equally, let it be said that the terminological variability that attends the use of the concepts of 'class' and 'status' in sociology, and not least in respect of the sociology of education, may be calculated to confound even the well-meaning. At the same time, it is difficult not to believe that the Report systematically plays down the importance of social class in education. To conceive of it simply in terms of the Registrar-General's occupational groupings is to conceive of it very narrowly. Such a view will tend to conceal differences acknowledged to be important for education. Even however in the Report's usage, there are differences revealed both by the 1964 National Survey reported and analysed in Volume 2, Appendices 3 to 7, and the Manchester Survey reported in Appendix 9, which would make it exceedingly difficult to ignore the importance of class both in respect of opportunity and educability. Evidence will be adduced below upon this point.

First of all, let us ask why class differences are treated in the Report in this way. One possible reason may be the seduction of a dual commitment to the developmental view of the child described above and to a belief in egalitarianism (that social differences 'ought not' to exist) that makes psychological reductionism appealing. The more acceptable reason may be a lack of sociological insight at points of construction and interpretation of the Survey work. Regression analysis in the National Survey suggests the grouping of variables bearing upon children's progress in school into three categories representing (1) parental attitudes, (2) home circumstances, (3) schooling. The major conclusion reached as the result of the Survey is that 'variation in parental attitudes can account for more of the variation in children's school achievement than either the variation in home circumstances or the variation in schools'. Further, that there is no doubt that attitudes have changed and are changing (Plowden, 1967, Vol. 2, App. 4, p. 181, para. 6). Moreover 'family size does not explain the children's test performances as effectively as the attitudes of their parents' (Plowden, 1967, Vol. 1, para. 90). On the question of 'whether the differences in circumstances account for the differences in attitudes . . . (the) . . . evidence . . . suggests that parent's occupation, material circumstances and education explain only about a quarter of the variation in attitudes' (para. 100). Attitudes may therefore be alterable by persuasion.

Parental attitudes account in fact for 28 per cent of the variation in educational performance for all pupils between schools and for 20 per cent within schools. Thirty-five per cent of the variation between schools and 54 per cent within schools is unaccounted for (Plowden, 1967, Vol. 1, p. 33, Table 1). The Manchester Survey in respect of both school and pupil analyses underlines the same factors, that 'economic level and social class are much less important than aspects of parental attitude' (Plowden, 1967, Vol. 2, App. 9, p. 381). Peaker, in his discussion of the National Survey, suggests that the inclusion of attitudes for the first time in such a survey adds a new dimension to the evidence of Crowther and Newsom (Plowden, 1967, Vol. 2, App. 4, p. 184, para. 18). It necessarily leaves open, however, in terms of the Survey, speculation about the origins of the attitudes which parents exhibit. No one would wish to espouse a deterministic argument concerning the relationship between socio-economic status and attitudes to education. But one would wish to guard against an argument that avoided including attitudes as a dimension of class differences. It would be as well to look very closely at this vital question of their relationship in the National Survey.

The total sample of parents taken as the basis for the Survey shows some discrepancy from the Registrar-General's percentage figures given for the married male population aged 20–64 (Plowden, 1967, Vol. 2, App. 3, p. 100, para. 2, 3). More important than this, the argument advanced that the connection between home circumstances, parental attitudes and children's achievement 'is analogous to the relations between the statuses of fathers, mothers and children' (App. 4, p. 184, para. 18), involves a rather misleading depiction of factor analysis. The 'mother' and 'father' of children's achievement, that is to say, parental attitudes and home circumstances, are constructs rather than givens. Concretely, one is inclined to quarrel with the treatment of variables such as whether parents have taken any recreational or leisure courses, whether the family goes on outings together, and even more strongly, literacy of the home and elements of the category of parental interest and support as attitudinal factors. (See the classifications of variables into factor groupings in Vol. 2, App. 4, Table 1). The criterion for allocating these variables appears to have become confused with a notion of their being 'less firmly anchored in the past' than are variables like parents' occupation and education which are classified under home circumstances (App. 4, p. 183, para. 11). To take one quite specific example, membership of a public library, taken as a component of literacy of the home and classed as an attitude factor in the Survey, shows class differences significant at more than the 0.001 level for both mothers and children in research undertaken by the Institute's Sociological Research Unit.

In other words, whereas social class is defined relatively unambiguously in terms of father's occupation, there is no clear definition of 'attitude'. It covers statements of fact, intention and disposition. On the basis of some rather inexplicit criterion of 'immediacy', important factors like the literacy of the home and paternal interest shown in the Survey and by other work (and further examined below) to be strongly linked to social class, have been arbitrarily assigned to the attitudinal factor in the regression analysis. To do this is to divorce class in an indefensible way from its behavioural concomitants.

That class (in the sense of the Registrar-General's groups) is systematically related to educational factors is not in any sense denied in the Survey work; it is merely systematically played down, particularly in the Report. In the summary of some of the interrelations between parental attitudes to education, home circumstances and class, there is a uniform gradient from Class I to V in respect of differences in responsibility and initiative taken by parents over the child's education, paternal interest and support, knowledge of work that the child was doing and the literacy of the home (Plowden, 1967, Vol. 2, App. 3, p. 147, Table 67). The strongest class gradients on the item clusters in fact appear in respect of paternal interest and literacy of the home. While these obviously imply attitudes, what they essentially refer to is the role system of the family and the range and quality of the communication it is transmitting. They reflect conceptions of how members of the family understand their rights and obligations rather than attitudes readily susceptible to change.

The Survey evidence concerning the role of the father in respect of the child's education is left particularly in mid-air. The National Survey established information about paternal attitudes and characteristics (as on all other aspects of parental attitudes) via the administration of a structured questionnaire by Social Survey Interviewers to mothers. It is important to be explicit upon this point; the data that we have upon the paternal role is essentially the opinion of wives delivered to what may in many cases, have been perceived as officialdom. The evidence gathered reveals strong social class gradients in respect of both husband's interest in the choice of school that the child went to and as to whether the husband had talked to the head of the child's school. The difference is less marked between classes in respect of father's interest in the child's progress with 68 per cent even of Class V fathers reported as taking an interest (Plowden, 1967, Vol. 2, App. 3, p. 118, Table 21). The average score on the item cluster 'paternal interest and support' shows the general class trend (App. 3, p. 147, Table 67). On the less specifically educational question, however, of whether the husband took a big part in controlling the children, responses for Class I to V are, in fact, uniformly high and show no significant trend (App. 3, p. 118, Table 21). On the evidence given, it is clear that, generally, responsibility for the child's education becomes more exclusively maternal as the class scale is descended.

It would seem that many working-class fathers do not support and develop the educational role of their children. It may well be that as a result, the working-class boy does not come to value his educational role as this is not identified with his most significant male relation. The father may point here to the occupational role without it being connected to the educational role. This situation may well be reinforced by the almost totally feminine world of the infant school. It would not be surprising, therefore, to find girls over-represented increasingly down the class scale, for these sorts of reasons, in 'good pupil' success roles, and boys similarly under-represented. Plowden does not present evidence broken down by age, sex and socio-economic category, which would allow such a view to be tested. In Volume I, the discernible references to sex difference amount, in fact, to noting differences in physical rates of maturation, 'the poorer resilience of boys than girls under adverse circumstances' (Plowden, 1967, Vol. I, p. 7) and that the games that girls and boys tend to play at the top of the Junior School are different (p. 258, para. 708).

There are equally striking class gradients exhibited over differences between the type of school parents hoped that their child (when in the final junior year) would go to and the type that the child was in fact going to (Vol. 2, App. 3, p. 122, Table 28. The interview of parents took place at the end of the school year when the 11+ results were known.); or again, as to 'whether any type of secondary was particularly disliked' (Vol. 2, App. 3, p. 123, Table 32); in terms of parent's preferences for streaming by ability (App. 3, p. 142, Table 60); or as to 'other things' which worried parents, indicating that parents highest up in the class scale worry most about things like size of school class. Deprivation is indeed a relative thing (App. 3, p. 144, Table 65). Factors which might count in interpreting these differences probably relate to a whole range of variables. Particularly highlighted are differences in parent's objective knowledge of the situation in schools, in their relative feelings of power or ineffectiveness in respect of school and their ability to express those feelings. It is particularly difficult to understand the failure in the Report to connect up the finding of the National Survey (App. 3, p. 121, Table 27) in respect of parents' attitudes toward their children 'staying on' with the suggested importance by the Manchester Study of preferred age of leaving as the best single indicator of favourable parental attitudes and hence attainment for the average or backward child (App. 9, p. 382, para. 109).

It may be as well to repeat that one is not attempting to deny the importance of parental attitudes for the child's educational attainment. Rather, one is suggesting that to underestimate the social principles which are responsible for the shaping of attitudes may make the problem of their change more difficult. The Report, although hopeful that these attitudes may be favourably manipulated, has virtually no positive evidence to rely upon. Peaker points out that 'such evidence as we have on this point is not very encouraging' (Vol. 2, App. 4, p. 181). (The little encouragement available is reported in Vol. 1, p. 43, paras. 113–117.) The limited evidence given appears open to several interpretations. As a striking example of the danger of the self-fulfilling prophecy in sociology, see Hornsby-Smith (1968). More importantly, the findings of Young and McGeeny (1968), signally fail to clarify this area. Particular attention should be paid to their presentation and discussion of test-score evidence between pp. 91 and 95. There are two sorts of considerations that appear to be important here. In the first place, it must be borne in mind that the relationship established between parental interest and school attainment is correlational rather than causal. In other words, the Report tends to suggest that greater parental interest leads positively to improved attainment. It is, of course, possible that the link in some instances runs the other way; that good attainment by the child leads to increasing parental interest.

One must assume that the link is at least partly reciprocal. Links between small family size and relatively high education aspiration for children must be thought of in the same way. If this is a possibility, then the attempt to 'generate' interest on the part of schools among parents by means described in Chapter 4, may prove a great deal more difficult than is envisaged in the Report or in much subsequent comment (see Blackstone, 1967, p. 300). Moreover, such interest if produced may be more transient than the 'spontaneous' sort.

The second consideration relates to how clear we can be about the proper relationship of the parent to the school. The Report is not without its difficulties in this matter. We shall see presently that its attitude toward Parent-Teacher Associations is ambivalent. This is merely one aspect of the complex of issues relating to parents' actual knowledge of school matters, the desirable extent of that knowledge from the school's point of view and the use to which increased knowledge may be put by parents. It is clear that many parents simply do not know enough about school and that the tendency for this to be the case increases with occupational descent. The Report acknowledges this in several places (Plowden, 1967, Vol. 1, paras. 102–106). What it fails to see is that among parents whose objective knowledge of school affairs is extensive, pressures to achieve may be equally (though more insidiously) hurtful to the child. In the general sense, the development of modern methods, particularly in the Infant School, has probably made it more difficult for parents to co-operate in an active capacity in their child's education. Current pedagogy, with its requirement of specialized teaching techniques which are difficult for the parent to learn, may have led to a greater exclusion of the working-class parent from the child's school experience. If this is the case, then it will be positively dangerous to raise the aspirations of parents unless schools can work out a genuinely meaningful area of shared concern. If this can in fact be done, then it may help to remove the wedge which exists in certain cases between the role of child and that of pupil – another less palatable fact concerning the existing discontinuity between home and school, of which the Report remains largely unaware.

In conclusion of this section, it is possible to agree strongly with the Manchester study's descriptive comment upon the importance of parental interest as a factor in children's brightness which suggests that 'the situation might not be quite as simple as it looks' (Plowden, 1967, Vol. 2, App. 9, p. 382, para. 110). The whole picture presented in the Report of the attitudes which are taken to lie behind and regulate that interest in parents is blurred. Moreover, the conception of 'the child' presented tends to overshadow the cultural and social shaping of the roles of children of different sexes from differing class backgrounds.

The situation insofar as they both bear upon children's school progress is indeed more heterogeneous than Plowden discerns.

Schools

Social aspects of school organization are relatively neglected in Plowden. The implicit picture that one comes away with from its pages is of children in the majority of schools happily progressing in self-regulating groups. As a picture, this is deceptively superficial. At the general level, although the Report talks explicitly about aims and purposes in education, it fails to distinguish these from 'functions' in the social sense. A link between schools and society is acknowledged, couched in the sort of inexplicit terms which only Crowther (Crowther, 1959, Vol. I Ch. 5) among Central Advisory Council reports on schools managed to surmount. In Plowden, schools have the task of preparing children to fit into a society which is rapidly changing, becoming more affluent and which will demand flexible though balanced people (Plowden, 1967, Vol. 1, p. 185). The difficulty of reaching statements upon aims (used in the sense of consensus as to goals to be pursued) is acknowledged, although a statement of goals whose acceptance and pursuit represents 'a general and quickening trend' is offered as a check-list (p. 187, para. 502). One such goal which schools pursue is the attempt 'to equalize opportunities and to compensate for handicaps' (para. 505). The normative intention of this and the whole paragraph in which it is embedded, despite its misleading opening, is clear. Education does offer an increasingly important avenue of social mobility and probably does on balance lessen overall deficiencies in life-chances. Unless, however, the meaning of 'compensate for handicaps' is made much more explicit and the social organization of the school is observed in terms of how it perpetuates such handicaps, we have few clear guides to amelioration. In wider terms, the section on goals in the Report falls short of an objective appraisal of the social functions of primary education. (For a view of the US elementary school see Parsons, 1961. For a specific discussion of the functions of the English primary school see Blyth, 1965, Vol. 1, although the discussion is marred by a peculiar use of terminology. For a wider discussion that fails to avoid a shading off from the empirical to the normative, see Goslin, 1965.)

The only general attempt to describe schools is contained in the evaluation of all primary schools by HMIs who suggest a classificatory scheme of nine intuitive, hazy categories (Plowden, 1967, Vol. 1, p. 100, para. 267 seq.). This is supplemented by the description of three good, 'composite' schools. The whole section is closed by the suggestion that 'what goes on in primary schools cannot greatly differ from one school to another, since there is only a limited range of material within the capacity of primary school children' (para. 289), a comment which epitomizes the triviality of this whole area of the Report.

Streaming is virtually the only aspect of school organization (barring the study of management reported in Appendix 13) given detailed consideration. The Report on balance rejects streaming (para. 833). The N.F.E.R. study on the effects of streaming in junior schools (App. 11), which is the preliminary report of a fuller work due for publication this year, would not of itself sustain this conclusion. It offers only the judgement 'that the question – to stream or not to stream? – reveals itself as the research continues – to require a far more complex and nuanced answer than the propagandists on both sides would have one believe' (Plowden, 1967, Vol. 2, App. 11, p. 555, para. 1.2). What the research reported does tend to suggest is that teachers' attitudes, values and practices are more significant than the form of school organization. This will be commented upon below. Without offering any social class data, the Report accepts that the research shows 'some evidence which suggests that achievement in the limited field of measurable attainment is higher in streamed schools. It is not so marked as to be decisive' and as 'organization can reflect and reinforce attitudes', those schools 'which treat children individually will accept unstreaming throughout' (Plowden, 1967, Vol. 1, p. 291, paras. 818–19). The survey itself points out that the test of attainment used may tend to favour children in streaming schools subject to more traditional forms of curricula and teaching and fail to record abilities which unstreamed schools may foster (Plowden, 1967, Vol. 2, App. 11, p. 574, para. 3.1).

There is a wider issue here which the Report does in fact discern, although it is not clear whether it sees all of its implications. It is felt that schools should work out their own tests for children (Plowden, 1967, Vol. 1, p. 201, para. 551) and that authorities who retain interim secondary selection should cease to rely upon external tests (p. 471). At the same time, it is recommended that 'there should be recurring national surveys of attainment' (p. 473). The wide issue at stake is the question of the sort of attainment that primary schools are working to in the first place. How are standards to be defined in the 'discovery' ethos proposed? What are their relationships to the teacher's classroom objectives? And what sort of testing procedures are appropriate to attainments which result from the school processes envisaged? From the point of view of the teacher, the answers to these questions are of vital importance.

In the same sort of context, the urge to achieve continuity between stages in education leads to the suggestion that 'there should be a detailed folder on each child which could provide a basis for a regular review with children's parents of their progress' (p. 471). The details of what the folder should contain are fully specified (pp. 161–2). The organizational imperatives of the 11+ are to be replaced by individualized rule by dossier. It is interesting to speculate upon the possible mechanics and consequences of keeping such folders. There would be questions of who wrote them up and controlled them; the problem of the evaluative categories to be used in them; difficulties of confidentiality and access. None of these problems are considered in the Report. (For a notion of some of the problems that might arise in this respect, albeit discussed in the context of the US high-school, see Cicourel and Kitsuse, 1963.)

The question of 'who decides what?' in schools is also generally neglected. There is no systematic exposition of the role of either the head or assistant teacher. It is strongly argued that schools need to be permeable to parents and a very large number of devices are discussed in Chapter 4 for improving their knowledge of and participation in school processes. The argument stops short, though, of universally endorsing Parent-Teacher Associations, despite members having been impressed by their high quality 'as much as any aspect of education' in the USA (Plowden, 1967, Vol. 1, p. 39, para. 111) and the generally glowing examples of English P.T. A.s cited (paras. 107–10). The main reasons for this attitude are given as the danger of cliques of dominant parents arising, the failure of the lower working class to participate, but most important, the danger that the head might not be able to give 'good leadership' or delegate P.T.A. running effectively (para. 111). Given the positive fervour with which the Report espouses other methods of parent-participation, one suspects a capitulation here to professional dislike of the P.T.A. One surmises that behind that dislike lies a genuine difficulty of defining the legitimate boundaries of parent-teacher interests and competencies. Our primary schools have only recently begun to move away from being relatively 'closed' social institutions (our secondary schools in the main still are) and in all but a few cases, there is genuine lack of clarity about the boundaries and content of roles to be played by staff and parents toward one another. This is without doubt an area of great difficulty. Nevertheless, by failing to complement its other measures for parental-participation with a more positive affirmation of P.T.A. work, Plowden is risking the build-up without the pay-off. It is also failing to recognize the different nature of the boundaries and contents of the roles of parents from varying social class backgrounds vis-à-vis the school. It merely accepts in this respect the importance of 'habit' in schools and the particular risk that innovation tends to run aground amid the conservatism of teachers (p. 187, para. 503). It is nonetheless prepared to run the risk of upsetting habits in respect of punishment (p. 269, para. 743 seq.). In both of these cases, the situation begs for at least a recommendation to further research on the extent and function of habit, stereotypes and ideology in schools, especially as they bear upon resistance and change. There is not even a hint that those teachers in school who are recognized as having to lean habitually upon coercion may not instantly accept the new forms of control implicit in the superior types of pupil–teacher relationships envisaged in the Report. Or that they may still be inclined, with physical coercion ruled out, even as a last resort, to lean on measures designed to produce psychic pain which may be equally or more undesirable than that induced by corporal punishment.

That there are limits to parents' rights in general in primary schools is a position parallelled in the Report by its proposal in respect of nursery schools to limit children's entry. Here where mothers 'cannot satisfy the authorities that they have exceptionally good reasons for working', the entry of their children is to be given low priority (p. 469). There might be considerable difficulty in rendering this administratively possible without great arbitrariness of definition. The Report believes it proper, in fact, to wash its hands of responsibility for the dangers of the 'alternative arrangements' that it knows in some cases will be made (p. 127, para. 330).

At the same time, the Report's notions upon educational priority areas and the need for positive discrimination toward them go in the right direction and the slogans are probably necessary spurs to public policy. The suggestion of a 'sustained effort . . . to diversify the social composition' of these districts happily amounts to no more than a desire to provide houses for teachers (p. 67). The areas are to be defined in terms of a battery of criteria (pp. 57–9). In general, they will be marked as places where children are most severely handicapped by home conditions. The areas are viewed as needing more teachers, aides, money, college links and teachers' centres. They should see the first developments in social work and community schools. The vital consideration of deciding why some of the schools in these areas *do* in fact work, and building upon this knowledge rather than shunting in extra resources willy-nilly, is in fact recognized as a priority for further research (p. 426, para. 1165 (d)).

The community school as presently envisaged is merely a new name for play centres, youth clubs and evening institutes, with lip-service to Henry Morris, meeting on school premises (pp. 44–6). It is difficult to see them making any significant short-run contribution to education itself in the EPA.

There are relatively straightforward proposals which will bear upon schools which are well conceived and ought to be welcomed. The introduction, for instance, of the single-term entry will provide a more satisfactory basis for the organization of the infant school. It will at the same time end the serious disadvantage of present arrangements to the summer-born child (p. 136), affirmed by numerous studies of streaming and attainment. Equally the call for a uniform, national policy on structure and transfer ages is both overdue and highly necessary in a country where even short-range geographic mobility by parents can transport a child to a completely different standard of provision. Such mobility is likely to increase and the disadvantage of changing schools ought not to be accentuated by gross variation in authority provision which has long been the scandal of the secondary sector.

The curriculum

There is no justification for treating the curriculum apart from the school, nor indeed from considerations of pedagogy. A fully worked out sociology of the school would attempt to relate the nature of the beliefs and skills which are transmitted to the curriculum and pedagogy on the one hand and to the authority relationships and organizational structure of the school on the other. The Report's view of the curriculum is inextricably linked to its view of child nature and the learning process. Its ideas upon child nature have been discussed above. Upon learning, it states that 'Piaget's explanations appear to most educationalists in this country to fit the observed facts of children's learning more satisfactorily than any other' (Plowden, 1967, Vol. 1, pp. 192–3). Play and interest are key aspects of the continuous process of learning. The rigid, subject-divided curriculum and time-table are rejected. In the free-day during which children take every opportunity to experience their environment, learning by discovery will take precedence over learning by description.

Essentially, the Report dichotomizes 'being told' and 'finding out' rather crudely. Its rationale is the pursuit of the long-term objective of living in and serving society being most probably achieved by happy adults who have lived fully as children (p. 188). The child lives most fully by finding out.

There are several far-reaching implications of this position. For the teacher, it indicates quite specifically the role of arranger of context (discussed below). It crucially heightens the problem of the evaluation of children's progress and that of the pedagogy itself. It will serve to reduce the salience of traditional attainments in the evaluation of children. Pupil success will be defined less sharply in terms of the efficient recall of conventionally taught material. For certain sorts of children, there will be the necessity to learn specifically an unaccustomed 'play culture'.

The great bulk of curriculum information in the Report comes in Chapter 17, which is divided into 'traditional' subjects. Robert Dearden [Dearden, 1972] has dealt at length with the possible objections to the Council's views, particularly upon religious education. While there are almost Durkheimian echoes in some of the passages upon the school community and the Act of Worship, it may be held that the views expressed in these areas are platitudinous rather than prescriptive. One would argue that the infectious theory of value-transmission expressed in the belief 'that children will catch values and attitudes far more from what teachers do than what they say' (p. 312) is much nearer the heart of the Council's general notion of learning and the child than is its lapse into moral fervour.

Broadly then, the instrumental order of the primary school is envisaged as non-compartmentalized. Achievement will be thoroughly individualistic though not competitive. The expressive order is seen as informal and nonritualized. Pupil-teacher relationships will tend to be friendly and therapeutic. Control measures will relate to individuals rather than to groups. Schools will be relatively open and fluid institutions. This prospect is regarded by Plowden as wholly pleasing and few would disagree over it. However, it would be as well to acknowledge that the 'open' school will bring with it a different set of problems as well as its expected benefits.

Teachers

The school and curriculum envisaged will, it is repeatedly acknowledged, depend upon the teacher. At the risk of the accusation of waywardness, one would point out that in the forty-six plates which occupy virtually the whole of the chapter on 'Aids to Learning and Teaching', only two contain a teacher. One might be forgiven for imagining therefore that teachers are aids to neither. At least, the balance struck is consonant with the view, already noted, of the teacher as an arranger of context or as a problem setter. This view springs from the premium placed upon 'readiness', which is a notion offered for critical guidance in the teaching situation without any evidence offered as to its signs or any systematic answer to the question of 'for what?' The logical conclusion of this excessive commitment to individual differences can only be a one-to-one teaching relationship.

The hard fact is that even when questions of content are answered, the signs of readiness are not always easily seen. Especially in the context of the large infant school, the teacher may sometimes confuse the inability of the child to master a particular skill either with his lack of interest or a failure on her part to present material in a meaningful way. This is all part of the view that on no account should the teacher impose anything upon the child – 'until the child is ready to take a particular step forward, it is a waste of time to teach him to take it' (Plowden, 1967, Vol. I, p. 25, para. 75). She must wait until the child himself determines what should be made available to him. Sin and virtue have changed sides in the teaching transaction.

However, this latter possibility is swiftly corrected by a positively Chaucerian picture of a typical classroom situation where 'the teacher moved among individuals and groups doing these and other things, and strove to make sure that all were learning' (para. 288). This teacher, like any other, the Report explicitly points out, is responsible for the worthwhileness of what the children are learning (para. 553). However, it is impossible to discover in the Report what this entails, unless implicitly that what children learn is by definition worthwhile.

In the very short introduction to Part Six, we are told that the role of the teacher is less crucial than was formerly thought, that the teacher is in some respect a parent-substitute, that he must be nurturant yet capable of evaluation in respect of the child, that he must have a highly individualistic approach to children's learning, that he must 'lead from behind' and perforce serve as a value-model. The teacher's role is 'bound to be at one and the same time satisfying and yet over-demanding'. 'The teacher's work can never be seen to be completed.' They run the danger of becoming child-like 'the more sensitive and conscientious (they) are' (pp. 311–12). This is once more a curious jumble of fact, myth and prescription but only more confused in degree than parts of the frequently quoted, short sociological analyses of the role (e.g., Wilson, 1962). There is nothing to be found in the Report upon teacher's career lines (not even comparable data on holding power of schools over staff, by areas, as provided by Newsom, 1963, Ch. 3, p.23), upon the consequences of teaching for different lengths of time in different sorts of schools, typical success patterns in teaching or upon informal staff relationships and their possible differences by age, training or sex. We cannot therefore evaluate the effects of any of these things upon children. There is very little in the Report, other than in purely administrative terms, about the head teacher or the existing implications of the pattern of rewards in primary schools. One quite fascinating discovery in respect of Appendix I, 'A Questionnaire to Some Teachers', to which all replies are printed which 'have proved to be of interest' (Plowden, 1967, Vol. 2, App. I, p. 1, para. 2), is that only two out of forty-one questions have been omitted. The first asks for opinions upon the basic salary scale, posts of responsibility and long service awards, the second asked whether men should be encouraged to teach infants (p. 11, Questions 28–9). It must be an exceedingly odd profession that fails to provide interesting opinions upon its own salary position or that fails to reflect upon this omission.

Contained in Plowden's view of the teacher there is an inexplicit assumption of role consensus, no questioning of how it is learned and no elaboration of its strains and satisfactions, of a systematic kind. One might have expected some reference to the way in which changes in science, maths and language teaching in the primary school are likely to strengthen the professional component of the role and perhaps weaken the stereotype of the infant school teacher as a surrogate mother. The practical survey of teacher training, the urge to have it examined and the endorsement of the greater need for a variety of intakes of teachers to primary schools all appear good sense (Plowden, 1967, Vol. I, Ch. 25). One suspects that research undertaken upon colleges of education and training departments will highlight a fundamental tension between the theoretical, liberal orientation of college staff and the more traditional orientation of teachers in practice schools in which students tend to get caught in a rather deadening and unproductive way.

Systematic information on one aspect of teachers is available in the research associated with the streaming study upon characteristics and attitudes exhibited in streamed and unstreamed schools (Plowden, 1967, Vol. 2, App. II, pp. 557–84). Exploratory research of fifty matched pairs of streamed and unstreamed schools by the N.F.E.R. led to the view that 'this difference in organization was reflected in, or arose from, very different views held by the teaching staff which in turn affected the choice of teaching methods' (p. 557). A complex piece of research which uses the rather unfortunate terms 'obsessive' and 'permissive' to dichotomise teaching characteristics, concludes that 'streamed and non-streamed schools embody different philosophies'; that although not all teachers conform to the predominant pattern of their school, 'the streamed school seems to be more systematic, concentrates more on conventional lessons, gives more attention to the 3-Rs and is likely to be more traditional'. The non-streamed school has younger teachers 'who hold more permissive views on such things as manners, noise and cleanliness. . . . Their teaching tends to place more emphasis on self-expression, learning by discovery and practical experience' (p. 589). The survey offers no opinion upon the fascinating alternative posed above as 'reflected in, or arose from' but emphasizes that differences in streamed and unstreamed schools arise not only from organization but 'the whole climate of relationships built up by what teachers say and do and what they appear to their pupils to imply' (p. 573). The research hints at the importance of a whole nexus of relationships between values, recruitment, professional socialization and organizational arrangements and offers an insight to the possible sorts of built-in resistances to any change envisaged in schools. And yet this fails to be even mentioned in the areas for further studies in the body of the Report.

It may be thought that too much space has been devoted to negative criticism of the Report in these comments. This has not been the aim. There are a number of very positive features and recommendations within the body of the Report and these have been referred to by numerous commentators. All that has been attempted here is to try and show the type of questions which can be raised as a result of adopting a sociological standpoint.

References

Berger, P. L. (1966) *Invitation to Sociology,* London: Pelican Books.
Bernstein, B. B. (1967) 'Play and the infant school', *Where* supplement.
Blackstone, T. (1967) 'The Plowden Report', *British Journal of Sociology,* Sept., 1967.
Blyth, W. A. L. (1965) *English Primary Education: A Sociological Description,* London: Routledge & Kegan Paul.

66   4 *Some sociological comments on Plowden*

Burns, T. (1967) 'Sociological explanation', *British Journal of Sociology*, 18, 1967.

Cicourel, A. V. and Kitsuse, J. I. (1963) *The Educational Decision Makers*, New York: Bobbs-Merrill.

Crowther Report (1959) *15 to 18*, Central Advisory Council for Education (England) London: HMSO.

Dearden R. F. (1972) 'The aims of primary education', in R. S. Peters (ed.) *Perspectives on Plowden*, London: Routledge & Kegan Paul.

Goslin, D. A. (1965) *The School in Contemporary Society*, New York: Scott, Foresman.

Hornsby-Smith, M. P. (1968) 'Parents and primary schools', *New Society*, 11 Jan.

Newsom Report (1963) *Half Our Future*, Central Advisory Council for Education (England) London: HMSO.

Parsons, T. (1961) 'The school class as a social system', in A. H. Halsey, J. Floud and C. A. Anderson (eds) *Education, Economy and Society*, Glencoe, Ill.: Free Press.

Plowden Report (1967) *Children and their Primary Schools*, Central Advisory Council for Education (England) London: HMSO.

Wilson, B. R. (1962) 'The teacher's role', *British Journal of Sociology* **8**, No. 1.

Young, M. and McGeeney, P. (1968) *Learning Begins at Home*, London: Routledge & Kegan Paul.

5

Political ends and educational means
Educational priority: EPA problems and policies

A. H. Halsey (ed.)

Preface

This report has its origins in the immediate aftermath of the publication of the Plowden Report in 1967 when Anthony Crosland was the Secretary of State at the D.E.S., I was his part-time adviser, Michael Young was the Chairman of S.S.R.C., and the informal seminars on problems of educational policy described elsewhere by Crosland[1] were in full swing.

Two things particularly impressed me in the Plowden Report – the principle of positive discrimination as applied to slums and the call for action-research. The Plowden Committee had drawn attention to the schools in run-down areas which had grim buildings, high staff turnover, and teachers liable 'to become dispirited by long journeys to decaying buildings to see each morning children among whom some seem to have learned only how not to learn'.[2] Positive discrimination was advocated 'to make schools in the most deprived areas as good as the best in the country'. Within the limits of the tiny resources made available to us the first aim of the programme reported here was to do just that, and much of our report is made up of descriptions of our successful and unsuccessful efforts.

This aim of action may be thought of as the primary interest of the D.E.S., backed by a grant of up to £100,000. But the second aim, which perhaps belongs more properly to the S.S.R.C. and its £75,000, was to transform action into action-research. The Plowden Committee had made a plea for 'research to discover which of the developments in the educational priority areas have the most constructive effects so as to assist in planning the longer term programme' which they hoped was to follow. The evaluations (a term with a range of strong and weak senses), which appear at various points in [Volume 1] and subsequent volumes, are our contribution to Plowden's plea. In the context of the programme as a whole they constitute a pioneering effort in the use of the action-research method in Britain.

This extract forms the Preface and Chapters 1 and 2 of A. H. Halsey (ed.) *Educational Priority Vol. 1: EPA Problems and Policies,* Report of a research project sponsored by the Department of Education and Science and the Social Science Research Council, London: HMSO, 1972, pp. vii–xi, and 3–30.

The programme

The slow progress of negotiating a grant began after the 'Plowden seminar' in 1967 and involved correspondence and discussion between Michael Young, Anthony Crosland, Sir Lionel Russell, the S.S.R.C.'s Educational Research Board and various Chief Education Officers of the local education authorities. The Secretary of State declared willingness to consider an action-research proposal in October 1967 and the E.R.B. approved the idea of an E.P.A. programme the next month. Protracted negotiations with L.E.A.s and nearby universities[3] followed in 1968. An H.M.I., John Gregory, was seconded to us from May 1968. The districts in London, Birmingham, Liverpool and the West Riding were chosen, parallel Scottish arrangements were made at Dundee,[4] and a grant for the English programme of up to £175,000 for a three-year programme was made at the end of May 1968.

The next few months were taken up with negotiating detailed arrangements with the L.E.A.s and the appointment of staff. The Liverpool project director, Eric Midwinter, took up his post in September 1968, Charles Betty went to Deptford in October, and Randall Lines and Mike Harvey to Birmingham and the West Riding respectively on 1 January 1969. There was thus a staggered start in the four areas, but the National Steering Committee fixed a common terminal date – the last day of 1971.

While staffing arrangements were being made in the autumn of 1968 George Smith had been looking closely at the American literature on 'compensatory education'. Then, in January 1969, Mr Smith, Dr Alan Little and I attended a conference under the auspices of the Centre for Educational Research and Innovation of O.E.C.D. and the Ford Foundation at which we discussed with experienced Americans the relevance of their programmes for the E.P.A. programme on which we were about to embark. Mr Smith and Dr Little subsequently visited a wide range of American projects with a view to preparing an extended report for O.E.C.D.[5]

By this time we were reaching the end of a series of plenary conferences attended by the staff of all the projects as they were appointed, by the Dundee project group, by Alan Brimer and his colleagues from the University of Bristol and by Michael Young and Jack Tizard from the E.R.B. There were also smaller conferences especially between the research staffs. The general character of our collective approach is fairly accurately reflected in my summary of the concluding plenary conference in January 1969* [which] shows how early we focused on the idea of a multiplier of educational effort from our own initial input and on the idea of the community school, [and] also [shows] the divisions within the project teams concerning the balance between action and research. Already I had become convinced that local autonomy and initiative could not and should not be

---

*See Appendix 1 to the report.

subjugated to central direction in the interests of evaluation in its strongest sense, i.e. within the rigorous constraints of a national experimental design. Rather was it that five case studies with evaluation in the weak sense of orderly description of the area, the schools and the action programme were assured and beyond this I encouraged co-operation towards inter-project co-operation and comparison. . . .

The differences between the teams were a function of both situation and personality. Charles Betty came to London from a primary school headship and was strongly teacher-oriented in an organisational setting which was unfamiliar to him and where a strong research department existed within the L.E.A. Randall Lines was an experienced chief education officer with a strong sense of the financial constraints on educational innovation, and he was partnered in Birmingham by a teacher and psychologist, Paul Widlake, with passionate interests in children who have to struggle with the elementary skills of language and number. Eric Midwinter came from a college of education and with a deep knowledge of the culture of Liverpool 8 and the E.P.A. school. His research officer, Keith Pulham, had had planning experience and, with the other members of the team, worked loyally and closely to Midwinter's leadership. Their co-operation with the L.E.A. was powerfully supported by the Chief Inspector, Tom MacManners. Mike Harvey was a young man with successful experience in the teaching of 'difficult' children, and his research officer, George Smith, was a classicist turned sociologist who had taught in India and whose wife was a trained social worker. The team was thrown closely together by the circumstances of an isolated and close-knit mining community at some distance from the centre of educational administration in Wakefield whence Sir Alec Clegg generated benevolent interest.

At all events differences on conceptions or priorities were obvious in the four projects from the beginning. Liverpool was action dominated from the start. The problem in Eric Midwinter's view was to get something done. As he wrote at the end of his interim report, 'so pressing is the need, both for the practical purpose of avoiding permanent social dislocation and for the moral purpose of ensuring an elementary system of social justice, that it would have been preferable to have come up with an answer in three weeks'. In fact and plan, however, the projects went on to the end of their three years with increasing pressure from the centre towards strengthening the evaluation side of the programme. An interim report was submitted to the D.E.S. and S.S.R.C. via the National Steering Committee in the autumn of 1970 at which point the budget for the final year was allocated.

During the third and final year, while the main effort has, of necessity, been concentrated on the action and research programmes which had been developed in the first two years, we have also done what we could to ensure that what has been successful among our innovations should not end with our formal departure from the four districts. The result so far lies between the height of our hopes and the depression of our expectations. Our attempt to persuade the S.S.R.C. to finance continuation of action-research in Birmingham, Liverpool and the West Riding failed despite the backing of the National Steering Committee – a bad omen for both the realisation of Plowden reform and for the progress of action–research. The only gain on this front was a small grant towards the completion of the Home Visiting and follow-up testing programmes in the West Riding.[6] On the other hand we have been encouraged by another arm of government – the Community Development Projects of the Urban Programme which have increasingly incorporated E.P.A. elements into their development, especially in the Vauxhall district of Liverpool and at Coventry. Moreover, after our final report was submitted, the D.E.S. gave us serious and sympathetic interest leading to discussions with officials and the Secretary of State which are continuing.

Important parts of the work in all four areas will continue to be financed by the Exchequer under the Urban Programme for at least five years. The I.L.E.A. will continue its action programme and will benefit, as do all the innovations of that Authority, from the established existence of Alan Little's research department.[7] The West Riding (regrettably to be broken up in 1974) will carry on its support to Red House, thereby essentially continuing the project. Birmingham is continuing some of the work in Balsall Heath, and Liverpool is contributing towards a new organisation for the national promotion of E.P.A. policy and practice, *Priority*. *Priority* promises to be a notable success and is owed first and foremost to the ceaseless and infectious enthusiasm of Eric Midwinter. Given our claim to have put substance on to the skeleton of the Plowden conception of the community school, it was essential to provide for the dissemination of successful practice to all E.P.A. schools, indeed to all schools, in the country. That is the essential funtion of *Priority*. In Dundee the education authority and other agencies have made provision for carrying on and extending E.P.A. work.

Meanwhile we can reasonably claim that a more or less permanent mark has been left on the schools, the communities, the teachers and the colleges of education where our action programme has taken us. The desirability of an evaluative revisit in, say, two years' time is almost too obvious to mention.

The other gain which deserves a mention is that the programme has developed experience and expertise in the skills of action-research which scarcely existed before the D.E.S. and S.S.R.C. financed this first venture. Some of the staff, and especially the younger research workers, are now highly valuable resources. They are the first generation of what I hope will become an important branch of the social sciences with its great potential utility for government, administration and constructive social criticism. We have now established a 'Social Evaluation Unit' in the Department of Social and Administrative Studies at Oxford which is concerned with the study of action-research methods and their application to various fields of public policy.

Our thanks are due to all those teachers, administrators, parents and their children whose participation made our work both possible and enjoyable. For my own part I want to record that the result which appears below owes much more to the labour of my colleagues than to me. The field work was enjoyable and enjoyed but it was nonetheless arduous: but despite the solemn warning of the American experience we never lost a single member of the team before the study was completed.

Finally we are grateful to the D.E.S. for arranging publication for us through the Stationery Office. The opinions expressed in this and subsequent volumes are, of course, ours and in no way represent policies or commitments of Her Majesty's Government.

Political ends and educational means

To find a strategy for educational roads to equality! That has been a central theme of educational discussion from the beginning of the twentieth century. It has produced a prolific sociology of education over the last generation in which the centrality of educational systems to the structure and the functioning of industrial societies has become a commonplace. In the 1950s education in these societies was seen as having a crucial role for economic growth and change. More recently the emphasis has shifted to the part played by formal educational organisations in defining what is and what is not knowledge, and as selective agencies allocating individuals to social positions, moulding their social personalities and their definitions of the world around them. But the underlying question is whether, and if so under what circumstances, education can change society.

The answer, whatever its form, has been controversial in two apparently different ways. Debate has turned on the *desirability* of using educational means for political ends. But also, and much more fruitfully, it has turned on the feasibility of different educational means towards agreed ends. Thus 'keeping education out of politics' can be a crude evasion of the incontrovertible fact that, in a modern or a modernising society, educational arrangements are an important determinant of the life and livelihood of individuals: education is a social distributor of life chances. In its more subtle forms, however, this political or moral stance may be a protest against narrow definitions of the social consequences of educational reform. As such it belongs neither to the political right nor to the political left. It is of course associated with such writers as T. S. Eliot,[8] Professor Bantock[9] and the authors of the Black Papers,[10] but there are equally important radical criticisms of narrowness in the sociological imagination; for example reform in the direction of meritocracy may fail to take account of those ramified consequences which Professor Bernstein has referred to as 'the individualisation of failure' and there is a good deal of current writing from an interactionist or phenomenological point of view which insists on the importance of education as structuring reality for those exposed to it in broader terms than that associated with a definition of schooling as the agency through which individuals are allocated to the labour force.

The problem of the entanglement of analysis with value assumptions is intrinsic to sociological study. To get it straight we must first distinguish the 'scientific' from the 'value' problem: to ask separately what is possible and thereby, with the issue and alternatives sharply defined, to decide on preferences and priorities. In this way the challenge to social science becomes clear and the task for the sociologist is, literally, to inform the political debate. Of course the distinction between sociology and politics is much less easy than a naive positivism would presuppose. It is necessary at every step to try to make explicit what are the implicit assumptions of political aims and the value premises of sociological analysis. There is no final or ready-made procedure for either of these tasks. We have only imperfect aids beyond the injunction to constant vigilance.

One aid of particular relevance to our problem in this book can be taken from John Goldthorpe's discussion of futurology.[11] Goldthorpe distinguishes between futurology as *prediction* and futurology as *design*. Conventional futurology is essentially extrapolation to the future of trends from the recent past. It therefore tends to carry with it the value assumptions of the status quo and is in that sense conservative. That is why the book covers of this literature (*U.S.A. 2000*) are, as Raymond Aron has remarked, so much more exciting than the pages. The future is only the present, usually writ slightly larger. Futurology as *design* is quite another matter, and not only because it is inherently more radical in its political possibilities. It is scientifically much more challenging in that it directly requires the social scientist to state clearly what he knows or does not know about the possibility of moving from the present state to a postulated, presumably desired, future state.

Political aims and programmes in general and the aim of educational equality in particular, together with the various programmes for its attainment, lend themselves fairly readily to translation into futurology as design. The translation can be used to define the critical and constructive role of the social scientist, in this case with relation to the problems of educational reform through political and administrative action. And action–research, as we understand it, is an experimental or quasi-experimental version of futurology as design. Ends are stated together with means to their achievement. In this case the ends are greater social equality of educational opportunity and attainment and the means are Plowden's positive discrimination for educational priority areas. Ends and means are modified and explicated in a programme of action and the relation between them is analysed by research monitoring of the action programme.

A second and related aid to understanding the social science task is the Popperian distinction between holistic and piecemeal reform. The general arguments against holism cannot be rehearsed here. What is relevant, however, is not a debate over the dichotomy but over the appropriate scale of the piecemeal. It is not so much a question of whether education can change society: it is a question of the level of ambitiousness of social engineering which may be required to change an undesired state of affairs. The Plowden analysis of low educational standards in E.P.A.s points to causes outside the school in the neighbourhood structure of life and therefore calls for a widely based programme of social reform alongside positive discrimination in education. Within this framework Plowden postulates that 'what these deprived areas need most are perfectly normal, good primary schools'. There is in other words a belief here in educational cures for educational evils. Some of the early American compensatory education programmes seem to have gone much further and approached the belief that poverty can be completely abolished through educational reform. Others take an opposing and more radical view of the changes necessary to ameliorate either poverty in general or educational poverty in particular. K. Coates and R. Silburn have expressed this view in a recent comment on the Plowden ideas.

... *the schools themselves could become, to a degree, centres of social regeneration: growth points of a new social consciousness among the poor, which might at last bring poverty under attack from its sufferers, no less than from the all-too-small battalions of liberal welfare workers and social administrators.*

Obviously many of these are sensible aims. Yet it is important at the same time to state baldly what these aims could not achieve. Education, in itself, will not solve the problem of poverty. The social structure that generates poverty generates its own shabby education system to serve it; and while it is useful to attack the symptom, the disease itself will continually find new manifestations if it is not understood and remedied. The solution to poverty involves, of course, the redistribution of effective social power. Self-confidence, no less than material welfare, is a crucial lack of the poor, and both can only be won by effective joint action. More contentiously, it seems to us that educational provision alone cannot solve even the problem of educational poverty, if only because in this sphere there are no purely educational problems.[12]

Our own view in undertaking the E.P.A. action–research was cautiously open-minded on the capacity of the educational system to reform itself, dubious about an educational approach to the abolition of poverty, but at least as optimistic as Plowden about the primary school and pre-schooling as points of entry for action-research aimed at inducing changes in the relation between school and community.

In principle, action–research can approach the holistic end of the continuum. In practice it usually operates at the other extreme though often with implicit holistic expectations of the kind reflected in the early euphoria and rhetoric of the American Headstart programme. Perhaps it is mainly the confused contradiction between astronomical ends and miniscule means that underlies the asperity of such criticisms as Bernstein's 'education cannot compensate for society'. We have to know what is sociologically and politically possible. In part the answer to both questions turns on the willingness and power of a society to define education imperiously in relation to the other social organisations which carry educative or culturally transmitting functions, especially the family but also classes, neighbourhoods, ethnic groups and local communities. This depends again in part on economic and technical means. Obviously the feasibility of education as the dominant means to a particular social design is eased by wealth and growth, but the crucial factor here is political – the political structure and the will of political leadership.

Perhaps the importance of the economic and technical base for educational development is exaggerated. There are conspicuous variations in the level of educational development between countries of similar income and wealth per capita. And the remarkably durable success of classical China in using her educational system to create and maintain a ruling administrative class of mandarins was, it should be remembered, the invention of a pre-industrial society. Perhaps also the serviceability of education as an agent of social selection and distribution is exaggerated until one examines the evidence: for example it was shown in the Robbins Report that two-thirds of *middle-class* children with I.Q.s of 130+ who were born in 1940/41 did not go on to a university education. Nevertheless it still remains a crucial question as to how seriously a society determines to realise the values in which the use of the educational system as a means is involved. That is the crux of the problem of educational inequality and the ultimate determinant of whether or not Plowden's positive discrimination will bring about its intended effects.

What, then, are the sought ends in the politics of education in modern Britain? The dominant slogans are combinations of efficiency and equality. Efficiency for modernity. Equality for efficiency and justice. But both the meaning of these combined ends and the means postulated as adequate to their attainment remain dubious and confused. Thus the combination of equality of educational opportunity with the goal of national efficiency has led to policies designed to create and maintain a meritocracy – a principle which by no means commands universal acceptance.

However, the essential fact of twentieth-century educational history is that egalitarian policies have failed. This must be the starting point for understanding the significance of our studies and to reach it we must review past principles and policies. There appears to us to have been a developing theoretical and practical debate in three stages about the way education can be used as a means towards the political and social end of equality.

In the first phase, from the beginning of the century to the end of the 1950s, the definition of policy was liberal – equality of opportunity. It meant equality of access to the more advanced stages of education for all children irrespective of their sex or social origin in classes, religious and ethnic groups or regions. It therefore expressed itself in such measures as building the scholarship ladder, abolishing grammar school fees, doing away with a system of separate secondary education for the minority and elementary education for the majority and substituting a system of common schooling with secondary schools 'end-on' to primary schools. In the later years of this phase it also meant expansion of higher education.

The logical end of the first phase, when equality of opportunity is combined with national efficiency, is meritocracy. In its most advanced educational expression this essentially liberal principle is to be found in the Preface to the Newsom Report written by the then Minister for Education, Sir Edward (later Lord) Boyle: 'The essential point is that all children should have an equal opportunity of acquiring intelligence, and of developing their talents and abilities to the full.' But the inexactitudes of psychometrics, the capriciousness of late developers, the survival of the private market in education along with the continuous renewal of non-educational avenues to higher social positions – all these factors together have prevented the emergence of an educationally based meritocracy.

The liberal notion of equality of opportunity dominated discussion at least until the 1950s. But it was never unchallenged by those who wrote in the tradition of R. H. Tawney and it was effectively lampooned in Michael Young's *Rise of the Meritocracy*. Writers like Tawney and Raymond Williams[13] always sought for an educational system which would be egalitarian in the much broader sense of providing a common culture irrespective of the more or less inescapable function of selection for different occupational destinies. There is a broad distinction of political and social aims here which, in the end, come to the most fundamental issue of the purposes of education in an urban industrial society and about which judgements are explicitly or implicitly made in any action–research programme of the type we have undertaken. One way of putting the distinction is that the liberal goal of efficient equality of opportunity is too restrictive: we have also to consider liberty and fraternity. Properly conceived the community school, an idea which we discuss in detail below, reflects the attribution of value to these other two great abstractions of the modern trilogy of political aims.

All this is to say nothing about the problem of feasibility of either narrowly or broadly conceived egalitarian aims. Tawney took it for granted that the processes of parliamentary democracy, serviced by the British type of civil administration, would be adequate as means to these ends. There is less confidence now and much more questioning as to what it might mean politically to achieve what Coates and Silburn have referred to as 'the redistribution of effective social power'. Questioning of this kind comes from many sources, but not least from recognition of the failures of past policies directed towards a greater equality of educational opportunity.

The essential judgement must be that the 'liberal' policies failed even in their own terms. For example, when, in a large number of the richer countries during the 1950s, a considerable expansion of educational facilities was envisaged, it was more or less assumed that, by making more facilities available, there would be a marked change in the social composition of student bodies and in the flow of people from the less favoured classes into the secondary schools and higher educational institutions. This has certainly not happened to the degree expected. While expansion of education was accompanied by some increase in both the absolute numbers and the proportions from poor families who reached the higher levels and the more prestigious types of education, nevertheless progress towards greater equality of educational opportunity as traditionally defined has been disappointing. It is now plain that the problem is more difficult than had been supposed and needs, in fact, to be posed in new terms.[14]

Too much has been claimed for the power of educational systems as instruments for the wholesale reform of societies which are characteristically hierarchical in their distribution of chances in life as between races, classes, the sexes and as between metropolitan/suburban and provincial/rural populations. The typical history of educational expansion in the 1950s and 1960s can be represented by a graph of inequality of attainment between the above-mentioned social categories which has shifted markedly upwards without changing its slope. In other words relative chances did not alter materially despite expansion. No doubt, the higher norms of educational attainment contributed something towards raising the quality of life in urban industrial society – that, at least, is the faith of the educationist. But in terms of relative chances of income, status and welfare at birth, the impact of the educational system on the life of children remained heavily determined by their family and class origins. From the same point of view, what appears to have happened was a general adjustment of the occupational structure such that entry to it was in process of continuous upward redefinition in terms of educational qualifications. The traditional social pattern of selection remained remarkably stable. The school is only one influence among others, and, in relation to the phenomenon of social stratification, probably a fairly minor one. Attitudes towards schooling, and actual performance in school, reflect children's general social milieu and family background, and probably most important of all, the expectations, built in by constraining custom, of his teachers. School reform helps, but the improvement of teacher/pupil ratios, the building of new schools and even the provision of a wider variety of curricula have at best a limited effect as counterweights.

Moreover, there has been a tendency to treat education as the waste paper basket of social policy – a repository for dealing with social problems where solutions are uncertain or where there is disinclination to wrestle with them seriously. Such problems are prone to be dubbed 'educational' and turned over to the schools to solve. But it was now increasingly plain that the schools cannot accomplish important social reforms such as the democratisation of opportunity unless social reforms accompany the educational effort. And it also became more evident that the schools are hampered in achieving even their more traditional and strictly 'educational' purposes when, in societies changing rapidly in their technologies and in the aspirations of their populations, a comparable effort to make the required change in social structures and political organisation is lacking.

In summary, it may be said that liberal policies failed basically on an inadequate theory of learning. They failed to notice that the major determinants of educational attainment were not schoolmasters but social situations, not curriculum but motivation, not formal access to the school but support in the family and the community.

So the second phase began with its new emphasis on a theory of non-educational determination of education. In consequence of the experience of the first phase in trying to bring about greater equality of educational opportunity, there had to be a change in the meaning assigned to the phase. Its earlier meaning was equality of access to education: in the second phase its meaning gradually became equality of achievement. In this new interpretation a society affords equality of educational opportunity if the proportion of people from different social, economic or ethnic categories at all levels and in all types of education are more or less the same as the proportion of these people in the population at large. In other words the goal should not be the liberal one of equality of access but equality of outcome for the median member of each identifiable non-educationally defined group, i.e. the *average* woman or negro or proletarian or rural dweller should have the same level of educational attainment as the average male, white, white-collar, suburbanite. If not there has been injustice.

This important social-cum-educational principle, with its radical implications for both social and educational policies, was graphically illustrated in the findings of the American Coleman Report[15] where educational attainments were compared as between northerners and southerners of white and non-white race. The graph (Fig. 5.1) shows that schooling between ages 6 and 18 (Grades 1–12 in American schools) is associated with a divergence of the mean attainment of four categories of children who are not directly defined in educational terms.[16] The radical goal of educational equality of opportunity would, if realised, produce converging as opposed to diverging lines.

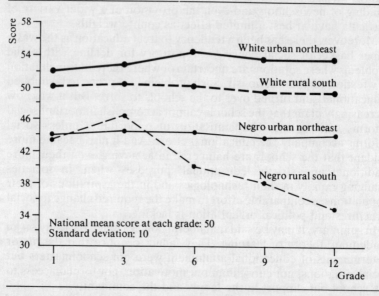

Fig. 5.1 Patterns of achievement in verbal skills at various grade levels by race and region.

The Plowden Report belongs to this phase in the development of our understanding of the egalitarian issues in education and relates them to the social setting of the school.

With Plowden the close relationship of social deprivation, in neighbourhood and home, and educational attainment was well-founded in research. Equally valid is the corollary that, if social conditions and parental interest could be improved, achievement might be expected to rise. One or two examples must suffice. J. W. B. Douglas in 1964 set the attainment scores of a large sample of upper primary children against a number of social factors.[17] From this survey certain extreme cases might be extrapolated. At eleven years of age and with 50 as the average mark, lower manual working-class children in unsatisfactory housing were scoring on average 46.66 as against the 56.91 of upper middle-class children in satisfactory accommodation; as between the same groups divided by low and high levels of parental interest the scores were 46.32 and 59.26; polarised by 'very disturbed' and 'undisturbed' assessments, the two groups averaged 44.49 and 57.53; while the seventh child of the lower bracket of parents obtained

42.19 over against the 59.87 of the first child in the higher social category. Eleven per cent of the lower manual group and 54.3 per cent of the upper middle group obtained grammar school places. Only 4.8 per cent of the children in a poorly assessed lower working class school as opposed to 53.22 per cent of those in a highly assessed upper middle class school obtained places in grammar schools. Just below the cut-off point for selection, 1.4 per cent only of the 'lower manual' children and as many as 42.9 per cent of 'upper middle' children were in grammar, technical or independent schools.

These admittedly are deliberately extracted extremes, but the E.P.A. projects were planned to consider one of these extremes. A very disturbed child of unskilled parents, who showed no interest in his schooling and who lived in unsatisfactory accommodation was, for example, no rarity in Liverpool 7. In 1967, the Ministry of Social Security reported that 7 per cent of families were at or below the poverty line. Either figure would include a large number of the study area's population; indeed, in 1968, the Merseyside Child Poverty Action Group found that one in three in Liverpool 8 were living in poverty as defined by the Ministry of Social Security, while, in 1971, the Child Poverty Action Group claimed that one in every six children in the nation was on or below the poverty line.[18]

Professor Wiseman argued convincingly that '"home" variables have, pro rata, twice the weight of "neighbourhood" and "school" variables put together' when correlated with educational attainment.[19] His research indicated that it was parental attitudes rather than social levels which were more important in the home. Again, the National Child Development Study showed that parents in the highest occupational grouping were much readier to initiate school contacts than those in the lowest grouping, and there was a similar social gap in terms of adjustment to school.[20] A recent examination of truancy suggests that gross absenteeism is solidly linked with unsatisfactory home life and uninterested parents.[21]

We are not here, it must be added, embracing the view that the pre-Plowden literature had over-emphasised the part played by class in determining educational performance. On the contrary we agree with the sociological critique of the Plowden Report by B. Bernstein and B. Davies, in which they expressed the view that, by its concentration on child centredness, Plowden had underestimated class distinctions.[22] As these writers argue, 'evidence suggests a strong relationship between social class and the extent of the mother's preparation of her child for school' and that 'one would wish to guard against an argument that avoided including attitudes as a dimension of class differences'.

At all events, in reading the Plowden Report, one could hardly escape the view that equality of opportunity was without equality of conditions, a sham. Home circumstances were obviously critical and these in turn were adversely affected by class and neighbourhood patterns. The school, where, after all, the children spent only five hours of the day, seemed comparatively powerless to alter matters radically of its own volition. Assuredly, a decision to consider the E.P.A. school in its communal setting was a wise one, and the Plowden Committee had been well advised to recommend that community schools should be developed in all areas but especially in E.P.A.s.

Our own definition of the problem in 1968 was consonant with the debate up to this point and was in accord with the Plowden approach accepting that positive discrimination held out the hope of further steps towards the new definition of equality of opportunity.

But in the early months of our work we began to realise that there were unsolved issues behind the equality debate even in its advanced formulation and especially when applied to the children of the educational priority areas. The debate could be taken beyond equality of educational opportunity to a third phase which involves reappraisal of the functions of education in contemporary society. Education for what? The debate over equality as we have summarised it – a movement from preoccupation with equality of access towards concern with equality of outcomes as between social groups – is essentially a discussion about education for whom and to do what. In planning our intervention in schools we were forced sooner or later to consider both questions and in doing so to question whether an E.P.A. programme is anything more than a new formula for fair competition in the educational selection race.

What assumptions could or should be made about the world into which our E.P.A. children would enter after school? Were we concerned simply to introduce a greater measure of justice into an educational system which traditionally selected the minority for higher education and upward social mobility out of the E.P.A. district, leaving the majority to be taught, mainly by a huge hidden curriculum, a sense of their own relative incompetence and impotence – a modern, humane and even relatively enjoyed form of gentling the masses? Or could we assume a wide programme of social reform which would democratise local power structures and diversify local occupational opportunities so that society would look to its schools for a supply of young people educated for political and social responsibility and linked to their communities not by failure in the competition but by rich opportunities for work and life? Even short of the assumption of extra-educational reform how far should we concentrate on making recognition easier for the able minority and how far on the majority who are destined to live their lives in the E.P.A? And if the latter did this not mean posing an alternative curriculum realistically related to the E.P.A. environment and designed to equip the rising generation with the knowledge and skills to cope with, give power over and in the end to transform the conditions of their local community?

It was, and is, commonly felt that a discriminatory boost was needed in the backward areas to bring education up to scratch so that, for instance, the thousands leaving school at fifteen who had the potential to benefit from advanced schooling might stay on. The Plowden Report argued this respectable and widely held thesis with admirable spirit. It detailed a programme of 'positive discrimination' and 'a new distribution of educational resources', through priority building and minor works, improved staffing and auxiliary help, supplemented salaries and so on. This was designed to cater for 'a great reservoir of unrealised potential', for 'what these deprived areas need most are perfectly normal good primary schools'. Twice over Plowden decreed that the E.P.A. schools should be as good as the best in the land.[23]

Because the national system of education was seen not to operate efficiently in its uniform application across the country, it was accepted that a differential application would help close, to quote Plowden again, 'the gap between the educational opportunities of the most and least fortunate children . . . for economic and social reasons alike'. But, logically, an alternative existed. It was worth considering that what was wrong was a uniform system, and that differing areas required differing educational formats.

This viewpoint, Eric Midwinter insisted in our early conferences, does no disservice to the pioneers who campaigned for parity of opportunity. They doubtless imagined that equality of opportunity would beget conditions in which forthcoming generations would automatically start at par. This has not, unhappily, transpired. Those working in a deprived area are typically sympathetic to the egalitarian tradition and find the alarums and the postures of the anti-egalitarian commentators laughable.[24] They shout before they are hurt. One might recall the words of R.H. Tawney: of the nation's children, he wrote '. . . if, instead of rejuvenating the world , they grind corn for the Philistines and doff bobbins for the mill-owners, the responsibility is ours into whose hands the prodigality of nature pours life itself'.[25] Eventually an E.P.A. community must stand on its own feet like any other and rejuvenate its world, and that is a dogma which might hold good on both political wings.

Poverty and American compensatory education

The failure of past policies for more equal educational opportunities in Britain was an essential background to the inauguration of our work in four educational priority areas. But so too was the transatlantic hubbub which followed President Johnson's declaration in 1964 of 'unconditional war on poverty in America', followed by a plethora of legislation, government programmes and social science literature. A new generation had rediscovered poverty and educational remedies were fashionable. But there was no guarantee that either new politics or new social science or their partnership would banish poverty from unprecedentedly rich societies.

On the political side we were working within assumptions concerning the attainment of the welfare society through the welfare state which were increasingly questioned. As we saw it, the project was a pioneering venture in Britain in experimental social administration, or futurology as design, in which the partnership of ourselves as social scientists and educationalists with politicians and administrators was assumed to be viable. But we were under no illusions. We were well aware that only in the loosest sense could the projects be described as experimental. The laboratory for testing 'Plowden hypotheses' was natural, not experimental. There were political as well as academic determinants of the districts which were chosen. The desired outcomes of action were not always precisely defined and in some cases resistant to precise measurement. We could not hope for complete control of relevant inputs to the local social and educational systems and so the relation between our input and the outcomes was to that extent bound to be uncertain . Nevertheless we took up the challenge – to contribute to developing a theory of poverty in its educational aspects and to test it in the very real world of the urban twilight zones.

The theory of poverty

What then is a viable explanation of poverty? First, poverty is not adequately conceived in the singular, either in its manifestations or its causes. We must speak of 'poverties' and we must recognise multiple if related causes with the implication that a war on poverty is indeed a war and not a single battle. A panel of the Social Science Research Council recently produced a discussion of current research which identified six types of poverty:

(a) crisis poverty;
(b) long-term dependency;
(c) life-cycle poverty;
(d) depressed area poverty;
(e) down-town poverty; and
(f) 'the culture of poverty'.[26]

The classification put forward by the committee, and the fact that the six types are not clearly distinguishable in practice, may help us to relate the American experience of 'compensatory education' to our own work in the four E.P.A.s. Three of these projects addressed themselves primarily to the fifth type, 'down-town' poverty, and all assumed the validity of a description of the poor which permits effective intervention using 'communities' or local administrative units as the appropriate arena of battle. On this view the problem is formulated as one where under modern urban conditions, social deprivation tends to be geographically concentrated, especially in the decaying inner ring of conurbations, in such a way as to reduce the quality of environmental service and opportunity. All local institutions, it is argued, are defective – the family, the school, the welfare agencies, the job market and the recreational organisation.

Moreover, the situation is seen as self-perpetuating; those most capable of doing so move out to take advantage of the opportunities provided elsewhere, be they residents moving to better jobs or better houses or be they school teachers or social workers who live in more salubrious districts and are concerned with this problematic territory only in their professional capacities. And the least capable move in, those most in need of and least able to avail themselves of education, housing, jobs and other publicly provided amenities and opportunities (e.g. immigrants and the downwardly mobile). Thus the inhabitants of the priority areas are thought of, correctly or incorrectly, as a sub-working class formed by selective migration with a distinctive set of economic, social and cultural attributes.

The theory of 'down-town' poverty begins with an elaboration of this description. Its factual base is surprisingly little explored in Britain. In America the description is heavily influenced by concern with the social conditions of negro ghettoes in the northern industrial cities, and the question therefore arises of how far it is relevant to British cities, either generally or more particularly to the districts inhabited by immigrants whose origins and characteristics cannot be equated with those of American negro migrants from the south. It is significant that the label given to this kind of poverty by the S.S.R.C. panel is clearly a transatlantic importation: and though Americans have, in the past few years, begun to produce a description of their version of the sub-working class,[27] to transplant the description without careful enquiry could be disastrous for both analysis and remedy.

On the basis of a review of American social science literature, Rossi and Blum have summarised the characteristics of the poor as follows.

1. **Labour-Force Participation.** *Long periods of unemployment and/or intermittent employment. Public assistance is frequently a major source of income for extended periods.*
2. **Occupational Participation.** *When employed, persons hold jobs at the lowest levels of skills, for example, domestic service, unskilled labour, menial service jobs, and farm labour.*
3. **Family and Interpersonal Relations.** *High rates of marital instability (desertion, divorce, separation), high incidence of households headed by females, high rates of illegitimacy; unstable and superficial interpersonal relationships characterised by considerable suspicion of persons outside the immediate household.*
4. **Community Characteristics.** *Residential areas with very poorly developed voluntary associations and low levels of participation in such local voluntary associations as exist.*
5. **Relationship to Larger Society.** *Little interest in, or knowledge of, the larger society and its events; some degree of alienation from the larger society.*
6. **Value Orientations.** *A sense of helplessness and low sense of personal efficiency; dogmatism and authoritarianism in political*

ideology; fundamentalist religious views, with some strong inclinations towards belief in magical practices. Low 'need achievement' and low levels of aspirations for the self.[28]

As a general description of the poor in any advanced industrial society this summary would command the assent of most social scientists. However, the description of down-town poverty which developed during the 1960s in relation to the American poverty programme is more dubious. It is well expressed by H. Gans, who distinguishes between a working class and a lower class. 'The former is distinguished by relatively stable semi-skilled or skilled blue-collar employment and a way of life that centres on the family circle, or extended family. The lower class is characterised by temporary, unstable employment in unskilled – and the most menial – blue-collar jobs and by a way of life equally marked by instability. Largely as a result of a man's instability, the lower class family is often matrifocal or female-based. This is most marked among the negro population, in which the woman has been the dominant figure since the days of slavery, but it can also be found in other groups suffering from male occupational instability. Although this type of family organisation has some stable and positive features, especially for its female members, the hypothesis has been suggested that it raises boys who lack the self-image, the aspiration, and the motivational structure that would help them to develop the skills necessary to function in the modern job market. Also it may prevent boys from participating in a "normal" family relationship in adulthood, thus perpetuating the pattern for another generation. These conditions are, of course, exacerbated by racial and class discrimination, low income, slum and overcrowded housing conditions, as well as illness and other deprivations which bring about frequent crises.'[29]

The matrifocal family is also described in English studies, for example Madeline Kerr's *Ship Street* in Liverpool, but the essential point here is the juxtaposition of uncertain occupational opportunities with an unstable family structure. In this connection S. M. Miller has drawn the contrast between W. F. Whyte's *Street Corner Society* which described men in an Italian slum in Boston in the late 1930s and Elliott Liebow's *Tally's Corner* (1967) which offers a vivid portrait of a Washington negro ghetto in a blighted section of the inner city in the early 1960s. 'Whyte's men were unemployed casualties of the Depression, and members of strongly-knit families. Most of them went on later to employment. On Tally's Corner the men have much less favourable relationships with each other and with their families; their hopes for a different and better future are constantly frustrated. The shift in these two books from the emerging Italian temporarily blocked by an economic depression to the thwarted negro of the affluent society captures the change in the social issues facing American society.'[30]

The theory is then, that of a vicious cycle of lack of opportunity and lack of aspiration, so that the 'pathologies' of rejection of the world and the search for gratification in alcohol and drugs, the apathy, drifting and dependence on public aid, are to be seen as adaptations to a life of exclusion from the main stream of society.

It is an open question as to how far British city slums resemble either those of Boston in the 1930s or Washington D.C. in the 1960s, though the signs that coloured immigrants are developing into a 'thwarted social stratum' are clear enough in E. J. B. Rose's *Colour and Citizenship*. But whether or not the theory can be properly applied to the British scene, it corresponds in many respects to the S.S.R.C.'s sixth type – the 'culture of poverty' – and as such has been the subject of a developing debate in America during the 1960s. All agree that the poor are different. But the explanation of these differences by those who insist on a situational rather than a cultural theory have profoundly different implications for the strategies of action against poverty.

The culture of poverty[31] insists in its simplest form that the poor are different not primarily because of low income but because they have been habituated to poverty and have developed a sub-culture of values adapted to these conditions which they then pass on to their children. It was this definition of the problem which dominated the war on poverty in America and the Economic Opportunity Act of 1964 – providing a convenient rationalisation for the emphasis on community action and social work rather than on employment policies and the redistribution of income.[32] Recent contributors, however, have returned in one form or another to a situational approach. Thus O.D. Duncan asserts that 'if there were any chance that the slogan-makers and the policy-builders would heed the implications of social research, the first lesson for them to learn would be that *poverty is not a trait but a condition.*'[33]

Out of this debate so far we must conclude that the 'poverties' to which urban industrial populations are prone must be understood to have their origins in both situational and cultural characteristics of those minorities which suffer disadvantage and discrimination and to have their cures in both economic and cultural reform, not only at the local or community level but also in the total structure of society.

Application of the theory

In social action–research, theory is applied in a political context. Within the framework of the theoretical discussion of poverty there are large political implications according to whether the emphasis is put on changing the structure of opportunities or raising levels of motivation. Clearly our E.P.A. programme was so conceived – in being confined to small geographical areas and endowed with very limited resources – that it had to focus mainly on the second alternative. A possible assumption of the E.P.A. programme is that the most effective point at which to break into the vicious poverty circle is in early childhood, in the primary school or in the pre-school period: and this approach tends to lead to considerable emphasis on work with families, thus raising fundamental questions about the right of the state, through its agencies, to intervene in the relation between parents and children.

But quite apart from this fundamental issue there are three partial interpretations of the general theory which may be distinguished and which have political consequences. On the first view, the cause of poverty is 'cultural deprivation' in the sense of inadequate social parenthood, and the cure consists of improved socialisation with the implication that the main thrust must be towards family casework. In the E.P.A. context this means that the sub-working-class family is held to be the major villain of the piece, failing to provide the early training in literacy, numeracy, and acceptance of work and achievement habits which constitute the normal upbringing of the middle-class child and which prepare the child to take advantage of the opportunities provided in school. An example and an elaboration of this point of view, directed towards the more pathological aspects of 'cultural deprivation', would be Sir Alec Clegg and Barbara Megson's *Children in Distress*[34] with its description of neglectful, cruel and workshy parents.

The second interpretation focuses on the other socialising institution – the school. It is the theory that the cause of poverty is educational deprivation. The blame is transferred here to the school teacher who fails to provide adequate educational stimulus to the sub-working-class child. Although they both concentrate on the socialisation process these two interpretations of the theory are often opposed in practice, at least in their emphases.

For our own part we have linked these two interpretations, emphasising both pre-schooling and the development of the so-called community school. Pre-schooling is a possible means of arousing community support for improved education: to reverse the process whereby the deprived child is one who has been prepared not for learning but for failure. Here is one of Clegg's infant school head-teachers:

We have children starting school for whom the words 1, 2, 3, 4, 5 represent a new language, children who are so unawakened to the world around them that the meaning of the colour words, red, blue, etc. is not known. Of the 19 children admitted in September this year there are eight who could not fit red to a red jersey or blue to a blue bead. Looking at a book, having someone read a story from it, or talk to them about it, is a new experience, as is the handling of a pencil or crayon. For some, communication by speech is an art to be acquired in school, toilet training has not been established, and the handling of cutlery needs to be taught. . . .

Playgroups, nursery classes and nursery schools can directly repair these deficiences; and the effect can multiply. If there is forbearance from the professional teachers and charity from their trade unions, then parents can learn to teach and the primary schools can begin their own task without a crippling handicap of ineducability among their five-year-olds.

A force possibly more significant is the community school. It is typical that contacts in slum schools between parents and their children's teachers are either non-existent or farcical. At worst the teacher drives through enemy-occupied territory at 9 a.m. to withstand siege until the 4 p.m. withdrawal. At best the occasional 'open evening' attracts the respectable and aspiring mother, sometimes accompanied by an embarrassed father, to a ritual and uncomprehending inspection of the pupils' exhibits while they queue for an inhibited account of their child's progress from the class teacher. Odd exceptions here and there suggest that it is possible to overcome this travesty of partnership between parent and teacher. The Plowden Committee found one school in its national survey where 'there is after-school activity on almost every evening during the year when groups of children meet voluntarily for pottery, drama, recorder playing, gardening . . . football, athletics, jumping and agility work. Parents are welcome.'[35] *Genuine* participation could provide the multiplier here. The traditional isolation of school from community reflects the uneasy relation between, on the one hand, the legally protected autonomy of the family and, on the other, the political state committed to the provision of individual opportunity through selective education. Within the traditionally isolated school, chances could be given to the exceptionally able or highly motivated individual, but all too often by subversion of the family (a process as rarely successful as it is inefficient).

The community school holds out the promise of peace and co-operation between teacher and parent. The first dove must be flown by the teacher, ideally one who is appropriately trained. The development of courses designed for teachers intending to go to E.P.A. schools and their link to community oriented curriculum change was an innovation we were keen to test. But the teacher cannot reconstruct the community unaided. If he is successful at all, the needs of the neighbourhood for health, housing, employment and other services will be found to impinge directly on his teaching tasks. The implication is clear: educational priorities must in the end be integrated into community development. The E.P.A. school is impotent except in the context of a comprehensive organisation of social services in the community.

The third interpretation of the theory of poverty, however, puts the emphasis on the opportunity structure of society and in this sense is opposed to both of the first two interpretations. On this view, high achievement orientation and performance on the part of the sub-working-class child would be irrational until the structure of opportunities for jobs, and indeed all the other elements of citizenship in the affluent society, are provided equally for all, independently of their social, familial and racial origins. There was very little that could be done directly in order to apply this side of the theory within the framework of an E.P.A. action programme. All that can be said is that no amount of success with work on either the cultural poverty of the home or the educational poverty of the school will result in anything but frustration if socialisation cannot be translated into opportunity at the end.

All these three interpretations are explanations of poor school performance. A parallel can, however, be drawn with independence or dependence on the social services. The view may be taken first, that cultural deprivation leads to both dependence on and incapacity to use the social services intelligently. For example, failure to take up the statutory entitlements may be regarded as a failure on the part of the individuals concerned. A second view, equivalent to the educational deprivation view, regards these services as inadequate for the needs of slum dwellers, for example, the gap between need and supply is interpreted as a failure of comprehension and communication on the part of the welfare bureaucracies. Another example would be that housing services are too narrowly defined, concerning themselves with the letting of council tenancies and not with the search for accommodation, mortgages, etc. in the private as well as the public market. Then the third and radical interpretation would suggest that social services are no more that a palliative while the structure of opportunity, especially opportunities for employment, and discrimination against coloured immigrants, continue. This third point of view may be taken to the point of seeing the whole apparatus of E.P.A. as a diversion from the pursuit of genuine egalitarian policy into the obscurities of unnecessary research.

We were prepared to take this risk. But we by no means accepted the ideal that either the inner rings of the conurbations or all of the designated E.P.A.s were wholly inhabited by a sub-working class approximating to American descriptions of the poor. [. . .] In the four areas and their schools we expected to find, and found, the recognisable descendants of Hoggart's Hunslet[36] as well as the hopelessly downtrodden, the shiftless and the abandoned. Moreover, one of our districts, and the one most community-like, was in the mining towns and villages of South Yorkshire, far removed from the inner ring of a conurbation.

American compensatory education

That 'compensatory education' in the United States has failed is a well-established belief in this country: indeed for some people it is almost the only thing known about American compensatory programmes. Many refer to the failure of compensatory education without having grasped the complex variety of educational developments and innovations loosely grouped under this heading.

When we were exploring the American experience in 1968–69,

morale among those connected with the American poverty programmes had probably reached its nadir. Moynihan's *Maximum
Feasible Misunderstanding*[37] gives a clear account of the politics of
disillusionment felt by those who had been involved in the early,
optimistic stages of the war on poverty. And at the same time the
massive Westinghouse Report on the national pre-school programme
Head Start[38] completed a series of negative findings on the long-run
effects of pre-school programmes. The Report showed that the project
did not make any substantial long-term impact on children's
intellectual and social development. And evaluation of other programmes, both national and local, had not produced much clear-cut
evidence of success. A study of a thousand selected projects[39]
identified only 21 studies where there was clear evidence of success –
and many of these were small-scale research projects affecting only a
few children.

It was this series of negative findings that stimulated Jensen[40] to
reopen the debate on the relative importance of genetic and
environmental factors in intelligence and to question a basic
assumption of compensatory educational programmes – that the
differences between social and ethnic groups on measures of
educational attainment were primarily caused by environmental
factors and could be influenced by educational programmes.

Meanwhile social and educational programmes connected with the
war on poverty had their funds reduced as the war in Vietnam
expanded. Race relations in many of the northern cities had worsened
sharply, and race riots were common. Schools had become centres of
conflict. The pressure was for increasingly radical solutions to the
problems of poor educational attainment by deprived children – for
free schools run by the community,[41] for community control of state
schools and for decentralisation and desegregation. Demand for these
changes led in turn to increased conflict between parents, community
groups, teachers and administrators, resulting in teachers' strikes,
school lockouts and boycotts.

Thus, in the years 1965–69, there had been a rapid shift from high
optimism to profound pessimism. It is these extreme positions that
have most successfully penetrated into this country and there is probably far less knowledge of what actually took place, or its detailed
results.

The difficulties of making any overall assessment of compensatory
education in the United States are formidable. Certainly the early
optimistic expectations have not been realised. And there are many
who would share Professor Bernstein's distaste for the notion of compensation on the grounds that it is difficult 'to talk about offering
compensatory education to children who in the first place have not, as
yet, been offered adequate educational environment'[42] as well as the
argument that the phrase tends to direct attention away from the
internal organisation and the educational context of the school and to

focus attention on the shortcomings of families which is a partial interpretation of the general explanation of poverty that we have outlined above.[43] Moreover where rigorous evaluation has been conducted, results have often been disappointing, or where significant, have not been maintained for any length of time. As Light and Smith note, 'our ability to detect failure has outrun our power to instil success'.[44] They attribute part of the problem to the 'make or break' method of the traditional evaluation approach, and suggest the need for 'improved development and evaluation strategies'. Others would lay most of the blame on the design of the action programmes, for inadequately using research evidence, or working within a limited frame of reference that neglects the child's wider experience outside school. And others would criticise the overall level of resources and the short time span within which measurable return was expected. More fundamentally, it may be argued that the educational system alone has little independent effect as an agent of social change, and that improvements, however radical, in educational facilities could never achieve the kind of objectives that were set; for even if these objectives were apparently 'educational' themselves, for example, an increase in pupil performance, the influence of the other social factors far outweighed the influence that schools could wield. In the face of such basic criticisms, it may well be asked whether the whole compensatory education movement has not in fact been a series of 'paper programmes' founded on inadequate assumptions and poorly articulated theory.

Some programmes have set themselves unrealistic objectives. This problem is particularly marked where vague non-educational goals are put forward – for example 'breaking the poverty cycle'; and in general, the more extensive and varied the programme, the more likely it is to have such objectives. Thus 'umbrella' programmes such as Head Start or Title I of the Elementary and Secondary Education Act of 1965 almost inevitably become associated with broad objectives as a way of including the varied components of such programmes. The relationship between these objectives and the educational changes promoted by the programmes was never spelt out, and, as in the case of the 'poverty cycle', the theories on which such relationships were based were often very inadequate. Yet it would be wrong to dismiss compensatory education as a series of 'paper programmes' because of weaknesses at this level of theory. Clear knowledge about such relationships is inadequate on any analysis, and it is perhaps only by experiment and research in this way with educational change that better theory will be developed.

At a lower level, there is no doubt that several compensatory programmes have demonstrated that the findings of social research can be used to produce more effective educational experiences for disadvantaged children. Though no single panacea has been discovered and it seems unlikely that any will, a number of promising innovations have been developed and tested. If several of these were tried out on an extensive scale, it is possible that educational performance would improve, and that the educational system would become more responsive to changing social needs.

In summarising the American experience of compensatory education, it is important not to underestimate the social changes which accompanied its development. These were primarily changing patterns of urbanisation as negroes moved in to central urban areas, and whites moved to the suburbs. Between 1950 and 1960 the city centres of the 24 largest metropolitan areas lost nearly $1\frac{1}{2}$ million whites to their suburbs, and gained more than 2 million negroes. These rapid movements were reflected in changing school populations in the inner cities. One consequence was that the differences in school performance between black and white pupils were underlined as teachers were faced with changing school populations. Lower school performance, however, was only one aspect of a series of social and economic inequalities experienced by the black population, by other ethnic minorities and by low-status whites, many of whom also came from depressed rural areas.

Though educational performance was only one aspect of such disparities, it appeared to be one where improvement could be achieved, with some hope that better job opportunities would result and thus a general reduction in inequality. Educational theory, too, was beginning to indicate ways in which basic changes in ability might be achieved, if the right kinds of educational environment could be created. The child's early years were isolated as those in which such changes were most likely to occur. The work of Hunt[45] and Bloom[46] was particularly influential in this respect. Other educational research was documenting, with increasing precision, the ways in which the child's experience outside the school, particularly in the home, affected his development in school. This suggested that the school could somehow 'compensate' for inadequate external experiences, or could influence the home in such a way as to bring about change for the better.

The Coleman Report[47] added extensive information about the disparities in educational performance between black and white children and the factors that were most highly correlated with school performance, indicating that the effects of home background and the characteristics of fellow pupils were far more marked than variations in school or teacher quality. These findings underlined the three general strategies of action that could be taken to improve educational outcomes: improvements within the school, increased educational influence in the home, or changes in the background of fellow pupils that could be achieved by altering pupil composition to include a more socially and ethnically heterogeneous group. Also, as we have noted, the Coleman Report gave impetus to the conception of equality of educational opportunity as equality of outcome rather than equal chances of access to educational facilities – and this implied policies of positive discrimination as well as desegregation.

The terms that came to be adopted to describe such programmes, 'compensatory education' and 'the disadvantaged', are essentially vague in reference. Neither clearly indicates an underlying theory, though several critics have restricted the term 'compensatory education' to strategies which confine change to the school curriculum. Such terms, though helpful in focusing attention on the problem and eliciting funds, have added confusion. Thus the use of the term 'disadvantaged' has tended to give a spurious unity to a group distinguished on broad social and economic criteria: it has concealed the diversity between groups, and, more importantly, the diversities of individuals within any group so classified.

Compensatory educational programmes in one way embody a continuing debate about educational change, with particular reference to social groups which have benefited least from previous educational development. Each new project has therefore tended to mark a point in the debate at which new assumptions were introduced or new theories came into fashion. It is difficult to offer a clear but brief chronology of a debate so confused and conflicting. As Deutsch[48] notes, no orthodoxy of compensatory education has yet emerged. The sudden increase in resources available for special programmes positively encouraged experiment and diversity. A strong motive for many participants was a desire to 'get into the action' and demonstrate that they had solutions and innovations to offer. The risk, and indeed the reality, was of a mass of small independent schemes which impeded the necessary replication and extension of successful programmes.

However, for purposes of exposition, the American projects can be grouped into three broad strategies of change. First there were changes within the school, particularly the development of new curricula, and the extension of formal schooling to younger age groups. Second there were changes in the relationship between schools and their social setting, for example improved home-school links; and third, as a special case of the second type, there was the strategy of integrating schools racially or socially when the communities themselves were not integrated. Each of these strategies has its own pattern of development as the initial belief that the problem would be quickly solved by goodwill, better communication and a small increase in resources, has had to be abandoned in favour of more complex and radical solutions.

Though pre-school education has not turned out to be as effective as many hoped, there are consistent indications that certain types of programme can produce gains in cognitive abilities. The more intensively the programme is geared to such intellectual development as language skills, the more substantial the gains that have been achieved. The work of Bereiter and Engelmann[49] is among the best known in this field, but several other research studies have shown considerable gains in children's ability at the end of the programme, for example, the Early Training Project in Nashville,[50] the work of Deutsch and his associates at the Institute for Developmental Studies in New York, the various pre-school projects run at Ypsilanti, Michigan by Weikart and his colleagues, the individual tutorial scheme carried out by Marion Blank in New York,[51] and many others.

In general, traditional pre-school methods have not compared favourably with more structured programmes of intervention, though the findings of Weikart,[52] who compared three different pre-school approaches, the traditional and two structured methods, suggest that where planning time, resources, and teacher motivation are equal, very similar results can be achieved with different types of programme. The overall results of large scale pre-school programmes such as Head Start have proved to be disappointing, in comparison to those of smaller experimental projects. These differences must in part reflect the problem of mounting a large-scale programme and the uneven quality of people and approaches to be found in Head Start centres. In its first summer of operation, more than 560,000 pre-school children were enrolled for an eight-week summer programme; and by 1967, about 215,000 children were enrolled in more than 13,000 different centres for a full year programme.

Follow-up studies of children who have attended pre-schools have also produced disappointing findings; in general gains are not maintained significantly for any length of time. These findings have indicated the need to look closely at whether pre-school work has made a real impact on development, and suggested that programmes will have to be maintained into the elementary grades if the negative effects of later schooling are to be counteracted. The child who moves from a well staffed reception pre-school atmosphere to a conventional school class with a high pupil-teacher ratio may be more at a disadvantage than one who has not been to pre-school. Equally these findings indicated the need for even earlier intervention – home visiting for very young children, and, as a logical extension, 'parent training' programmes for teenagers.

At school level, programmes have in general not been able to achieve the type of gains in performance seen in the small pre-school projects. One reason may be that changes at this level often have been too piecemeal. No overall change in curriculum and method has been made. However the strategy of the 'Follow-Through' programme, the extension of Head Start to the elementary grades, is geared to bring about this overall change by providing curricula along the lines of the experimental pre-school projects. But at this level too there have been spectacular failures, with projects such as the 'More Effective School' programme in New York which sought to increase substantially the school's resources by virtually doubling the numbers of teachers. The evaluation[53] of this project indicated that despite changes in teaching ratios, teachers were using the old methods only with smaller classes. As the researchers pointed out, what may have been a dramatic change for the adults involved may have made little impact on the children in the school. However, at higher levels, programmes which have provided college entrance courses have at times been successful in achieving substantial advances in academic skills. Thus the College Board programme in New York was able to demonstrate that the students had made considerable gains in a short space of time.

Many programmes have avoided involvement with the existing teaching force in schools by working outside schools or by appointing new staff specifically for the project. However, such programmes have uncovered a number of ways in which the teaching staff can be supplemented and reinforced. The use of aides or sub-professionals, often from depressed areas themselves, is common both at pre-school and school level. Students in training have also been involved in several projects. An alternative method of increasing the 'teaching force' and one that begins to undermine the traditional distinction between 'teacher' and 'pupil' is to use one student to teach others. This can either take the form of older children working with younger groups – for example teenage girls in pre-school – or genuine 'peer teaching' within the same class or age-group. Plans for a 'tutorial community project'[54] outline a school organisation in Los Angeles built on this concept of older pupil and peer teaching, using a wide variety of different teaching techniques involving different age-groups in the teaching and learning relationship.

The second broad strategy is to change the relationship between the school and its social setting. Here there is evidence that carefully worked out programmes of parental involvement, as for example in the Nashville pre-school project[55] and the Bloomingdale family programme[56] can produce measurable change in parental behaviour and attitudes towards education, and even produce I.Q. gains among the parents as well. The development of home visiting schemes, initially as an adjunct to pre-school work, for example in Nashville and Ypsilanti, but later as an alternative strategy, has also produced successful results. The 'diffusion effect' noted in the Nashville 'Early Training Project', whereby younger siblings of the children in the project and other children in the community appeared to progress more rapidly, may well indicate an effect of home visiting. Where the mother is closely involved in the teaching programme, it is possible that the long-term impact can be maintained by periodic visits. This suggests an alternative strategy to concentrating resources in the formal educational system, and deploying them instead to make a direct impact on the child's educational experience in the home. Many argue that such programmes may well be more effective than those based within the school system. Successful programmes are reported by Gordon in Florida,[57] Weikart and Lambie in Ypsilanti,[58] and Shaefer[59] in the Infant Education Project in Washington D.C. Generally these home visiting programmes have concentrated on younger children, either from birth or in the infancy period from 18 to 36 months.

Another way to increase educational influences within the home is to change school organisation and control in such a way that it is more open to the influence of the community. As the school becomes more involved in the community through the development of community study and programmes of parental involvement, further changes may occur. Thus several projects, notably the Head Start group in Mississippi, have argued that schools must be concerned with general community progress, rather than education alone. The idea of the community school as an agency concerned with general community welfare and development is closely related to this approach. Community oriented curricula for such schools has emphasised the need to inform students as to how change in their community can be achieved. 'A Book about New York City and How to Change It' is the title page of one such community textbook.

More radically, such links with the community are taken to imply that formal control over the school should be vested in the community rather than in a central authority. This is the method of 'community control' or 'decentralisation'. The results of such changes in control are not, so far, clear. Schools involved have become centres of conflicting groups of parents, teachers and administrators. In the past, schools have been insulated from strong social and political pressures; the traditional expectation of an orderly learning environment held by both teachers and parents does not respond well to the unpredictable and sudden changes that many 'community schools' or 'community controlled' schools have experienced. Such changes in the organisation and control of schools are more closely concerned with wider issues of political power than with programmes to improve the outcomes of schooling for disadvantaged groups. Many, however, argue that until such groups are given more control over institutions which shape the lives of citizens, programmes of educational reform will continue to be ineffective.

Schemes to integrate schools or school systems entail a very different conception of the relationship between school and community; here 'community' represents a much wider cross-section of society than that normally found in the catchment area of a single school. To achieve this balanced group within schools, children have to be bussed to other areas, catchments re-zoned, massive new schools or educational parks have to be built. The belief that the performance of deprived children will improve once they join an integrated school has been a powerful factor in developing such programmes. In fact, the evidence of research studies on this issue is not clear cut, and where pupil performance has increased it may be that the new schools to which they are bussed are of generally higher quality. Many integration programmes have only been able to move a token number of pupils, and there are few schemes as comprehensive as that of Berkeley, California, which planned to integrate all its elementary schools. Other areas have planned more comprehensive schemes, involving 'educational park' complexes, which are large enough to draw from integrated catchment areas, though the more residential segregation there is, the larger such institutions have to be.

The building of new institutions has been another response to the problems of getting schools to adopt innovations: 'model' or 'demonstration' schools are a way of showing the feasibility and effectiveness of new ideas, at a relatively local level. Such development can apply equally to curriculum innovation and to more general changes in school organisation and control. Thus the 'free' schools demonstrate that members of minority groups can run schools effectively; while another type of 'model school' emphasised the working of new curriculum approaches or organisational methods.

Examples of free schools are to be found in many large city centres: model or demonstration schools have also been tried in a number of areas – for example the 'World of Inquiry' school in Rochester which aims to take a cross-section of the city population and makes extensive use of activity methods and flexible organisation. Another much publicised example is the Parkway project in Philadelphia, a school without a building for those who have left school, which uses the resources of central Philadelphia, libraries, museums, research institutes, commercial and industrial firms to provide courses for students. Another method is the 'model district', for example the Cardozo district of Washington D.C., where a small team works with a number of schools, introducing teachers to new methods and providing the necessary materials, workshop sessions, and classroom support, so that teachers can experiment in their own schools.

Compensatory programmes have drawn on research, both to design and to evaluate new educational programmes. The experience of combining action and research in this way has at times been uncomfortable for both parties. Each exposes vulnerable positions in the other; the methods of research introduce uncertainty into action, and undermine the needs of the decision-making process for clear cut results. And involvement in action by research may challenge the basic distinction between fact and value that underlines many research procedures. Many of the requirements of research for control over the development of the action and for the systematic allocation of children to one group or another cannot be met in large-scale action programmes for social and political reasons. Though small-scale studies, for example at pre-school level, have managed to approximate to experimental design and have produced relatively clear cut results, there is need for more information about the reasons for such results – for the study of 'process variables'. In the context of large-scale programmes such as the Head Start pre-school project there are strong arguments that overall evaluation of the final outcomes is in many cases premature; there is need for detailed examination of whether the programme has been adequately implemented, and for research strategies that identify successful elements in the programme. Overall evaluation of final outcomes tends to encourage an over-simplified response to programmes in sharp success or failure terms. Evaluation of educational programmes for the disadvantaged has increased the demand on research resources, and new research and evaluation centres have been created to respond to this need. Basic research has also been stimulated, and a hopeful development has been the increasing interaction between basic research findings and the evaluation and development of action programmes.

Running through both action and research approaches to the problems of education for deprived groups, there appear to be two contrasting themes, based on different assumptions about the potential for development. Illustration of these approaches will serve to round off this summary of American experience in this field. The first example concerns the length of time a child should ideally take part in special programmes. One response to the apparent failure of short-term intervention projects has been to press for more total programmes; for the child to join almost at birth, and ideally to be in some form of residential care. The aim, here, is clearly to minimise the effects of other influences on the child. He is in a 'controlled environment' for as long as possible. A different response to the problem of ineffective short-term programmes is to try to change the dynamic forces in the child's experience – to 'multiply' the effects of the programme. A home visiting strategy that seeks to improve the educational content of interaction between mother and child in the home is clearly of this kind. Programme effects may be maintained through the mother with a relatively low level of support from the home visitor.

Similar differences of standpoint can be seen in the methods of introducing new curriculum to teachers: one approach here is to work out a complete curriculum package, where the teacher only has to monitor its operation in the classroom; for example the Individually Prescribed Instruction Programme developed at Pittsburgh, where each child follows a set course of study, only calling upon the teacher when he cannot understand something in the programme, or to have his work checked. Another method seeks to involve teachers in the development of the curriculum, accepting that each teacher will introduce her own variations. These differences of approach are reflected in the methods of organisation set up to stimulate innovation on a wider basis; the 'model school' approach can be similar to the development of a 'package'; teachers in effect are asked whether they wish to adopt the approach or not. In the 'model district' strategy, however, there is an attempt to build a curriculum with teacher involvement at the start; there is in fact no precise 'model' or 'package' – but a series of ideas and guidelines within which teachers are free to develop their own approaches.

In research strategy, too, similar distinctions can be seen. A major requirement of 'experimental' procedures is that action develops in a predictable way; such an approach is more closely in accord with the development of curriculum 'packages'. Yet the experience of using such methods in evaluation has indicated the need for more information about how the programmes actually developed, for this is not always in accordance with the predicted course. Teachers, for example, may use kits or 'curriculum packages' in quite different ways, and consequently with different effects. This possibility underlines the need for alternative research strategies to aid in programme development, and to identify successful programme elements. Such research strategies are likely to be more amenable to the more 'organic' methods of curriculum development outlined above.

This summary of American experience has deliberately selected some of the more optimistic outcomes of compensatory programmes. These developments occurred at a time of worsening race relations in the cities, and it would be easy to outline a more depressing picture. Changing political conditions have made it impossible in some areas to revert to earlier methods of compensatory education. Black militant groups may block programmes aimed at the cognitive 'deficits' of the disadvantaged child, and both black and white militants oppose integration programmes that involve bussing.

Though there have been some 'paper programmes', it would be wrong to use this description to cover 'compensatory education' in general; for there are a set of positive findings. If this is thought to be a small return for the amount of money invested in such programmes, it would be interesting to compare the 'return' from the general educational budget. The range of innovations in curriculum and school organisation must be hard to parallel in any comparable period of time. Indeed the extent and diversity of programmes, as we have noted, makes any overall assessment extremely difficult.

Compensatory education has not produced clear cut answers to such questions as the relative importance of genetic or environmental factors in intelligence, or the relationship between education and the occupational structure. It is interesting that the genetic-environmental controversy has been opened again, at a time when experimental pre-school programmes, part of 'compensatory education', have demonstrated that considerable improvements in intelligence test scores can be achieved and maintained. Attempts to improve the educational experience and qualifications of disadvantaged groups may well help to clarify the complex relationship between education and the occupational structure, particularly if research and evaluation are a part of them.

To simplify our description of American compensatory education programmes we can say that the movement began with what appeared to be a simple educational problem, the fact that certain social groups on average had a lower level of educational performance. Attempts to solve that problem were forced to go further and further outside the educational system, as the ramifications of the initial problem were uncovered. In this process the most basic questions are raised about the nature of social organisation, and about the reasons why lower social status should be associated with lower educational performance. These developments indicate that a purely educational response to the initial problem is unlikely to succeed. Action programmes have tended to follow this pattern, first seeking to introduce changes in the child's experience in the formal school setting, and then increasingly to widen their approach, so that larger areas of the child's experience are affected. Educational underachievement has become merely one manifestation of a series of social and economic disparities experienced by disadvantaged groups. The long-term solution must be a comprehensive policy which strikes at these political, social and economic inequalities. Nevertheless many participants at the New York conference, while recognising the need for comprehensive programmes of this kind, underlined the important role that educational reform would have to play. It is possible, too, that educational programmes may make considerable impact on the political consciousness of the poor, a process that has certainly accompanied the development of compensatory education in the United States. Such political awakening may be the most effective means of ensuring that the gross inequalities between social and ethnic groups are eradicated.

Notes and References

1. Edward Boyle and Anthony Crosland in conversation with Maurice Kogan, *The Politics of Education,* Penguin Education Specials, 1971.
2. *Children and their Primary Schools,* Central Advisory Council for Education, Vol. 1, p. 51 (Plowden Report 1967).
3. It turned out in the end that, apart from helpful contacts with particular individuals, the university departments as such offered little or no help to the local project teams. By contrast colleges of education were, in many cases, extremely helpful.
4. The Scottish project is not dealt with here [. . .]
5. G. A. N. Smith and A. Little, *Strategies of Compensation: A Review of Educational Projects for the Disadvantaged in the United States,* O.E.C.D., 1971.
6. In effect this was a time extension only as we had not spent all the original grant.
7. Dr Little has since left the I.L.E.A. to join the Community Relations Commission.
8. See *Notes Towards a Definition of Culture,* Faber, 1948.
9. G. H. Bantock, *Education and Values,* Faber, 1965, especially Ch. 7.
10. C. B. Cox and A. E. Dyson (eds), *Fight for Education,* and T. E. B. Howarth, *Culture, Anarchy and the Public Schools,* Critical Quarterly Society, 1969.
11. J. Goldthorpe, 'Theories of industrial society: Reflections on the recrudescence of historicism and the future of futurology', *European Journal of Sociology,* **12** (1972), 263–88.
12. K. Coates and R. Silburn, 'Education in poverty', in David Rubinstein and Colin Stoneman (eds), *Education for Democracy,* Penguin Education Special, 1970.
13. See, for example, Raymond Williams, *Culture and Society,* Penguin Books, 1966; *The Long Revolution,* Penguin Books, 1965.
14. Cf. Charles Frankel's and A. H. Halsey's introduction to *Educational Policies for the 1970s,* OECD, 1971, pp. 14ff.

15. James S. Coleman *et al.*, *Equality of Educational Opportunity*, US Government Printing Office, Washington D.C., 1966.
16. We found some evidence, discussed in Ch. 5, of similar patterns in our E.P.A. schools.
17. J. W. B. Douglas, *The Home and the School*, MacGibbon and Kee, 1964.
18. R. Boyson (ed.), *Down with the Poor*, CPAG, 1971.
19. S. Wiseman, 'The Manchester Survey', App. IX, *Plowden Report*, Vol. 2.
20. 1st Report of the National Child Development Study (1958 Cohort), April 1966, App. X, *Plowden Report*, Vol. 2, *Research and Surveys*, 1967.
21. M. J. Tyerman, *Truancy*, University of London Press, 1968.
22. B. Bernstein and B. Davies, 'Some sociological comments on Plowden', in R. S. Peters (ed.), *Perspectives on Plowden*, Routledge & Kegan Paul, 1969, pp. 58–77.
23. Plowden, *op. cit.*, Ch. 5, especially paras. 136–52 and 158–73 (see Reading 1).
24. For instance, Cox and Dyson, *op. cit.*
25. R. H. Tawney, *The Acquisitive Society*, Bell, 1921, republished 1961 (Fontana), p. 81.
26. S.S.R.C. *Research on Poverty*, Heinemann, 1968, p. 9.
27. See the essays by P. H. Rossi and Z. D. Blum, Oscar Lewis, H. J. Gans, L. Rainwater and W. Miller in D. Moynihan (ed.) *On Understanding Poverty*, Basic Books, 1969. See also H. Gans, 'Urban poverty and social planning', in Lazarsfeld *et al.* (eds) *The Uses of Sociology*, Free Press, 1967, pp. 437–76.
28. Z. D. Blum and Peter Rossi, 'Social class research and images of the poor: a bibliographical review', in Moynihan *Understanding Poverty* (1969), pp. 351–2.
29. Gans, *loc. cit.* (1967).
30. S. M. Miller, 'Invisible men', *Psychiatric and Social Science Review*, 2, No. 5, May 1968, p. 14.
31. See Oscar Lewis, 'The culture of poverty' in Moynihan *Understanding Poverty*, pp. 187–200.
32. Thus in presenting the case for the Economic Opportunity Act to Congress in 1964, Sargent Shriver argued that 'being poor . . . is a rigid way of life. It is handed down from generation to generation in a cycle of inadequate education, inadequate homes, inadequate jobs and stunted ambitions. It is a peculiar axiom of poverty that the poor are poor because they earn little, and they also earn little because they are poor.'
33. Otis Dudley Duncan, 'Inheritance of poverty or inheritance of race', in Moynihan, *Understanding Poverty*, p. 88.
34. A. Clegg and B. Megson, *Children in Distress*, Penguin, 1968.
35. Plowden (1967, Vol. 1), para. 122.
36. Richard Hoggart, *The Uses of Literacy*, Chatto and Windus, 1957.
37. D. P. Moynihan, *Maximum Feasible Misunderstanding: Community Action in the War on Poverty*, New York: Arkville Press, 1969.
38. V. G. Cicirelli *et al.*, 'The impact of Head Start on children's cognitive and affective development', Westinghouse Learning Corporation, Washington D.C., O.E.O., 12 June 1969, mimeo (The Westinghouse Report).
39. D. G. Hawkridge *et al.*, *A Study of Selected Exemplary Programs for the Education of Disadvantaged Children*, US Department of Health, Education and Welfare, Sept. 1968 (2 vols.).
40. A. R. Jensen, 'How much can we boost I.Q. and scholastic achievement?', *Harvard Educational Review*, 1969.
41. See for example George Dennison, *The Lives of Children*, Penguin Education Special, 1972.
42. Basil Bernstein, 'A critique of the concept of compensatory education', in Rubinstein and Stoneman, *op. cit.*, p. 111.
43. *Supra*, pp. 81–8.
44. R. J. Light and P. V. Smith, 'Choosing a future: strategies for designing and evaluating new programs', *Harvard Educational Review*, 1970, 40(1), 1–28.
45. J. McV. Hunt, *Intelligence and Experience*, New York: Ronald Press, 1961.

46. B. S. Bloom, *Stability and Change in Human Characteristics,* New York: Wiley, 1964.
47. Coleman *et al., op. cit.*
48. M. P. Deutsch, Preface to J. Hellmuth (ed.) *The Disadvantaged Child,* Boston: Brunner-Mazel, 1967.
49. C. Bereiter and S. Engelmann, *Teaching Disadvantaged Children in the Pre-school,* N. J.: Prentice-Hall, 1966.
50. S. W. Gray and R. A. Klaus, 'An experimental pre-school program for culturally deprived children', *Child Development,* 1965, **36,** 887–98.
51. M. Blank and F. Solomon, 'A tutorial language program to develop abstract thinking in socially disadvantaged pre-school children', *Child Development,* 1968, **39**(2), 379–89.
52. D. P. Weikart, 'A comparative study of three pre-school curricula', Ypsilanti Public Schools, Michigan, 1970, mimeo.
53. D. J. Fox, 'Expansion of the more effective school program', Center for Urban Education, Sept. 1967, mimeo.
54. R. J. Melaragno and G. Newmark *et al.,* 'Tutorial community project: Progress Report 1968', Santa Monica, California: Systems Development Corporation, 1968, mimeo.
55. Gray and Klaus, *op. cit.*
56. A. B. Auerbach, 'Parent development through active involvement with their children in an integrated pre-school education and family recreation program', paper presented to the American Orthopsychiatric Association, 21 Mar. 1968.
57. I. J. Gordon, 'A parent education approach to provision of early stimulation for the culturally disadvantaged', Final Report to the Fund for the Advancement of Education of the Ford Foundation, 30 Nov. 1967, mimeo.
58. D. P. Weikart and D. Z. Lambie, 'Pre-school intervention through a home teaching project', paper presented at the American Education Research Association convention, 1968, mimeo.
59. Hawkridge *et al., op. cit.*

Formulating the problem

6

Alienation, anomie and industrial accidents

W. Baldamus

Introduction to Reading 6

It is rare (if not unknown) for a social scientist to report the truly early stages of a major research project. You will look in vain in professional journals for an account of the dead-ends entered, the fortuitous coincidences discovered or the striking connections made with other problems which mark the way in which social scientists translate a bright idea into a piece of research as conventionally reported in the professional journals.

Professor Baldamus' article has several merits, not the least of which is that it takes us from the position which the social scientist starts from, before he knows whether or not he has a problem which is worth researching or what the 'problem' is. He notes two puzzles with which he started his research. The first is the 'public' one of the startling rise in industrial accidents reported to the Factory Inspectorate in the 1960s. The second is a more private puzzle (arising from earlier research by Professor Baldamus) the similarity between the variations by days of the week in the patterns of absenteeism and industrial accidents. For both absenteeism and accidents, the frequency peaks on Mondays and declines steadily to Fridays. Absence may be presumed to be a 'voluntary' matter, certainly in contrast to accidents which in English (as Professor Baldamus notes) are, by definition, without apparent cause. Why then should the patterns be so much alike? No obvious explanation presents itself as the answer to this joint puzzle, and when Baldamus adds some data from Oldham to show that even suicides have the same weekly pattern we begin to feel more than a little perplexed.

The reader might be tempted to think that the industrial accident figures are an artefact, produced by some changes in reporting which took place in the mid-1960s.

Industrial accidents are legally notifiable to the Factory Inspectorate (under the 1961 Act which consolidated many earlier pieces of legislation) if they occur in any factory (defined as employing one or more workers in manual labour to produce or adapt any article for sale) and result in death or in more than three days' absence from normal work. So we are not dealing with cuts

This is a previously unpublished discussion paper from the University of Birmingham.

and scratches requiring a few minutes to deal with. On the other hand, we are dealing with a category which ranges from fatalities and serious injuries to 'backaches and sprains'. A possible answer is that there was a rise in the rate of *reporting* of accidents in the 1960s, rather than in the rate of accidents themselves. But the rise is documented across a wide range of industries and across nearly all the districts of Britain into which the Factory Inspectorate divides the country. If there is a cause to do with the *reporting* of accidents acting so uniformly over the range of industry it should be easily detectable.

There are many possible causes of a *reported* rise in accident rates, rather than a real rise in the frequency with which accidents occur. The move from piecework systems of payment to daywage systems may be associated with a greater willingness for workers to report minor accidents since their earnings will not suffer from time lost to report and treat minor injuries (Wrench 1972). The 1960s saw the introduction of daywage systems in many industries, notably in vehicle manufacture; the 'climate' of management opinion in British industry on pay changed generally in this period thanks to books such as Wilfred Brown's (1962).

Another possible cause of a rise in reported accidents could be legal changes in what constitute notifiable accidents. You will see that Professor Baldamus uses all reported accidents in factory processes as the time series to follow trends in accident rates. There was no change in notifiable accidents between the 1961 Factories Act and the 1974 Health and Safety at Work Act, yet the time series shows its steepest rise during this period.

Perhaps we are dealing with such a few cases that a handful more will wildly inflate the incidence rates? Not so, since there are around 250,000 industrial accidents each year at the present time. A rise from 19.9 reported accidents per 1,000 employees at risk in 1962 to 31.7 per 1,000 employees at risk in 1967 represents an enormous increase. What is more, this rise has been sustained since the last year for which Professor Baldamus reports figures (1967). In 1971, the last year for which figures exactly comparable to Professor Baldamus' can be obtained from the *Annual Report* of the Factory Inspectorate, the rate was 32.7 accidents per 1,000 employees at risk. From 1972 onwards the source for British industrial accident figures (the Factory Inspectorate) appear to go to some lengths to avoid giving a *rate* (as contrasted to reporting an *absolute* figure) for all notified accidents. However, a figure for all notified accidents can be extracted after 1972 but it differs from Baldamus' series in two ways. Firstly it is based on a 5 per cent random sample of notified accidents and will thus be subject to sampling error. Secondly, the rates are calculated for manufacturing industry rather than factory processes. The category 'manufacturing industry' covers 90 per cent of the premises within the category 'factory' as defined in the Factories Act 1961. 'Manufacturing industry' excludes small premises in which reported accidents seem to be fewer anyway (*Annual Report* 1974, App. 4). How these differences affect a comparison of accidents in manufacturing industry with accidents in factory processes is not clear, but it cannot be a big discrepancy. Therefore, we can use the rate for manufacturing industry as a reasonable estimate of later figures in Baldamus' time series:

	1971	1972	1974
Incidence rate for all reported accidents/1,000 employees in manufacturing industry, all districts, based on 5 per cent sample.	32.4	33.2	33.2

I conclude that the all accident rate has not declined from the level of 1967 reported by Baldamus.

The Factory Inspectorate was embarrassed by the (to them) inexplicable rise in accidents in the 1960s which is easily traced to a rise in minor accidents rather than in serious ones. It is minor accidents which Professor Baldamus shows in a related paper to the one reprinted here (Baldamus 1969b) which follow the same weekly cycle as for voluntary absenteeism.

The Factory Inspectorate's reaction to Professor Baldamus' work seems to be one of the few cases in which ' . . . an official administrative body is influenced by a piece of academic sociological research . . . ' (Baldamus 1969c). In the 1968 *Annual Report* (published at the end of 1969) the Factory Inspectorate produced a new classification of industrial accidents:

Group 1. 'Those which are both severe and *unambiguously the direct and undoubted* result of an accident at work. Fatalities are included in this group, though also separately tabulated.' (18.4 per cent of all notified accidents in 1972.)

Group 2. 'Those which although severe in that they resulted in absence for more than 28 days or admission to hospital for in-patient treatment, cannot be *objectively* so described. These include a proportion, particularly strains and sprains, where there is legitimate doubt whether they were caused by a truly accidental happening at work.' (27.3 per cent of all notified accidents in 1972.)

Group 3. 'Those which are not severe and which do not result in absence for more than 28 days or in admission to hospital for *in-patient treatment.*' (54.3 per cent of all notified accidents in 1972.)

(*Source: Annual Reports of H.M. Chief Inspector of Factories,* 1968 onwards) (all italics are mine – *editor*)

Readers should compare this classification – an innovation introduced by the Factory Inspectorate itself – with the criterion of a notifiable accident laid down in the 1961 Factories Act and summarised on page 105 of this introduction.

Why introduce this new more severe classification of industrial accidents (based upon a detailed inspection of a 5 per cent random sample of notified accidents)? H.M. Chief Inspector of Factories argued in his 1968 report that the use of *all* reported accidents was a misleading index of safety performance since 'changing social conditions over the years have altered the meaning of the three day absence criterion of reportability'. (*Annual Report of H.M. Chief Inspector of Factories,* 1968, p. xii.) Quite what the changes in 'social conditions' have been has never been further itemised by the Factory Inspectorate except in so far as the Inspectorate's views were reflected in the

Robens report on Health and Safety at Work in 1972: ' . . . (the) criterion for notification – absence from work for more than 3 days – is subject to influences which have nothing to do with safety performance, i.e. it is affected by changes in social attitudes to, and social provision for sickness absence. Different individuals react differently to injuries of a similar nature and our present social organisation is such that the individual has a considerable measure of choice as to whether and how long he will stay away from work following a slight accident.' (Robens 1972).

Although the Robens Committee received written evidence from Professor Baldamus on 'absenteeism – accidents' (Baldamus' concept) they chose to ignore it as did the Factory Inspectorate, except to endorse implicitly the Inspectorate's concentration on the causes of serious accidents and how they might be diminished. The Factory Inspectorate views 'truly accidental' accidents as (a) objectively serious in the injuries suffered, and (b) as reducible by the adoption of safe working practices on the part of both management and workers. The Factory Inspectorate offers to Parliament and the public as a measure of its effectiveness, the way in which Group 1 accidents have been reduced over the last few years:

Group 1 Accidents/100,000 persons employed*						
	1969	1970	1971	1972	1973	1974
In manufacturing industry	710	680	610	600	560	554

*Including fatalities.
(*Source: Annual Reports* of H.M. Chief Inspector of Factories, 1969–74.)

At the same time, the failure of 'all accidents' to diminish significantly is played down, partly by the lack of attention paid to them in *Annual Reports* and partly by making it impossible for researchers to calculate a rate for all accidents (dominated as they are by minor accidents) comparable to the figures published up to 1967 which Baldamus uses as his major time series.

As Baldamus points out, the Factory Inspectorate is committed conceptually (and therefore in practical terms as well) to viewing accidents as being caused by either the technical hazards of the job or by personal negligence or both. The possibility that minor accidents are used to justify absenteeism is something outside the Factory Inspectorate's intellectual and organisational terms of reference. This position is understandable in the light of the history of the Factories Acts and the background of inspectors, but the efforts of the Inspectorate to gloss over (if not to actually hide) certain figures such as the trend in all notified accidents per 1,000 employees at risk, is hardly forgivable to researchers.

Readers will find Professor Baldamus' tentative explanation of the phenomenal rise in minor accidents in his discussion of the concepts of alienation and anomie. That this paper is not conclusive must be put down, in part, to the fact that his research funds were cut off in 1968, and detailed studies of the workers at particular factories could not be undertaken.

Readers may also care to note that this occasion is the first time that any of Baldamus' articles on industrial accidents have been published in a form other than by mimeographing (which thus reached only a limited audience).

References and Further Reading

Adorno, T. *et al.* (1950) *The Authoritarian Personality*, Harper.
Annual Report of the Inspector of Factories, London: HMSO 1968, Cmnd 4146 and *Annual Report:* 1969 Cmnd 4461; 1970 Cmnd 4758; 1971 Cmnd 5098; 1972 Cmnd 5398; 1973 Cmnd 5708; 1974 Cmnd 6322.
Baldamus, W. (1969a) 'Alienation, anomie and industrial accidents: an essay on the use of sociological time series', University of Birmingham, Faculty of Commerce and Social Science, *Discussion Papers*, Series E, No. 12, June.
– (1969b) (June), 'On testing hypotheses', *op cit.*, No. 13, July.
– (1969c), (June), 'The concept of truly accidental accidents', *op. cit.*, No. 14, Oct.
Brown W. (1962) *Piecework Abandoned, the effect of wage incentive systems on managerial authority*, Harper and Row.
Nichols, T. (1975) 'The sociology of accidents and the social production of industrial injury' in G. Esland *et al.* (eds) *People and Work*, Milton Keynes: Open University Press.
Robens, Alfred (1972) *Safety and Health at Work*, Report of the Committee 1970–72, under the chairmanship of Lord Robens. Vol. I. *Report*, London: HMSO,; Vol. II. *Selected Written Evidence*, London: HMSO.
Wrench, J. (1972) Speed accidents: a study of the relation between piecework and industrial accidents', University of Birmingham Faculty of Commerce and Social Science, *Discussion Papers*, Series E, No. 17, May.

I. Accident time series as an index of industrial behaviour

In its wider implications, this paper is concerned with methodological issues inherent in studies on social change. More specifically, it advocates the use of sociological time-series.[1] As very little has been done to explore this device, my objective amounts to a preliminary assessment of its advantages and limitations. It will be seen that statistical technicalities are not the main problem at the present stage;[2] nor is the availability of adequate data a serious question. What does matter is the surprising lack of awareness among contemporary sociologists and social administrators of the potential usefulness of the method in the analysis of social change. This is particularly surprising since, with the marked decline of interest in the predominantly static version of functionalist theory, the central focus of modern sociology has clearly moved towards a concern with the dynamics of changes through time, towards social and political trends, social development, institutional change, cultural lags, and so forth. [. . .] The most profound and most recent studies in this perspective are Dahrendorf's

Essays in the Theory of Society. In an unmethodical and impressionistic manner, social changes through time are being taken into account in all recent enquiries wherever the role of new social and political factors happens to be sufficiently obvious.

But while the strategic significance of change and development can hardly be doubted, the realization of this perspective through empirical work is fraught with difficulties. I shall limit myself to discussing at present only such obstacles which are apparent rather than real. My illustrations will be taken, as far as possible, from a current study on industrial accidents; this will automatically bring into the forefront the question of sociological relevance.[3] Since time series methods are widely used *outside* the realm of sociological enquiry, notably in Econometrics, Business Studies, Industrial Economics, Demography, Social Medicine, etc. we should start by asking, in what sense is a specifically sociological utilization of this method possible?

Part of the answer is simple enough. However controversial the criterion 'sociological' may be in epistemological terms, as regards concrete research practice, the prevailing pattern is remarkably consistent. The consistency rests on a widely shared agreement in the choice of explanatory variables. To take the survey method as the most representative type among all sociological methods, a firmly established paradigm has emerged over the past 30 years which revolves on a highly standardized set of explanatory variables, used singly or in various combinations: *social class*, *occupational status*, *level of education*, *urban-rural community*, *religion*, *political orientation*, *marital status*, *ethnic origin*, *sex* and *age*.[4] Thus while the selection of dependent variables in social research is immensely complex, arbitrary and unlimited, the list of *independent* variables is small and rigidly prescribed by the consensus among sociological practitioners. Ostensibly it is therefore not the subject matter as such, but merely the use of a prescribed range of particular variables for explanatory purposes which determines whether or not a piece of research is sociologically relevant.

The remarkable consistency and completeness of the standard list of sociological parameters is not by any means the result of systematic methodological thought. It is merely the product of a long process of trial and error in the development of routine survey research. This explains why as yet next to nothing is known about the logical status of such variables; their existence and approved usefulness is simply taken for granted. It also explains why the nature of time series in this realm is still obscure. But even as brief and preliminary a discussion as the present can bring to light certain basic shortcomings.

The role of time sequences in survey data is of course well recognized. Since the object of survey methods is the causal analysis of correlated observations, the time order among variables is important. But this problem concerns solely the analysis of change within the precincts of the *dependent* variables. The most typical case is that specific changes in, say, voting behaviour, religious practices, work attitudes, etc. have been observed in a group of people, and the investigator then tries to correlate these with a cluster of possible determinants chosen from the standard repertoire of independent variables, such as class (measured by a variety of indicators) occupational status and so on. It follows that any manifestation of change among our sociological (i.e. independent) variables is treated simply as a datum, not as a problem! The question: *what determines the determinants*? is systematically excluded by the very nature of survey designs.

It would be extraordinary if a methodological tradition that is incapable of grasping what are surely the most salient social issues could survive for long. As a matter of fact a curious device to conceal this deficiency has been developed. Briefly it works like this. It is observed in a given sample that the aspirations of skilled and semi-skilled workers reveal more middle-class orientations than those of unskilled labourers; since it is generally known that there is a secular trend towards status-upgrading throughout modern industry, certain macrosociological conclusions about fundamental changes in class-structure may then be inferred, without further enquiry. Hence there is in this roundabout way considerable scope for discussing long-term social change in terms of major issues, even when primarily the available data are unsuitable for such purposes. But the fact remains that on methodological grounds the device is patently inadequate. A great deal of the current criticism of survey research appears to be rather trivial once we recognize this more profound deficiency which affects the whole paradigm. The endlessly repeated cliché that statistical measurement leads to a preference for insignificant problems is obviously misplaced and superficial in view of the fact that in principle the *whole* phenomenon of macrosociological change is intractable by the conventional method of survey design. It has nothing to do with techniques of measurement and levels of precision.

The systematic weakness inherent in contemporary empirical sociology has a number of far-reaching implications which I cannot follow up in this paper. The search for remedies seems the most urgent task, and here is the point where the use of time series methods may open up a new perspective. Even at a first glance, it is plain that each one of the survey parameters presents a complex that is essentially dynamic. Each one is subject to secular trends. Indeed, with little exaggeration one can say the only thing that is really important about class, occupation, religion, educational politics and so on, is the dimension of change through time. In view of this it appears that the conventional survey paradigm is designed precisely so as to *eliminate* this dimension: every piece of survey research is wholly based on a particular *ceteris paribus* clause, the tacit assumption that the fundamental structural forces controlling the sociological parameters are being kept constant. The most serious difficulty of incorporating time series is therefore the structural interdependence between the various parameters. How can we enquire into the effects of long-term changes in, for example, the distribution of occupational status without knowing how this is related to all the other concomitant changes in the structure of society? In posing this large question, we can see at least one thing clearly. The only way of coping with any sorts of structural interdependencies in social change must be a concern with (macrosociological) theory.[5] To put it the other way round, the static bias of traditional survey methods with its concealed *ceteris paribus* clause amounts to an ingenious device of dispensing with any kind of explicitly formulated theory. (This, incidentally, is the true reason for the much lamented divorce of theory and research.) It follows that the introduction of a time dimension into empirical work will automatically enforce a sharper awareness of the indispensable role of explicit theory construction.

II. Accidents trends and industrial alienation

I will leave it at that, and instead of pursuing these formidable issues any further, I shall now try to illustrate some of the more obvious methodological implications by recourse to a concrete case. For the past two years I have been conducting, on the basis of survey methods, a large-scale enquiry into industrial accidents.[6] As this investigation has abruptly come to an end on account of insuperable administrative obstacles, it lends itself ideally for the present purpose. It has in fact turned out to be a pioneering experiment in the utilization of sociological time series. From the very start, it was a particular kind of trend data that formed the background of the study: as Table 6.1 indicates, the national average of officially reported accident rates of factory workers has been increasing from 19.9 per cent in 1962 to 31.7 per cent in 1967. The table includes a number of Factory Inspectorate districts where the increase was even more pronounced. The rising trend of industrial accidents had already started to alarm industrialists and Ministry of Labour officials around 1964. From then on the problem aroused more and more interest, a considerable amount of research funds became available from public sources, and in due course, several large projects got under way. There was a good reason for the abundance of research money: the alarming rise of accident rates was completely inexplicable!

From a sociologist's point of view the situation was even more puzzling. Accident rates have never been the subject of systematic sociological enquiry. For over 50 years, they had remained exclusively the domain of applied psychology, in particular industrial psychology. The fact that the knowledge available from past research in this field offered no explanation is of course no reason to argue that the true explanation must be sociological. My own motive for taking up the

Table 6.1 Reported accidents in factory processes, 1962–67. Incident rates per 1,000 workers employed.[7]

District	1962	1963	1964	1965	1966	1967
Wakefield	41	42	71	97	99	104
Sunderland†					*	86
Rotherham	53	56	67	73	74	79
Swansea	38	44	57	65	69	74
Cardiff	38	45	60	71	69	70
Fife	44	40	57	68	62	67
Tyne†					*	65
Darlington	38	37	53	61	*	64
Sheffield North	30	34	43	57	60	63
Stirling	28	36	53	61	62	61
Newport	30	35	53	57	56	60
Carmarthen	39	51	60	64	57	58
Middlesbrough	30	32	46	50	*	57
Sheffield South	30	34	41	46	48	54
Lanarkshire	26	28	45	55	53	51
Newcastle†					*	51
Average rate for all Factory Inspectorate districts	19.9	21.6	27.7	30.0	30.2	31.7

*Figures not available because of mid-year boundary changes.
†Figures not available for 1962–66 because of boundary changes which produced three districts in place of two.

matter was at the time extremely tenuous. In 1966, I had come across a conspicuous similarity between certain aspects of industrial absenteeism and industrial accidents (which I shall discuss presently). Data on absenteeism has been used by Blauner, among others, as an index of industrial alienation, and this had been done implicitly with a view of changes through time. Could it not be possible that – somehow – accidents, too, may be connected with the concept of alienation (in one or more of its various connotations)? We can see here very clearly the point I made earlier on: even the mere contemplation of utilizing time series for sociological purposes immediately necessitates a concern with formal theory. Of course one can always postpone such issues. One can start with a vague theoretical hunch, leaving the working out of a theoretical model to a later stage when a sufficient amount of data has been analysed to guide the formation of suitable theoretical concepts. What matters more is that 'theorizing' at this early stage really amounts to a basic clarification about value premises:[8] as soon as one tries to grasp the *possible* meaning of a given set of time series, a decision enforces itself as to whether or not the phenomenon is worth investigating, and this unavoidably depends on value-determined standpoints in favour of or against specific macrosociological theories. In the present case I would never have dreamt of concerning myself with industrial accidents as such, unless there was a prospect, however uncertain, of a link with alienation trends or a similarly significant theoretical problem. And this in turn was simply the manifestation of the kind of personal value-commitment which arises from a fundamental critical attitude towards advanced capitalist society. It is interesting to note here that the very nature of long-term time series, in so far as they are sociologically relevant, makes them particularly attractive from such a point of view.

But there was also a more tangible reason that suggested a possible connection between industrial alienation and accident trends. Previous research on absenteeism in British industry had established a peculiar pattern in the frequency distribution of absence by days of the week.[9] Total absences are highest on Monday and then decline in regular steps to Friday or Saturday. Moreover, the downward gradient varies by occupational status and also according to the level of employment. Thus the weekend effect on absence is more pronounced with unskilled workers than with craftsmen, and, again, it increases with a rise in the level of employment. These observations are easily interpreted in the light of a broad notion of industrial alienation, and the phenomenon of absenteeism has of course been frequently discussed in that context. Nevertheless, a precise interpretation of the cyclical day-to-day pattern has never been worked out. I tried, several years ago, to account for it in terms of cyclically varying normative expectations of earnings and effort; as the week goes by and pay-day approaches, the worker's definition of his financial rewards becomes more and more favourable; conversely, his perception of the disrewards, such as effort, tedium and fatigue, is most acute at the beginning of the week. The combined effect is a gradual increase in the degree of disparity between rewards and disrewards as it is experienced from day to day. This interpretation, however, had remained rudimentary and tentative for lack of sufficiently elaborate data. An opportunity for taking the matter up again seemed to arrive when in 1966 data on industrial accidents became available which appeared to support the absence cycle in a most remarkable manner.[10] As a matter of fact, when I first saw the table shown here as Table 6.2, my immediate reaction was that the apparent cycle must be statistically spurious.

Table 6.2 Total industrial accidents (2,991,000) by days of the week in the German Federal Republic, 1964.

	All Acc. (%)	Fatal Acc. (%)
Monday	20.0	17.3
Tuesday	18.9	16.9
Wednesday	17.8	16.3
Thursday	17.4	15.4
Friday	17.4	17.5
Weekend	8.3	16.6

It will be seen later that the explanation for the surprising similarity between the day-to-day cycles of absence and accidents is exceedingly simple. Yet it was discovered only two and a half years after publication of the German data. Until then, everybody working on the project or otherwise connected with it had been completely in the dark about the meaning of the weekly accident cycle. I have collected a number of excuses for our conspicuous lack of perspicuity: (1) The concern with alienation trends, induced by previous work on absenteeism, created a strong bias in favour of a 'motivational' theory of accident causation. The idea, was, to put it crudely, that accidents may be determined not only by occupational (technological) hazards, but also by certain psychological dispositions which in turn might be associated with the motivation to work, and hence with industrial alienation. Such a theory not only would have thrown new light on the whole problem of accident causation, but would also have lent support to my earlier explanation of the absence cycle; (2) Despite the vast amount of previous research on accidents, no explicit and comprehensive theory of accident causation has ever been formulated. The dominant orientation was centred on the concept of 'fatigue' ambiguously defined and strongly dependent on elements of common-sense knowledge. Thus I started off in a theoretical vacuum; there seemed to be a serious gap and this made it all too easy to envisage a novel theory of accident motivation; (3) While academic research had little to offer by way of explanatory theories, industrial practitioners had no need for them. Safety officers, factory inspectors, personnel managers, shop stewards, and foremen, they all appeared to have their own explanation – a common-sense explanation that is as persuasive and simple as it is fallacious. Aided by a strange fluke in the English language, they are able to argue that all accidents are an 'accidental' occurrence. They have no causes. They are 'occupational hazards'. The Oxford Dictionary puts this very clearly: 'an event without apparent cause, unexpected, unintentional act, chance, fortune, mishap. . . .' For a sociologist, this was unmistakably a powerful piece of deeply ingrained folklore, fascinating on its own account and yet challenging him to replace it by a verifiable theory of motivation.

The combined effect of the three factors created a kind of smoke-screen that bedevilled the early stages of the research. Later I came to realize that they are of larger significance as they affect, jointly or separately, all discussions on industrial accidents. It will therefore help the subsequent analysis, if each one is given a label for brief reference. The first could be called 'sociological causes' with particular emphasis on social trends. The second factor refers to the fatigue syndrome chiefly used among industrial psychologists, including a more recent concern with 'emotional stresses'; all this may be summarized under the blanket term of 'psychological causes' in the sense of a strictly non-sociological approach to the explanation of accidents. The third factor concerns the notion of 'occupational hazards' for which I shall substitute the wider concept *'technological causes'*.

III. Conflicting explanations of industrial accidents

Anyone who approaches the problem of accident causation is bound to come up against an astonishing lack of theoretical and conceptual analysis. This is all the more irksome as there is an abundance of statistical data. The absence of theoretical clarification may not be apparent at first sight, for the field is also saturated with an unusually large amount of undefined common-sense notions, such as 'fatigue', 'occupational hazards', 'irresponsibility', 'intention', 'lack of neuro-muscular coordination', 'absentmindedness', 'excitement', 'loss of practice', 'lack of interest', and so forth. These terms appear to be so obvious, that an explicit theoretical definition seems superfluous.

A deeper reason for the lack of theoretical sophistication is a peculiar form of inherent complexity. It manifests itself in two ways which provisionally may be described as 'causal' and 'organizational' complexity. The first refers to the intricate chain of causation that determines a particular accident in a given organizational environment. Here we may distinguish first of all between proximate and remote causes. The implication here is that each accident is the joint product of multiple causes whereby some exercise a proximate, direct or manifest effect, and others a more remote, indirect or latent effect. For instance, whatever 'fatigue' may mean, it is clear from the technical literature that it involves a relatively remote condition, as compared with such specific and proximate conditions as 'inattention', 'lack of coordination' or 'absentmindedness'. Thus, for each type of remote cause, there may be many proximate ones. This dimension may be combined with another aspect of the causal complexity, the distinction between *precipitating events* and *underlying causes*. It means that an accident occurs only when a given complex of underlying causes, previously described as remote and proximate, coincides with an external set of events that act as a sort of release mechanism. The main illustration for these precipitating events is the common-sense construct of 'occupational hazards'. In other words, such hazards are not by themselves a causal factor, they become effective only in conjunction with certain underlying causes that are already existent before a specific hazard occurs. Basically, the causal chain may be visualised from the scheme given in Fig. 6.1.

Although greatly oversimplified, the scheme shows clearly that an explanation of accidents by recourse to hazards alone is as easy as it is superficial, while the remote underlying causes (e.g. alienation, fatigue) are most difficult and intractable.

As regards the other aspect, organizational complexity, the overriding difficulties are methodological rather than conceptual. All

Underlying causes		Precipitating events
Remote	Proximate	
Fatigue	Inattention	Faulty machine
		Ineffective guards
		Crowded workplace
	Carelessness	Excessive speed
		Excessive noise, heat
Alienation	Faulty attitude	Uncoordinated processes
	Boredom, weariness, frustration	Weather conditions
		Etc.
Etc.	Etc.	Etc.
		Etc.

Fig. 6.1 The causal chain of industrial accidents

accidents are intrinsically interlocked with the organizational environment of industrial work. As a consequence, it is impossible to compare the distribution of accidents between different groups of workers by assuming that the environment may be kept constant; thus, one cannot isolate the effect of class, occupational status, sex, age, ethnic origin, etc. on the relative frequency of accidents because all these groups differ also in the type of work they are doing. Equally disturbing is a special form of organizational complexity which may be termed the 'work-volume' effect. By necessity, the amount of accidents occurring in a given work period, say a week, is a direct function of the amount of work having been done in that period. If a worker happens to be absent for a day in that week, his liability of having an accident is accordingly reduced.

Nevertheless there are ways and means to overcome the disturbing influence of organizational complexity. The use of time-series presents the most important tool in this respect. For example, if we compare the relative frequency of two groups of workers, e.g. skilled and unskilled, or male and female, at two different points in time, we can make a reasonable assumption that the organizationally determined nature of their work has not changed substantially. The most widely used time sequences for this purpose are hourly and day-to-day cycles. When longer periods are used, such as annual trends, the assumption that the type of work remains constant naturally becomes dubious.

We are now ready to introduce a simple statistical technicality. Time series are merely a set of measurements recorded at certain intervals of time. If we connect the points representing the measured quantities, the resulting curve will have either an irregular shape, or form a definite pattern which can be expressed mathematically. For the purpose of causal analysis, only the regular shapes are of any use and there are various ways of classifying these into different types. For our purpose it is sufficient to distinguish between cyclical curves and trend curves. In principle, the length of the time intervals is immaterial for this distinction, but as regards sociological relevance, we shall find that cycles are more interesting in short-term, and trends in long-term, applications. Up to this point, the incorporation of time series into conventional survey analysis means no more than that the dependent variables are expressed in the form of cycles or trends over time. This does not affect the basic procedure of cross-tabulations in terms of the usual type of multivariate analysis.

A considerable refinement, however, is now possible by contrasting simple and compound time series. The latter are constructed by superimposing series of different intervals upon each other. A simple example may take the place of a more technical definition: the combination of hourly, day-to-day and annual variations in the frequency rates of accidents. Ample illustrations of this method will be shown presently, but first I wish to emphasise the sociological implications. It goes without saying that sociologists are particularly interested in long-term *structural* developments. The usual assumption here is that although such developments are manifest (i.e. observable in time series) only as long-term trends, they are nonetheless a *latent* determinant of social behaviour at a given moment of time. The difficulty of identifying latent structural determinants has been for a long time the most serious obstacle to the causal analysis of survey data. In theoretical terms the corresponding difficulty adheres to such concepts as 'social norms'; it is assumed, for example, that structures of normative expectations are relatively stable and subject to long-term changes only; thus, at a given point of time the task is to gauge their effect on the more flexible elements such as attitudes towards a specific situation. The use of compound time series simplifies this problem enormously, because, as we shall see in a moment, on that basis long-term changes become immediately visible in the configuration of related short-time series. As the statistical terminology is sometimes misleading, I shall borrow from classical economics the term 'secular trends' to describe long-term structural developments, while the word 'cycles' will be reserved for the particular form of short-term periodicities which is relevant in this context. Our problem is then to trace the *interrelation of cycles and secular trends*.

I have in front of me an inexhaustible supply of data. Most of this is from the Accident Project; another lot has been extracted from published official statistics; a great deal has accumulated from official or research data published in other countries (chiefly Germany, Sweden, Poland, the USA and Spain). I shall pick out from this material just those bits and pieces which seem to make sense in the light of the few general concepts which I suggested earlier. There is no question of 'testing' specific theories of accident causation.[11] At the most we are dealing with what Dahrendorf has called 'para-theoretical' orientations.[12] I have already mentioned three of these orientations, characterized by the key-concepts 'occupational hazards', 'fatigue' and 'alienation'.

1. Technological causes

The hazards factor may serve as a counter-instance to both the fatigue and the alienation problem, for it does not lend itself to be measured by trends or cycles. But this is not to say that the technological aspect of accidents stands outside the dimension of social change. It is merely due to a particular bias that conventionally the discussion of occupational hazards and safety measures has been confined to a peculiarly static perspective. The prevailing idea is that occupational hazards are unevenly distributed over the range of different industries and processes and that this is a sort of immutable law: coal mining is necessarily more dangerous than food processing. Similarly, a certain amount of accidents, including fatalities, is unavoidable. The object of safety devices and factory inspection is to keep this amount as small as possible. But it can easily be seen that in fact the whole complex is permeated with cultural and normative expectations, and thus subject to structural development. Clearly, there are powerful secular trends. The hazards to the life and health of coal-miners that seemed 'normal' a century ago have given way, slowly but consistently, to much lower limits of acceptability and correspondingly higher standards of safety. It is equally obvious that these norms present a complex structure which comprises numerous sectional interests and expectations, all of which are subject to social changes. In that sense the control over hazards is inseparately a component of the overall development of industrial conflict. The employer's and the wage-earner's definition of what constitutes a tolerable amount of danger, a fair compensation for injuries, an effective standard of safety measures, must necessarily be in conflict. But there are also institutional factors pointing towards a consensus of interests. Under piece-work conditions, for instance, there are situations where a relaxation of safety rules may be condoned by both sides for the sake of increasing output per man. Moreover, a deeper lying consensus governs the basic definition of the employment contract: accidents are, on a par with frustration, tedium and fatigue, conceived by employers and workers alike as an element of the aggregate disrewards of work for which the payment of wages is expected to compensate. It is merely the quantitative substance of the contract, not the underlying principle of 'exchange', that generates conflicts. Here is one important link with the long-term trend of industrial alienation.

The technological orientation towards accidents in the sense of occupational hazards tends to conceal the intrinsic connection between conflict and change. By over emphasizing the role of superficial precipitating factors at the expense of underlying causes, an ideological bias reveals itself. The hazardous effects of technical and organizational factors are basically conceived as unavoidable. This attitude is reinforced by the difficulties obstructing their statistical measurement. Voluminous official statistics are compiled in every industrial country and most of them have a long history; but the underlying purpose is narrowly descriptive, not analytical. In England, the first attempts towards systematic recording originated with the Factories Act of 1844, though the coverage was very small. From then on, the history of accident statistics mirrors closely the growth of factory legislation: the centralized compiling and publishing of figures developed as an unintended byproduct of the Factory Inspectorate's administrative functions.[13] Still, the annual reports remain an invaluable, yet rarely utilized source for gaining an insight into the precise impact of industrial development on the technological conception of accident causation. From 1913 on, a remarkable comprehensive and complex tabulation by industries, processes and geographical divisions has been available which grew from year to year into an increasingly unwieldy system of classification. As a result of the dominant administrative aspect, very little attention was paid to comparability over time; even less to the use of figures for a causal analysis. The first serious endeavour occurs as late as 1966. The Annual Report of the Chief Inspector of Factories for 1966 contains a short paragraph, entitled 'Geographical Variations', which comments on a detailed table showing the changes in accident rates per 1,000 persons employed from 1965 to 1966, comparing the main geographical divisions. It is pointed out that the variations, both by district and over time, are too large to be explained by reference to lack of safety measures and generally to accident prevention performance. The section ends with the conclusion: 'The situation that has emerged is puzzling in the extreme and must certainly be given further study' (p. 97).

The results of the promised studies are presented in the Annual Report for 1967, where the section on 'Geographical Variations' now covers four pages. It starts with an abbreviated table (see Table 6.1) of 16 districts in which the frequency rates in 1967 exceeded 50 per 1,000 workers employed and the changes of these rates from 1962 to 1967 are shown. The Report then goes on to search for the causes. The method of analysis consists of close-up studies of a large number of individual factories, selected from the high accident rate 'black spots' (Wakefield, etc.). Throughout this analysis, the main emphasis is on occupational hazards and safety performance. Thus the question is examined whether the cause lies in the nature of the factory processes or the size of the plant. The possible effect of the difference between day shifts and evening shifts is explored. Similarly, in one firm where the rate was as high as 325, the working conditions such as lighting,

Table 6.3 All reported accidents, 1963 analysed by the nature and site of injury and industry.

| | | | Vehicles | | | | | |
| Nature and site of injury | Shipbuilding and marine engineering | Total accidents | Motor vehicle manufacturing | Motor cycle, three-wheel vehicles and pedal cycle manufacturing | Aircraft manufacturing and repairing | Locomotives and railway track equipment | Railway carriages and wagons and trams | Perambulators, hand trucks, etc. |
S.I.C. MLH No.	370		381	382	383	384	385	389
Head and neck (excluding eye and socket)								
Fracture	27	39	18	1	8	3	8	1
Dislocation without fracture (neck and jaw)	2	—	—	—	—	—	—	—
Scalp injury, without fracture	63	51	24	2	15	5	5	—
Concussion, without fracture	24	61	37	—	11	7	6	—
Open wounds, laceration	139	259	158	7	50	17	24	3
Surface injury (excluding scalp)	130	155	92	1	31	12	17	2
Foreign body in ear, nose or mouth	1	2	—	—	—	—	1	1
Burns	30	38	17	1	4	5	10	1
Not otherwise specified	28	16	5	—	2	1	8	—
Total	**444**	**621**	**351**	**12**	**121**	**50**	**79**	**8**
Eye and socket								
Open wound, laceration	28	70	34	2	14	6	12	2
Surface injury	72	84	55	1	7	9	12	—
Foreign body	174	487	310	14	69	43	51	—
Burns	38	87	44	10	20	5	8	—
Not otherwise specified	36	28	10	2	6	2	8	—
Total								

Spinal column								
Fracture	4	6	2	–	2	–	2	–
Strains of joints	9	18	11	–	2	2	3	–
Not otherwise specified including displacement of inter-vertebral disc	18	87	51	–	23	4	9	–
Total	**31**	**111**	**64**	**–**	**27**	**6**	**14**	**–**
Trunk								
Fracture	67	82	55	1	15	4	7	–
Strains of joints	1,008	1,831	967	35	304	180	332	13
Internal injury (excluding hernia)	5	13	5	1	2	3	2	–
Open wounds, laceration	7	13	10	–	1	–	2	–
Surface injury	493	621	351	10	85	59	110	6
Foreign body in orifice	–	3	–	–	2	–	1	–
Burns	8	12	5	–	2	1	4	–
Not otherwise specified	136	245	136	4	49	22	34	–
Total	**1,724**	**2,820**	**1,529**	**51**	**460**	**269**	**492**	**19**
Upper limb (excluding hand and wrist alone)								
Fracture	56	124	65	3	26	10	17	3
Dislocation without fracture	20	26	11	–	4	5	6	–
Sprains, strains of joints	120	227	125	3	41	20	37	1
Amputation, open wounds, laceration	29	167	131	3	14	6	13	–
Surface injury	217	316	163	10	66	27	48	2
Burns	32	55	35	2	6	6	6	–
Not otherwise specified	18	42	18	–	5	8	10	1
Total	**492**	**957**	**548**	**21**	**162**	**82**	**137**	**7**

Table 6.3 All reported accidents, 1963, analysed by the nature and site of injury and industry, cont.

	Nature and site of injury	370 Shipbuilding and marine engineering	Total accidents	Vehicles					
S.I.C. MLH No.				381 Motor vehicle manufacturing	382 Motor cycle, three-wheel vehicles and pedal cycle manufacturing	383 Aircraft manufacturing and repairing	384 Locomotives and railway track equipment	385 Railway carriages and wagons and trams	389 Perambulators, hand trucks, etc.
Hand and wrist (alone)	Fracture	300	652	368	15	93	75	96	5
	Dislocation without fracture	9	24	8	–	6	5	5	–
	Sprains, strains of joints	116	233	112	15	43	17	46	–
	Amputation, open wounds, laceration	745	2,293	1,331	140	372	189	237	24
	Surface injury	676	1,052	572	37	177	121	137	8
	Burns	83	126	62	3	14	21	25	1
	Not otherwise specified	64	132	79	4	12	12	25	–
	Total	**1,993**	**4,512**	**2,532**	**214**	**717**	**440**	**571**	**38**
Lower limb (excluding foot and ankle alone)	Fracture	50	88	52	1	17	7	10	1
	Dislocation without fracture	8	10	6	–	2	–	2	–
	Sprains, strains of joints	203	355	169	11	75	28	72	–
	Amputation, open wounds, laceration	94	169	100	11	25	15	18	–
	Surface injury	491	643	336	16	140	59	85	7
	Burns	15	27	13	–	–	6	8	–
	Not otherwise specified	42	54	19	2	6	13	14	–

Fracture	368	791	409	19	131	115	114	3	
Dislocation without fracture	1	11	5	–	2	1	3	1	
Sprains, strains of joints	416	496	245	11	90	58	90	2	
Amputation, open wounds, laceration	115	293	176	8	33	22	52	2	
Surface injury	881	1,368	746	37	241	151	184	9	
Burns	63	75	27	2	7	22	17	–	
Not otherwise specified	47	61	25	–	6	5	24	1	
Total	**1,891**	**3,095**	**1,633**	**77**	**510**	**374**	**484**	**17**	
Multiple fractures	16	10	10	–	–	–	1	–	
Multiple dislocations	–	–	–	–	–	–	–	–	
Multiple sprains or strains	6	8	5	–	1	2	1	–	
Multiple amputations or lacerations	15	6	5	1	13	–	–	–	
Multiple surface injuries	84	70	36	–	–	9	11	–	
Foreign bodies – multiple orifices	–	1	1	–	–	–	–	–	
Poisoning	9	15	11	2	2	1	2	–	
Multiple burns	29	32	19	2	7	1	3	–	
Other injuries and effects difficult to localize	85	78	44	–	21	5	6	–	
Grand Total	**8,070**	**14,438**	**7,936**	**450**	**2,423**	**1,431**	**2,100**	**99**	

Foot and ankle (alone)

Table 6.4 All reported accidents, 1966: analysed by the nature and site of injury and industry.

		S.I.C. MLH No.			Vehicles					
	Nature and site of injury	370/1 Shipbuilding	370/2 Marine engineering	Total accidents	381 Motor vehicle manufacturing	382 Motor cycle, three-wheel vehicles and pedal cycle manufacturing	383 Aircraft manufacturing and repairing	384 Locomotives and railway track equipment	385 Railway carriages and wagons and trams	389 Perambulators, hand trucks, etc.
Scalp	Fractures and dislocations	11	2	19	8	–	7	1	3	–
	Open wounds and surface injury	126	19	178	122	5	30	7	14	–
	Concussion and bruising	62	3	96	49	2	31	3	11	–
	Burns	–	–	1	–	–	1	–	–	–
	Other (including multiple) injuries	3	1	17	9	–	2	5	1	–
	Total	**202**	**25**	**311**	**188**	**7**	**71**	**16**	**29**	**–**
Eye and socket	Open wounds and surface injury, bruising, etc. (including removal of eye)	85	13	158	98	1	20	10	27	2
	Foreign body	156	46	633	420	17	101	30	57	8
	Burns	26	5	92	50	3	12	11	14	2
	Other injuries	42	8	47	21	1	7	3	13	2
	Total	**309**	**72**	**930**	**589**	**22**	**140**	**54**	**111**	**14**

Category	Injury type									
Other head injuries	Fractures and dislocations	16	3	25	14	—	1	5	5	—
	Open wounds, surface injury, bruising, etc.	266	34	391	252	8	60	25	43	3
	Foreign body in ear, nose or mouth	1	1	2	1	—	1	—	—	—
	Burns	29	4	54	32	—	7	3	12	—
	Other (including multiple) injuries	15	4	32	16	—	3	6	6	1
	Total	**327**	**46**	**504**	**315**	**8**	**72**	**39**	**66**	**4**
Spinal col. and adj. muscles	Fractures and dislocations	17	4	40	22	1	11	—	5	1
	Strains of muscles	1,119	163	2,007	1,256	46	277	134	283	11
	Other (including multiple) injuries	92	8	194	128	4	41	10	10	1
	Total	**1,228**	**175**	**2,241**	**1,406**	**51**	**329**	**144**	**298**	**13**
Trunk (other than spinal column)	Fractures and dislocations	87	14	147	87	5	30	14	9	2
	Strains (including hernia)	471	87	1,121	714	17	191	71	124	4
	Internal injury	—	—	2	1	—	1	—	—	—
	Open wounds and surface injury, bruising, etc.	623	76	786	506	14	104	63	92	7
	Foreign body in orifice	1	1	—	—	—	—	—	—	—
	Burns	12	—	25	17	1	1	1	5	—
	Other (including multiple) injuries	13	—	48	31	—	11	1	4	1
	Total	**1,207**	**178**	**2,129**	**1,356**	**37**	**338**	**150**	**234**	**14**
Hand	Fractures and dislocations	232	70	595	377	16	81	57	58	6
	Sprains and strains of joints	67	12	157	97	2	33	9	16	—
	Amputation	43	4	209	145	12	35	7	9	1
	Open wounds and surface injury, bruising, etc.	1,333	337	3,507	2,263	138	570	207	297	32
	Burns	105	27	135	72	3	23	12	20	5
	Other (including multiple) injuries	22	7	110	74	8	20	3	3	2
	Total	**1,802**	**457**	**4,713**	**3,028**	**179**	**762**	**295**	**403**	**46**

Table 6.4 All reported accidents, 1966: analysed by the nature and site of injury and industry, cont.

				Vehicles					
Nature and site of injury	370/1 Shipbuilding	370/2 Marine engineering	Total accidents	381 Motor vehicle manufacturing	382 Motor cycle, three-wheel vehicles and pedal cycle manufacturing	383 Aircraft manufacturing and repairing	384 Locomotives and railway track equipment	385 Railway carriages and wagons and trams	389 Perambulators, hand trucks, etc.
Upper limb (other than hand)									
Fractures and dislocations	125	24	272	161	8	51	19	32	1
Sprains and strains of joints	177	29	375	226	8	59	29	50	3
Amputation	1	–	1	–	–	1	–	–	–
Open wounds, surface injury, bruising, etc.	259	42	717	510	22	99	32	47	7
Burns	46	1	75	45	1	12	3	13	1
Other (including multiple) injuries	23	1	65	40	2	16	1	6	–
Total	**631**	**97**	**1,505**	**982**	**41**	**238**	**84**	**148**	**12**
Toes									
Fractures and dislocations	199	57	527	305	14	82	51	69	6
Sprains and strains	1	–	4	3	–	–	1	–	–
Amputation	1	–	4	3	–	–	–	1	–
Open wounds, surface injury, bruising, etc.	299	68	727	458	20	132	45	62	10
Burns	1	–	1	1	–	–	–	–	–
Other (including multiple) injuries	4	3	12	6	–	5	–	1	–
Total	**505**	**128**	**1,275**	**776**	**34**	**219**	**97**	**133**	**16**

Foot (other than toes)									
Fractures and dislocations	95	25	265	159	3	17	43	38	5
Sprains and strains	111	11	133	82	1	8	25	15	2
Amputation	–	–	1	–	–	–	–	1	–
Open wounds, surface injury, bruising, etc.	579	106	1,061	676	25	73	155	119	13
Burns	65	5	79	52	3	8	6	10	–
Other (including multiple) injuries	22	2	46	27	–	2	11	5	1
Total	**872**	**149**	**1,585**	**996**	**32**	**108**	**240**	**188**	**21**
Lower leg and/or ankle									
Fractures and dislocations	96	13	140	79	5	16	29	11	–
Sprains and strains	526	82	630	364	10	53	114	85	4
Amputation	–	–	1	–	–	–	–	–	1
Open wounds, surface injury, bruising, etc.	376	51	635	425	13	32	96	61	7
Burns	28	3	31	20	1	2	2	7	–
Other (including multiple) injuries	13	1	28	16	–	3	7	1	1
Total	**1,039**	**150**	**1,465**	**904**	**29**	**106**	**248**	**165**	**13**
Other and multiple lower limb injuries									
Fractures and dislocations	22	4	54	31	1	1	15	5	1
Sprains and strains	275	50	367	199	7	27	69	64	1
Amputation	1	–	–	–	–	–	–	–	–
Open wounds, surface injury, bruising, etc.	440	70	586	401	8	30	85	57	5
Burns	9	2	13	7	1	–	1	5	–
Other (including multiple) injuries	30	4	45	23	–	2	13	6	–
Total	**777**	**130**	**1,065**	**661**	**17**	**60**	**183**	**137**	**7**
Other injuries									
Multiple fractures and dislocations	7	1	4	3	1	1	1	–	–
Multiple burns	26	2	32	22	1	3	6	–	–
Other multiple injuries	168	22	155	89	2	17	33	11	3
Poisoning	14	2	10	5	–	–	5	–	3
Other injuries and effects difficult to localize	61	4	66	43	–	4	17	1	1
Grand Total	**9,175**	**1,638**	**17,990**	**11,363**	**460**	**1,177**	**2,902**	**1,924**	**164**

heating and ventilation, the standard of housekeeping, the attention devoted to safety measures and so on were carefully investigated. Yet despite all this, the entire analysis turns out to be a complete failure: the relevant causes appear to have remained as mysterious as before. The last sentence of the chapter states: '... important as these accident prevention techniques are for the avoidance of certain types of injury, they may have little impact on many of the incidents which go to make up the total of reported accidents' (p. 126).

Considering the large experience and resources available to the Factory Inspectorate, such an astonishing failure of the attempted causal analysis may have deeper reasons. One would have thought that even within the severe limitations of the technological approach, *some* insight into accident causation must be available from the wealth of published data on the different types of injuries in different industries on the basis of comparative time series. The information necessary for this purpose may be compiled from an exhaustive survey which is published every three years. In what follows I am presenting a small extract from this material, namely the accident data for the category of 'vehicles', in 1963 and 1966 (Tables 6.3 and 6.4).[14] Since many of these figures may appear quite unbelievable, I am reproducing an extract by way of photocopies. The reader is invited to compare particularly the figures under the headings 'spinal column, strains of muscles', etc. It appears that there has been a fantastic increase from 1963 to 1966 in injuries, somewhere in the range of up to 10,000 per cent. This, of course, cannot possibly be true – or if it were, it could hardly have escaped the attention of the Factory Inspectorate and there would have been a similar special enquiry to that concerning the puzzle of the 'Geographical Variations'. Partly the mystery resolves itself if we notice that there are also considerable *decreases* from 1963 to 1966 under the rubric of 'trunk strains'. Moreover, the contrast between the trends of the two rubrics repeats itself virtually throughout the entire sets of data. In all probability, therefore, we are dealing with an error of classification, albeit a serious error. It seems reasonable, then, to group the two rubrics together and as definitional accuracy is impossible anyway, to aggregate them under the heading of 'backaches'. Even then, the resulting increases from 1963 to 1966 are very large and possibly exaggerated. I am suggesting that these injuries are predominantly of a slight and vague nature. Now we may juxtapose the increase of such minor injuries with a category of relatively serious and more clearly defined injuries. I have chosen eye injuries for the purpose because the subdivisions of this rubric show fewer alterations from 1963 to 1966 than any other. The result of this comparison is shown in Table 6.5. Evidently, throughout all industries the increase in 'backaches' has been consistently and noticeably larger than the change in eye injuries. It is still puzzling, of course, that there has been a conspicuously large increase of almost all types of injuries from 1963 to 1966 (the national average is 45 per cent), but I cannot pursue this any further at the moment. The purpose of this discussion is merely to stress the advantages of a time-series analysis in pointing out unresolved and unnoticed, yet obviously important problems. I will come back to this in a different context in Section IV.

Table 6.5 Reported accidents in 1963 and 1966[14]; 'Backaches' (strains to muscles and joints of spinal column and trunk) and eye injuries.

	'Backaches'			Eye injuries		
	1963	1966	% increase	1963	1966	% increase
Food, drink, etc.	1,690	2,910	72.2	227	345	52.0
Chemical industries	1,166	1,903	63.2	351	522	48.7
Metal manufacturing	2,856	5,313	86.0	1,015	1,478	45.6
Engineering and electrical goods	3,563	6,940	94.8	1,636	2,429	48.5
Vehicles	1,849	3,128	69.2	756	930	23.0
Other metal goods	1,050	2,259	115.1	497	715	43.9
Textiles	1,213	1,992	64.2	248	277	11.9
Clothing and footwear	103	243	135.9	50	73	46.0
Bricks, pottery, etc.	1,152	2,529	119.5	259	379	46.3
Timber, furniture, etc.	350	890	154.3	144	204	41.7
Paper, printing, etc.	881	1,458	65.5	152	216	42.1
Building, etc.	3,361	7,591	128.8	1,133	1,597	41.0
Shipbuilding, etc.	1,017	1,841	81.0	348	381	9.5
Other manufacturing industries	604	1,301	115.4	172	235	36.6
Miscellaneous services	2,806	3,344	60.3	474	684	44.3
All industries	24,044	45,599	89.6	7,699	10,824	40.6

2. Psychological causes

The problem of psychological causes is no less complex than that of the technological aspect of accidents. Once again the primary objective must be to put some sense into the accumulation of disjointed pieces of research data, concepts and unstated assumptions. To start with a somewhat drastic simplification, I shall disregard the question of personality factors, among which accident proneness[15] has produced the greatest amount of research. My reason for neglecting this aspect is partly that it extends far beyond the realm of industrial accidents and partly that the technical literature is very controversial and contradictory. As regards the psychological component of specifically *industrial* accidents, the dominant theoretical orientations have for a long time been associated with the concept of 'fatigue', while the main empirical basis has been derived from a unique type of time series hourly cycles. The explanatory principle which has inspired the relevant research is as simple as the data are complicated and confusing. From hour to hour as the day goes on, the worker's physical and mental capacities are increasingly impaired by fatigue and hence the frequency of accidents increases correspondingly. One would expect, therefore, an ascending curve. The outstanding merit of this method is that it eliminates the larger effects of occupational hazards; as the crucial element of the hourly cycle is solely the *relative* variation over time, the typical direction of the curve would be the same, however different the technologically determined accident liability may be. At the same time, the cycle would still reveal those components of the physical environment of work which are controlled by organizational factors, as the hours of work, the distribution of rest pauses, the speed of work and so on. The more fatiguing these conditions the steeper the curve would be.

Investigations of this kind are numerous and they have a long history. The results have been disappointing. Even the earliest reports, dating from the beginning of this century, are lacking in definite evidence of typically rising accident curves.[16] But the connection between fatigue and accidents seemed so obvious, that the idea continued to guide all research of this kind, and moreover made a strong impact upon the movement towards shorter hours. It had become clear, however, that all sorts of refinements of the method were called for. For instance, it was realized that variations in the amount and the speed of work must have a disturbing effect and that therefore the accident rate should be corrected by output per man-hour. These and similar reflections formed the background of extensive investigations in munition factories carried out in England and the USA during the First World War. As a result, a number of observations did in fact strengthen the fatigue hypothesis. But there was also a growing amount of evidence suggesting non-fatigue elements in so far as many accident curves contained substantial sections in a *downward* direction, chiefly towards the end of the working day. Finally, in 1918 H. M. Vernon discovered an even more disturbing anomaly. He found that during night shifts, apparently the most fatiguing work of all, some accident cycles have a downward instead of an upward trend.[17] By the end of the 1920s, the overall picture of hourly accident and output cycles had become so bewildering, that any kind of empirical generalization had to be expressed with great caution and numerous qualifications. Even so, it was not until 1947 that the theoretical basis of this approach was called into question. This was done by T. A. Ryan who demonstrated irrevocably that the concept of fatigue covered a number of unstated assumptions connected with various subjective factors in the motivation to work, that are unobservable and unmeasurable.[18]

Several devices are available today for making a fresh effort in facing up to the inherent complexity of the problem. The task of identifying the more general, deeper-lying determinants of accidents is first of all a statistical issue. With modern sampling methods, sufficiently large populations can be analysed to be able to separate the particular from the universal causes. Obviously, the conflicting results of past research were to a large extent due to the smallness and the haphazard nature of the data. A further refinement would be the use of test-variables in conjunction with successive two-variable runs as developed by survey research. And this could be improved still further by superimposing long-term trends on the cyclical patterns. This may be illustrated by a simple model. Assuming that the upward sloping components of the hourly cycle reflect those elements of physical impairment which are related to long hours and strenuous work, we can reasonably argue that the secular trend towards shorter hours and lighter work must have progressively reduced their incidence; conversely, the downward slope, associated with the unexplained residual of 'non-fatigue' would be expected to become more pronounced. Schematically the shape of the cycle in Fig. 6.2 would change from A to B.

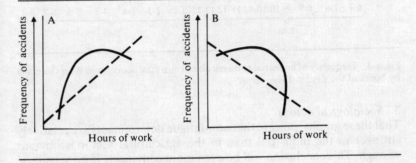

Fig. 6.2

The suggested combination of cycles and secular trends must seem outrageously unrealistic without the support of facts. I have been searching through the mass data on hourly accident cycles published during the past 50 years. But the available sources are so eclectic and fragmentary that they provide no more than the vaguest impression of the postulated trend. I found at last some confirmation in a recent official report of the German Federal Republic[19] which is based on a representative 10 per cent sample of the total working population. The tables present the hourly distribution of accidents for 24 hours, sub-divided by fatal and non-fatal injuries, men and women, and industrial and agricultural workers. As is to be expected, there is a marked volume effect throughout these figures in the distribution of the 24 hours: among the industrial section, the accidents before 7 a.m. and after 6 p.m. are below 2 per cent; this corresponds to 6 a.m. and 8 p.m. for the agricultural occupations. I have extracted from these tables comparative figures of non-fatal accidents so as to contrast the industrial with the agricultural section (Fig. 6.3).

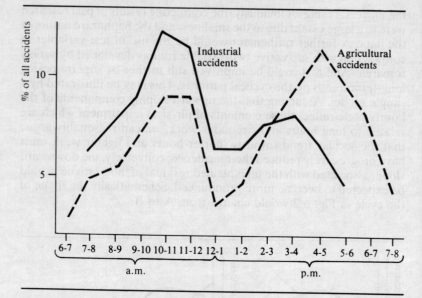

Fig. 6.3 Frequency of industrial and agricultural non-fatal accidents in West Germany by hours of the day, in 1966.

3. Sociological causes

That these graphs indicate that non-fatigue determinants are relatively stronger in the industrial than in the agricultural sector is obvious enough. This conclusion will be even more convincing if we substitute

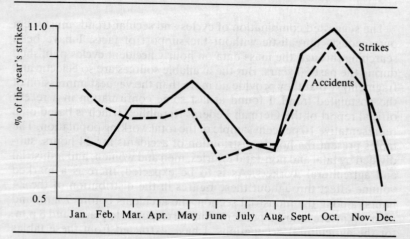

Fig. 6.4 Monthly variations of strikes and accidents, Birmingham district, 1963 (correlation coefficient $r = 0.85$; $p = 0.05$).

'alienation-effects' for the empty term 'non-fatigue'. But there is no proof. The suggestion seems acceptable merely because it goes along with what we know about alienation trends. A more stringent analysis is, however, possible. This would have to follow the usual pattern of further subdividing the data, especially by sex, level of skill and age; one other criterion, severity of injury, will be discussed later.

A great deal more could be said about this, even from the kind of limited data on hourly accident and output curves that are available from past research. As space is scarce, I shall instead add one observation which occurred by chance in the course of the Accident Project. By way of data dredging, we experimented for a short time with monthly accident cycles. And here we found a startling correlation with monthly frequency rates of *strikes* (see Fig. 6.4). So far as this kind of evidence goes, we can at least say that the feasibility of an alienation hypothesis is not quite as far-fetched as the current emphasis on the more tangible accident causes would suggest. But there is other evidence which lends support to this possibility. The latest German official report (see Table 6.6) represents day-to-day accident data for three consecutive years.[20]

Table 6.6 Variations in accident rates by days of the week (West Germany).

	1964	1965	1966
Monday	20.0	19.9	20.1
Tuesday	18.9	18.7	19.0
Wednesday	17.8	18.0	18.2
Thursday	17.4	17.4	17.4
Friday	17.4	17.5	16.9
Saturday/Sunday	(8.5)	(8.6)	(8.3)
Total	100	100	100

If we now recall (see above, 129), that the shape of these accident cycles is significantly similar to the day-to-day absence cycle, the suggested connection between accidents and alienation appears to be more acceptable. Although a significant annual trend does not emerge from the German accident cycle, the data are strong enough to encourage further investigation. It would be interesting to know whether or not the combined day-to-day and annual series would reveal something like the pattern (as shown in Fig. 6.5), which emerged from a study on absenteeism in a German steelworks.[21] Perhaps this will suffice to illustrate the argument that in addition to fatigue (and its concomitants), alienation, too, could be envisaged as a remote, underlying cause, as is suggested by the theoretical framework outlined on p. 134. The overriding difficulty with this is certainly not an empirical one. The scope for further data in the form of various time series is unlimited. What really blocks any further progress at the moment is the astonishingly large gap between theory and research in

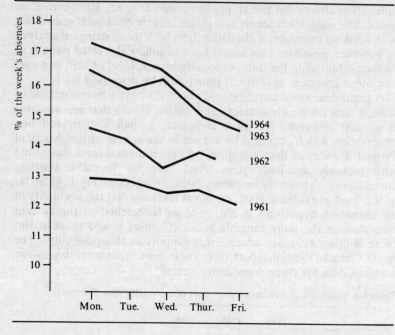

Fig. 6.5 Day-to-day cycle of absence in a West German steelworks, 1961–64.

this particular area. The growing complexity and uncertainty surrounding the concept of alienation has often been deplored. In the area of political sociology alone, there are, as Ken Newton has put it, 'as many, if not more, definitions of alienation as there are political sociologists who have used the concept'.[22] The most recent attack on the problem appears in a paper by H. Barakat.[23] This is an attempt, in parts quite ingenious and resourceful, to integrate a large variety of present conceptions and meanings by way of a comprehensive conceptual framework. He even contrives to stretch his global concept of alienation so far that it encompasses several meanings attached to a very different, if equally ambiguous concept: *anomie*. One interesting consequence of the enlarged concept of alienation is that it now reaches far beyond the familiar ground of absenteeism, strike-proneness, restrictive attitudes, etc. into the causal mechanism underlying the phenomenon of *suicide*: 'For acutely alienated people, life might become so unbearable and meaningless that suicide alone could provide an exit' (Barakat,[23] p. 9). Somewhat ironically, I happen to be in a position to provide the necessary data for making this assertion a little more relevant. Assuming that the correlation between the day-to-day cycles of absence and accidents points in the direction of alienation, then the same cycle of suicide rates would seem to clinch the argument (see Figs 6.6 and 6.7).

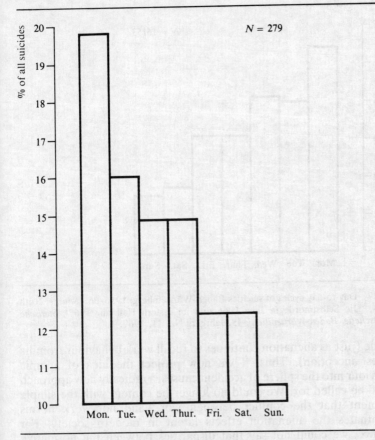

$N = 279$

Fig. 6.6 Day-to-day cycles of suicides in Oldham county borough, 1946–60. (*Source*: Jennings and Lunn, 'A study of suicide in a northern industrial town, 1946–60', *The Medical Officer*, 28 Dec. 1962.)

IV. Accident cycles and industrial anomie

But there is another possibility. The similarity between the weekly suicide and accident cycle is so striking that it raises a new question. Instead of stretching the concept of alienation far beyond its original core meaning, would it not be better to treat anomie as a separate cause of accidents in its own right? Once again it is awkward to avoid getting involved in the endless terminological wrangles which have become the fate of every classical concept. By way of a short cut, I shall propose that the central meaning of anomie has retained throughout its history a specific empirical reference: however one tries to define it on theoretical grounds, it remains associated with the phenomenon of

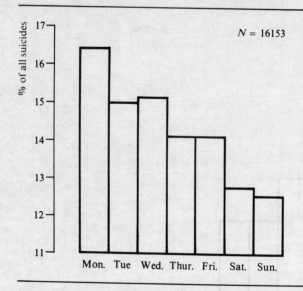

Fig. 6.7   Day-to-day cycles of suicides Baden-Württemberg, 1956–66. (*Source*: Ruth Paulus, 'Die Selbstmorde in Jahr 1966 und im erstern Halbjahr 1967', *Statische Monatschefte, Baden-Württemberg,* **15,** Jahrgarg No. 11, 1967.

suicide (just as alienation continues to recall work behaviour from its earliest inception). Thus, if we now project the idea of anomic behaviour into the sphere of accident causes, a radically new approach would be called for. We could no longer be content with the simple argument that the conflict between work and non-work norms accentuates the alienation effects latent in modern society. For instance, we could not say that disparities between the normative expectations of work and leisure are the *only* sociological determinants of accidents. From the moment that we introduce the notion of anomie an alternative sociological approach is invoked, and it is one that is fundamentally different. No matter how alienation is defined, the concept implies a rational calculus: the actor somehow strives to obtain a balance of inputs and outputs. Anomie, however (again, in whichever direction a sophisticated definition leads) transcends rational behaviour. It results from an inescapable, head-on collision between ends and means, and thus presupposes a normless situation. There is a corresponding contrast in macrosociological terms. The calculus of the alienated worker is an essential component of the motivational forces which keep the whole system going. The very mechanism that impels the development of capitalist society revolves upon institutionalized alienation. Anomie, by contrast, implies a breakdown of the normative basis of the total system. We may remember, for instance, that among the crucial elements of Durkheim's definition is a strong emphasis on total societal disorganization: 'the state of crisis and anomie is constant and, so to speak, normal'.[24]

There is one further contrast between alienation and anomie which, though patently obvious, has frequently been neglected. While the concept of alienation, when used as a central issue aligns itself readily with an anti-capitalist ideology, the opposite is true of the core meaning of anomie, because it is based on the postulate of a conflict-free society and hence points to a politically reactionary standpoint.

Supposing, then, that we allocate anomie a place among the remote underlying causes of industrial accidents, what would the concomitant, proximate aspect be? It would have to be a motivational factor which equally well fits the condition of anomic suicide as it does that of industrial accidents. It is doubtful whether Durkheim's much-criticized 'intervening' determinants would be very helpful here. Nevertheless, for the sake of historical interest, one of these intervening variables may be mentioned, especially as it happens to concern both suicides and industrial accidents. In trying to interpret cyclical variations of suicides by hours of the day, Durkheim refers to the vacillations in the intensity of 'social life', 'general activity' or 'public activity'. He argues that there are relatively few suicides during midday because general activity is then at a low level. (Durkheim, *Suicide*, p. 118).[24] And then he adds a footnote:

'Another proof that social life experiences a rhythm of rest and activity at the different times of day is the variations of accidents by hours. They are distributed as follows according to the Prussian Bureau of Statistics:

From 6 to noon   1,011 accidents per average hour
From noon to 2   686 accidents per average hour
From 2 to 6   1,191 accidents per average hour
From 6 to 7   979 accidents per average hour'

Fortunately, to fill this gap in a more convincing way is not as difficult as it seems. I suggest that here is in fact the place where the contemporary notion of psychological 'stress' can be usefully employed.[25] To put it briefly, this approach to psychological accident theory puts the emphasis on the relation between environmental–physical conditions and an individual's adjustment (or lack of adjustment) to the environment in terms of 'stress-tolerance'. Disregarding individual differences, a 'stressful situation' can thus be treated as a specific determinant of accident liability. The particular kind of stress-generating situation which is relevant to anomie may be constructed as follows. Maintaining Durkheim's basic assumption of 'insatiable', 'uncontrollable', 'unlimited' passions, and projecting it into the realm of industrial work, we may argue that anomic behaviour presents a form of irreparable instability; the actor strives at one time towards maximizing his earnings and at another time towards maximizing his non-work satisfactions (consumption, leisure, etc.) In the absence of specific normative expectations stabilizing either of the incongruent goals, he would find himself in a perpetual crisis and therefore in a situation of intolerable psychological stress.

No doubt, given time and opportunity, this theory could be worked out more carefully. For instance, even from a layman's limited understanding of diverse schools of contemporary psychology, one possible refinement suggests itself from the curious similarity between environmentally conditioned stress and environmentally induced neuroses on the basis of irreconcilable goals. However, at the moment it is sufficient to realize that the importance of all this hinges upon one single methodological point. No matter how sophisticated and careful such theorizing may be, it will always require the assumption that the occurrence of accidents is a form of human behaviour; in other words, part of the causation of accidents rests on *motivation*. Since this in turn necessarily implies that the event of an accident can be made comprehensible or understandable to the observer, it constitutes an approach which radically contradicts everything that has ever been assumed by common sense. And, as we know, the element of common-sense explanations has been of overwhelming influence in this area. By far the strongest manifestation of this element is the theory that accidents are caused by occupational hazards inherent in the technological-organizational environment of work. The model of the hazard theory treats accidents as a direct function of 'safety performance': given a minimum of 'unavoidable' accidents, the average rate of accidents would move up or down in accordance with the average degree of effectiveness of safety measures. Accidents are, then, essentially a component of the total technological-organizational apparatus; they are as much an integral part of the machinery as the safety devices themselves. Methodologically, therefore, accidents are, according to the model, strictly a physical spacio-temporal event, a chance occurrence that transcends human understanding and which can be analysed solely in terms of a statistical probability calculus. The most tangible expression of the hazards theory is the vast accumulation of descriptive statistical data in the official reports published regularly in all advanced industrial nations throughout the world. The fact that this wealth of data has remained completely useless for any causal analysis is suspicious enough. Worse still the common-sense plausibility of the theory is so powerful that the question of validity never seems to arise. Obviously, the authors of these reports do not realize that the hazards theory is a theory.

The upshot of this paper is that we are finally confronted with a surplus of possible theories. At the start, we found ourselves in a theoretical vacuum. Above all, the possibility of a *sociological* theory of accident causation was virtually unthinkable. Now we are forced to decide between two competing sociological approaches which appear to exclude each other; one derived from alienation, the other from anomie. They certainly imply conflicting value premises. According to conventional method texts this sort of dilemma cannot be solved by recourse to empirical tests, for scientifically validated facts are believed to be ethically neutral. However, as the new facts discovered by the Accident Project appear to be relevant to both theories the time has come to challenge this belief. But this is another story.[26]

Notes and References

1. Although written under the impact of my recent research experiences, the paper in fact continues the discussion of general methodological issues which I started in two previous papers: 'The category of pragmatic knowledge in sociological analysis', *Archiv fur Rechts- und Sozialphilosophie*, **53** (1967), 31–51, and 'The role of discoveries in social science', *Discussion Paper, University of Birmingham* Series E, No. 2, July 1966.

2. For a simple, non-mathematical introduction cf. W. J. Reichmann, 'Time series, and arithmancy', in *Use and Abuse of Statistics*, London: Chapman and Hall, 1961, pp. 172–88. Not unexpectedly, economists have given the widest recognition to the role of time series; occasionally even in the context of sociologically relevant factors. In this respect, my exposition has been greatly stimulated by the following pioneer work in the socio-economic analysis of wage structure: Wolfram Mieth, *Ein Beitrag zur Theorie der Lohnstruktur*, Gottingen: Schwartz, 1967.

3. Criteria of research relevance have been very much neglected in current methodology. For a recent, incisive discussion cf. Nathan Glazer, 'The ideological uses of sociology', in Lazarsfeld *et al.* (eds) *The Uses of Sociology*, Basic Books, 1968.

4. Only a few of the numerous contributions to the methods of survey analysis have realized that this paradigm is based on tacit agreement among its users rather than on conscious deliberation. Cf. notably, William W. Cooley and P. R. Lohnes, *Multivariate Procedures for the Behavioural Sciences*, New York, 1962, W. G. Cochran, 'The planning of observational studies of human populations', *J. Roy. Sta. Soc.*, A128 (1965) 234–65. T. Hirschi and H. C. Selvin, *Delinquency Research: An Appraisal of Analytic Methods*, New York.: Collier-Macmillan, 1967.

5. Here and henceforth the term 'theory' is deliberately left vague. It simply alludes to the familiar dichotomy 'theory versus research'. A serious treatment is impossible at present in view of the confusion brought about by such methodologists as D. Willer, Glaser and Strauss, R. Dubin and others.

6. This research is based on two approaches: (*a*) a large-scale statistical analysis of official accident records, and (*b*) a series of intensive studies of accident data from selected firms. I wish to acknowledge the valuable assistance and criticism that I have received throughout this work from Miss. S. Anisulowo, Mr R. D. Ballantyne, Mr M. Barhoum, Mrs H. A. Cowie, Mrs J. M. Davies, Miss Ailsa Duff, Mrs C. Houlton, Mrs J. Lowe, Mr M. Minards and Mr R. Rowe.

7. *Source: Annual Report of H.M. Chief Inspector of Factories, 1967*, London: HMSO, Cmnd 3745, 1968.

8. The most pertinent recent contribution to this question is R. Dahrendorf's ingenious concept of 'para-theory'; cf. his *Pfade aus Utonia*, Piper, 1967, p. 336, and *Essays in the Theory of Society*, London: Routledge and Kegan Paul, 1968, pp. 106, 141, 176, 229. Among earlier analyses of the problem, John Rex's *Key Problems of Sociological Theory* (Ch. 6, pp. 96–114), London: Routledge and Kegan Paul, is still by far the most penetrating.

9. W. Baldamus and H. Behrend, 'Variations in absenteeism during the week: an index of employee morale', *Nature*, **165,** 1950. W. Baldamus, *Efficiency and Effort*, Tavistock, 1961. H. Behrend, 'Absence and labour turnover in a changing economic climate', *Occup. Psychol.*, **27,** 1953.

10. Deutscher Bundestag, 5. Wahlperiode, V/152, 1966.
11. The whole issue of hypothesis construction will be treated separately in a forthcoming discussion paper entitled: 'On testing hypotheses', *University of Birmingham, Discussion Paper,* Series E, No. 13.
12. Cf. above note 8.
13. Cf. F. Tillyard, *The Worker and the State,* London, 1948, pp. 178–242. W. M. Cooper and J. C. Wood, *Outline of Industrial Law* (3rd edn), London, 1958, pp. 307–75.
14. Source: *Annual Report of H. M. Chief Inspector of Factories,* 1963 and 1966, London: HMSO, 1964 and 1967.
15. Cf. in particular M. Greenwood and H. M. Woods, 'The incidence of industrial accidents upon individuals with special reference to multiple accidents', *Industrial Fatigue Research Board, Report No. 4,* London HMSO, 1919. A. G. Arbous and J. E. Kerrich, 'Accident Statistics and the concept of accident-proneness, *Biometrics,* **14** (1951), 340–432. A. B. Cherns, 'Accidents at work', in A. T. Welford *et al.* (eds) *Society, Psychological Problems and Methods of Study,* London: Routledge and Kegan Paul, 1968, pp. 206–28.
16. See for instance, *Nineteenth Annual Report of Interstate Commerce Commission, No. 195, 1905—1906; First Report of the Industrial Accident Board, Massachusetts, 1912—1913.*
17. First reported in Memorandum No. 21 of Health of Munitions Workers Committee, 1918 and summarized in his book *Industrial Fatigue and Efficiency,* London: Routledge, 1921, pp. 186–194.
18. T. A. Ryan, *Work and Effort,* New York, 1947.
19. Deutscher Bundestag, 5. Wahlperiode, Durcksache V/3745, Bonn, 1969.
20. Source: see note 19.
21. W. Zimmermann, 'Fehlzeiten im Industriebetrieb', *Soziale Welt,* 1966.
22. K. Newton, *The Sociology of British Communism,* London: Allen Lane, 1969, p. 112.
23. H. Barakat, 'Alienation: a process of encounter between utopia and reality', *B. J. S.,* 20, No. 1 (Mar. 1969).
24. E. Durkheim, *Suicide, a study in sociology,* trans. J. A. Spaulding and G. Simpson, Free Press, 1951.
25. I am indebted to Mrs H. Cowie who enlightened me on the recent development of this concept. Cf. for example, L. Brody, 'Methodology and patterns of research', *Annals of N.Y. Academy of Sciences,* **107**(2), 1963.
26. See 'On testing hypotheses', *Discussion Paper, University of Birmingham.* Series E, No. 13, July 1969. It should be noted that the present paper has confined itself to the discussion of facts (e.g. the German accident cycle, the suicide cycle, the relation between strikes and accidents) which were *not* the central issue of the Accident Project which concerns the British evidence on accident cycles, and is the empirical focus of 'On testing hypotheses'.

7

Justice and the comprehensive ideal

J. Ford

Introduction to Reading 7

Comprehensive secondary education has spread generally throughout England and Wales in the last twenty years. Its beginnings were slow at first, with some rural areas such as Anglesey introducing it in the 1950s as a way of coping with highly dispersed rural populations for whom the provision of three types of schools would have been unduly expensive. The only city regions in England and Wales to have comprehensive secondary education in the 1950s as a matter of social and educational policy were Leicester and the old London County Council. Even so, in these two areas, the comprehensive schools still existed side-by-side with selective secondary schools.

The movement towards comprehensive secondary schooling has accelerated tremendously in the 1960s and 1970s. Although only 28 per cent of secondary school children were in comprehensive schemes in 1968, now the majority of children between eleven and the compulsory school-leaving age of sixteen years attend such schools. The pressure to go comprehensive is now a political one which cuts across the two main political parties (with some right-wing Conservative opposition). The pressure now comes not from a belief in its cost-effectiveness (though that has played a part), but from the belief that education can and should be used to create a 'fairer' society, and that comprehensive education is the means to the end.

The belief in the role of education as the engine of social change towards true equality of opportunity for children, based only on the meritocratic criterion of ability, comes from two sources. From the research of social scientists, and from the redefinition of goals and means in the Labour Party and in the liberal wing of the Conservative Party.

The academic attack on the liberal ideas of 1944 Education Act (itself a joint production of the three main political parties) established that 'the essential judgement must be that "liberal policies have failed in their own terms" ' (Halsey, reprinted in this reader pp. 67–101). The education scheme laid down in the 1944 Act failed to bring about that true equality of opportunity that its proponents desired. The chance of a child's passing the selective

From J. Ford, *Social Class and the Comprehensive School*, London: Routledge & Kegan Paul, 1969, Ch. 1, pp. 1–19.

examination for the most prestigious of the three forms of state education (the grammar school) was shown to be strongly conditioned by its social origins, even when measured abilities were equal (Douglas 1964). The research of academics was noted by politicians, particularly by Labour politician Anthony Crosland, in the late 1950s and early 1960s who articulated the doubts of academics in their political programmes. Political demands such as comprehensive education at secondary level were responses both to expert opinion and to the disquiet felt by certain social groups in the electorate. These political programmes reacted back on academic thinking about education and redirected the research effort in sociology and psychology.

Ford reflects the dual – both political and academic – pressures behind the drive to comprehensive education. She is unable to state the theory of how comprehensive education would equalise opportunity without drawing on both political and academic sources. The interaction between political programmes and academic research which lies at the heart of the comprehensive debate is shown most clearly in Ford's need to *create* a theory (in order to test it) from a variety of sources. There exists no clear and well-worked-out theory of how comprehensive education leads to a juster society, precisely because notions of 'justice' can be both moral (as in the political debate) and sociological.

Only by addressing herself to what people think *ought* to be a 'just' society can she bring a sociological technique to bear. Ford formulates her research problem in the context of the political debate about the goals of comprehensive education. She asks why there should have been political pressure in the 1950s against the eleven-plus selection of children for grammar schools and secondary moderns. She finds the answer in the 'bulge' of children passing through the educational system in the 1950s who had restricted chance of qualifying for grammar school because of the failure by local education authorities to expand grammar-school places to compensate for the larger age group. This was a historical injustice, but there also existed geographical injustices as well which she does not point out. Many counties in Wales accepted nearly 30 per cent of the age group for an academic education, while at the other extreme, Hertfordshire accepted less than 18 per cent.

Ford's explanation of why this demographic accident resulted in political pressure rests on two related sociological theories: that of relative deprivation, and that of status inconsistency. In relative deprivation it is argued that individuals assess their own satisfaction not by reference to any fixed norms of consumption or social mobility, but by reference to how well others are doing with whom they feel some sense of likeness. Status inconsistency stems from an individual's unmatched statuses in the various social hierarchies such as income, occupational status, ethnic standing, and so on. Lenski (1954) among others has pointed out that those with inconsistent statuses will be more radical, even though their income (for example) is higher, than those who occupy equivalent positions in the various social rankings of society.

Ford, having dealt with the background of the comprehensive education movement, turns to her central research problem; does comprehensive education produce a fairer society? She recasts this question – which is unanswerable as it stands because of the philosophical range of meanings given to 'fair' – into a more sociological form which is in principle an answerable question. The question then becomes will comprehensive education meet the definitions of what people regard as 'fair'? She then proceeds formally to articulate seven propositions which she creates from her reading of the academic and political literature. The only question which the critic can ask at this stage is, do these propositions correspond to what was expected of comprehensive reorganisation? In short, does her formulation of the theory (what she calls her creative act) cover the main currents of thought which resulted in the move to comprehensive education? This she calls an ideal-type theory (after Weber). Ideal types are tools which social scientists use to study the world. In the form of theories (such as Ford's) they are clearer and more internally consistent models than any of the varied sources which she drew on would have held. Ideal types are the creations of the social scientists, and the only question which one can ask about them is – are they useful? If they are such strong distortions of thought that few if any thinkers ever subscribed to parts of them we can reject them as a useful starting point. Beyond that one cannot judge ideal types.

There remains an ambiguity in her use of ideal type for the intended effects of comprehensive education. It probably does correspond to the rationalised collective opinion of those who advocated comprehensive schools, but does it describe the intentions of the local education authorities who had the task of creating a comprehensive system in their regions? The retention of some direct-grant schools alongside so-called comprehensives makes a mockery of the intention to have schools with an intake covering the whole range of ability. In other words, are the effects of comprehensive education as it actually exists those which its advocates intended? Her ideal type is a model of the intentions, not of the practice. This makes the evaluation of her findings (which are not extracted here) more difficult. We can perhaps reformulate Ford's research question from 'Does comprehensive education satisfy the notions of justice which political programmes offered?' to 'Does comprehensive education in practice satisfy notions of justice . . . ?'

Much of the current political debate on comprehensive education is in just these terms – that is, 'Does comprehensive education meet the demands for social justice which its advocates have made?' Any answer now must be tentative because truly comprehensive education for secondary school pupils has yet to emerge on a national scale. Those local educational authorities which have opted for complete comprehensive education have too little experience for them (or us) to assess the effects yet, and many have not even completed the move to full 'comprehensivation'. In either case it is too early for a useful judgement to be given, although social scientists are pressed for interim judgements if only because our children have but one educational life to live.

References and Further Reading

Crosland, C. A. R. (1956) *The Future of Socialism,* London: Jonathan Cape.
Douglas, J. W. B. (1964) *Home and the School: A Study of Ability and Attainment in the Primary School,* London: McGibbon and Kee.
Lenski, G. (1954) 'Status crystallisation: a non-vertical dimension of social status', *American Sociological Review,* 19.
Runciman, W. (1966) *Relative Deprivation and Social Justice,* London: Routledge and Kegan Paul.
Weber, M. (1947) *The Theory of Social and Economic Organisation,* trans. T. Parsons, New York: The Free Press.
Weber, M. (1949) *The Methodology of the Social Sciences,* trans. E. Shils and H. Finch, New York: The Free Press.

Among parents and teachers, as well as Labour Party idealists and educationalists, discontent with the tripartite organization of secondary education in England and Wales is very evident. But criticism of the present system of selection does not stem so much from a rejection of the general principle whereby rewards, material and symbolic, are unequally distributed in society, as from a distaste for the current bases of discrimination. Thus, as Pedley puts it, 'The Englishman of the 1960s does not believe in equality. What he wants is equal opportunity to be unequal.'[1] On closer examination, however, even the argument for equality of *opportunity* is seen to be a cover for a yet more limited plea. For, as Benn and Peters have noted, the cry for equality of opportunity refers in practice to the desire to accord individuals the same opportunities 'only in the sense that they are all entitled to be treated alike until *relevant* grounds are established for treating them differently'.[2] In the English situation relevant grounds are almost invariably considered in the context of ability. Thus we can see the main body of current criticism of the tripartite system of education, in sociological as well as political and administrative circles, as stemming from the view that selection should be based on the sole criterion of 'ability'[3] and that this cannot be adequately ascertained by an examination at Eleven-Plus.[4]

Now it should be made clear immediately that this is always an ideological position, a bid to remove an injustice, a statement that discrimination is being made on irrelevant grounds and that this should be replaced by efficient selection on relevant and reasonable criteria.[5] Sometimes the ideological flavour of such a criticism is disguised in a variant of the fuctionalist view. For example, Floud and Halsey[6] argue that the 'efficient division of the working population requires both that there should be the right numbers of workers in each occupation and that the qualities of workers in each occupation should be as appropriate as possible – in short that 'ability' and 'opportunity' should be matched as closely as possible.'[7] They claim that under the present system this requirement is not being met adequately, and that a closer adherence to this ideal could be attained by comprehensive reorganization. Yet on closer inspection this argument is not entirely convincing. Floud and Halsey may consider the present system to be unjust, but they have not demonstrated that it is inefficient.

Consider, for example, the situation where the proportion of individuals with abilities relevant to high status jobs exceeds the number of those jobs. In this case, so long as all those who actually attain high status jobs do have the requisite abilities, 'the efficient division of the working population' is effected – but some individuals with the 'ability' to become brain surgeons have to be content with sweeping roads. Furthermore, the actual brain surgeons could have been selected from the universe of potential brain surgeons on entirely ascriptive, that is 'unreasonable', grounds; but the requirements of efficiency in the division of labour would not be threatened so long as they could actually function adequately as brain surgeons. There is no reason to assume that roadsweepers of brain-surgeon capacity would be inefficient at sweeping roads. Nor does it salvage the argument to introduce the idea of 'wastage of ability'; for, while the supply of skills or potential skills in the population exceeds the demand for such skills which is generated by the occupational structure, there will always be 'wastage of ability' regardless of the mode of selection through education.[8]

So, rather than wasting intellectual effort in attempts to rationalize ideological commitments and to present the conclusions from normative assumptions as though they were derived from value-neutral deductions, it is clearly more economic to state these value assumptions in explicit form.[9] Let us recognize that, in our discussions of the processes of educational and occupational selection, it is justice which is at issue, not efficiency. There is no fear that by formulating the argument in these terms we are relegating it to idealists and politicians; such a discussion does not lie outside the province of sociology, for our ideas about justice in general, and our mobility ideologies in particular, are important aspects of our culture which themselves merit study.

There are two opposed approaches to the study of justice among sociologists: one empirical, the other moral. The empirical position is exemplified in the work of Homans.[10] For Homans' norms of justice are determined by the empirical conditions of exchange in social relationships; 'what *is* determines what always *ought* to be.'[11] Thus what a man expects, what he considers just, is determined by his actual experience: he comes to learn that generally it happens that rewards are proportional to costs: 'if one man is "better" than another in his investments, he should also be "better" than the other in the value of the contribution he makes and in the reward he gets for it.'[12] Thus an empirical expectation, a conception of *probability*, gives rise to a normative expectation, a conception of what *ought* to be done.[13] This can be expressed by the more general Aristotelian notion that 'if (a man) is better on one count, he ought to be better on both: his rankings on the two counts should be in line with one another'.[14] On the empirical view, then, justice is a matter of expectations and the sense of injustice is aroused when expectations are defeated.[15]

The empirical approach has been attacked by Runciman[16] who, drawing on Benn and Peters,[17] stresses that just differentials in rewards are based, not on *any* differences in status or investment, but on *relevant* differences. Runciman's personal sense of justice is outraged by the denial of reward to an individual in one of Homans' examples[18] on grounds he does not see to be relevant. 'By normal standards of justice,' says Runciman, 'this is transparently unfair.'[19] But what are 'normal' standards of justice? Clearly, if we understand 'normal' in the statistical rather than the clinical sense, there is the possibility that what other people consider to be just, what is normal to a particular culture or subculture, is 'transparently unfair' to Runciman. Of course the bases of discrimination must be relevant in some sense to the discrimination in question before a difference in reward is described as just. But what are the criteria of relevance? Runciman seems to consider that there are absolute criteria which must be obvious to all reasonable men. Yet even if we were to accept this philosophically intuitionist position[20] we would still be left with the task of explaining what actually happens in the world. For these purposes Runciman's personal conception of what kinds of differences between human beings are relevant bases of differential reward is of no interest; we are asking, rather, what criteria of differentiation are popularly held to be relevant to differences in reward. Thus the moral conception of justice is antipathetic to sociological explanation since conceptions of what the standards of justice ought to be are irrelevant to an understanding of the views of justice which people in fact hold.

Curiously Runciman's own *Relative Deprivation and Social Justice*[21] provides a most enlightening explanation of the way in which popular conceptions of justice actually change based on the very idea of status inconsistency which is so central to the Homansian approach to justice. Basically his argument is that 'objective' inequalities in life-chances of all kinds – the sorts of situations which liberal sociologists might describe as 'transparently unfair' – are not themselves sufficient to produce a sense of injustice in the deprived individuals. The intervening variable is the notion of *relative deprivation*.[22] Relative deprivation arises when individuals perceive inequalities between their positive reference groups and their membership groups.[23] For example, when individuals are placed in marginal positions,[24] one attribute or status making them eligible for membership in a more highly valued group in which they are not wholly accepted while other attributes assign them more firmly to a less highly valued group, they will feel relatively deprived. The debilities ascribed to them because of their membership of the less highly valued group will now come to be defined as intolerable and unjust. Thus in societies where there is a high degree of status crystallization,[25] where individuals' rankings on the various hierarchies of prestige, power, wealth, race and so on tend to be highly correlated, relative deprivation, and hence the sense of injustice, will tend to be low. On the other hand in societies undergoing more rapid social change, where mobility between statuses is greater and where consequently there is a low degree of status crystallization, there will tend to be groups and individuals who are continually redefining traditional conceptions of justice, and rejecting as unfair what was formerly accepted as right.

We have seen that our ideas about equality of educational opportunity are aspects of our more general cultural conceptions about justice, and that changing ideas of justice in society can be explained with reference to the ideas of status crystallization and relative deprivation. We are now in a position to examine changing conceptions of justice in the sphere of education in terms of this explanatory framework.

Changing attitudes to education can be seen as changing ideas of what are *just* bases for educational discrimination. The sense of injustice arises because the sorts of differences between individuals which have been determining their educational opportunity are now seen as irrelevant. Thus the charter of the Butler Act of 1944 was to neutralize the impact of wealth on educational attainment as wealth came to be an unacceptable determinant of educational success. However, the Act did not remove, nor was it designed to remove, differentials in educational opportunity, for educational chances were now to be determined by measured intelligence, and since this attribute was considered to be relevant to educational success, this new discrimination was seen to be just.

Now, while it is true that there has been some disquiet deriving from the suspicion that the Eleven-Plus test is not an accurate measure of innate intelligence,[26] it is generally agreed that this test is the best instrument yet devised to measure 'intelligence' and that alternative attempts at selection for secondary school, such as teachers' recommendations are less 'fair'.[27] How is it then that people have come to define the present system of educational selection as unjust? Their sense of injustice stems from a redefinition of 'intelligence-as-measured-by-Eleven-Plus-tests' as an irrelevant basis of discrimination. And their argument is that a new and just differentiation should be on the basis of 'real ability' rather than measured intelligence.[28]

The explanation of this changing conception of educational justice must be sought in the conditions which gave rise to a sense of relative deprivation among those not favoured by the tripartite system. It is the working class which is, and always has been, most educationally deprived.[29] But, as we have seen, deprivation is not in itself sufficient to produce the sense of relative deprivation. Since the majority of secondary modern school children have always been from working-class homes and their low educational status, and consequent low anticipations of occupational status, have been quite in accord with their parents' occupational prestige, we would not expect them or their parents to define their circumstances as unjust. This *consistently* deprived group then is not a likely source of the pressure for change; our search for an explanation of the innovation in educational attitudes becomes the search for a marginal group: a group with inconsistent status rankings.

When we consider the effects of the post-war 'Bulge' in the birth rate a possible answer suggests itself. The first wave of the Bulge reached the age of eleven in 1957 but there was no substantial increase in the number of places available in grammar schools. This had a two-fold impact on the intake of the secondary modern schools: they began to receive more middle-class pupils and more pupils of higher than average ability than had formerly been the case. For the first time then middle-class families, in relatively substantial numbers, were experiencing the effects of having one or more children receiving an 'inferior' education, and one which was not generally intended as a preparation for middle-class occupations. This situation of status inconsistency may well have resulted in a feeling of relative deprivation among these families, and eventually this rather vocal section of society may have come to define as unjust a system of education where children are almost certainly doomed to low status jobs by the failure of an examination at the age of eleven.

At the same time the addition of relatively able pupils to the secondary modern school may have been working in another way to introduce discontent with the system. For it has been argued[30] that headmasters of secondary modern schools took advantage of this opportunity to distinguish their schools in public examinations, entering more and more pupils for 'O' level G.C.E.[31] In 1954 the number of secondary modern schools entering pupils for G.C.E. was only 357; this figure had risen to over 1,350 by 1959 – over one-third of all secondary modern schools. The growing demand for qualifications is probably reflected in the increasing percentage of pupils staying for a fifth year in secondary modern schools. Dent notes that this rose from 3.5 per cent in 1949 to 7 per cent in 1959,[32] and by 1964 the proportion had reached about one in ten.[33] Thus a further source of criticism of Eleven-Plus selection is suggested. Growing awareness that some pupils, though rejected by the Eleven-Plus were capable of G.C.E. success may have led to a suspicion that this examination was somehow an inaccurate measure of 'ability'. Thus in two ways the effects of the Bulge may have operated to thwart individuals' expectations in the field of education and hence to produce a feeling of injustice resulting in rising criticism of the tripartite organization of secondary education.

So far we have considered only the negative side of our changing attitudes about education: the redefinition of tripartite education as unjust. The other aspect of current educational thought is, of course, the advocacy of comprehensive education as an alternative, which, it is believed, will abolish the unjust features of the present system and hence produce the 'Fairer Society'.

There is fairly general support for the idea of comprehensive education in this country. A recent opinion poll carried out by *New Society* and Research Services produced the following distribution of responses to the question 'Are you in favour or against comprehensive education?'[34]

Table 7.1 Social class*

	AB	C₁	C₂	DE	All	N = 1,331
%						
In favour	46	51	58	51	52	
Don't know	17	29	27	38	29	
Against	37	20	15	11	19	

*Standard Market Research categories.

There is then substantial acceptance of comprehensive education across all social classes. Rejection, however, is clearly related to social class, for, while in the AB category only 9 per cent more accept than reject, in the DE category the difference between acceptance and rejection is 40 per cent ($p = 0.001$). Members of the social class categories who might be seen as having most to lose by comprehensive reorganization favour this policy significantly less than members of those which are seen to have most to gain. Attitudes to comprehensive education were also shown by the survey to be related to political party allegiance, 60 per cent of Labour Party, 55 per cent of Liberal Party, but only 45 per cent of Conservative Party supporters expressing acceptance of comprehensive education ($p = 0.001$).[35]

So support for comprehensive reorganization of secondary education, while not homogenous, is fairly general and such reorganization is the expressed policy of the political party which forms the present government.[36] Yet there has been very little research into the effects of comprehensive schools,[37] and even less into the question as to the extent to which they can be expected to produce the 'Fairer Society', an expectation which is arguably the basic rationale behind this reorganization.

In order to examine this question empirically it is first necessary to clarify the precise theory on which the hypothesis *Comprehensive schools will tend to produce the 'Fairer Society'* is based. At this point the discussion turns from popular attitudes about comprehensive schools to the published literature on the subject. For there is, of course, no reason to suppose that 'the man-in-the-street' has explicitly formulated ideas about the relationship between education and 'equality', although aspects of the more academic discussion on the matter may filter into his consciousness through the media of opinion leaders.[38]

If one turns to the published work of the advocates of comprehensive schools, any hope of discovering this theory is, however, soon disappointed. The connection between comprehensive education and the 'Fairer Society' is nowhere made clear, in fact it is often taken to be self-evident, and the connection is considered to be so obvious that no explanation is required. Thus, for example, Armstrong and Young in their Fabian pamphlet[39] assume that comprehensive schools will produce a better society, and merely discuss the various alternatives within the broad comprehensive ideal. Floud and Halsey also advocate comprehensive reorganization, with the proviso that this would produce the desired results 'only if the spirit as well as the form of English secondary education were changed',[40] yet their reasoning is entirely based on criticism of the tripartite system.

However, while I have not found a complete theory of the effects of comprehensive schooling in any single work, it is possible to build up a sort of *ideal type* theory from the suggestions in the various sources. Such a theory, of course, will never conform completely to the views of any one author, but it should be a reasonable representation of the general line of thought which is current.

The key to the theoretical link between the tripartite system and the 'Unfair Society' seems to lie in the idea of early selection. Few critics reject selection *per se*, however, their objections are specifically to *early* and relatively final differentiation on the basis of measured intelligence. Taylor, for example, argues that

if we no longer possess a criterion that will legitimize early selection, allocation and the subsequent differentiation attendant upon them, then it becomes morally imperative to shift the basis of allocation procedures from performance in intelligence and attainment tests and response to primary schooling to a more flexible procedure operating within secondary and post-secondary education, where the range of choices available is such as to make it easier for child, parent and teacher to match interests and attainments and a suitable type of course.[41]

This rejection of early selection is very often accompanied by a rejection of traditional forms of streaming as bases for grouping within the new comprehensive schools. Many writers advocate, and some schools operate, methods of breaking up the school on horizontal lines, not in any way related to academic performance, such as house systems. For it is clear that a rigid system of streaming in comprehensive schools amounts to tripartite differentiation with the sole exception that grammar, technical and secondary modern schools are housed in one building. Nevertheless, completely unstreamed comprehensive schools are rare and it does seem to be government policy to pursue the comprehensive ideal to its logical conclusion.[42] Thus Crosland has said, 'Both common sense and American experience suggest that (unstreaming) would lead to a really serious levelling down of standards and a quite excessive handicap to the clever child. Division into streams according to ability, remains essential', and in a footnote he adds, 'some (enthusiasts), their heads perhaps a little turned by too much sociology, even insist on classes being not known by numbers but by the teachers' names lest any mark at all of superior or inferior status be conferred. This is simply egalitarianism run mad!'[43] Where unstreaming does not accompany comprehensive organization the principle of abolition of early selection is often claimed to be protected by the fact that mobility between streams within one school is easier than mobility between schools.

Having identified the major variable in the theory which our ideal-typical advocate of comprehensives might put forward, it is now necessary to spell out the remaining intervening variables and the relationships between them. The actual arrangement of propositions in a theory is, of course, a creative business, very much a personal, even artistic endeavour. Two theorists approaching the same problem from similar perspectives could never produce the same theory, just as two painters from the same school could not, without collaboration, paint substantially similar portraits of one woman. Thus the deductive scheme suggested below, while inspired by the arguments which can be found in the literature, does not spring directly from those arguments. It is, like all ideal types, an imaginative reconstruction, a product of selective emphasis and exaggeration.

The theory

Proposition One Early selection of children into groups with differential educational and occupational prospects
  (i) prevents the fullest development of talent,
  (ii) inhibits equality of educational opportunity for those with equal talent,
  (iii) prematurely confines children's occupational horizons,
  (iv) segregates potential occupational 'successes' from 'failures', hence echoing and reinforcing the system of stratification in the wider society.

Proposition Two Where conditions (iii) and (iv) occur children's perceptions of the structure and meaning of stratification tend to take the form of rigid dichotomous models.

Proposition Three Where (iii) and (iv) do not occur children's perceptions of the structure and meaning of stratification tend to take the form of flexible hierarchic models.

Proposition Four Under a tripartite system of secondary education early selection of children into groups with differential educational and occupational prospects is present.

Proposition Five   Under a comprehensive system of secondary education early selection does not occur to such a great extent.

Proposition Six   Movement from a tripartite to a comprehensive organization of secondary education will therefore cause
(a) a greater development of talent,
(b) a greater equality of opportunity for those with equal talent,
(c) a widening of children's occupational horizons,
(d) a relative decline in the social interaction in school which takes place within the boundaries of anticipated occupational strata, and a relative increase in interaction across such strata.

Proposition Seven   Conditions (c) and (d) will produce a tendency to greater frequency of flexible hierarchic models of stratification over rigid dichotomous models.

None of these propositions is inherently untestable; however, I will be concerned with testing only propositions six and seven, as any refutation of these would be sufficient to throw doubt upon the whole theory. Naturally the theory would be even more fundamentally questioned if the fifth proposition were to prove false. While this has not been specifically tested there is sufficient evidence available to give strong grounds for *suspecting* it to be false. Studies of the determinants of educational success in primary schools[44] suggest that academic successes and failures are largely selected long before the stage of entry to secondary school, and it might be argued that, for this reason, reform of secondary education is irrelevant. However, for present purposes it will be assumed that there is less early selection under comprehensive educational schemes. [. . .]

Returning to the sixth and final propositions we see that these two statements suggest five hypotheses:

1. Comprehensive schools will produce a greater development of talent than tripartite schools.
2. Comprehensive schools will provide greater equality of opportunity for those with equal talent.
3. The occupational horizons of children in comprehensive schools will be widened relative to those of children in tripartite schools.
4. Comprehensive school children will show less tendency to mix only with children of their own social type than will tripartite school children.
5. Comprehensive school children will tend to have views of the class system as a flexible hierarchy, while tripartite school children will tend to see this as a rigid dichotomy.

Hypothesis One   The idea that early selection prevents the fullest development of talent derives from a rejection of the notion that ability is a fixed genetic quality, a notion that was behind the provisions of the 1944 Act. Burt, in his report to the Consultative Committee in 1931 stated, 'Before this age (12) is reached children need to be grouped according to their capacity, not merely in separate classes or standards but in separate types of school.'[45] The similar argument put forward in the Norwood Report, that the three types of schools were designed to cater for three types of minds, is by now infamous.[46] Against this the argument has recently been advanced that the attainment of different standards by children selected for different types of education is no more than a self-fulfilling prophecy: that children do as well as they *think* they can and their perceptions are shaped by the way the educational system defines them.[47] In fact, [. . .], there is as yet no definite empirical evidence in support of this argument. However, in so far as it is now widely believed that talent is produced by school experience rather than given exclusively by birth, then norms of equality will be concerned with the provision of equal opportunity for each individual to *develop* his talent to the full, rather than the more limited notion of equal opportunity for those with equal talent.[48]

Hypothesis Two   The more limited notion that early selection actually inhibits equality of educational opportunity for those with equal talent is a common one. This will be discussed in Chapter 3, where evidence from a sample of fourteen and fifteen year olds in tripartite and comprehensive schools will be brought to bear on the question whether or not comprehensive schooling increases the possibility that equal opportunities will be available to children of equal talent.

Hypothesis Three   Another aspect of the self-fulfilling prophecy notion as it relates to early selection is contained in the idea that different types of school 'feed' different occupations, not only because of the differences in the actual educational content provided – an effect specifically fashioned by the Butler Act – but also because of children's definitions of their ability. Research in England and Scotland has demonstrated the way in which type of school determines children's occupational horizons relative to their parents. Working-class boys in a London grammar school were found to have 'unrealistically' high expectations of social mobility[49] while secondary modern school children were found to set their sights 'realistically' low.[50] In Chapter 4 occupational plans and aspirations of children in tripartite and secondary modern schools will be examined and compared in an attempt to test the hypothesis that comprehensive schooling effects a widening of occupational horizons.

Hypothesis Four   It is a well documented fact that, in schools with early selection, friendships within school tend to occur among children of similar social-class background, and tend also to be confined to children with similar educational and occupational prospects.[51] However, no study has been published which tests the hypothesis that comprehensive schooling will reduce these effects, thus undermining the way in which school experience reinforces the class structure. This hypothesis will be examined in Chapter 5 where the attempt to undermine vertical stratification by breaking up the school into horizontal house groups will also be discussed.

Hypothesis Five   In Chapter 6 the way in which perceptions of social stratification are related to educational experience will be discussed and a typology of stratification maps suggested. The specific hypothesis that children who have experienced comprehensive schooling will be less likely to hold rigid dichotomous models of social class than tripartite school children will then be tested.

Notes and References

1. Robin Pedley, *The Comprehensive School*, Pelican, Penguin, 1963, p. 11.
2. S. I. Benn and R. S. Peters, *Social Principles and the Democratic State*, Allen & Unwin, 1959.
3. The relationship between the concept of 'ability' and that of 'intelligence' will be examined and discussed in Chapter 2.
4. A common theme in such criticisms concerns the plight of the late developer, prematurely abandoned by tripartite but encouraged to attain his maximum potential in the comprehensive school.
5. Thus in the Labour Party Manifesto *Signposts for the Sixties*, London, 1961, we read: 'To achieve genuine equality of educational opportunity we require . . . to reorganise the State secondary schools on comprehensive lines, in order to end the segregation by the Eleven-Plus examination which is now almost universally condemned on educational as well as social grounds.' A similar argument appears in C. A. R. Crosland, *The Future of Socialism*, London: Jonathan Cape, 1956.
6. Jean Floud and A. H. Halsey, 'English secondary schools and the supply of labour', in A. H. Halsey, J. Floud, and C. A. Anderson, *Education, Economy, and Society*, Free Press, 1961, pp. 80–92.
7. *Ibid*, p. 80. Note the similarity here to the argument of K. Davis, and W. E. Moore, 'Some principles of stratification', *Amer. Soc. Rev.*, **10** (1945), 242–9.
8. This line of argument is somewhat similar to that advanced against the functionalist theory of stratification by Buckley who points out that the functionalist approach leaves out the whole question of how individuals get into positions in the occupational structure, i.e. it confuses an epidemiological with an aetiological level of analysis. See W. Buckley, 'Social stratification and the functionalist theory of social differentiation', *American Soc. Rev.*, **23** (1958), 369–75.
9. A celebrated exponent of this idea is Gunnar Myrdal. See his 'The relation between social theory and social policy', *Brit. Journ. Sociol.*, **23** (1953), 210–42; *Value in Social Theory*, New York, 1958, and *An American Dilemma*, Harper, 1944.
10. The major argument is presented in G. C. Homans, *Social Behaviour: Its Elementary Forms*, Routledge & Kegan Paul, 1961, pp. 232–64.
11. G. C. Homans, 'Fundamental social processes', in N. J. Smelser, *Sociology*, Wiley, 1967, p. 64.

12. Homans, *op. cit.* (1961), p. 245.
13. For an interesting discussion of the distinction between 'ought's of empirical and normative expectations' see N. Gross, N. S. Mason, and A. W. McEachern, *Explorations in Role Analysis,* Wiley, 1958, Ch. 4.
14. Homans, *op. cit.* (1967), pp. 64–5. See also Aristotle, *Nichomachean Ethics,* Bk V, Ch. 3 and 4. Homans notes also the similarity to Jouvenel's 'What men find just is to preserve between themselves, as regards whatever is in question, the same relations that exist between them as regards anything else', *op. cit.* (1961), p. 245.
15. For other discussions of the empirical conception of justice and its relationship to social exchange see P. M. Blau, *Exchange and Power in Social Life,* Wiley, 1964, especially pp. 156–8 and 228; and Julienne Ford, *et al.,* 'Functional autonomy, role distance and social class', *Brit. Journ. Sociol,* **18** (4) (1967), 370–81. Both these stress norms of justice as aspects of culture deriving from patterns of social exchange. See also the interesting phenomenological approach to ideas of equality in Alfredo Schutz, *Collected Papers,* Vol. II, The Hague: Nijhoff, 1964, especially pp. 239–44, and 257–73.
16. W. G. Runciman, 'Justice, congruence and Professor Homans', *Archiv. Europ. Sociol.,* **8** (1967), 115–28.
17. Runciman, *op. cit.*
18. This example was taken from W. F. Whyte, *Street Corner Society,* Chicago U. P. 1943. Whyte noted that Alec, who had low status in the gang failed to do well in bowling tournaments between all members of the gang, although his performance in friendly matches indicated that his bowling skill was quite high.
19. Whyte, *op. cit.,* p. 118.
20. Runciman's philosophical intuitionism draws heavily on the work of John Rawls. Very briefly the argument is that fairness could be intuited by rational and impartial men if they were required to agree on principles by which they would be prepared to make and concede claims. As Runciman puts it, 'To make a claim on the basis of justice, therefore, is not merely to claim what is seen as a right, but to claim what is a right only if it derives from a *principle* to which the claimant could have subscribed before knowing whether he might not be the loser, rather than the gainer, by the acceptance of it', *op. cit.,* p. 253. See Rawls' three articles, 'Justice as fairness', *Philosophical Review,* **67** (1958), 164–94; 'The sense of justice', *Ibid.,* **72** (1963), 281–305; and 'Constitutional liberty and the concept of justice', *Nomos,* **6** (1963), 98–125.
21. Routledge & Kegan Paul, 1966.
22. This concept was first introduced by S. A. Stouffer, *et al., The American Soldier,* Vol. 1, Princeton U. P., 1949. See also the experimental demonstration of the relative deprivation hypothesis in A. J. Spector, 'Expectations, fulfilment and morale', *J. Aborm. Soc. Psychol.,* **52** (1956), 51–6.
23. Runciman distinguishes between three types of reference groups: membership, comparative and normative (*op. cit.,* pp. 9–16). However, this is a little confusing as the types are not mutually exclusive. It is perhaps more enlightening for this discussion to think in terms of a two-dimensional typology. Any particular group to which any specific individual refers may be classified according firstly to whether or not he is *accepted* as a member of it, and secondly to his *evaluation* of membership of it. It is, then, the feeling which arises when an individual compares a group of Type 2 with one of Type 3 which is described as relative deprivation.

    This typology does not in any way exhaust the meaningful distinctions which can be made between different types of reference groups; for example, some groups provide normative standards for their members while others do not, in addition one could distinguish between reference groups according to their saliency for the individuals involved. For a fuller understanding of the concept of reference group than can be provided here, the reader should consult H. H. Kelley, 'Two functions of reference groups', in G. H. Swanson *et al.* (eds), *Readings in Social Psychology,* 2nd edn, N.Y., 1952, pp. 410–14; and Erwin L. Linn, 'Reference group: a case study in conceptual diffusion', *Sociological Quarterly* **5** (1964), 489–99, where a summary of the previous literature is provided.

	Accepted into group	Not accepted into group
Positively evaluates membership	1	2
Negatively evaluates membership	3	4

24. For definitions of the concept of marginality and summaries of the vast literature on the subject see H. F. Dickie-Clark, *The Marginal Situation,* Routledge & Kegan Paul, 1966, and Steven Box and Julienne Ford, 'Commitment to science; a solution to student marginality?', *Sociology,* **1** (3) (1967), 225–38.
25. The concept of status crystallization was recently popularized by Gerhard Lenski, see for example his 'Status crystallization: a non-vertical dimension of social status', *Amer. Soc. Rev.,* **19** (1954), 405. However, the concept is by no means a new one and there are a multitude of terminological synonyms. The major alternative terms are *Status Consistency* probably first used by W. F. Kenkel, 'The relationship between status consistency and politico-economic attitudes', *Amer. Soc. Rev.,* **21** (4) (1956), 265–8; *'Goodness of Fit',* which is used by Broom who clearly differentiates between crystallization on macro and micro levels – a distinction ignored by some of the writers above, see 'Social differentiation and stratification' in Robert K. Merton, Leonard Broom, and Leonard Cottrell, *Sociology Today,* Harper, 1959. An earlier usage is to be found in Benoit-Smullyan's introduction of the concept of *Status Equilibration,* which refers to the process of adjusting the lower to the higher status; E. Benoit-Smullyan 'Status, status types and status interrelationships', *Amer. Soc. Rev.* **9** (1944), 151–61. The earliest version, however, is probably Parsons' *Vagueness of Class Structure* in his 1940 essay 'An analytical approach to the theory of social stratification', in Talcott Parsons, *Essays in Sociological Theory,* Free Press, 1964, pp. 69–88.
26. The Crowther Report found that nearly one-third of the R.A.F. recruits' performances in their I.Q. tests on entering the service indicated that they had had the 'wrong' type of schooling: *15 to 18,* Vol. 1, HMSO (1959), p. 72.
27. See A. Yates and D. A. Pidgeon, 'Transfer at eleven-plus', *Educational Research,* **1** (1958), 13. See also Floud and Halsey's comparison of 'class chances' of entry to grammar school in an L.E.A. operating teacher recommendation in 'Social class, intelligence tests, and selection for secondary schools', Halsey *et al., op. cit.* (1961), pp. 209–15.
28. The notion that measured intelligence is not an epistemic correlate of 'real ability' will be discussed in Chapter Two.
29. For two excellent studies of the formidable number of separate pieces of evidence on this issue see Glen Elder, 'Life opportunities and personality: some consequences of stratified secondary education in Great Britain', *Sociology of Education,* **38** (3) (1965), 173–202; and A. Little, and J. Westergaard, 'The trend of class differentials in educational opportunity', *Brit. Journ. Sociol.,* **15** (1964), 301–15.
30. Steven Box and Douglas Young, 'Reform of secondary education in Britain', unpublished monograph, London: The Polytechnic, 1963.
31. See William Taylor, *The Secondary Modern School,* Faber, 1963, also the Beloe Report, HMSO, 1960. Of course, similar pressures may also have been coming from secondary school teachers. For, once the syllabus of the modern school began to resemble that of the grammar school, their personal chances of career mobility were increased.
32. H. C. Dent, *The Educational System of England and Wales,* London: ULP, 1961.

33. Rough estimate based on the number of children leaving school at age 16 or later, *Educational Statistics*, 1964.

34. From D. V. Donnison, 'Education and opinion', *New Society*, 26 Oct. 1967.

35. This finding is, however, probably on artifact of social class which was not simultaneously controlled.

36. Of course this does not mean that comprehensive reorganization had not got under way before the election of a Labour government. For the progress made up to 1963, see Pedley, *op. cit.*

37. Most of the research available has taken the form of impressionistic surveys such as T. W. G. Miller, *Values in the Comprehensive School*, Oliver and Boyd, 1961, and K. Currie, 'A study of the English comprehensive school system with particular reference to the educational, social and cultural effects of single sex and co-educational types of school', Ph.D. (Ed.), London, 1962.

38. See Elihu Katz and Paul F. Lazarsfeld, *Personal Influence*, The Free Press, Glencoe, 1955.

39. Michael Armstrong and Michael Young, *New Look at Comprehensives*, Fabian Research Series 237, 1964.

40. Floud and Halsey, *op. cit.* (1961), p. 89.

41. William Taylor, 'Family school and society', in Maurice Craft *et al.* (eds.), *Linking Home and School*, Longmans, 1967, p. 233.

42. In the L.C.C. publication, *London Comprehensive Schools* (1961) we read, 'None of the schools bases its organisation upon the impractical assumption that teaching groups covering the whole range of ability are suitable or desirable', p. 32.

43. C. A. R. Crosland, *The Future of Socialism*, Cape, 1963, p. 202.

44. See for just a few examples, Basil Bernstein, 'Social class and linguistic development: a theory of social learning', in Halsey *et al.*, *op. cit.*, pp. 288–314; J. W. B. Douglas, *The Home and the School*, MacGibbon and Kee, 1964, pp. 60–5 and 159–62; Brian Jackson, *Streaming: An Education System in Miniature*, Routledge & Kegan Paul 1964.

45. *The Primary School*, HMSO, 1931, App. III, p. 258.

46. *The Norwood Report*, HMSO, 1943.

47. This was noted in the Crowther Report, *op. cit.*

48. The distinction between equality of opportunity for equal talent and equality of opportunity to develop equal talent is attributed to Crosland. Cited in John Vaizey, *Britain in the Sixties: Education for Tomorrow*, Penguin, 1962, p. 16. But see also R. H. Tawney, *Equality*, New York, 1931, p. 123.

49. H. T. Himmelweit, *et al.*, 'The views of adolescents on some aspects of the class structure', *Brit. Journ. Social.* 3 (1952), 148–72.

50. G. Jahoda, 'Job attitude and job choice among secondary modern school leavers', *Occupational Psychology* (July 1952), 125–40; M. D. Wilson, 'The vocational preferences of secondary modern school children', *Brit. Journ. Educ. Psychol.* (June 1953), 97–113 and Nov. 163–79.

51. See for example David H. Hargreaves, *Social Relations in a Secondary School*, Routledge & Kegan Paul, 1967, especially Ch. 4. The existing literature on sociometric relationships in school will be discussed in Chapter 5.

The design of research

8

Problems of sociological fieldwork: a review of the methodology of 'Hightown Grammar'

C. Lacey

Introduction to Reading 8

Lacey's research – Hightown Grammar – is a form of educational sociology which contrasts sharply with the quantitative, survey-based approach exemplified by the National Survey of Primary School Children commissioned by the Plowden Committee (see the introduction to the Plowden Case Study in this book).

It is research like the National Survey which Lacey calls the 'black-box' model of research, and this model is one for which 'elaboration has almost ceased to be useful' in Lacey's words. Both Plowden (implicitly), and Lacey (explicitly) were concerned with the same issue of the poor attainment of working-class children at school in comparison with the children of the middle class. It is useful, then, to ask why survey-based research might be less fruitful as an approach to explaining this problem than the participant observation method which Lacey used.

The first contrast in methods is that Lacey used a longitudinal approach while the National Survey studies samples of different age groups at primary school. The contrast here is between Lacey who followed a cohort (a school class) for three years, and Plowden who compared cross-sections of pupils at different points in the primary school. Longitudinal studies allow the researcher to trace the process through which individuals move over time. In Lacey's case, he could compare a working-class pupil who entered grammar school performing well academically, with what became of the same pupil three years later when he had dropped to near the bottom of his class and developed strong anti-school attitudes. Longitudinal studies use repeated measures of the same individual through time and allow us to make strong inferences about causes.

Longitudinal *surveys* are possible, though it is expensive to re-contact a sample later, and are sometimes used (e.g. Douglas 1964). What distinguishes Lacey's work is not simply the use of a longitudinal method but his use of continued observation of pupils in the classroom over the full time span of the research.

From M. Shipman (ed.) *The Organisation and Impact of Social Research*, London: Routledge and Kegan Paul, 1976, Ch. 4, pp. 63–88.

His discovery of the processes which he calls 'differentiation' and 'polarisation' could only be made by a method of observation applied in time. Differentiation is the 'separation and ranking of students according to . . . criteria which make up the normative, academically orientated value system of the grammar school' (Lacey 1970, p. 57). Differentiation is the teachers' labelling of pupils in moral and intellectual terms in such a way that the pupils grow to fit these labels even if they did not at first.

Polarisation, on the other hand, 'takes place within the student body, partly as a result of differentiation, but influenced by external factors and with an autonomy of its own' (Lacey 1970, p. 57).

The pupils themselves formed cliques and groups (which changed through time) which developed their attitudes to the official culture of the school. Anti-school groups developed which resulted in their members sometimes leaving school early without 'having taken advantage' of the grammar-school system.

Lacey makes two major points about the importance of pupil groups to behaviour (social and academic) at school. Firstly, there is little association between IQ and attitude to school (though the small IQ range at grammar school would make an association unlikely) – secondly, though there is an association between boys of working-class background and membership of an anti-school pupil group it is by no means perfect. Lacey documents isolates in class or members of anti-school groups who became 'failures' in grammar-school terms, as well as working-class boys who accept the values of the school.

The Plowden analysis which shows a correlation between low social class and poor pupil attainment is misleading if it is interpreted to mean that low social class is always a handicap to academic attainment.

Classroom culture affects boys' aspirations, boys' academic performance, and boys' personal behaviour in school, and is a variable which is *autonomous*. That is, it is an aspect of social interaction which must be taken into account in framing an explanation of the causes of pupil performance. It cannot be reduced to an aspect of the variable 'social class' because it is independent of social class. Lacey points out in this connection that he would expect public schools to show the same processes of differentiation and polarisation, based on factors other than the social-class origin of the pupils, since public schools will have a homogeneous intake in terms of social class.

It is no accident that the Plowden National Survey of Primary School Children did not look at classroom processes or at processes within the school generally. To have done so, and over a representative sample of schools and classes, would have demanded research time and resources which were not available. By not doing so, their research results consisted of a model which implicitly assumed the pupil to be a 'black box' into which went such inputs as family social class, size of school class, quality of teacher, parental attitudes to education, parents' own education, etc. Out of the 'black box' (the pupil) came the output of the child's attainment.

Now, if we could always perfectly predict the output (i.e. the child's scholastic score) from a knowledge of the input values, then the Plowden model would be an adequate explanation of the causes of the differences in children's attainment. But the Plowden model accounted for 54 per cent of the variance in pupils' scores (this is the within-schools figure, Plowden, Vol. 2, App. 4, 1967), leaving 46 per cent of the variance unexplained.

Thus the statistical model developed for the Plowden Committee explained just over half of the variance in pupils' scores. Social scientists argue that such a model is inadequate because it (a) leaves a significant proportion of the score variance unexplained, and (b) some social scientists argue also that a model which fails to show how and why variables are connected to perform- ance is inadequate in itself. Lacey, in criticising the 'black-box' approach belongs to the second group of social scientists and he is on strong ground because his research adds knowledge of a new set of variables which can only be discovered by non-survey methods. The concepts of differentiation and polarisation help to explain differences in pupils' performances over and above the Plowden variables.

It could be that Lacey's concepts could be operationalised in a way that would permit them to be used systematically in a longitudinal survey of school performance by pupils. In which case, the 'socially deterministic' model would be usefully elaborated and could be expected to improve its predictive power. Or, as Lacey seems to say, such a model is better substituted by a different kind of model in which the processes of adaptation to school by pupils is carefully described and documented in the methods which Lacey used in Hightown Grammar. In the terms of the introduction to this book, Plowden based its models on covering-law schemes of explanation while Lacey favours explanation-by-understanding. The choice between these two positions in social science must be made on philosophical grounds of what an adequate explanation should be, rather than on technical grounds of how good the explanation is. Lacey's work could be used to improve the Plowden type of approach, or it could be the model for further research using the method of participant observation.

References

Douglas, J. W. B. (1964) Home and The School: A Study of Ability and Attainment in the Primary School, London: McGibbon and Kee.
Lacey, C. (1970) Hightown Grammar, Manchester: Manchester U.P.
Plowden (1967) Children and Their Primary Schools, Vol. 2, App. 4, Central Advisory Council for Education (England), London: HMSO.

M. Shipman's introductory note

Hightown Grammar was published in 1970 by Manchester University Press. It was based on research conducted between 1962 and 1966 in a Northern grammar school. This was one of a number of research projects organised within the Department of

Sociology in the University of Manchester, all concerned with the relation between schooling viewed as a social process and social structure. The book deals primarily with an intake into the grammar school in 1962 and the progress of the boys through the junior forms. The information on pupils and staff from observational studies, interviews and questionnaires was related to the historical and contemporary context of the school to give an insight into the way selective schooling operates.

The book, and the article which preceded it ('Some sociological concomitants of academic streaming in a grammar school', *British Journal of Sociology*, Vol. 18, 1966) had an impact on two levels. First, the longitudinal enquiry enabled the processes of differentiation and polarisation to be mapped and analysed. Second, the drive and achievement of the boys selected for the school was shown to be accompanied by the demoralisation of some through their failure relative to others. Despite the high ability of these boys, they were often subject to stress leading to failure. This detail and the context to which it is related have made this a most influential study of the differentiating pressures within schooling.

In this reading I will interpret methodology in its broadest sense, to include methodological aspects of theory. I do not intend to dwell on the non-strategic details of the methodology of the study. The review that follows is a personal statement. In it I explain some of the factors that led up to and shaped the study, and which are seldom discussed in sociological monographs. I hope to make clear the central ideas underlying my methodology and how these were developed during the research. This reading has a broadly chronological structure and shows how a general concern with the problems of society shaped by my experience within the Department of Social Anthropology and Sociology at Manchester, and finally moulded into a methodology through my study of Hightown Grammar. In addition, I feel it is necessary that the study is seen within the broader framework of my continuing research.[1] I have approached the task in this way because I believe it is important that students realise they are able to pursue their deepest concerns about society through sociological research.

To write about one's own methodology and the problems of doing empirical research is inevitably to make gross assumptions about one's own theoretical orientations and even one's biography. While it is impossible in a short chapter to trace out the full implications of these two factors, I think it is important to outline some of the basic strands of my intellectual development. In this way I can provide the material for developing an internal as well as external critique of my methodology and view of sociology. This is the sort of exercise from which both reader and author can benefit.

I was in my second year of a university degree in geology (geophysics) before the accumulation of a number of trends convinced me that I could never proceed into an academic or civil service career as a geologist. I could not even consider industry. It seemed to me that for a number of years I had been living a schizophrenic existence in which the major developing interests and preoccupations of my life did not feed into any of my career expectations. I had got to this point, like many boys of working-class/lower middle-class origin, by myopically pursuing those academic subjects – at grammar school and then at university – at which I happened to perform best.

In contrast with the essentially narrow, competitive, crossword-puzzle, problem-solving world of the grammar school in which 'society' is static, or ignored, my interests developed through the political and union activities of my family and in reading Marx, Shaw and Russell.[2] These writers, from very different vantage points, have a purposive, change-orientated view of society. All imply that it is pos-sible to intervene into the dialectic relationship between personality and social structure, or, put in more recent terminology, into the intricacies of the social construction of reality. My concern was to promote those sorts of intervention that would lead towards an egalitarian society. It seemed to me self-evident that greater social and economic equality would lead to greater democracy and greater potential for the full development of individual personality, in turn leading to greater diversity and richness in social life.

This concern has remained a central underlying purpose. It predates my interest in sociology as such and it provides a support for my continuing interest. In fact, I feel sure that my interest in sociology depends on my seeing it as a tool, as a means for progressing towards a realisation of this purpose. If I felt that sociology was not 'useful' in this way, I would probably turn to politics or journalism, or something.

If this perspective – sociology as a 'means' rather than an 'end' – implies that my involvement is peripheral, a dilettante interest, I must challenge the assumption. I see sociology as a vital analytical tool in the reconstruction of our society. As such, I am centrally interested in all aspects of its development, its theory, methodology and technology, its legitimation and status, not just in the eyes of an elite group of academics, but also the wider society. I see sociology developing to provide a basic ingredient in a generally available education in a self-understanding society.[3] In my view, the converse is also true; sociology as an end in itself, as an academic exercise among many others, is to run the risk of reducing its status to that of a hobby for secure academics.

There is one set of concerns within sociology that is cut off by my perspective: the internecine wrangles between schools of sociology – conflict theory versus functionalism, symbolic interactionists versus positivists, ethnomethodologists versus symbolic interactionists, social anthropologists versus sociologists, Manchester School versus LSE, Chicago versus the rest, and so on. These seem to me to be a product of introverted intellectualism (a young man's proxy for an ivory tower), an over-concern with sociology for itself. They result in the spinning of over-elaborate cocoons of terminology which isolate the sociologist from his wider audience and deflect energies that should, in my view, be used to attack problems of perspective and communication with this wider audience.

Unfortunately, the 'schools' do have the effect of providing security in an insecure world and the wrangles do ensure a never-ending source of final-year exam questions.

It would seem that each of these systems of belief, procedural exhortation and terminological elaboration which constitutes a 'school', is based around a set of coherent and more or less useful statements about society, the nature of man and ways of investigating both. Each has its strengths and none has all the drawbacks elucidated and endlessly propounded by its enemies. It seems to me to be a time for turning outward – synthesising from the strengths available to us and tackling the problems of the wider society.

My own experience has led to a particular blend or synthesis of methodologies and approaches and, before embarking on the central core of the paper, it is perhaps important to know in outline what these were, up to the point at which I undertook my study of Hightown Grammar.

In 1960, after teaching for three years in Birmingham and London, I joined the Department of Social Anthropology at Manchester to read for an MA. Manchester at that time was diversifying. Max Gluckman had encouraged Tom Lupton to start micro-studies of shop-floor organisation. In particular, they were concerned to apply the careful fieldwork techniques of the social anthropologist to the attainable areas of industrial society. Participant observation is a much maligned word but in Manchester at that time it involved the fullest possible transfer; that is, the transfer of the whole person into an imaginative and emotional experience in which the fieldworker learned to live in and understand the new world he had chosen. I have not used the term 'role-playing'. I think in retrospect I would use the term 'role-taking' (or role-making in the sense used by Turner) because this implies involvement of the self in an exposed and vulnerable position. There could be no clinical distancing, the fieldworker was expected to enter in and take punishment until he or she had learned to survive.

The analyses of a wide range of fieldwork situations were united by Manchester's own peculiar blend of conflict theory and functionalism. The mix varied. The Marxists pushed criticisms of the structural reification, timelessness and ossification apparent in the earlier studies, and at one time a fruitful line in MAs developed in which classical anthropology, was reanalysed using a conflict framework.[4] The idea of the study of Hightown Grammar grew out of this mix of social anthropological fieldwork techniques, a theoretical concern for social processes and social conflict and my own experience within schools.

Manchester expanded rapidly. Two professors of sociology were appointed in about as many years. Both wrote articles on the 'death of social anthropology within months of arriving, and neither article was fruitfully discussed. Sociologists and social anthropologists caricatured each other over coffee and a promising development slowly died. The sociology and social anthropology departments have since separated completely.

When in 1963 I started fieldwork in Hightown, this was seen as an extension of the department's work of carefully executed microstudies into industrial society. In fact the developing split between the social anthropologists and sociologists meant that I was about the last fieldworker with a complete background in social anthropological techniques[5] to begin work in what came to be seen as a sociological domain.

The Hightown study was always part of a broader study of schools, for which Ronnie Frankenberg and Valdo Pons were responsible. This project was at first confined to grammar schools (one girls' grammar school studied by Audrey Lambert and one boys' grammar school studied by myself), but when David Hargreaves was appointed a year later it became possible to extend the study to include a secondary modern school. It is not possible to deal with many of the team aspects of the research in this chapter,[6] but it is clear from the similarities in the published results of the studies that the team members learnt a great deal from each other.

General aims

It is easy to guess from what I have said already that a major concern of the study would be with the under achievement of working-class children in grammar schools. Behind this lay an unworked-out set of assumptions that if schools changed sufficiently to allow radically different rates of upward mobility, there would be a chain reaction in which sets of unchallenged assumptions about the structure of our society would be examined and criticised; for example, the public schools (privileged education) and eventually the inheritance of wealth (privileged social position). It seemed to me that the internal logic of a meritocratic society would bring about changes that were an essential precursor to the posing of problems relevant to an egalitarian society. Until those steps were taken most people would be unable even to understand this later stage. It would remain in the realms of utopian philosophy until the necessary experiences, gleaned from the 'meritocratic versus inherited social position' battle, had become a common occurrence. I was not unduly worried by some of the results of Dennis Marsden and Brian Jackson's work[7] which revealed the strains experienced by working-class families through the upward mobility of one of their sons. They were both walking contradictions of the 'defection' argument.

Problems of bias

Even before the study began a number of colleagues expressed opinions about the viability of the research. There were two strands of this opinion that foresaw as inevitable a broad irreducible streak of bias running through the study.

One group, made up mainly of the more traditional social anthropologists, argued that given my experience and closeness to schools, I could not obtain the necessary distance and therefore objectivity to make a study.

Another group expressed the view that it would be important to 'open up' grammar schools to criticism and implied that a hefty dose of the 'right' bias would be a good thing.

I disagreed with both these views. I could not agree that the 'outsider' had to be totally outside the culture (for some social anthropologists an outsider also meant an outsider from the point of view of race and language) in order to achieve 'distance' and make so called 'objective' judgments. Even at the planning stage of the study I felt disinclined to go along with the notion of 'objectivity'. Instead I saw it as my job to develop views of the system from a number of points of view – those of the parent, the teacher and the child. It was, I believed, through presenting these views and, more importantly, the intersection of these views that the researcher could illustrate the dynamics of the system. This task seemed to me to call for a specific approach to fieldwork requiring sympathy, naivete, openness, a willingness to help where possible, and an ability to let people talk.

I had rather more sympathy with the second view. After all, every study is constrained by the limitations of the researcher and those limitations extend to the constraints imposed by the researcher's values. These may limit his insights and curb his imagination. This criticism made me determined to go beyond the usual social anthropological methodologies and construct models that could be tested at various points in the analysis. In this way my biases could perhaps lead to omission, but they could hardly lead me to constructing an account based simply on my prejudices. There are many instances of these tests within the book; the subjective connection between 'performance' and 'behaviour' of pupils made by the teachers and the construction of sociometric indicators to test 'differentiation' and 'polarisation', for example. The chapter most affected by social anthropological criticism and which itself contains an implied criticism of much social anthropological writing, is chapter 7 where case studies are presented within an analytical framework to counteract the tendency to make 'apt illustration' from fieldwork notes.

Choice of school

We chose to work initially in grammar schools for a number of reasons:

1. We felt that the problems experienced by working-class children would be posed in a more acute form in grammar schools. Also their organisations were simple and traditional compared with the

complexity and flux of the large new comprehensives. I was interested in defining and delineating the problems that the comprehensive schools would, in their day, have to solve – not in whether they had the answer. It seemed to me that the definition of the problems came prior to the solutions.

2. We wished to study the school within its community. Grammar schools and secondary moderns (to a lesser extent) had relatively stable relationships with their communities. Comprehensive schools lived in a flux of make-believe and achievement that would have required either a massive study or a very long-term design.

3. We further simplified our problem by separating the problems of boys and girls and by choosing a 'one-grammar-school town' so that we could study the actual community that related to the school. The statistics relating to Hightown, therefore, had a decipherable relationship with the community served by the school.

In my view the simplification of the problem – by eliminating sex differences within the one school, for example – the strategic site of the study, at the apex (in conventional wisdom) of the town's secondary system, proved invaluable. It enabled the development of a hybrid methodology which in turn enabled me to link various levels of generality in the final analysis.

The field of study

The merging of one's own value orientations and the work already accomplished in the chosen field of study is a complex interaction to unravel. However, it bears directly on the development of my methodology and needs some explanation.

The major weakness of existing research in the field seemed to me to be its adherence to a simplistic theoretical model, around which elaboration had almost ceased to be useful. Bernstein has described this as an input–output model. I prefer the term a 'black-box' model of research because it describes more accurately the nature of its limitations. The model assumes that in order to demonstrate an effect it was only necessary to show correlations between inputs and outputs. The contents of the black-box, the social mechanisms and process, are neglected and not without cost. At whatever level of generality the model is used, societal or institutional, the element of social determinism is extremely strong. There is nothing to counteract it. Nor is there anything inherent in the model to challenge the notion that the factors considered by the researchers are necessarily the salient ones as far as the social actors are concerned. The framework of variables to be considered is imposed; there is little chance of developing an alternative perspective from these research reports. There is one further drawback to this type of research. It produces descriptions of the school system that document, for example, the under-achievement of working-class children but give very little indication of how the school system or individual teachers can change in order to alter or modify this effect. In fact, because of the 'social determinism' element and the imposition of an analytical framework which rarely contains variables relating to the school or the classroom, the implication for many teachers is that it cannot be changed. The idea that the causes of under-achievement are to be found solely in low material standards or attitudes held by working-class families, I found totally unacceptable. Elaborations of this model can only take place in three directions:

1. Superimposition of different scales of black-box model.[8]
2. Elaboration of input and output variables.
3. A moving black-box, a follow-through cohort study.

In the period leading up to the study the major effort of researchers in this field had undoubtedly been in the direction of the elaboration of variables. Asher Tropp had attempted to put almost all the variables anyone had ever heard of in a complex model of causation. Stephen Wiseman had attempted a similar exercise with ecological units and in the USA number crunching proceeded on a grand scale.

It seemed useful, therefore, to work within the framework of established black-box findings and to use if necessary the first alternative of different scales of application of the model, but to work in the opposite direction, that is, from within the black-box out towards the community and wider society. The implication of this direction was that I would need to immerse myself within the system in order to be able to feel, recognise and describe the constraints of the various roles within the school and be able to put together a descriptive model or series of models of the processes that I recognised. The idea was to describe the system from a number of perspectives. Only in this way did I feel that I could include an analysis of how the perspectives intersected to produce a social process.[9]

The research strategy

There are two schools of thought which relegate carefully thought-out research strategies to a low priority in participant observation studies:

1. the 'go through the motions' school;
2. the 'be natural' school.

The first needs little consideration. It is based on a mistrust of participant observation as a research tool and the researcher simply goes through the motions before collecting 'real data' with questionnaires.

The second has a lot more to recommend it, especially to inexperienced researchers, and can give excellent results[10] but seems to me to have many serious drawbacks. One of which is that it is based on an illusion. The argument goes that the researcher should be 'himself' and be 'honest' and therefore to adhere to a research strategy is somehow dishonest.[11] The illusory aspect of this is the belief that to be 'natural' and 'honest' means to be without a strategy. In fact, social life demands that people choose or develop social strategies. If they don't, then a strategy is usually allocated to them.[12] The dangers of the 'be natural' school are threefold:

1. The researcher is apt to take personally rejections or evasions on the part of the people within the system, i.e. instead of seeing those rejections as evidence indicating the working of the system.
2. The researcher has many hidden agendas but is not sufficiently clear about them to take them into account when assessing evidence.
3. The researcher can waste time, meander round and get drawn away from central issues. He has no central plan to which to relate and becomes more like a participant and less like a participant observer.

The broad strategy which we worked out for Hightown was as follows:

1. To choose the school carefully with advice from HMIs and the local authority and present definite reasons for our choice.
2. To enter the system above the school in the authority system and move down through the authority system to the school.
3. To teach (participate) and observe, but to move slowly out of the teacher role towards a research role with much greater flexibility and access to pupils.

The decision to teach was reached through a number of lines of reasoning:

1. Entry to the school would be facilitated if the headmaster felt he was getting additional, worthwhile teaching assistance.
2. Long-term participation (a three-year period of association was initially proposed) in a school would require the researcher to build up in the first period a fund of goodwill on which to draw to support his later roles. These would be incomprehensible to the staff of the school unless they were developed out of an established relationship. Within the last year of the study it was expected that the contact would be attenuated and a monitoring relationship set up. This attenuation could, it was felt, put some strain on the relationship with the school. If a considerable fund of goodwill had been created, this would not be so marked.
3. Most importantly, to gain a teacher perspective as one of the essential elements in putting together a pattern of interacting perspectives.

My operational strategy was designed to examine the 'process' of grammar school education as it developed from the lower school, through the middle school to 'O' level and the sixth form. I therefore selected three points in the school from which I could eventually cover the whole school during a three-year period, albeit at different intensities of participation and observation (see Table 8.1).

Table 8.1

Start with	(3 years later) ————▶	Finish with	Methods
1 1st year (120 boys)	————————▶	3rd year	Teach and observe
2 4th year (120 boys)	————————▶	6th formers or leavers	Observe
3 Lower 6th form (50 boys)	————————▶	Leavers	Teach and observe

The intention was to teach for the first year and then give up most of my teaching to move towards a freer research role in the second and third years. In the third year in particular I planned to move outside the school into the community and the home.

The plan was far too ambitious. In my desire to include everything I saddled myself with a killing workload and a far too attentuated contact with any one form at any time. It required a tremendous effort to keep going on all fronts and learn in some detail the personal data for 300 boys. By the second term I had given up the detailed study of the sixth form. Looking back, it is easy to see this mistake in the context of a common participant observer syndrome. The feeling develops very vividly at times that the real action, the real social drama is going on somewhere else. While you are in the staffroom there are important discussions in the headmaster's study; while you observe 3A, a really critical series of lessons is being taught in the room next door. The root of this feeling is in the nature of one's task. The participant observer records as accurately as possible selected aspects of the everyday life of people in everyday situations. There is rarely anything dramatic, there is rarely anything of outstanding interest taking place.[13] Classrooms can be incredibly boring places. The interest in the situation emerges as the observer puts together the pieces of an amorphous and intricate puzzle in which even the pieces are not defined. Until this is done the tensions and strains on the researcher are considerable and the 'it is all happening somewhere else' syndrome flourishes.

There is an interesting divergence between my version of the planning process and that given by Hargreaves in his book *Social Relations in a Secondary School*. I report giving over two months of my time in the school to consciously working out a strategy that was acceptable to the school and capable of meeting my research aims. I saw this as an integral part of the research process and that it was necessary to work this out within the school so that the sort of conflict reported by Hargreaves was avoided:

When the study was planned it seemed that the assumption of a teacher-role would be the best way in which the participant observation could be effected, but it was not foreseen that the assumption of a teacher-role, whilst facilitating my relations with the staff, would seriously inhibit my relations with the pupils. A choice had to be made, and I decided to abandon my carefully nurtured teacher-role. . . .[14]

In part, this problem relates to Hargreaves's late entry into the team. The discussions on research strategy were largely over and the discussions about the emerging theoretical models were predominant. The difference also illustrates an important point about operational strategies. They must be personal strategies and relate to the skills and experience of the researcher as well as the demands of the institution. My transition from a London comprehensive school to Hightown Grammar was an easy assignment by comparison with Hargreaves, who moved from teaching in a grammar school to a tough secondary modern school. Even so, I decided against a regular year-long teaching commitment with forms other than the first and second year and sixth form. I felt that with the first year and sixth form in particular I could establish the sort of teaching relationship that would not interfere with making a more relaxed person-to-person relationship outside the classroom. I did not, for example, feel threatened by these groups as Hargreaves obviously felt threatened by the fourth year at Lumley: 'The delinquent group, for example, began shouting out to me "Hello Sir" in a rather cheeky way, which I would have immediately crushed as a teacher.'[15] The need to 'crush' or 'be crushed' was not so immediate with the forms I chose to teach.

Change of research role

The movement from a teacher role to a freer research role was accomplished smoothly without too much strain on my relationships with the staff. Several incidents did, however, illustrate the potential dangers of living within the informal worlds of both staff and pupils. Before relating these incidents, it is necessary to describe the actual changes that took place in my research role.

Even during my first year at the school my role differed considerably from a normal teacher role:

1. I was not employed by the local authority and had a special negotiated relationship with the headmaster, which staff and pupils knew about.
2. I observed classes on a regular basis, something other teachers never did.
3. I was more available to staff and pupils, who found me interested in matters not usually discussed by teachers.

This interest gradually established a flow of information from both staff and pupils about things they thought would interest me, from formal events like public speaking competitions to informal events like fights in the park. My change in role was accomplished by building on these existing differences and moving out of my classroom teaching role (I retained some sixth-form teaching). I held informal discussion groups, which were established during school hours (boys could be excused Religious Education) but continued during lunch-time on an informal basis. I visited the homes of boys to talk over problems with them or their parents. I entered informally into conversations with boys in and around the school and invited boys to my home, which was only a few hundred yards from the school. I entered into informal activities after school and eventually ran a school cricket team (second-year). The final stage of this change of role was never achieved. I had planned to move out of the school and meet boys in clubs, coffee bars and informal out-of-school groups like regular street football games. It was during the second year of the research that I began lecturing at the university and had to confine my participation at the school to mornings and some afternoons. A much reduced version of the final stages of the study was eventually accomplished with the aid of a second research grant which financed an interview study.[16]

The change in role brought an increase, gradual at first and then steep, in the amount of information received about pupils. The discussion group ranged over topics from marriage and sex through general questions about the school and its relation to jobs and earning a living, to individual masters and the boys' relationships with them. One of the groups had been 'set up' to include most of the anti-group boys from one fifth-year class and this group of between six and eight boys provided without doubt the most stimulating and entertaining discussions I enjoyed in the school. The discussions had a life of their own.

It was this group that proposed and carried out an experiment within the classroom to 'prove' that Mr Bradley 'had his knife into' Morris, one of the boys in the group. Morris was programmed to keep quiet and work diligently for the first part of the lesson. Then when the classwork had been set and the customary buzz of conversation had established itself, he was to start talking like the rest of the class. According to the boys in the group, Mr Bradley noticed him immediately and told him off. They were delighted with their experiment and its result.

The completely informal, relaxed relationship with this group of boys contrasted with the classroom role of the teacher and the formal relationship generated through the teaching persona. The group was noisy, frank, sometimes lewd, but always (in marked contrast to the classroom) interested and sincere. I was constantly surprised by the degree to which they appreciated their own position in the school, and the way in which they were prepared to examine and discuss it. One discussion centred on the extent to which they felt they would now need to compromise in order to get some examination success. This contrast with the classroom was brought home to me when I was asked to stand in with the whole class for a teacher who was absent. When I got in the classroom I was greeted by one of the boys from the group: 'Hello Colin, what are you doing here? Willy has not turned up yet.' After I had explained that I would be sitting in, the reaction was immediate:

Group member: Come on, let's have one of our discussions.
Me: We can't, the rest of the class have not been in on them. In any case Mr W. has set you some work.
Group member: Come on, John, let's get a group over this side of the class; they can get on with the work.

I thought for a moment that this might just be a solution, but the rest of the class had got over their amazement and were beginning to get in on the act. They did not want to work while a group, who normally had low status in the classroom, had a cosy discussion with the 'teacher'. Noisy disputes developed in all sections of the class as 'the group' organised their discussion and the rest of the class opposed the idea. My role as a 'teacher' was clear: I should have organised a class discussion or Mr W.'s set work, but since 'the group' were opposed to either of these I would have had to sanction them fairly severely to do so.[17] I chose not to do so and the lesson proceeded in turmoil with some working and some discussing, and most just making a noise. This role conflict, similar to that described by Hargreaves, had been avoided during the main research period for the purpose of obtaining a teacher perspective. It did, however, occur during the transition period. This small social drama highlighted for me the constraints affecting the teacher in Hightown Grammar in his relationship with pupils inside and outside the classroom.

A second incident posed a dilemma in a different context. For some days, boys had been telling me that Marston and Badman were going to fight in the park. 'Marsey' had turned up two nights in a row but Badman had always slipped away. Feeling was so strong that a large group of boys escorted Badman from the school to the park and formed a ring so that the fight could proceed. The fight had been a good one and was in full flight when the park keepers had intervened. Such was the excitement and annoyance of the boys that some had attempted to arrange a temporary diversion by starting a fire under a park keeper's hut.

Next morning the headmaster was presented with a list of serious crimes by the park keeper ranging from abusive behaviour, through trampling flowers to arson. An outside complaint of this sort clearly required swift and effective action. As was pointed out to me, press reports of this type of incident could quickly sour a school's relations with the community and affect it in a number of ways (recruitment of pupils from respectable families, for example).

The day after the fight I happened to be talking with the headmaster when a boy was brought into his study and accused of fighting in the park. He had clearly been involved in a fight. His face was badly bruised and cut and he had an enormous black eye. For some twenty minutes I listened to him being accused of taking part in the fight and threatened with the cane. He steadfastly refuted the accusations and said that he had been beaten up by two boys from another school, whom he would not name. In the end the headmaster believed his story and he was allowed to go, but for some moments in the interview I felt torn between betraying the confidence of the boys who had told me about the fight and saving a particular boy from the cane.

My participation and involvement in these situations demonstrated more clearly than any other method the way some aspects of the pupil/adolescent world are cut off from the teacher and the school. They also demonstrated the way the teacher role is shaped and constrained by pressures outside the classroom emanating from the community, mediated by the headmaster and to some extent enshrined in the behaviour codes and punishment system.

Classroom observation perspective versus teaching perspective

I hope it is still clear at this stage that although there were numerous supporting reasons for the decision to teach, the main purpose was to explicitly take on a teacher perspective. This linked into the theoretical orientation of examining the system in action and describing the dynamic interaction of perspectives.

(a) The classroom observation perspective
The question of how much I as an observer altered the teachers' or children's behaviour in the classrooms I observed seemed secondary to the question of how I interpreted what went on. After I had observed all the masters teach it was quite clear that I could fairly easily observe in most of the classes within the school. However, there were some masters who were going to be constantly worried by my presence. One began by asking me 'What are you doing?', asked three or four times 'What shall I tell the boys?', and finished after the lesson by asking pointedly, 'What can you possibly get out of it?' He conveyed such a strong sense of discomfort that I felt I could not possibly impose myself. Afterwards, a group of masters asked me about what went on in his lesson. Hardly waiting for an answer, they told me that he once made a boy stand in the corner for a whole lesson holding a sand bucket in one hand and a water bucket in the other. He tried to teach ecology by linking it with the Queen's progress round Australia. 'What do these boys care about the Queen's visit? He's a nut.' It was quite clear that the man was under pressure from both his fellow teachers and his pupils and I decided I could not increase the pressures he already felt.

The contrast between my observer position, feeling free from the responsibilities of classroom control, and his tense irritability, worried by problems of the classroom and lack of support from his colleagues, highlights the problem of the observer versus the teacher perspective. Remarks from boys that I interpreted as lacking menace or threat obviously stung him into reprisals of sarcasm or anger.

During my first weeks in the school a whole series of incidents made it apparent that the observer role would enable me to achieve a pupil perspective far more easily than a teacher perspective. An example from my field notes illustrates this:

Mr P.   *was shouting at a pupil, already in tears, as I went into the staffroom.*

Mr P.   *(bursting into the staffroom with great energy and in great anger)*: *Hill, been at it again — truanting!*

Mr J: *What again — not for a whole day!*

Mr P: *No, he's been in the toilets for my lesson. He'd lost his exercise book and was frightened to face up to it. I asked him whether he thought he'd get away with it — he said 'No'.*

Mr J: *He was caned about a fortnight ago for truanting.*

Later, I left the staffroom and passed the boy in the corridor.

Mr P. was ranting at him in a loud voice:

Mr P: *What sort of trick do you think this is — deceitful, low, sly — shows you've no back-bone.*

Hill was crying — tears streaming down his face.

Mr J.   *(later)*: *The only way to cure it is to cane him and cane him every time he does it.*

(Later): Mr P. laughed about his 'go' at Hill and said it was all a big act.

(b)The teaching perspective

An important finding from teaching at Hightown was that even with a strong desire to break out of an authoritarian mould – as I had – my teaching represented only a modified version, a more permissive version, of this style. And I had not been subjected to pressures from the bottom streams of the third and fourth years.

This experience led me to observe the socialisation of young teachers. I noted their timetables, the gossip about them, the sort of advice they were given and finally, when they were judged to be ready, their induction into the 'hard core' – that is, the group of teachers who were central to the running of the school.

All these investigations showed that their induction was also structured by the processes of differentiation and polarisation. Young teachers had to deliver their message, define and do battle with the enemy. The enemy had to be the right enemy. Young teachers were sanctioned (as I was) for helping the wrong types. Interestingly enough, they were also sanctioned for being too emotionally involved and too zealous in their punishment of wrongdoers. The contrasting examples of Mr P. and Mr L. illustrate this last point.

As I described previously, Mr P. pointed out that his outburst had been 'all an act'. In doing this he was distancing himself from the person we had all seen ranting in the corridor. That person had been an aspect of the 'mask', the 'teaching persona', and the act had been a necessary unpleasant act that did not, however, reflect on the personal qualities of Mr P. In this Mr P. had been successful. Other masters had made it clear that they were on his side by suggesting the cane and also by allowing the remark to go unchallenged. Mr L., describing a similar incident, told how he had caught a boy called Chegwin in some wrong-doing by standing in a doorway and grabbing him as he passed. Mr L. spoilt the whole story as far as the rest of the staff were concerned by ending with an emotional outburst: 'I despise him, detest him and loathe him.'

This lack of 'professional distance' led a senior member of staff to interrupt Mr L. with a long discourse on how to handle Chegwin. 'He is a decent boy at heart, despite a poor home background, and a limited ability – we will have to ride him with a light rein.' He carried on in this way until Mr L. left the room. His departure was marked by the raising of eyebrows, the puffing of cheeks and the shaking of heads.

I still remember vividly incidents like those described by Mr P. and Mr L. As an observer of these incidents, I felt little affinity with the teachers – all sympathy for the pupils. Yet, as is clear in the description above, many of these teachers were sincere in their desire to help and encourage their pupils to learn. I had to teach in order to appreciate the strains that on occasion turned reasonable, kindly men into bellowing, spiteful adversaries. They left the staffroom in good order; it was in the classroom that they went wrong.

The section in Hightown on the teaching persona was the outcome of that experience. It was only through the creation of a second 'me' that I could survive. Every event within the classroom had to be judged on two criteria: first, its own merit; second, its effect on the classroom order. It is the second criterion that is difficult to understand as an observer.

Why did Mr A. suddenly pounce on Jimmy Green? Answer – because Jimmy Green was venturing, perhaps unwittingly, across a threshold that Mr A. judged was essential for his control. Practically all the teachers at Hightown were domino theorists and most had learned their lesson through hard experience.

Mr L. failed to develop this second self. He was progressively sanctioned by other teachers not so much for the intensity of his outbursts or the punishments he inflicted, but for the fact that they were 'real'. They were spiteful and vindictive. Finally, he was humiliated by his exclusion from the staff cricket XI which was to play the school First XI. He had failed to develop a 'teaching persona' acceptable to staff and pupils. My participation as a teacher enabled me to watch with a certain amount of apprehension but with fascination the way in which small group pressures were manipulated by prominent members of staff. The manner of his exclusion illustrated the working of these informal pressures.

The staff team [18] had been put up in the staffroom. Mr L. came into the room and all went quiet. He went over to the notice board and looked at this list. He turned angrily to the staff who were there and complained that there were some people in the team who were not really 'staff' (I was not in the room), and with a 'flourish' took out his pen and crossed off his name as twelfth man. As he left the room there were guffaws of laughter and a number of choice comments.[19] Mr L. left the school for a job 'nearer home' that did not involve a promotion. I felt it important not to underestimate the pressures on the new staff to conform to staff mores.

Participant observation and other methods

The core methodology of the study was without question participant observation and observation. Yet in a sense the most important break-through for me was the combining of methods, and the integration of these in the analysis.

The observation and description of classrooms led quickly to a need for more exact information about individuals within the class. I used school documents to produce a ledger of information on each boy, for example, address, father's occupation, previous school, academic record, and so on. I built on this record as more information became available from questionnaires. This information enabled me to check immediately any change taking place in seating arrangements or pat-terns of association outside the classroom and, most importantly, to interpret the significance of the development within the established structure of the classroom.

During the early period of observation a high proportion of the incidents and interaction I observed were simply not interpretable. I could see one boy punch another, or two boys joking; I could record the interaction between a master and a boy; but very little added up to produce a structure, or even more important, the sorts of processes I was attempting to unravel.

The key series of observations for me was in the music teacher's class as described in Hightown. He simplified the pattern of interaction by imposing his mental picture of the class on to the physical layout of the classroom. This idea of the teacher having a crude conceptual picture of the class began to fit into my own developing ideas of the classes I taught. I had vivid impressions of the 'clever boys', the 'good boys', the ones that 'rarely understood', the 'bad boys' and the 'characters', but the others, probably between a half and a third of the class, fell into the undifferentiated middle. Even after teaching them for some months it was difficult to recall their names.

The idea of the master imposing his view of the class on to the pupils in the class followed quickly from this and soon I was looking for a way to check how far this imposition[20] actually affected the way children thought of each other, interacted with each other, maybe even made friends with each other. The idea of using sociometric indicators for this purpose, therefore, evolved from the problem and my relationship with it.

The analysis of the sociometric data was a completely new experience. I can still remember the excitement as one after the other of my ideas about the patterns of relationships held up during the analysis. The conceptualisation of the processes of differentiation and polarisation grew out of this interplay between observation and analysis of sociometric data. Looking back, I now feel that I under-utilised these findings in my subsequent fieldwork (by this time I was also teaching at Manchester University). I collected no direct interview evidence on the complexities of the structure. I watched for changes and knew about quarrels, fights and emerging friendships, but I omitted to ask questions about how other boys viewed boys outside their own group. I did this in a formal questionnaire (can't get on with choices and diaries, etc.) in a systematic way, but could, given more time, and should have done much more in following up particular insights from the analysis in informal but patterned interviews. The next strategy would have been to explain my analysis to some of the boys who were closest to me so that they would also act as observers of the process. I began this with two boys, one who was having difficulty within the sixth form and for whom the analysis provided an explanation of his difficulties, a form of therapy, and one who did in fact start to provide me with a self-generated analysis of his own classroom.

What I did was to 'escalate insights' through moving backwards and forwards between observation and analysis and understanding (see Fig. 8.1). This diagram could obviously be complicated by adding a

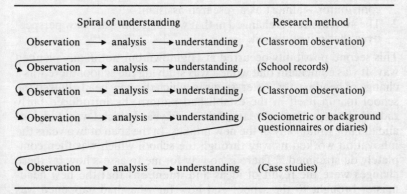

Fig. 8.1

large number of cycles in this process,[21] as I built upon certain methods and insights to achieve a deeper understanding. An important point to notice is the way certain insights or levels of understanding are associated with certain methods of data collection. In other words, just as methods like classroom observation or participation as a teacher have important theoretical repercussions, so other methods like the use of sociometric data and its analysis using sociomatrices can have important effects on the shaping of concepts and the deepening of one's understanding (which is perhaps another way of saying the same thing). I feel very strongly that the world under investigation seen through one method of collecting data becomes enormously distorted by the limitations of that data and the available methods of analysis.

The extension of this process that I began at Hightown and would certainly advocate in any similar study can be portrayed schematically as shown in Fig. 8.2.

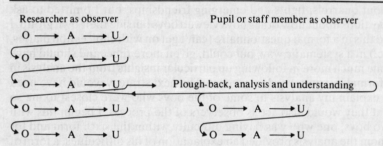

Fig. 8.2

The effect of this strategy is twofold:

1. The pupil or teacher is brought into the analysis as a positive contributor – almost as a research assistant.
2. The system itself is changed in that within it there are new perspectives that might alter it.

This second possibility occurred at Hightown but not in any planned way. It was coincident that while I was studying the school there was a change of headmaster. After a year in which the new head allowed the school to run itself in the established pattern, he introduced fairly radical changes. He de-streamed the third year (which I was studying) and did not stream any of the new intakes. In the span of two years the innovation worked its way through the school which was then completely de-streamed.[22] There is no way for me to assess how far these changes were the result of ideas and intentions that the new headmaster brought to the school and how far what had happened was influenced by the results of my analysis of differentiation and polarisation, of which he was aware. In any event, it does provide us with a paradigm for the study of innovation and an interventionist research strategy (see Fig. 8.3).

In other words, episodes of innovation and change can occur through research and augment that research. These innovations need not occur by chance – they can be planned episodes in research designs.

It will be some time before local government administrators, teachers, pupils, their parents, and researchers have enough confidence in each other to plan this sort of research in a co-operative enterprise. Yet this degree of co-operation is a necessary first step in understanding, if not controlling, the effects of innovation.

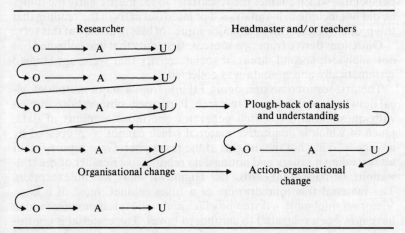

Fig. 8.3

Levels of analysis

I dealt early on with the problem of bias and my desire to combine so-called subjective participant observation methods with tests of the models produced using so-called objective indicators. There is also a second dimension on which it is possible to obtain a critical appraisal of the explanations produced by the research. The research was planned to integrate a number of levels of analysis from the macro to the micro levels. It is therefore possible to test this research by examining the compatibility of the models produced at these different levels. In the book *Hightown* I begin by describing the community and the school within the community, and taking an historical view before moving into the school. Within the school I investigate one cohort, then a single class within the cohort, and finally I move on to individual case studies. In the final chapter on staff–pupil relations I link back again to more macro levels when I consider the career and professional aspects of the teacher role. A useful critical exercise is to read the book from this point of view to establish how far the six to eight models used in the description of Hightown Grammar contain mutually contradicting or reinforcing elements. In order to use the book as a sociological tool (as opposed to using it to learn about schools), and it was certainly intended as such, it seems essential to approach the book critically in this way.

Omissions

Looking back at the research after a period of six years provides a perspective which enables the researcher to see more clearly the things he did not include in his analysis. I pointed out early in the reading that this probably constitutes the major source of bias in a study of this sort.

Omissions derive from two sources: first, data that was collected but not analysed; second, areas of social activity that were not studied systematically and no data was collected.

The first sort of omission stems, I think, from a major methodological drawback of this type of research. Participant observation coupled with questionnaire research generates enormous amounts of data, much of which is qualitative material which cannot be processed by anyone who has not the insights of the researcher. Gans reports[23] that after reading his diary and noting data relating to a number of generalisations, he had 2,000 cards. The Hightown study was no exception. The material fills four drawers of a filing cabinet, most of a large Victorian sideboard, a dozen box files and some questionnaires which have now been relegated to cardboard boxes. The material is enormously varied. It contains my own fieldwork diary ledgers in which I made classroom observations to use for reference, eighty-plus diaries kept by pupils, nearly twenty reels of tape-recordings, detailed records of a cricket team, names of boys who used the school library, boys who were punished, boys who gained school honours and boys who were absent or late. This is not an exhaustive list.

I believe that this proliferation of types of data in a number of areas within the system under study is inevitably part of a participant observation study. It is important that the researcher develops insights and enthusiasms and is prepared to follow them along new and sometimes not very promising paths. If the path simply leads back to the main avenue after a tiring and gruelling detour, then the data can be put on one side. I had no way of knowing whether collecting sociometric data from pupils would turn out to be a promising or self-defeating activity until I had done it and invested an enormous amount of time in it. However, once the data collection is completed and it is being analysed and shaped for writing up, it is essential to be selective. Material that is omitted can be written up later as chapters or articles. Omissions of the first kind are therefore a considered aspect of the presentation of the data.

Omissions caused through failing to collect data are obviously more serious. They cannot be remedied. They are also more likely to reveal the deep-seated orientations of the study. It is clear to me that were I involved in a similar study today I would collect far more data on the content of lessons and the curriculum,[24] especially in the context of a field of study in which Hightown and a number of other school studies have already been made. It is important to bring light to bear on sets of hidden assumptions about the nature of knowledge and understanding and about the construction of superior and inferior levels of knowledge and understanding. In addition, the process I described earlier in the chapter as the battle between the 'meritocratic' and 'ascriptive' philosophies has proceeded in the twelve years since the study was planned. The meritocratic philosophy is under attack in society at large, in schools and within sociology, from elements of an emerging but now developed and pervasive egalitarian philosophy. For example, within a comprehensive school known to myself, the future of the school is debated largely in terms of a meritocratic philosophy versus an egalitarian philosophy. Within this new context it is important that sociologists ask new questions about how subjects are taught and whose standards are dominant. These new questions challenge the established hierarchy of knowledge and are related to the emergence of an egalitarian philosophy within schools and society at large.

The models produced: some substantive and methodological consequences

Models are a form of explanation and are therefore closely related to understanding. The models produced in Hightown Grammar have an interventionalist purpose and are therefore designed to be as close as possible to the everyday world of the teacher and the pupil, while still retaining analytical penetration. It was not the intention of the research to be directly interventionalist (the changes initiated by the headmaster ran counter to the planned research design) but to provide teachers and students in general with an insight into their own world that would lead to further debate, the redefinition of problems and the development of new solutions. There was also an attempt to diagnose the points at which intervention is possible.

The model of the classroom as a competitive arena, presented in Hightown Grammar, is a good example of this aspect of the study. The analysis shows how the teacher perspective transforms competition between individuals with markedly different resources relevant to the competitive process, into a competition of equals. In other words, the dynamics of the classroom situation make demands that cause the teacher (often despite his private feelings) to ignore the fact that the unequal resources of his pupils are relevant to the classroom.

Fig. 8.4 shows the classroom within the community. The pupil–parent teams are included in shaded areas that represent the size of each team's resources. The teacher frequently conducts the competitive aspects of the classroom process as though the differences made explicit in the diagram do not exist. My interest in the classroom situation has developed out of this early insight. It has involved me in two lines of enquiry and in developing new models of co-operation between sociologists and educationalists.

One line of enquiry has been into the training and professional socialisation of teachers. The question that intrigues me is how far the teacher and the school can modify the classroom role of the teacher in the face of community, professional and situational pressures. The possibilities of change seem to exist at three different levels:

1. A modification of the competitive process, to produce less differentiation and polarisation. This would involve a modification of the teacher's role within the classroom and perhaps some organisational change.
2. A reversal of the usual allocation of resources – that is, a compensatory strategy – in the face of pupil and community pressures.
3. A redefinition of the teacher role and the part played by education within the community.

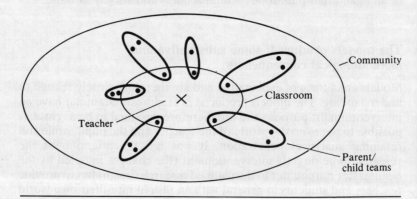

Fig. 8.4

Most innovation and change within our schools aims at levels 1 or 2 above,[25] yet each year a large number of student-teachers leave universities and colleges ideologically committed to level 3 change. This process of change and the way in which the ideological commitment of young teachers merges with the gradually changing practice within our schools have become some of my central sociological concerns. Future research of this problem seems to me to require co-operative work including social scientists, curriculum analysts, pupils and teachers. The practical forms of co-operation have still to be worked out but the theoretical notion behind this co-operation has been suggested earlier in this section.

The second set of ideas that emerged from the Hightown study and have continued to involve me have been the concepts of differentiation and polarisation. These processes resulted from a particular and perhaps peculiar set of pressures on a group of individuals, held together in an organisation over a considerable period of time and for long periods of each work day. They therefore emerged clearly within an observational study and were capable of documentation using sociometric techniques, despite the inaccuracies of the technique and 'noise' created by other processes at work within the classroom. Viewed at a higher level of abstraction these processes are, however, a universal characteristic of human relationships. Actors within social settings pursue social strategies that derive from the actors' experiences and expertise, are relevant to the social situation and are an attempt to achieve the often complex and unworked-out aims of the actor. The peculiar nature of Hightown Grammar rests in the similarity of the pupils' previous experience and expertise, the uniformity and prevasiveness of the academic and behaviour norms imposed by the school and the persistence of the social situation (the classroom) over a period of years.[26] In these conditions the strategies chosen by individual pupils have a regularity and persistence and sometimes a generality that persuades the teacher (or the observer) that what he is observing is the individual and not simply strategies adopted by that individual; that is, strategies that are sometimes chosen, sometimes forced on him in the situation in which he is observed. I think there were times when I made this mistake and there are perhaps points in Hightown Grammar when the analysis comes close to obscuring this important distinction. There are times, however, when the distinction is clear. It is made clear by describing incidents where individuals manipulate one set of subcultural understandings in one situation and then partake actively in another – for example, when the teacher leaves the room. It is made clear at a theoretical level by using the term subculture to represent a set of ways of behaving and understanding, and not a group of individuals who are indelibly marked by experiences of personal characteristics. An important realisation gained during the Hightown study was the extent to which the selection and adoption of a social strategy was part of a competitive process (another competitive element in the classroom is the battle to define the situation so that strategies over which one has established a claim are seen to be the most relevant to the situation). Changes in the social setting could markedly upset even well established structures made up of stable patterns of adopted strategies. This was obviously the case within the discussion group I describe in this reading. I also have records of a case study where I experimented with the usual situational constraints affecting the selection and running of a cricket team. My team of 'playground'[27] cricketers brought forth a new set of relationships and behaviours on a Saturday morning that again had little relationship to the usual school-day patterns.

These insights have had important repercussions on the way I now view adolescent and adult socialisation. I have developed the concept of situationally constrained social strategies in my study of the professional socialisation of teachers, and it has been able to show why, for example, many of the ideas adopted by students during their training year are relatively quickly modified during their early years of teaching.

The connection between the individual and the social setting has been illustrated by these researches. My conception of the problems we face in attempting to change the social world has been sharpened.

The main purpose of this reading was to review my study of Hightown Grammar in broadly methodological terms. In doing so, I illustrated the way in which my own values and preoccupations fed into the research and were developed and refined during and through the process of the research.

Finally, I described how these developments directed me into new channels of enquiry.

If a student can obtain a feeling for the movement from ideas to research — a realisation that his deepest concerns about society can become the basis for his research — then he need see no dichotomy between these two. If he can come to see, in time, that the research, grounded in these deep concerns, is his principal means of refining and developing them, then he will hardly settle for their separation.[28]

Notes and References

1. I have just completed a three-year research project into student teacher socialisation, 'The Tutorial Schools Research Project'. Many of the concerns which lay behind this study developed out of my work in Hightown Grammar.
2. I had no idea that it was possible to study the works of these writers within the framework of a university degree. At this stage I saw the university simply as an extension of school quite separate from my developing concerns about society.
3. See R. J. Frankenberg, 'The sociologically-minded person and the self-understanding society', University of Keele Inaugural Lecture, 1970.
4. See Peter Worsley's MA thesis and the Curl Bequest Essay. My own MA thesis would have been an application of Weber's paradigm of authority types to a Nilotic tribe in which institutionalised leadership failed to develop.
5. I am not making claim to a highly sophisticated arsenal of techniques. I was ready on the department's own reckoning to begin fieldwork and this could just as easily have been among the Eskimo as among the inhabitants of Hightown.
6. See p. xii of Preface to *Hightown Grammar*.
7. B. Jackson and D. Marsden, *Education and the Working Class*, Routledge & Kegan Paul, 1962. See also M. Young and P. Willmott, *Family and Kinship in East London*, Routledge & Kegan Paul, 1957, for the effects of upward mobility on the working-class families.
8. The model can be applied to the education system as a whole (Coleman's *Equality of Opportunity* Report), grammar schools (*Early Leaving Report* – probably the purest 'black-box' design), or individual schools (Ford's *Social Class and the Comprehensive School*).

9. I was anxious to present more than a simple 'underdog' perspective. The discussion between Alvin Gouldner and Howard Becker on this issue is illuminating with respect to many facets of the problem but overlooks the central issue. If sociologists are involved (for whatever reasons) in 'understanding' social behaviour, then it is important to understand the full complexity of the problem. The intersection of perspectives seems essential to this end. See J. D. Douglas (ed.), *The Relevance of Sociology*.

10. W. F. Whyte's *Street Corner Society* could be classified under the 'be natural' school.

11. David Hargreaves (*Social Relations in a Secondary School,* Routledge & Kegan Paul, 1967) comes close to this position when he criticises Frankenberg's view that: 'If the observer cannot participate with the knowledge and approval of the people to be studied he should not be there at all. The observer has a positive duty to be open that his intentions are to observe, to report and to publish an account of what he sees.'

    Hargreaves complains that this is not simple. 'In light conversation with a teacher one cannot suddenly point out that what he has just stated is sociologically important, for this could seriously inhibit future relations. If the observer really does have "a positive duty to be open in his intentions", then he must constantly remind the people he observes of this fact, whereas in reality they adjust to the observer's presence and cease in part to treat him as such.'

    If we place this notion of 'honesty' into everyday life it would require the actor to explain that a particular piece of information from colleague A in one situation might be useful elsewhere in one's relationship with colleague B. He would not have many social relationships at all!

12. Foot-Whyte's role in Doc's gang can be seen as being allocated to him.

13. Bill Watson summed up this aspect of fieldwork in a remark made in a seminar. He was describing how he arrived in an African village full of romantic notions of what he would find. 'What did I find? A load of unemployed bums!'

14. David Hargreaves, *Social Relations in a Secondary School*, Routledge & Kegan Paul, 1967, p. 204.

15. *Ibid.,* p. 203.

16. DES Report, *A Sociological Study of the Connection Between the School and the Community it Serves.*

17. I did appeal to them to understand my position in charge of another teacher's class. Afterwards they argued that they just could not see why they should. They were sorry at a personal level but they reckoned that the chaos would re-occur if the situation presented itself again. In any case, they felt that the chaos was caused by the rest of the class. They did not treat me like a 'teacher' outside the classroom, so why should they do so inside?

18. The staff team had a regular fixture list and Mr L. had played on a number of occasions. He had bought all the correct kit and had taken lessons in his own time. He was very keen and had let this be known. The staff/school match was a special fixture. The whole school turned out to watch and there was competition for places in the team.

19. The incident was described to me later by teachers who were obviously satisified by the way things had gone.

20. In Hightown Grammar I made a clear distinction between 'differentiation' – imposed by the teacher – and 'polarisation' – a product of pupil interaction. I have modified my position slightly and now see differentiation to be in part produced by intro-group competitive pressures. In other words, the children themselves bring into the classroom some of the criteria which will be used in judging them. They use these criteria to judge each other.

21. The process is portrayed here as inevitably progressive. My filing system shows otherwise. On more than one occasion I worked hard and enthusiastically on a 'new' idea, only to find an almost identical analysis planned or even worked out in my filing system.

22. C. Lacey, 'Destreaming in a "pressured" academic environment', in S. J. Eggleston (ed.), *Contemporary Research in the Sociology of Education*, Methuen, 1975, pp. 148–66.

23. Herbert Gans, *The Urban Villagers*, Free Press, 1968.

24. I collected data on the content of lessons but this was mainly to identify the lesson and enable me to put the interaction I recorded into some sort of context.

25. It has been a characteristic of sociologists studying education that they have under-estimated the difficulties of bringing about even minor changes. They have not, therefore, made studies of innovation and change in educational institutions. This is an important gap in the literature.

26. Only the family presented the actor with a more consistent set of pressures over a longer period of time.

27. A term sometimes used to describe those boys who played cricket with a soft ball and an asphalt wicket. They specialised in fast bowling and big hitting and were regarded by some teachers (e.g. First XI coach) as poor cricketers in the proper sense. They were not normally chosen as school team members. I chose my second-year school team mainly from 'playground' cricketers. It was outstandingly successful.

28. J. S. Coleman, 'A research chronology', in P. E. Hammond, *Sociologists at Work*, Basic Books, 1964.

9

Self and identity in the context of deviance: the case of criminal abortion

D. W. Ball

Introduction to Reading 9

This reading reports a study of an illegal abortion clinic in the USA. The research methods used included observation of the clients and the 'doctors' in their natural setting, and interviews with the clients of the clinic.

The research tradition or style of Ball's work is firmly *ethnographic* as he points out himself. He claims the following strengths of an ethnographic approach to the study of deviance:

1. Deviance involves rule-breaking actions, sometimes criminal sometimes simply disapproved, and will be largely covert or hidden. It does not lend itself to investigation ' . . . by constructing questionnaires, sampling, and ringing doorbells to ask people about their participation in this activity' (Reading 9, p. 193).

2. A statistical approach to deviance must necessarily rely on official statistics which suffer from several deficiencies from the researcher's point of view:

(a) The statistics will usually be based on a biased sample because the less competent deviants will come to official notice more frequently than will the more intelligent or better connected ones. In types of deviancy which are just on the margins of criminality (such as abortions or homosexuality), the wealthier deviant can buy 'competency' easily in one way or another and so avoid coming to official attention. There is clearly a tendency for samples to be more biased in cases of marginal criminality than where the deviant acts are undoubtedly criminal, although any sample of offences and offenders will be biased to some degree if it is based on official statistics.

(b) Official classifications of deviant behaviour are based on legal definitions and these will not always be the same as social definitions of deviant or immoral behaviour. The current English law on abortion is a strong example of this point. What determines whether an abortion is legal or illegal (and thus one which *may* be recorded as a crime) depends on the willingness of doctors to certify an abortion as falling within the terms of the 1967 Abortion Act, and for another doctor to carry out the abortion

From R. A. Scott and J. D. Douglas (eds) *Theoretical Perspectives on Deviance*, New York: Basic Books, 1972, Ch. 7, pp. 158–86.

itself. The regional variations in the ease with which abortions are obtained is one of the weakest features of the 1967 Act. A woman is about four times likelier to obtain an abortion in Birmingham than in London. Thus, many more women could be labelled deviant in Birmingham than in London solely because of the arbitrary interpretation of the 1967 Act by the local doctors. Presumably the difference between the two areas in awarding the social label of 'deviant' to women having or seeking abortions is not going to be greatly different, certainly not four times greater in Birmingham than London. Thus, if one relied on those cases which were known to the police as illegal abortions, Birmingham would appear to be a black spot and London not. The difference in actual *behaviour* between the two cities will be, in fact, small if not zero.

(c) Interview material with those who are known to the authorities may be misleading in two ways: (i) the unlucky or the 'incompetent' or poor will be overrepresented for reasons noted above; (ii) interviews with those who have been 'caught' will be subject to a number of biases. Firstly, such interviews must be retrospective in nature when questions are asked about 'why?' or 'how?' the deviant became so. The tendency to recon- struct the past, in the light of *present* concerns is well known to psycholo- gists and sociologists, as is the effect of the interviewer on the material elicited. Secondly, every interview is an interaction in which the status characteristics of the interviewer may bias the responses. Where the respondent comes into a sample from his or her record in an official list of deviants the interviewer is, at the least tinged with official status, if not directly seen as an officer of an agency of social control. Accounts of deviancy given in these circumstances will clearly be biased.

3. The final strength of an ethnographic method is one which applies not only to deviancy but to any sort of human action. It is best captured by the quotation from Goffman in Ball (Reading 9, p. 199): '. . . the serious ethnographic task of assembling ways in which the individual is treated and treats others, and deducing what is implied about him through this treatment' . . . . Behaviour is largely situational. Given certain personality characteristics of the individual, he or she acts with and to others. One cannot predict behaviour from a knowledge of the individual's attitudes even if 'attitudes' are broadly con- ceived to include not only 'predispositions to behave in certain ways' but self-descriptions (what Goffman refers to as 'verbal trait lists' in Reading 9. p. 199). What an individual does, as opposed to what he or she might think they would do, depends as much on how other actors manage the interaction as on predispositions or personality characteristics.

In Ball's study, the clinic is organized to appear very like a normal doctor's practice. The patients are guided in their responses by the familiar routines of a (legal) doctor's surgery. What is a stressful experience for the client both because of what she needs (an abortion) and because it is illegal is managed in such a way that the normal middle-class patterns of doctor-patient roles and expectations are sustained. Ball argues that clients tacitly cooperate in this parody of an (expensive) medical clinic because it offers them (implicitly) a favourable image of themselves in a situation which is one of anxiety and self-doubt. These clients are, as Ball points out, respectable citizens usually, forced by need into contact with a criminal world with a seedy reputation. The 'self' which they are invited to present to themselves is their normal everyday one of self-respect and security. Ball's analysis can only be *deduced* from the patterns of behaviour and speech which he observes, it cannot be got by interviewing a sample of women who have had an abortion and the abortionists.

The reasons for this are two fold:

(a) Respondents cannot be expected to reflect on the significance of how they have behaved in an abortion clinic. To do so needs a degree of self-knowledge and detachment which they cannot be expected to show. To admit that the familiar symbols and practices of a doctor's surgery have effectively persuaded them that they have never left the secure world of their normal life needs an admission of a willingness to deceive oneself which might appear childish.

(b) The setting of the clinic is an important part of the illusion. The luxury of the waiting-room, the 'operating theatre', the white-coated receptionist, all contribute to the air of legal normality. These things can only be *observed* and their significance interpreted by a trained observer.

I

The following deals with some aspects of criminal abortion: practitioners, patients and their companions, and the place of such illegal work. More particularly, it is concerned with the management of respectable appearances in such an unrespectable situation – the problematic selves and identities of the actors so located, the presentational strategies and rhetorical devices, and the cooperative evasions used by these participants – to create and sustain legitimizing definitions of themselves and their audiences.

In this theoretical perspective self and identity are not synonyms, but differentiated conceptions. One may distinguish between *self*, ego as known to ego, and *identity*, ego and his self as he appears to alter, his audience (Stone, 1962). The coincidence of these two or the lack thereof is one of the central problems facing social actors in everyday life. We present our audience with a self, which is acknowledged by them in the making of an assignment of identity; one can ratify and confirm or deny and disconfirm the other.

Identity assignments are based upon presented self, social role, biographical knowledge about the actor and biographical experiences of the audience, and situational meanings available to the presenter and the audience. These identities are then available to the actor, ego, for incorporation or rejection in his definition of self. Self is then producer, product, and process: presenter and presented to the audience; consumed and reconstituted as an identity; and repossessed –

possibly in an altered state – by the presenting actor, now for his acceptance or denial as a definition of his self.

And the stuff of such continual negotiations is symbols: words, phrases, gestures, postures, dress, and other communicative acts, including the ecological and physical settings in which social actors situate and locate themselves. We may refuse our identities, reject them, and present selves that are otherwise; but we cannot ignore them. For they are the materials that structure our audiences' expectations about us, and their responses to us. For any line of action for our selves requiring the actions of our others, our assigned identities must at least overlap, if not coincide with our presented selves.

Central to the notion of defining one's self is the definitions of one's others, their identities. If one is known, given an identity, by the company one keeps, this knowledge is available to oneself, about one's self, to construct a definition of self, as much – if not more – than it is to anyone else. And if we get our identities and thus know ourselves, at least in part, by the company we keep, then in a sense we owe our selves to our others.

Such a model of self, identity, and others is not limited to the 'straight' world of fathers and mothers, sisters and brothers, enemies and friends alone, but is also applicable to those situations and settings typically categorized as socially wrong, immoral, illegal, deviant, and the like.

Abortionists get clients, clients get abortions, and in and from the process of these transactions, they both give identities and get selves. It is with such matters that this reading is concerned: the selves that eventuate from a particular kind of sexual outcome: an unwanted pregnancy and its illegal termination by a criminal abortionist.

An important *caveat* is in order. The data reported here were collected in 1965 and first described two years later (Ball, 1967b). The kinds of identities, the attitudes, considerations, and definitions of normality and morality available to social actors *then* are not necessarily the same construction materials for the building of selves that are available today. However, I have tried to maintain faithfulness to the historical reality that was then available to the participants' experience.

To the extent that the problems and dilemmas of self and identity presented herein may seem dated to the reader, that is what social change is all about. Empirically, I have no evidence that that which was either still is or now isn't. All social phenomena are rooted in time and space: so too should be their analyses.

II. A methodological excursion: problems of research strategy

Since criminal abortion is just that, illegal, it is a form of deviant conduct; rule-breaking activity officially labeled as morally wrong, and on that basis punitively sanctioned. Thus, there is good reason for persons so involved to hide their involvement, or deny it if accused. It is not, then – as is the difficulty with most hidden or secretive endeavors – amenable to study by constructing questionnaires, sampling, and ringing doorbells to ask people about their participation in this activity. This is a problem that plagues the study of most kinds of deviant conduct, not just abortion; as well as other activities that are considered personal and private, such as sexual relationships. Before turning to abortion, then, it seems advisable to consider some general issues and problems in the study of deviance.[1]

Typically, the study of deviant conduct, at least that which has the potential of evoking formal legal sanctions such as criminal abortion, has suffered from a dearth of primary data. Those materials most readily available and thus most often examined by students of deviance have usually, in some significant degree, been removed from the actual phenomena that are ultimately of basic interest.

Thus, all too frequently, sociological reports dealing with the deviant or unconventional in social conduct have been based upon (1) the official statistics issued by variously concerned control agencies; and (2) self-reports, often by the apprehended violators of formal rules and regulations of conventional society. Such a collection of data has disproportionately represented the technically unskilled and the politically unconnected; and neither of these sources is of the sort that is likely to aid in the constitution of a representative picture of deviant actors, their actions, or the social organization of such phenomena, let alone the selves and identities involved.

By now the sources of inaccuracies in official statistics have become legendary: differential administrative practices and applications by agencies of social control, class biases, unreported violations, lack of uniformity in the definitions of offenses, and so forth. Such statistics are, as Cicourel (1968) and Cicourel and Kitsuse (1963) have pointed out, *products manufactured by the organization issuing them*. And as regards self-reports, even when collected from other than only those actors whose contingency sequences have led them, through organizational differentials, to become labeled as 'official' deviants (Becker, 1963), that is, when gathered from unapprehended rulebreakers located in the conventional culture – they are still inadequate data.[2] If more interesting as to their implications regarding actual rates or incidences than the 'official statistics', such self-reports tell us little about the structure and process of deviant activities, that is, their social organization as contrasted to their simple statistical distributions, or the selves and identities of the persons involved. Such descriptive materials about people and their rates are only a first step toward sociological analysis of the persons and their social actions implicated in these rule-breaking modes of conduct.

For criminal abortions, frequently sought, frequently gotten, and almost always without legal complications, the biases of conventional data are particularly acute. And there is no evidence that recent changes in legislation regulating abortion (liberalization, tokenism, moral decadence – depending upon your viewpoint) have significantly altered the incidence of illegal pregnancy-terminations; an unascertainable matter anyway.

Alternatively, a less conventional method for pursuing the study of deviance such as abortion, but one which has, to date, unfortunately, been only rarely utilized, is the developing of contacts with unapprehended deviants themselves, that is, going directly to unconventional actors and their cultural milieux. Such a procedure ignores questions about rates, but it is only with such a procedure that the natural, the routine and everyday, the mundane context of deviance and deviant actors can be captured; this, rather than the typically biased picture provided by the conventional data for which we all too often settle. Such common strategies may be safer and easier, but they involve at best a serious compromise with accuracy, and all too frequently a degree of data distortion beyond utility for anything save the sociologist's own *vita* enlargement.

In recent years a few students of deviance have made use, either through design or circumstance, of the more direct approach involving actual observation, if not participation, in deviant subcultures: Becker's (1963) work on marijuana users, Hooker's (1963) studies of male homosexuals, and a few others. Most often, however, the direct method has been applied by sociologists to the study of only marginally or potentially deviant actors, their actions, and their settings, for example, Scott (1968) on horse racing, Polsky (1967) on pool hustlers, Cavan (1966) on bar behavior – topics where the risks and hazards are ordinarily relatively smaller.

We would argue that this less traditional, essentially *ethnographic approach* to the collection of sociological data on deviance is superior, particularly in terms of completeness, to the more conventionally used official statistics and self-reports; *especially as regards hidden deviance* (Becker, 1963: 19–20) such as rarely legally acted-upon criminal abortion. However, it should be obvious that this research strategy is not without its own attendant problems and dilemmas; the remainder of this section deals with some of these issues.

Ethics

First of all, there is the ethical problem. The investigator is, irrespective of any degree of personally experienced cultural integration or alienation, a member of the society that creates, maintains, and applies the definitions of who and what is or is not deviant, as well as the attendant penalties. As Ned Polsky has cogently noted:

If one is to study law-breaking deviants as they engage in their deviance in its natural setting, i.e. outside the jail, he must make the moral decision that in some ways he will break the law himself. He need not be a

*[participating observer] and commit the deviant acts under study, yet he
has to witness such acts or be taken into confidence about them and not
blow the whistle. That is, the investigator has to decide that when
necessary he will 'obstruct justice' or be 'an accessory' before or after the
fact, in the full legal sense of those terms. He will not be enabled to
discern some vital aspects of criminally deviant behaviour and the
structure of law breaking subcultures unless he makes a moral decision,
makes the deviants believe him, and moreover convinces them of his
ability to act in accord with his decision.*

Polsky goes on that, concerning the placing of the norms of science
above those of the community, that is, its laws:

*The last mentioned point can perhaps be neglected with juvenile delin-
quents, for they know that a professional studying them is almost always
exempt from police pressure to inform; but adult criminals have no such
assurance, and hence are concerned not merely with the investigator's
intentions [and discretion], but with his sheer ability to remain a 'stand-
up guy' under police questioning. [Personal Communication, cited in
Becker, 1963:171, note 7]*[3]

Thus, for the researcher interested in criminal abortion, direct contact
must involve getting his hands dirty, going to abortionists in their
natural habitat such as abortion clinics or mills, and compromising
himself legally if not morally and sticking to his commitment as he
violates the formal prescriptions of the culture vis-à-vis activities
defined as deviant. Such a dilemma can only be personally resolved,
for there are neither shortcuts nor handy rules for such situations.

Sources

Another dilemma is the problem of obtaining and maintaining contacts with the worlds of deviants. It may – or may not, and probably
should not – surprise us to find how rich our own acquaintances may be
as sources or leads to various rule-breaking actors and their subcultures. This is especially true of the more widespread criminal service
and supply networks such as abortion, prostitution and other sexual
services, soft (if not hard) narcotics, and gambling. Alternatively,
habituation of known resorts for such deviant endeavors and/or their
products may ultimately lead the researcher to the acceptance that is
necessarily adequate to generate access to the relevant actors and their
activities. More succinctly, if we don't already know, we probably
know who or where to ask (see Manning, forthcoming, and Howell, on
the strategies for finding an abortionist).

Disclosure

Once contact has been established, the investigator faces the usual
problem inherent in the observer role, that is, how much of one's own
purposes, motives, and role to reveal to one's subjects (Gold, 1958).

While ignoring, but not unaware of the problem of potential physical danger or violence in some settings, the degree of revelation is methodologically still a particularly crucial issue – since in studying deviance *in situ* one's legitimacy in the dominant law-abiding culture may be a discreditable stigma (Goffman, 1963:41–62) in the view of one's subjects. Parenthetically, this may be less of a problem regarding abortion than for many other *organized* criminal activities, since most persons seeking criminal abortions are otherwise conventional (Section III, of this reading). Again, the general problem probably must be solved by the individual investigator, weighing his own values, the maximization of an efficacious research strategy, and the consideration of an evaluation of his subjects as persons in some form of Benthamite moral calculus.

Reactivity

Yet, the dilemmas are still more complex, with other issues coexisting with, if not transcending, those of ethics, sources, and access There is the problem of reactivity (Webb *et al.*, 1967): the effect of the process of investigation upon that which is being investigated; not just the more or less straightforward one of subjects not talking or dissembling in the presence of an alien researcher, but a much more subtle one, best introduced by way of example:

About fifteen years ago, a young doctoral candidate at a Midwestern university decided to do for his dissertation an observational study of juvenile gangs. To this end the student, who looked less than his years, drifted into a predominantly blue-collar steel mill town and began hanging around a local pool hall frequented (just as folk-lore would have it) by delinquent adolescents (a site identified to him by local police, who were cooperating with the study). In relatively short order he made contact with members of an appropriate gang and was accepted into it by the members. The gang itself fell some place between the negativistic, vandalistic gangs delineated by Cohen (1955) and the instrumentally oriented theft-for-gain criminal gangs described by Cloward and Ohlin (1960).

It was as regards these latter kinds of activities that the researcher had his greatest problems in trying to avoid reactively influencing his subjects. As the gang members would formulate and discuss plans for their next adventure, usually on the order of knocking over a candy store while the proprietor was in the back room, the investigator – who was, after all, not unintelligent or lacking in analytical ability – would see flaws in these schemes; flaws serious enough to make apprehension an all-too-real probability. Needing to keep his subjects on the loose and unfettered by involvement with legal authorities, he would as gently as possible try to mend the holes in the gang's plans, but with an unanticipated consequence. In a short time the gang members began to defer to the investigator's organizational ability and to treat him as a leader. His desire to keep his subjects in a viable state, i.e uncaught and routinely engaging in their usual deviant activities, which in turn led to his forced demonstration of planning and administrative competence reactively affected the gang. Having gained access and acceptance, the researcher then faced a new and unexpected dilemma: avoiding the creation of a gang to study which was actually being led by a young Ph.D. candidate.[4]

The object of this little cautionary tale is simple. The reactivity problem, in the study of deviance and other areas as well, is not exhausted merely by the avoidance of having one's subjects 'clam up' or deceive in hopes of misleading, or alternatively, pleasing the investigator. Since deviant subjects in particular seem less likely than others in more conventional settings to learn or be informed as to the researcher's true intentions of identity, their direct study appears likely to magnify the dangers of reactivity even more than usual; both the investigator and his subjects are restricted, by a blanket of secrecy, from making the adjustive compensations necessary to assure 'normal' conduct in the field.

Scientific status

Finally, there is a collection of issues that may be subsumed more generally as the 'Scientific Problem'. It is frequently if not usually the case that for one reason or another the directly observing student of deviance will feel honor-bound not to reveal his sources or the specifics of his data-gathering procedures. Motivations for such strictures may range from moral obligation regarding the protection of subjects to a more mundane unwillingness to implicate one's self as a participant in, or an accessory to, deviant activities; especially if such disclosure is likely to invite criminal investigation. Until such time as some form of legal recognition of confidentiality, that is, privileged information and communication, and thus immunity is extended to sociologists and others investigating deviance in a manner analogous to that enjoyed now by physicians, lawyers, and clergymen, the risk of criminal prosecution will remain a very real hazard for those going directly to the source.[5] However, for whatever the reason, the *in situ* observation of the deviant and his milieu often precludes the complete reporting of method and the possibility of exact replication ordinarily demanded by the rules of scientific rigor.

Thus, the gemini issues of validity and reliability are raised – and as regarding the study of deviance to a much greater extent than is true of observational research in general. By its very nature, any kind of direct observation is open to question as to *validity*, for example, is what is reported an accurate account of events and relationships; and *reliability*, for would other observers and their observations generate the same set of data, always keeping in mind the dubious *ceteris paribus* qualification. Such problems are difficult enough to answer when the observations are drawn from nondeviant settings and methods are carefully described; they become even more important when full disclosure of procedural minutiae is deemed impossible, as in the following material on abortion – as is usually the case when the data concern deviant actors and actions and their organizations.

We would like to suggest, however, that important as these traditional methodological questions are, they should not be allowed to obscure the central issue. Although conventionally aggregated data may satisfy rigid criteria for statistical manipulation, they do so at the cost of a misleading, even atypical, portrait of the deviant actor – what might be called 'the-unable-to-make-the-fix-incompetent' – and that furthermore ignores the structural and situational context of such conduct. In studying nondeviant conduct, at least the central tendencies are frequently known or relatively easily determined; deviance such as criminal abortion, almost by definition is secretive. So too is much, if not most sexual conduct; often legal only if private and hidden. Readily or easily collected data on such phenomena are analogous to the exposed portion of the iceberg, and just as unrepresentative of the whole.

Basically the fundamental issue is age-old; one that has haunted sociology since its empirical beginnings divorced it from social philosophy and criticism. This is the ever-present dilemma of resolving, in some form of compromise, the mutual *desiderata* of richness and rigor; polarities for which a maximization of one can occur only at the expense of the other alternative. Although the phenomenological school – the ethnomethodologists *inter nos* - would argue that the richness-rigor dichotomy is a false one, they especially would also recognize its hoary existence as part of the folkloric sociological tradition. Unfortunately an examination of this debate is beyond the scope of this chapter.[6]

Since the moral statisticians, Durkheim (see Douglas, 1967:3–76) and Lombroso's early study of the physiological characteristics of imprisoned criminals (summarized, with others, in Vold, 1958:43–74), the sociology of deviance has historically stressed conventional methodological rigor at the sacrifice of substantive richness; even to the extent of utilizing data that are trivial if not completely misleading. Ultimately, sociologists seek maps and models of human social conduct, conventional and otherwise, not merely data that conveniently fit existing statistical models.

This should not be taken as a criticism of statistical method *per se*. Rather, it is a plea for a recognition of the unique, hidden character of much that is defined and responded to as deviant, and its lack of ready accessibility as data when compared with other areas of sociological inquiry. To repeat, almost by definition deviance is secretive; that which falls into the net of public information may be considered in a sense almost incidental, and certainly not a true picture of the state-of-affairs as it actually exists and is experienced by actors so situated.

To properly understand their selves, then, we must share their experiences, and learn what identities are available to them as well as what are their presentational resources. Remarking generally about the study of the self, Goffman's comments seem particularly cogent when the subject is involved in deviant doing:

Little help has been provided by paper and pencil students of the self who start with a subject's verbal description of himself, often based on his selection from verbal trait-list, instead of starting with the serious ethnographic task of assembling ways in which the individual is treated and treats others, *and deducing what is implied about him through this treatment.* [*Goffman, 1969:361, note 5, emphasis added*]

III. The data: an abortion clinic ethnography[7]

What follows is an effort to utilize direct contact with deviant actors in their natural habitat, to describe ethnographically certain aspects of a particular abortion clinic, especially as such data may illuminate the presentational strategies employed by a habitually deviant establishment in its dealing with a situationally deviant clientele. All of the methodological drawbacks discussed apply to this material; hopefully, so too do some of the substantive benefits.

For an abortion clinic's staff, participation in an action legally defined as deviant, that is, criminal abortion, is habitual. That is to say, it is regularly repeated on a routine, businesslike basis; it is a part, the occupational part, of their everyday world. For patrons, such involvement is at most occasional; if that, irregular; and for most, by contrast, however, a once-in-a-lifetime engagement in this form of deviance.

Furthermore, most patrons are members of otherwise law-abiding cultures. Unlike the staff, their involvement in this deviant setting is not an aspect of a career, but an accidental consequence of an unwanted pregnancy. And it is probable that in most cases abortion is the most serious, that is, legally and socially penalized activity in which they will be criminally implicated.

In the context of an abortion clinic, therefore, the deviant transaction ordinarily is enacted by two kinds of actors: those *habitually* involved in such exchanges, that is, the *staff*; and those only *situationally* deviant, the otherwise conventional actors in their clinic-related roles as *patrons*.[8] It becomes of some interest, then, to consider how an abortion clinic manages and fosters impressions for an audience of patrons constituted of actors drawn from outside its habitually deviant, abortion-oriented subculture; how patrons are similarly involved in impression management; and some of the characteristics of such strategies used by each. Stated differently, the focus will be upon (1) techniques used by the clinic to key itself to the demands and expectations of a patronage drawn from the conventional culture, (2) the devices used by patrons to deny the legal if not moral realities of the solution to their predicament, and (3) the consequences of these strategies for the selves and identities of both patrons and staff.

Suffice it to say (see Section II), strictures of confidence prevent any elaborate discussion of method, problems of access, and the like. Let it be noted, however, that the materials reported and interpreted herein are based upon: (1) sufficiently lengthy observation of a clinic's routine (exclusive of specifically medical procedures that are not strictly relevant to the problem) to establish the patterns of its everyday functioning, (2) extensive interviews with a necessarily small number of its patrons, some of whom were also observed within the clinic, and (3) limited discussions with some of the clinic's nonmedical staff. Additionally, supplementary and confirmatory data have been drawn from interviews with individuals who have utilized other, similar facilities. Unfortunately, any more detailed methodological description would, not surprisingly, violate promises of anonymity guaranteed to the persons involved.

Background

The clinic studied was located, along with several similar establishments, in a border town along the California–Mexico line. Its staff included two practitioners – abortionists – ostensibly physicians, the younger of whom was in an apprentice relationship to the senior man; a practical nurse, a receptionist-bookkeeper, a combination janitress and custodian, a chauffeur-errand boy, and a telephone-appointments secretary.

As costs for such procedures go, the clinic was a relatively expensive one, with fees averaging $500 per abortion. The rate, however, would be somewhat less for other medical personnel and students, who were eligible for a discount; and more for persons desiring postoperative overnight observation, as well as those beyond the tenth week of pregnancy. In terms of finances, the clinic studied was probably representative of others catering to a middle- and upper-class clientele at that time. Its patients were usually married; if single, they were the daughters of well-to-do parents. The few single adult females could be better categorized as 'career women' rather than 'working girls'.

In order to obtain a better picture of the establishment, a brief natural history of a typical involvement between clinic and patron is useful at this point. Preliminarily though, it should be recognized that the ideal-typical practitioner-patient model of the medical sociologist is not appropriate for the analysis of abortion. Like veterinarians and pediatricians, abortionists frequently have *patients* for whom financial if not moral responsibility is an obligation of the role of some other person, that is, a *client*. For abortionists these clients include boyfriends, husbands, and parents. Along with persons such as accompanying friends, they comprise for the patient what might be classified as *supportive others:* persons attending the clinic along with the patient in order to provide psychological support and reinforcement in this crisis situation. Not surprisingly, it is rare for a patient to go to the clinic completely alone, without some morally supportive other.[9] Thus, within the context of abortion, the typical practitioner-patient dyad usually becomes a triad, comprising practitioner, patient, and supportive other; these last two constituting the clinic's *patrons*.[10]

A *natural history*

After referral, usually by a legitimate physician, less often by a friend or an acquaintance, a patron would make original contact with the clinic by telephone. The typically tentative, noncommittal, but implicitly urgent communication of the patron was immediately treated in a matter-of-fact manner by the telephone girl.

Girl: Hello, Doctor —'s office. Can I help you?
Patron: Yes, I, er, uh, would like to make an appointment with the Doctor.
Girl: How long has she been pregnant?

The fact of pregnancy was thus immediately introduced by the staff-member. And in appropriate middle-class speech patterns she quickly and efficiently asked the length of the pregnancy, extolled the skills of the staff, set up a tentative appointment, and discussed the fee and its mode of payment by the patron. This treatment of the patron's problem as *routine* helped to minimize the anxiety inherent in such situations.[11] Parallel to this was a 'medicalization' of the situation, also helping to disarm the patron vis-à-vis the deviant nature of the proposed transaction; practitioners were always referred to as doctors, and at all times the terminology was that of conventional medicine and surgery. Later, ordinarily two or three days prior to the appointment, the patron again called the clinic, this time to get confirmation of date and time.

Patrons would usually spend the night before their appointment at a hotel or motel near the clinic. Early in the morning of the scheduled date they were to call the clinic once again, this time to get directions to the only then revealed place of rendezvous where they were picked up and transported to the clinic by one of the staff members in a large, late model station wagon.

It was at this time that the patrons would first find that they were not alone in their dilemma; for there would also be several other patrons picked up at the rendezvous site, filling the station wagon to capacity. Although propinquity seemingly might argue for it, there would be little deliberate interaction among patrons during the ride to the clinic; uncertainty, anxiety, and felt stigma, effectively socially immobilizing these situational deviants in the ambiguous situation into which they had placed themselves.

Upon arrival at the clinic, where the station wagon and all related cars of the staff would be hidden from street view, the patrons were ushered into a large, well-furnished waiting room. The clinic itself most resembled an extremely roomy private home, both externally and internally – in its non-medical areas – and was located in a prestigious residential neighborhood on a hill overlooking the community.

Once inside, the patrons would find seats for themselves and settle into a waiting period of hushed expectancy. Conversation was limited to patients and their respective supportive others, that is, only to those sets of persons previously known to one another. After a short interval of perhaps five minutes, the receptionist would appear and call out the name of the first patient. The pair, patient and receptionist, would then retire out of sight of the remaining patrons into the medical wing of the clinic.

The first stop in the medical wing was an office. After first explaining the procedure in explicitly medical terminology, the receptionist would shift to her bookkeeper role and request the fee (in cash or traveler's checks only) from the patient; frequently finding that it was being held by an accompanying supportive other still in the waiting room. Following this discussion and the collection of the fee, the patient was then sent to a bathroom, well appointed in terms of luxury rather than gynecology, to remove her street clothes and put on a surgical gown. Once gowned, the patient would be directed to the room where the actual abortion would take place.

Those specifically involved in this procedure included, in addition to the patient, the two practitioners, senior and apprentice, and the practical nurse. Although a spinal anesthetic was administered, at no time would the patient be allowed to lose consciousness; a necessity born of the possible need for quick removal in the event of visitation by legal agents. Immediately, upon completion of the procedure, the patient would leave the table and then be sent to another room to rest for from fifteen minutes to an hour-and-a-half. Finally, after receiving medication and instructions regarding post-operative care from the receptionist, the patient and any supportive others would be returned by a staff-member to the site of the original rendezvous and thus sent on their way back to their conventional worlds.

Description and analysis
With this brief, oversimplified picture it is now possible to turn to more specifically sociological concerns: the aforementioned presentational strategies that make up what may be called, for the clinic, a *rhetoric of legitimization,* and the selves and identities for staff and patrons so generated and cooperatively sustained.

Rhetorics
Sociologically, a rhetoric may be considered a vocabulary of specific purpose; that is to say, as a limited set of symbols functioning to communicate a particular set of meanings, directed and organized toward the representation of a specific image or impression. Such

vocabularies are not only verbal but also include visual symbols such as objects, gestures, emblems, and the like.

As a theoretical point it should be noted that rhetorics are not necessarily the same thing as ideologies, although empirically they may coincide. The conceptual difference between the two is that whereas rhetoric speaks to communication, both style and content (Simmel, 1950:22–23, 40–43; Wolff, 1959, several papers, especially those by Levine, Weingartner, and Tenbruck), ideology refers to perception and justification in terms of the ideologue's conception of relevant portions of his world. It is conceivable that individual actors, groups, or establishments will utilize a rhetoric without any ideological convictions as regards its validity, but with a recognition of its pragmatic efficacy. Similarly, ideological dedication does not automatically assume a developed rhetoric to attempt its maintenance or furtherance. The former may be illustrated by much of Madison Avenue advertising; the latter by the inarticulate responses frequently elicited by this form of commercial persuasion.

Returning to the case of the clinic: basically its rhetoric operated to subvert the conventional world's view of abortion, and to generate a picture of legitimate activity. Fundamentally, the question thus becomes: what techniques were utilized via this rhetoric to *neutralize* the context of deviance in which the clinic operated so as to enhance parallels with conventional medical and social situations and thus derive a kind of 'rightness' or legitimization?[12] How, in other words, were milieu and actions *qua* impressions manipulated in order to maximize the clinic's image over and above the successful performance of its task; and to contradict the stereotypic stigma of deviance? Particularly, how did the clinic (1) minimize the possibilities of trouble with frightened or recalcitrant patrons and thus maximize ease of work-flow, (2) generate the patron satisfaction necessary for referral system maintenance, and (3) present an image that would provide the most favorable selves and identities possible for the actors involved, whether patron or staff?

The second and third problems are, in effect, special cases of the first. Minimization of trouble was not motivated so much by fear of patron complaints to legal agents, which would involve the complainants in admitting complicity, but more by a desire to (a) maintain referrals and (b) maintain or enhance self-definitions.

Only additionally such minimization produced a smoother, easier workflow for the staff. A similar rationale in conventional medical settings sometimes dictates the use of general anesthetics when, in terms of patient pain, locals would be adequate.

For analytical purposes, the clinic's rhetoric of legitimization may be conveniently conceptualized by employing Goffman's (1956:13–14) delineation of front and its constituents of setting, appearance, and manner. This scheme formed an observational framework for data collection as well as a perspective for then analyzing it. Originally a framework for analyzing the presentation of a single self in interaction, this scheme seems extendible to the strategies of establishments and institutions as well; and thereby the selves and identities situated, developed, and given meaning within them.

Essentially, *front* consists of those communications that serve to define the situation or performance for the audience: standardized expressive equipment including (1) *setting*, the spatial/physical background items of props and scenery in the immediate area of the interaction, (2) *appearance*, the sign-vehicles expressing the performer's social status or type, and (3) those expressions that warn of a performer's demeanor, mood, and the like, that is *manner*.

Examining each of these elements for evidence of how they were manipulated to constitute a rhetoric allows the identification of the central themes and dimensions of the clinic's presentational strategies. Although the combination of the conceptions of rhetoric, neutralization, and front and its elements produces an admittedly loose theoretical scheme, the character of the data does not suggest the utility of further rigor in this case.

Setting

A paramount feature of the clinic's rhetoric was its physical and spatial characteristics. Especially important for patrons generally was the stereotype-contradicting waiting room, the first impression of the clinic itself – and the dominant one for supportive others. This waiting room was likely to be the only room in which supportive others would be present during their entire visit to the clinic, save for the possibility of a short interval in the office if they happened to be holding the fee (a frequent occurrence, especially if the other was also a client).

Spatially, the waiting room was L-shaped and extremely large; approximately seventy-five feet long and fifty feet wide at the base leg. Its size was accentuated by the fact that most of the room was sunken about three feet below the floor level at its perimeters. Fully and deeply carpeted, well furnished – with several comfortable couches and armchairs, large lamps and chandeliers, coffee and end tables – the room spoke of luxury and patron consideration. These were also implied by the presence of a television set, a small bar, and a phonograph; such items of decor in addition to the usual magazines present in more typical medical waiting-room situations (see Fig. 9.1).

I knew, for the first time, really, that the whole thing might work out after all. I mean when I saw those crystal chandeliers hanging there, and all that carpeting, I thought that I could come out of it O.K. It reminded me of what I imagine those clinics in Switzerland must look like.

Thus commented one patient about her first reaction upon stepping into the room and seeing it for the first time. It served to reduce anxiety for her, providing for the first time in her patient experience with the clinic the suggestion that she would be all right, that is, physically;

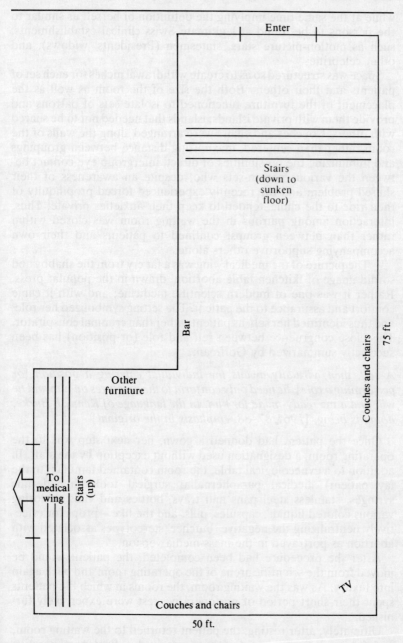

Fig. 9.1 The ecology of the clinic's waiting room

while at the same time implying the definition of herself as similar to the persons to be found at legitimate Swiss clinical establishments, such as motion-picture stars, statesmen (Presidents' widows), and other celebrities.

Space was structured so as to create withdrawal niches for each set of patients and their others. Both the size of the room as well as the placement of the furniture functioned to isolate sets of patrons and provide them with private islands; islands that needed not to be shared with others. Couches and chairs were arranged along the walls of the room rather than centered, maximizing distance between groupings and minimizing the possibilities of direct, intergroup eye contact between the various patron-sets who, despite an awareness of their shared problem and the recently experienced forced propinquity of their ride to the clinic, tended to keep their anxieties private. Thus, interaction among patrons in the waiting room was closed within rather than between groups; confined to patients and their own accompanying supportive others alone.

The picture of the medical wing was a far cry from the shabby and sordid image of 'kitchen-table abortion' drawn in the popular press. Rather it was one of modern scientific medicine; and with it came comfort and assurance to the patient. The setting symbolized her role, and thus identified her self, as patient rather than criminal conspirator. This close congruence between self and role (or position) has been succinctly summarized by Goffman:

A self, then, virtually awaits the individual entering a position [or performing a role]; he need only conform to the pressures on him and he will find a me *ready-made for him. In the language of Kenneth Burke, doing is being.* [1961:87–88, emphasis in the original]

Once the patient had donned a gown, her next step was to the operating room, a designation used without exception by the staff. In addition to a gynecological table, the room contained familiar (to the lay patient) medical paraphernalia: surgical tools, hypodermic syringes, stainless steel pans and trays, bottles and vials enclosing various colored liquids, capsules, pills, and the like – props for effectively neutralizing the negative 'butcher' stereotypes associated with abortion as portrayed in the mass-media version.

After the procedure had been completed, the patient would be moved from the scientific arena of the operating room and back again into luxury. As was the waiting room, the rooms in which the patients spent their short period of postoperative rest were expensively furnished.

Ultimately, after resting, the patient returned to the waiting room, and for most to supportive others, received a final postoperative briefing before being returned to the rendezvous site. Parenthetically, it may be noted that throughout the entire episode music had been piped into every room in which patrons, both patients and their others, were present.

In terms of setting, the clinic presented itself as not unlike a small hospital, albeit with a decorator-designed interior. For patient and supportive others the scenery and props functioned to communicate an image of assurance and protection through the devices of cost and luxury along with that of scientific medicine; to minimize the deviant nature of the transaction, to emphasize positive cultural values, thus efficiently counteracting stereotypic images, and thereby provide for the possibility of positively valued selves and identities for staff and patrons alike.

Appearance and manner

A widespread device for visibly differentiating various social categories or types is clothing (Stone, 1962; Roach and Eicher, 1965; Ryan, 1966). Items of dress may function as insignia or uniforms to label the persons so garbed as members of particular social groups, occupations, or the like. Such institutionalized symbols act as both identifiers and identities; to be attired in certain ways is to be a certain kind of person, thus to have a certain kind of self, not only in the identifying eyes of the audience, but also in terms of the actor's perception of himself. Dress is, then, an integral aspect of social identity and experienced self.

So it was with the clinic: practitioners, patient, nurse – all wore from the layman's point of view, the appropriate symbols of dress for surgically centered roles. White tunics were worn by the practitioners; patients were surgically gowned; the nurse and even the janitress wore white uniform dresses. This element of the rhetoric would be especially highlighted at the beginning of the procedure when both practitioners ostentatiously donned surgical gloves, visibly emphasizing their, and the clinic's, concern with the necessity of asepsis. This ritualistic activity also served to forcefully identify these actors in their medical roles as defined by the rhetoric, and thus the patient in hers.

The medical model was further underscored by the preoperative medical history that was taken and recorded upon a standard, multicarboned form (the destiny of these duplicate copies was never made known to the writer). Actions such as this, along with other aspects of appearance such as dress, provided major modes of keying symbols and stressing the medical legitimacy of the clinic, its staff, its task, and thus its clientele.

From the receptionist on up through the clinic's hierarchy, behavior, particularly verbal, emphasized medical and professional aspects of the clinic's operation. Nowhere was this more apparent than in the area of vocabulary; it was strictly medical, with no effort either made or implied to speak down to the less knowledgeable lay patron. It is also noteworthy that at no time was the word abortion *per se* used in the presence of a patron; rather, references were to the operation, the procedure, or a 'D and C' (dilation and curettage). Similarly, as noted, the room in which the procedure took place was at all times designated by members of the staff as the operating room.

Other elements of staff behavior that furthered the medical impression were (1) the postoperative consultation and medication that effectively contrasted with the popular view of abortion as an 'off-the-table-and-out' procedure, and (2) the presence of an apprentice practitioner and its obvious analogy, at least for the medically sophisticated, with a teaching hospital. For the patient, the teaching aspects of the senior practitioner's role helped to generate confidence in his skill, a matter that was also verbally reinforced by other staff members in their interactions with the patrons.

As with appearance, the manner of the staff was essentially directed toward the medical elements of the clinic's rhetoric; their demeanor was professional at all times, with one exception. This exception was the receptionist-bookkeeper, whose role was, by definition, outside the strictly medical aspects of the clinic. As a result, freed of the obligations of professional mien, the receptionist was able to interact with patrons in a reassuring and supportive manner; in effect, her presentation of the rhetoric was through expressive strategies of nurturance, whereas the manner of other staff members was more instrumentally oriented.[13]

Before turning to central symbolic themes appealing to the patrons that were engendered by the clinic's rhetorical strategies, it might be well to at least take note of some flaws in the presentation, even though they may have escaped the usual patron's attention. These may be considered under the general rubrics of pseudosterility and miscellaneous delicts.

Pseudosterility
Although ostentation was the rule as regards the emphasis of aseptic and antiseptic precautions, there were also omissions less readily obvious. It will be recalled that measures apparently designed to minimize infection and also at the same time maximize parallels with legitimate medicine included (1) the wearing of tunics by the practitioners, (2) their donning of surgical gloves prior to the procedure, and (3) the display of the tools and paraphernalia of medicine and surgery in the operating room.

It should be pointed out that, aseptically, tunics are no substitute for full surgical gowns, that full precautionary tactics would also include items such as face masks, caps, and the like; and that it is highly irregular for an operating room to lack an autoclave (for the sterilization of instruments) and changeable covering for the table, which that setting did; or for surgical instruments to stand on exhibition, exposed to the air for long periods of time, like a sales display at a medical convention. Additionally, it may be noted that those portions of the preoperative medical history that were taken by the senior practitioner were recorded by him – *after* his elaborate display of putting on the surgical gloves; a less than ideal practice for sterility.

These breaches of standard surgical procedure suggest that much of what passed for the lay patron as concern with aseptic and antiseptic practices was actually a calculated rhetoric, designed to communicate to the audience a sustained standard of professional medical rigor that did not in fact exist.

Miscellaneous delicts
Within this category are included additional practices at variance with the fostered medical impression, but not directly involving matters of sterility.

Perhaps the most glaring of these was the lack of privacy afforded the patient in comparison with more conventional surgical settings. The fact that patients were handled in groups and moved and serviced in what in comparison with a hospital was a small and not systematically designed space, led to a good deal of enforced contact between patients and staff involved in various stages of the process. Of necessity this led to frequent invasions of privacy, at least as open to perception and definition by patients accustomed to more traditional medical situations. Thus, for instance, the room used as the business office also doubled as a resting room, and a patient lying there for postoperative rest might suddenly find herself witness to a financial transaction as a later-scheduled patron made payment of the fee. The resting patient was thus treated, in effect, as an object, becoming, in Goffman's phrase, a *nonperson* (1956:95-96), that is, an actor not accorded the usual deferences given as minimal acknowledgment of a person's moral worth, simply by virtue of the fact of that person's being human.

Also of interest was the function of the *music*, piped into every room including the one for the procedure. When the patrons first arrived at the clinic the music would be quiet, soothing, and relaxing in style; but with the entrance of the first patient into the medical wing, the tempo and timbre both increased markedly. The volume of the music then effectively operated to drown out any untoward sounds that might emanate from the medical wing and alarm those patrons still in the waiting room.

Another delict involved the marked contrast in *vehicles* used in picking up and returning patrons to the rendezvous. In keeping with the symbolism of cost and luxury presented to the prospective patron, the station wagon which would bring them to the clinic was an expensive new model. By contrast, for the return to the rendezvous, which was not done *en masse* as was the initial pick up, and by which time presentational strategies were less necessary – the car driven by the chauffeur-errand boy was an old, rather decrepit foreign sedan of low cost and questionable reliability.

Still another item at variance with traditional medical procedures was the emphasis, especially by the practitioners, on the necessity of the patient's cooperation to assure the procedure's success. The patient was in effect invited, if not commanded, to become an active participant in the ongoing activity.[14] She would be told, for instance, of the desirability of her concentrating on other matters, for example, 'think of something else and all will go smoothly and rapidly'. This assigning of an active role of the patient stands in marked contradiction to her objectification as regards matters of privacy, and implies expediency as a more central concern of the clinic's operation than patient welfare.

Finally, it may be noted that although the practitioners were verbally represented by others on the staff as physicians, gynecologists in fact, no evidence of medical training in the form of certificates or diplomas was displayed and available for patron scrutiny.

Discussion

From this selective ethnographic description of various aspects of the clinic's front, two broad dimensions appear essential to its rhetoric of legitimization: (1) luxury and cost, and (2) conventional medical practices and procedures. It is these two themes that were most emphasized in the clinic's efforts to neutralize its aura of habitual deviance before an audience of only situationally deviant patrons drawn primarily from the world of conventional society. Thus, the rhetoric sought its vocabulary in meaningful and positive values of the patron's culture.

Within these master themes, four elements may be specified as contributing to the two broader dimensions of luxury and cost and conventional medicine: cleanliness, competence, conventionality, and concern for the patron.

Cleanliness and *competence* are both elements of the instrumental aspects of medicine. Albeit with significant flaws, unrecognized by most lay patrons, the clinic's presentational strategies enhanced these impressions, if not to the same extent their actualities. The obvious symbols of dress and equipment were presented to the patient in the medical wing of the clinic where anxiety and uncertainty were likely to be high. These symbols were readily recognizable and implied the normality of the situation; they provided, in effect, the cues for a set of familiar expectations drawn from past experience with legitimate medicine. In a similar allaying manner, the practitioner's skill and competence were repeatedly voiced by the staff from the time of the initial telephone contact until the beginning of the actual abortive procedure itself.

Conventionality here means a realization of the middle-class values of most patrons. One of these values is, of course, a positive view of professional medicine, a view that the clinic attempted to exploit. Throughout the patron's experience with the clinic, parallels with this model were highlighted; but it is in another area that this element of the rhetoric functioned most effectively – the waiting-room setting.

The obvious expense, comfort, and general decor of the waiting room were such as to disarm all but the most fearful and suspicious patron, as the earlier quotation implied. This room and the first impressions it presented were such as to immediately link the clinic to the safe, known world of respectable middle-class conventionality. In the process of this linkage, the clinic was, in the patron's perception, divorced from the usually illicit image conjured by abortion; if not rendered totally conventional the clinic was at least brought within the context of their definitions and expectations from more mundane, everyday experience. Because of its crucial location in the process, being the patron's first direct exposure to the clinic milieu, it is fair to say that this room was the most successful presentation strategy in the clinic's legitimizing rhetoric.

The comfort of the waiting room was but one of the forms of expression of *concern for the patron* that helped to create a legitimatizing presentation. Other strategies included the telephone girl's supportive routinization of the patron's problem at the time of the initial contact; the similarly solicitous demeanor of the receptionist; and the postoperative consultation. This involved not only the dispensing of drugs to facilitate the patient's convalescence but also a brochure specifically detailing an expected course of progress and steps to be taken in case of complications.

By demonstrating concern, the clinic affirmed its subscription to the values of its patrons, and thus asserted its basically conventional nature, that is, the congruence of its operation with the norms of those upon whom its income relied.

All of these factors combined to help construct a rhetoric of legitimacy: a set of presentational strategies that allowed the clinic to minimize problems inherent in typically anxious and fearful patrons, and thus to function more effectively. And in addition, to generate the reputation necessary for an establishment of its kind, dependent upon referrals from legitimate physicians (or satisfied patrons).

IV. Self, identity, and deviance

Additionally, whether manifest or latent, the rhetoric also had consequences for the selves and identities of the actors involved. Both habitual deviants, the staff, and situational deviants, the patrons, were able to partake of the rhetoric so as to enhance their own self definitions. The rhetoric helped the staff to define their participation in the clinic's habitually deviant activities, despite the occasional flaws, as involvement in a professionally functioning establishment with the trappings of legitimate medicine. For patrons, although they too were admittedly involved in a deviant situation, the rhetoric blunted this hard truth. By accepting the presentational strategies as part of the clinic's reality, the patron was allowed to define the situation through symbols drawn from his conventional everyday experience. Thus, for both patron and staff alike, the rhetoric allowed for a minimization of the threats to experienced self and imputed identities that were built into their illicit transaction.

Fundamentally, both patrons and staff were involved, at the inter-personal level, in mutual 'face-work', each building images of self delineated in terms of approved social attributes (Goffman, 1955:213). To do so required each team, one the patrons the other the staff, to cooperatively evade certain matters. This *cooperative evasion* took the form of the mutual disattending of information available to each; acknowledgment that could only eventuate in less desirable, actually less respectable selves and identities.

As the rhetoric highlighted certain themes such as luxury and conventional medicine, so too the participants had to look the other way, had to ignore blunt facts in order to make it work. Patrons cooperated with staff by evading or ignoring information in contradistinction to the medical model that the staff emulated; similarly, the staff treated the patrons 'as if' (Vaihinger, 1927) they were persons with or with persons with a legitimate medical complaint seeking a conventional, a legal course of treatment for their dilemma.

Respectability
Through mutual evasion of some information and the presentation and acceptance of a rhetoric involving other versions of their shared task, patrons and staff converted, at least for the moments of their face-to-face (or voice-to-voice in the case of telephone conversations) involvement, a context of illegality and deviance into one of respectability.

Sociologically, to be *respectable* is to be a person:

1. perceived-to-be-normal, thus possessing moral worth,
2. the appearance of which is thereby accorded through deferential displays, i.e. signs of person appreciation from others,
3. in socially situated encounters. [Ball, 1970:332]

Briefly, from a sociological perspective, respectability is not an attribute of persons but a relational category. Persons become respectable by virtue of the responses of others to them, at particular times and in particular places; they are seen as normally situated, and therefore moral, and thus respectable. Thus, therapeutic abortions are respectable and criminal abortions aren't – even though the same medical procedures are employed in both.[15]

The rhetoric rendered an illegal abortion clinic into a normal, respectable medical setting; and what the rhetoric couldn't completely hide: the provision and utilization of a criminal service; *cooperative evasion* served to deny. If one is given identity by the company one keeps, the more respectable the company, the better and more respectable the self available. If one's company is 'patients', then self can be more medical than criminal – and if company is 'medical', then self can be that of patient rather than law-breaking client.

The clinic setting merely highlights two fundamental characteristics of respectability: (1) as a fundamental dimension in the definitions of selves and identities, it is actively sought after rather than simply passively bestowed; and (2) it is always problematic, its presence is not automatically warranted; it is always contextually given meaning – whether in confirmation or denial.[16]

Temporal dimension

A pair of useful distinctions, those concerning the temporal dimensions of self, and perception of identities too – have been made recently by Turner (1968:94) concerning the former, and Douglas (1967:280–283) regarding the latter. Although we have referred to self and identity throughout in a gross, temporally undifferentiated manner, this is not experientially the case: they are both momentary and transitory as well as enduring and persisting over time.

The self, ego as known to ego, is known both as a stable, basic entity, the 'Real me' —— 'I-myself as I really am' (Turner, 1968:94). This Turner calls the *self-conception*, which he contrasts with the self of immediate experience, the *self-image* – the picture ego has of himself in the immediate present, specifically located in time and space. The relationship between these two is interdependent. The self-conception is the result of the accretion of a life-time of self images, gradually building up a biographical self for the person. And as these images contribute to the more basic self-conception, this latter forms a baseline for comparison and evaluation of momentary images. These are judged as true or false, desirable or undesirable as they contrast or complement the actor's conception of himself as a self, as an object-to-himself as well as an acting subject. Images too dissonant for incorporation in existing conceptions exert pressure toward change. Such change may, of course, be readily accepted or actively fought depending on the valence of the emotional freight it bears.

A similar distinction can be made regarding identities: they are both *situated* and *substantial*.[17] That is, identities are situated in time and space, and given meaning by that contextual location. At the same time there is, in North American Society

a general, implicit, non-theoretical assumption made in everyday communications (with oneself and with others) that each individual has, or is, a substance. This substantialist meaning of persons leads to judgements of persons as wholes ... independent of time, place, and situation. [*Douglas, 1967:281—282*]

These substantive judgments are definitions, demands, and expectations about persons – they are assignments of a substantial identity, against which situated identities play and reinforce or alter, just as do self-images with self-conceptions. The distinctions made by Turner and Douglas are, then, opposite sides of the same coin. Schematically, their relationship can be shown in a paradigm (see Table 9.1).

Thus, the mutual face-work of patrons and staff is designed to keep negative self-images and situated identities from intruding upon more

Table 9.1

Temporality:	Perceptual source:	
	From ego (actor)	From alter (audience)
Transient	Self-image	Situated identity
Enduring	Self-conception	Substantial identity

enduring self-conceptions and substantial identities. Cooperatively, positive situated identities are imputed to one another, and thus positive self-images derived. This is not, of course, to construe a rational bent to these phenomena, but a functional one; although calculation is much more a part of the staff-mounted production of the rhetoric of respectability than is the patrons' response to it.

Finally, another useful distinction is the one that has been made by Lemert (1951; 1967:40–64) between primary and secondary deviation, which seems particularly useful here. Broadly, *primary* deviation refers to the *act* of deviation; in this case, performing and procuring criminal abortions. *Secondary* deviation, on the other hand, refers more to the deviant actor; specifically to his acquisition of an identity – and thus potentially a self – as a deviant. It is the function of the rhetoric of legitimization and the operation of cooperative evasion to minimize the vividness of the primary deviation in order to avoid the problems, both interpersonal and intrapersonal, associated with deviance of the secondary order. If the primary deviance of illegal abortion cannot be denied completely, it can at least be disguised. And it is to such concerns that the rhetoric speaks and is attended to by both patrons and staff.

Unfortunately, the confidential and historical nature of this data and interpretation do not allow one of the usual canons of science to be met, that regarding exact replication; and no claim regarding the typicality of the clinic described herein can be formally made. Thus, if generalizations can be derived, they are of a conceptual rather than a statistical nature. Hopefully, however, the materials have shed some light on a relatively little-known area of social conduct.[18] Given the incidence of criminal abortion, it may be hoped that similar analysis can be conducted by others. Lastly, it may be suggested that hopefully the concept of rhetoric provides a useful tool for examining the dramas of social life and the selves and identities so implicated, whether these be deviant or conventional, spontaneous or routine, unusual or mundane.

Notes

1. Portions of this section are based upon a paper originally presented as 'Conventional data and unconventional conduct: toward a methodological reorientation', Section on Deviance, Pacific Sociological Association, Long Beach, California, March 1967 (Ball, 1967b).
2. For self-reports of women seeking and obtaining abortions, both therapeutic (legal) and criminal, see Gebhard *et al.* (1958: 189–214).
3. For an extended statement by Polsky, see 'Research method, morality, and criminology' (1967: 117–149).
4. The following two paragraphs are drawn from a class lecture by Donald Bowlus given in 1960. For examples and discussions of reactivity, even within the context of carefully controlled experimental research – involving both infrahuman and human subjects, see Rosenthal (1966) and Friedman (1967).
5. This legal problem is also sometimes encountered by journalists.
6. Among others, see Natanson (1963), Schutz (1962; 1964), Garfinkel, (1967), Hill and Crittenden (1968), and most recently Nicholson (1969).
7. The material in this section has been revised (from Ball, 1967a), primarily by a shift in tense to the 'ethnographic past'.
8. For the *habitually deviant,* their deviance takes on the aspect of a *career* (Becker, 1963: 24–25, 101–102), for the *situationally* deviant, their deviance is an *event.* For a similar interpretation of the contrasting Mertonian (Merton, 1938) and Durkheimian (Durkheim, 1951 edition: 241–277) views of anomie, see Scott and Turner (1965).
9. Only one exception was observed, and she stayed overnight.
10. This triad, practitioner-patient-client, is probably much more common and the doctor-patient dyad much less common than the use of the latter as the 'typical model' by medical sociologists would suggest. See, for instance, Bloom (1963: 40–42, 52–58).
11. Garfinkel (1963 and 1964) discusses and demonstrates the importance of routine in interaction, and the tension and anxiety its absence promotes.
12. Compare Sykes and Matza (1957) and Matza (1964), where the analysis is individual rather than institutional, also Lofland (1969).
13. Excluded from the consideration is the telephone girl who was never in face-to-face, but only voice-to-voice interaction with patrons, but who was both medical-professional and supportive in her verbal demeanor. I have dealt with some of the contrasts between face-to-face and voice-to-voice interaction brought about by telephones, particularly opportunities for deceit, in Ball (1968).
14. By way of contrast, see the discussion of the patient as basically passive and helpless in Parsons (1951: 439–447).
15. Technically, this is not true. Some criminal abortions may involve techniques other than the dilation and scraping of the uterus. This procedure is the safest though, and most probable technique for the 'better' abortionists.
16. The sociology of respectability is more thoroughly explored in 'The problematics of respectability', as well as other papers in *Deviance and Respectability: The Social Construction of Moral Meanings,* Jack D. Douglas (ed.) (New York: Basic Books, 1970), pp. 326–371.
17. In his original discussion Douglas referred to situated and substantial *selves,* meaning *ego* as known to *alter.* This kind of terminological imprecision is common in the literature, with a consequent blurring of the important difference between alter's and ego's perspectives. We have, therefore, substituted the term identity in interpreting his discussion.
18. For a relatively recent summary which demonstrates how little is still actually known, see the excellent review of the literature by Schur (1965: 11–66).

References

Ball, Donald W. (1967a) 'An abortion clinic ethnography', *Social Problems* **14** (Winter), 293–301.

– (1967b) 'Conventional data and unconventional conduct: toward a methodological re-orientation', Presented to the section on Deviance, Pacific Sociological Association, Long Beach, March.

– (1968) 'Toward a sociology of telephones and telephoners', in *Sociology and Everyday Life,* Marcello Truzzi (ed.), Englewood Cliffs, N. J.: Prentice-Hall, pp. 59–75.

– (1970) 'The problematics of respectability', in *Deviance and Respectability: The Social Construction of Moral Meanings,* New York: Basic Books, pp. 326–71.

Becker, Howard S. (1963) *Outsiders,* New York: The Free Press.

Bloom, Samuel W. (1963) *The Doctor and His Patient,* New York: Russell Sage Foundation.

Cavan, Sherri (1966) *Liquor License: An Ethnography of Bar Behavior,* Chicago: Aldine.

Cicourel, Aaron V. (1968) *The Social Organization of Juvenile Justice,* New York: Wiley.

Cicourel, Aaron V. and Kitsuse, John I. (1963) *The Educational Decision-Makers,* Indianapolis: Bobbs-Merrill.

Cloward, Richard A. and Ohlin, Lloyd E. (1960) *Delinquency and Opportunity,* New York: The Free Press.

Cohen, Albert K. (1955) *Delinquent Boys: The Culture of the Gang,* New York: The Free Press.

Douglas, Jack D. (1967) *The Social Meanings of Suicide,* Princeton: Princeton U.P.

Durkheim, Emile (1951) *Suicide: A Study in Sociology,* New York: The Free Press.

Friedman, Neil (1967) *The Social Nature of Psychological Research: The Psychological Experiment as a Social Interaction,* New York: Basic Books.

Gebhard, P. H. *et al.* (1958) *Pregnancy, Birth and Abortion,* New York: Harper.

Garfinkel, Harold (1963) 'A conception of, and experiments with, "Trust" as a condition of stable concerted actions', in *Motivation and Social Interaction,* O. J. Harvey, (ed.), New York: The Ronald Press, pp. 187–238.

– (1964) 'Studies in the routine grounds of everyday activities', *Social Problems* **11** (Winter), 225–250. Reprinted in Garfinkel, 1967: 35–75.

– (1967) *Studies in Ethnomethodology,* Englewood Cliffs, N. J.: Prentice-Hall.

Goffman, Erving (1955) 'On face-work: an analysis of ritual elements in social inter-action', *Psychiatry* **18** (Aug.), 213–31.

– (1956) *Presentation of Self in Everyday Life,* Edinburgh: Social Sciences Research Centre, University of Edinburgh.

– (1963) *Encounters: Two Studies in the Sociology of Interaction,* Indianapolis: Bobbs-Merrill.

– (1963) *Stigma: Notes on the Management of Spoiled Identities,* Englewood Cliffs, N. J.: Prentice-Hall.

– (1969) 'The Insanity of Place', *Psychiatry* (Nov.), 357–88.

Gold, Ray (1958) 'Roles in sociological field observations', *Social Forces* **36** (Mar.), 217–33.

Hill, Richard J. and Crittenden, Kathleen Stones (eds) (1968) *Proceedings of the Purdue Symposium on Ethnomethodology,* Lafayette, Indiana: Purdue Research Foundation (Institute for the Study of Social Change, Department of Sociology, Purdue University; Institute Monograph Series, Number 1).

Hooker, Evelyn (1963) 'Male homosexuality', in *Taboo Topics,* Norman Farberow (ed.), New York: Atherton, pp. 44–55.

Lemert, Edwin M. (1951) *Social Pathology.* New York: McGraw-Hill.

– (1967) *Human Deviance, Social Problems, and Social Control,* Englewood Cliffs, N. J.: Prentice-Hall.

Lofland, John, with the assistance of Lyn H. Lofland (1969) *Deviance and Identity,* Englewood Cliffs, N. J.: Prentice-Hall.

Manning, Peter K. (forthcoming) 'Fixing what you feared: notes on the campus abortion search', in the *Sociology of Sex*, James M. Henslin (ed.), New York: Appleton-Century-Crofts.

Matza, David (1964) *Delinquency and Drift*, New York: Wiley.

Merton, Robert K. (1938) 'Social structure and anomie', *American Sociological Review* **3** (Oct.), 672–82.

Natanson, Maurice (ed.) (1963) *Philosophy of the Social Sciences: A Reader*, New York: Random House.

Nicholson, Robert F. (1969) 'Sociological homunculi: professional dilemmas in taking Alfred Schutz seriously', Presented to the Second Annual Conference on Existentialism and the Human Sciences. San Jose, California, 14–16 Nov.

Parsons, Talcot (1951) *The Social System*, New York: The Free Press.

Polsky, Ned (1967) *Hustlers, Beats, and Others*, Chicago: Aldine.

Roach, Mary Ellen and Eicher, Joan Bubolz, (eds) (1965) *Dress, Adornment, and the Social Order*, New York: Wiley.

Rosenthal, Robert (1966) *Experimenter Effects in Behavioral Research*, New York: Appleton-Century-Crofts.

Ryan, Mary Shaw (1966) *Clothing: A Study in Human Behavior*, New York: Holt, Rinehart and Winston.

Schur, E. M. (1965) *Crimes without Victims*, Englewood Cliffs, N. J.: Prentice-Hall.

Schutz, Alfred (1962) *Collected Papers, I: The Problem of Social Reality*, The Hague: Martinus Nijhoff.

– (1964) *Collected Papers, II: Studies in Social Theory*, The Hague: Martinus Nijhoff.

Scott, Marvin B. (1968) *The Racing Game*, Chicago: Aldine.

Scott, Marvin B. and Turner, Roy (1965) 'Weber and the anomic theory of deviance', *The Sociological Quarterly* **6** (Summer), 233–40.

Simmel, Georg (1950) *The Sociology of Georg Simmel*, Kurt H. Wolff (ed.), New York: The Free Press.

Stone, Gregory (1962) 'Appearance and the self', in *Human Behavior and Social Processes*, Arnold M. Rose (ed.), Boston: Houghton-Mifflin, 86–118.

Sykes, Gresham M., and Matza, David (1957) 'Techniques of neutralization: a theory of delinquency', *American Sociological Review* **22** (Dec.), 664–70.

Turner, Ralph H. (1968) 'The self-conception in social interaction', in *The Self in Interaction*, Chad Gordon and Kenneth J. Gergen (eds), New York: Wiley, 93–106.

Vaihinger, Hans (1927) *The Philosophy of 'As If'*, New York: Harcourt Brace Jovanovich.

Vold, George B. (1958) *Theoretical Criminology*, New York: Oxford U.P.

Webb, Eugene, Campbell, Donald T., Schwartz, Richard D. and Sechrest, Lee (1967) *Unobtrusive Measures: Nonreactive Measures in the Social Sciences*, Chicago: Rand McNally.

Wolff, Kurt H. (ed.) (1959) *Georg Simmel, 1858—1918*, Columbus: Ohio State University.

10

Behavioural study of obedience

S. Milgram

Introduction to Readings 10 and 11

Milgram's now famous series of experiments took place in the early 1960s. His complete account of them was published in 1974 (Milgram 1974) and included his replies to the several criticisms levelled against him. The article reprinted here reports the first of his experiments on obedience to authority and the critical note by Baumrind is directed at Milgram's first report.

Milgram's work has had a considerable impact both professionally and within the lay world (e.g. a popular account of his experiments and their implications appeared in the *Sunday Times*). This need not surprise us since the obedience of ordinary people to the inhumane orders of a malevolent authority has been seen as the characteristic pathology of mass society in the modern world. I need only mention Hannah Arendt's (Arendt 1963) view of Eichmann as an efficient bureaucrat or Mary McCarthy's view of Lt. Calley in Vietnam as an ambitious but conformist officer, to remind us of the lengths to which very ordinary members of the public will go when their 'legitimate' superiors demand that they commit mass murder.

Given that such events as the My Lai massacre or the Nazi extermination programme can be considered 'normal' by their perpetrators, a systematic investigation in the psychological laboratory of the limits of obedience by subjects seems to be a reasonable line of enquiry and, furthermore, one which has the merit of uniting the precision of a controlled experiment to a central issue of humanistic concern in the twentieth century. This is itself a strong reply to those critics of psychology who see it as the exact measurement of trivial phenomena.

Yet Milgram has attracted many charges against his experiments and, important though the implications of his work are, its significance is strongly disputed. Let us look at these criticisms under two headings: those concerned with the internal validity of his experiments and those concerned with their external validity (these terms are due to Campbell and Stanley 1963).

From L. S. Wrightman and J. C. Bingham (eds) *Contemporary Issues in Social Psychology,* Monterey: Brooks/Cole, 2nd edn, 1973, Article 17, pp. 173–81. This article was first published in *Journal of Abnormal and Social Psychology,* **67** (1963), 371–8.

Internal validity

This concerns the question of whether another interpretation of the experiment's finding is as plausible as the one reported by the experimenter. Milgram draws the basic conclusion from his work that a subject will (1) impute legitimate authority to the experimenter given certain contextual cues, and (2) obey the orders of the 'legitimate' authority even though those orders conflict with their internalised values (conscience).

'Internally valid' means in essence that the experimental results are not ambiguous, but at least one examination of psychological experiments concludes that ambiguity of interpretation is not unusual but in fact the norm (Crowle 1976). As Crowle points out 'the fundamental problem is that the human subjects are of the same order of complexity as the experimenters'. What might seem to be the same operationalised variable in an experiment may change its nature because of the interpretation which subjects place upon the experimenter's words or because the subjects may deceive the experimenter. Crowle conducted an experiment in which he tested the hypothesis that subjects who were highly committed to taking part in his experiment would be dishonest when asked if they had prior knowledge of the (ostensible) purposes of the experiment. He conducted the experiment so that (using stooges) subjects did learn about it while they were waiting to take part. Forty-five per cent of the high-commitment subjects were dishonest when asked after the experiment if they had known the details of the experiment: 23 per cent of the low-commitment subjects were also dishonest. Crowle manipulated the (independent) variable of commitment by asking some subjects to return. Those asked to return – it was reasoned – would be more highly committed to the experiment than those who were told that their part was finished. Crowle finds his own experimental results (the hypothesis stated above) ambiguous in retrospect because the manipulation of commitment in the experiment depended on the *meaning* assigned to the experimenter's words by the subject and the interpretation by the subject of *why* he was asked to return could vary in an uncontrolled manner.

What implications does this have for Milgram's experiments? The finding that subjects were often dishonest and the more committed subjects were more dishonest (leaving aside whether it was commitment to the experiment or to something else) in confessing their prior knowledge is important. Milgram's experiments in all their versions relied upon the subjects' belief that they were really inflicting shocks on innocent victims. By the end of the series (which covered 1960–63) 1,000 subjects had been used in several American cities. It is certainly possible that some subjects knew beforehand that the 'shock treatment' was a fake. Milgram relied on post-experimental interviews with subjects to assess whether or not they believed in the genuineness of the shock generator. But we can suspect (after Crowle's work) that some subjects might have lied. A strong point in favour of Milgram's interpretation is that his results continued to show a high proportion of subjects were willing to go to extreme shock levels from his first experiment to his last. One would assume that knowledge of the key feature of the experiment from the subjects' point of view (the fake shocks) would become more diffused the longer that the experiments continued. Yet even this interpretation cannot be definite since later experiments changed the nature of the independent variable ('orders from legitimate authority') by, for example, removing the experimenter's presence throughout the experiment, or placing a 'common man' as an interpreter of the experimenter's orders when the experimenter was absent. Thus (as Milgram predicted), later experiments tended to reduce the proportion of subjects proceeding to high shock levels (the dependent variable) anyway, because the legitimacy of the experimenter's authority was reduced, or because the agony of the victim was made more obvious to the subject.

External validity

This is the most disputed feature of Milgram's experiments. By external validity we mean whether the interpretation of the experiment will stand for other subjects, whether similar results could be obtained for other sorts of authority, or whether we could generalise from the infliction of painful but non-lethal shocks to behaviour by subjects which causes death or permanent bodily harm. It is this aspect of Milgram's findings which has most interested audiences which do not consist of professional behavioural scientists, although professionals are as much interested in this aspect as in the design or internal validity of the experiments.

Let us take these issues of the external validity of Milgram's work in turn.

Other subjects

This is a question of whether Milgram's subjects were unusual in comparison to the general population. Did they share some characteristic which affected their behaviour in the experiment which is uncommon in the general population? Were they, for example, more often authoritarian, or sadistic, or submissive? Surprisingly Milgram did not attempt to measure the personality characteristics of his subjects and compare the results with the general population, although this would have been a major undertaking. The subjects were a non-random sample recruited by newspaper advertisement which offered $4.00 for an hour's participation in a 'scientific study of memory and learning'. Milgram deliberately planned for a better cross-section of ages and occupations than is usual in psychological experiments where students are very often used. He was here anticipating the problem of generalising his results from the sample of subjects to a wider population, although his methods do not constitute in any sense a probability sample which alone can give sure inferences from sample to population.

Although Milgram's subjects could have been unusual as a group in a way which affected the results, it is for a critic to point out a likely extraneous independent variable which could have produced the strikingly high levels of obedience which he found. A good candidate for this role would be 'authoritarianism' which is strongly related to a willingness to see moral responsibility as lying with the organisation rather than with the individual.

Authoritarian individuals would be more likely to obey in extreme conditions than those who were not authoritarian (Adorno *et al*. 1950).

Milgram did not check on personality characteristics in a systematic way, but his complete account of his experiments contains several ethnographic case-studies of the personality of his subjects. He was impressed by the stress shown by the majority of subjects when placed in the position of reconciling 'legitimate' but inhumane actions with the apparent 'suffering' of the victim, contrary to their internalised values. Now, this sort of stress would not be characteristic of an 'authoritarian personality' and thus the reporting of stress in subjects disposes us to think that, as a group, they were not particularly authoritarian. This conclusion rests on the assumption that Milgram reports *typical* case-studies of stress in his subjects. All that is reported of the typicality of stress symptoms in Milgram's accounts comes from the paper reprinted here:

Many *subjects showed signs of nervousness . . . especially upon administering the more powerful shocks.* **In a large number** *of cases the degree of tension reached extremes that are rarely seen in sociopsychological laboratory studies.* (Milgram 1963, p. 191, my emphases – *editor*)

My conclusion is that 'authoritarianism' as a confounding extraneous independent variable can be ruled out, even though Milgram uses vague language in reporting the proportion of subjects showing marked signs of stress. 'Stress', we have further to assume, is symptomatic of the subject's not being authoritarian. It would have been better had Milgram measured authoritarianism in his subjects directly and shown that it was not an alternative explanation. You will note that my discussion of 'authoritarianism' is connected both with the internal and the external validity of the experiments. The most important question to ask of Milgram's experimental results is this: can we say that ordinary, common, men and women will obey orders to inflict pain (or worse) on others if they perceive the authority which gives those orders to be legitimate, and what are the limits of their obedience? This is the central issue as Milgram defines it, and is rightly the one which has attracted most attention. Milgram writes:

The aim of this investigation was to find when and how people would defy authority in the face of a clear moral imperative. There are, of course, enormous differences between carrying out the orders of a commanding officer during times of war and carrying out the orders of an experimenter. Yet the essence of certain relationships remain, for one may ask of a general: How does a man behave when he is told by a legitimate authority to act against a third individual? If anything, we may expect the experimenter's power to be considerably less than that of the general, since he has no power to enforce his imperatives . . . Despite these limitations, I thought it worthwhile to start careful observation of obedience even in this modest situation, in the hope that it would stimulate insights and **yield general propositions applicable to a variety of circumstances.** (Milgram 1974, p. 4, my emphasis – *editor*)

Other forms of authority

Milgram pursued his investigations, then, in the hope that his work would have high external validity for other organisations and for other forms of authority. It is precisely on this point that Baumrind attacks Milgram (the other point of Baumrind's attack is the ethical problem of the possible harm done to subjects).

Baumrind argues that the psychological laboratory induces a special 'set' in subjects. By 'set' psychologists mean the frame of reference which subjects bring to the experiment. This particular frame of reference included (a) the subject's belief in the worthiness and mystery of science, (b) the high prestige accorded to Yale University and to one of its professors, (c) definition of the victim as an innocent participant, and (d) the subject's own internalised values and moral rules (e.g. we assume for American subjects that the infliction of pain on a third party is usually considered wrong).

Baumrind seems to be saying that the elements (a) and (b) of the set were dominant in the Milgram experiments and were strong enough to override (c) and (d). The conflict in the subject's mind between the two parts of his 'set' produced the stressed behaviour upon which Milgram comments. Baumrind then goes on to remark that in Nazi Germany, SS men experienced no internal conflict because the elements of belief and perception in their 'set' were mutually supportive. Though this was almost certainly the case (cf. Bettelheim 1961) its relevance as a negative criticism of Milgram is doubtful. Milgram shows that ordinary American subjects will continue to obey orders which they believe to be (at the least) extremely painful to innocent victims and even though it causes the subjects serious stress. Need we be surprised, then if Germans (or Russians or Americans for that matter) committed atrocities in a context where legitimate authority had gone to great lengths to resolve their subordinates' potential internal conflict by such ideas as *'untermenschen'*, 'enemies of the people', or 'gooks'?

Baumrind chooses the wrong comparison with which to attack the external validity of Milgram's findings. The 'special quality of the set' which he notes in the Milgram experiment is in fact the location of the experiment in the impressive Interaction Laboratory of the very prestigious Yale University. An experimenter in this setting will be clothed in the legitimacy of science without any doubt. A better question to ask is: will subjects defy authority if its legitimacy is less well founded? With this sort of question the limits to obedience may be better determined and the generalisability of Milgram's findings to other contexts will be better documented.

After the first experiment reported here (and the only one which Baumrind was able to review in 1964), Milgram ran further experiments on obedience in which he introduced a number of variations. In one major variation the experiment was conducted in rented offices in a nearby industrial city, under the name of 'Research Associates of Bridgeport'; a name which had been contrived for the purpose and which had no known connection with Yale or with university research at all. The same procedures of the experiment, of recruitment, personnel, and characteristics of subjects were used. The results showed a slight drop in the level of obedience by subjects but not a significant one. Milgram thus effectively answers Baumrind's question.

The issue raised by Baumrind, though he uses a poor example for his argument, does lead us to look more closely at the independent variable in Milgram's experiments.

In its broadest sense, the independent variable can be stated as 'orders from legitimate authority' as the (presumed) cause of obedient behaviour (the effect or dependent variable). The independent variable actually consists of *two* related variables:

(a) *The basis of legitimate authority.* – In Milgram's first experiment the basis of his authority was Science, though this is not explicitly stated.

(b) *The content of the orders issued by legitimate authority.* What constitute acceptable orders depends on a subject's perception of the *scope* of a particular form of authority. Military authority, for example, is traditionally very wide in scope so that a soldier's dress or personal demeanour can be legitimately controlled as well as his use of weapons or deployment in battle. In contrast, the authority of a traffic warden is very strictly limited to parking a vehicle or licensing offences. The scope (Dahl 1957) of authority of science is wide precisely because the authority of the experimenter is diffuse. Lay subjects are unsure as to what psychology is and what can be properly asked of them. When the authority which issues the orders is a lay one (and known as such to the subjects) obedience has much lower limits, as Milgram showed in one of his variations where the experimenter left the laboratory and an obviously lay individual gave the orders, in the experimenter's name. Subjects' obedience to the layman (who was, of course, another stooge) was much lower than it was to the experimenter.

Similarly, in other variations of the basic experiment, obedience was markedly lower where two 'legitimate' scientific authorities gave contradictory orders or where an authority played the (reluctant) victim. Another significant variation on the basic experiment was one where the subject was influenced by peer-group pressure, which ran contrary to the experimenter's orders.

To summarise, then, the variations on the basic experiment clarified the nature of the independent variable and allowed us to see some limits to the external applications of the experiment. Where the authority is legitimate and diffuse in scope obedience to unethical orders will be high. Provided, that is, that authority is univocal in its orders and the subject is not met with strong counter-pressure from a peer group. The other factor which leads to high obedience is remoteness of the subject from the effects of his actions, since where subjects could see and hear the pain of the 'victims' they were less likely to obey. Still at issue, of course, is how people obey different types of authority (e.g. military, bureaucratic, familial, etc.). Since Milgram did not attempt experiments with different sorts of authority we cannot be sure. It is my conclusion that the perceived (i.e. by subjects) *scope* of legitimate orders issuing from authority is the key part of the complex independent variable of authority. The main criticism of Milgram should be that he does not seem to have recognised the complexity of his independent variable and, therefore, his results are limited in their generalisability. Even so, his complete report (Milgram 1974) is suggestive of the limits of obedience and the reader is invited to consult it.

References

Arendt, H. (1963) *Eichmann in Jerusalem: A Report on the Banality of Evil,* Viking Press.

Bettelheim, B. (1961) *The Informed Heart,* Thames and Hudson, (1970) and Paladin.

Campbell, D. T. and Stanley, J. C. (1963) 'Experimental and non-experimental designs for research in teaching', in N. L. Gage (ed.), *Handbook of Research on Teaching,* Rand McNally.

Crowle, A. J. (1976) 'The deceptive language of the laboratory', in R. Harre (ed.), *Life Sentences: Aspects of the Social Role of Language,* Wiley.

Dahl, R. A. (1957) 'The concept of power', *Behavioural Science,* **2,** 201–15.

Milgram, S. (1974) *Obedience to Authority,* Tavistock.

Obedience is as basic an element in the structure of social life as one can point to. Some system of authority is a requirement of all communal living, and it is only the man dwelling in isolation who is not forced to respond, through defiance or submission, to the commands of others. Obedience, as a determinant of behaviour, is of particular relevance to our time. It has been reliably established that from 1933–45 millions of innocent persons were systematically slaughtered on command. Gas chambers were built, death camps were guarded, daily quotas of corpses were produced with the same efficiency as the manufacture of appliances. These inhumane policies may have originated in the mind of a single person, but they could only be carried out on a massive scale if a very large number of persons obeyed orders.

Obedience is the psychological mechanism that links individual action to political purpose. It is the dispositional cement that binds men to systems of authority. Facts of recent history and observation in daily life suggest that for many persons obedience may be a deeply ingrained behaviour tendency, indeed, a prepotent impulse overriding training in ethics, sympathy, and moral conduct. C. P. Snow (1961) points to its importance when he writes:

When you think of the long and gloomy history of man, you will find more hideous crimes have been committed in the name of obedience than have ever been committed in the name of rebellion. If you doubt that, read William Shirer's 'Rise and Fall of the Third Reich'. The German Officer Corps were brought up in the most rigorous code of obedience . . . in the name of obedience they were party to, and assisted in, the most wicked large scale actions in the history of the world [p. 24].

While the particular form of obedience dealt with in the present study has its antecedents in these episodes, it must not be thought all obedience entails acts of aggression against others. Obedience serves numerous productive functions. Indeed, the very life of society is predicated on its existence. Obedience may be ennobling and educative and refer to acts of charity and kindness, as well as to destruction.

General procedure

A procedure was devised which seems useful as a tool for studying obedience (Milgram, 1961). It consists of ordering a naive subject to administer electric shock to a victim. A simulated shock generator is used, with 30 clearly marked voltage levels that range from 15 to 450 volts. The instrument bears verbal designations that range from Slight Shock to Danger: Severe Shock. The responses of the victim, who is a trained confederate of the experimenter, are standardized. The orders to administer shocks are given to the naive subject in the context of a 'learning experiment' ostensibly set up to study the effects of punishment on memory. As the experiment proceeds the naive subject is commanded to administer increasingly more intense shocks to the victim, even to the point of reaching the level marked Danger: Severe Shock. Internal resistances become stronger, and at a certain point the subject refuses to go on with the experiment. Behaviour prior to this rupture is considered 'obedience', in that the subject complies with the commands of the experimenter. The point of rupture is the act of disobedience. A quantitative value is assigned to the subject's performance based on the maximum intensity shock he is willing to administer before he refuses to participate further. Thus for any particular subject and for any particular experimental condition the degree of obedience may be specified with a numerical value. The crux of the study is to systematically vary the factors believed to alter the degree of obedience to the experimental commands.

The technique allows important variables to be manipulated at several points in the experiment. One may vary aspects of the source of command, content and form of command, instrumentalities for its execution, target object, general social setting, etc. The problem, therefore, is not one of designing increasingly more numerous experimental conditions, but of selecting those that best illuminate the *process* of obedience from the socio-psychological standpoint.

Related studies

The inquiry bears an important relation to philosophic analyses of obedience and authority (Arendt, 1958; Friedrich, 1958; Weber, 1947), an early experimental study of obedience by Frank (1944), studies in 'authoritarianism' (Adorno, Frenkel-Brunswik, Levinson, and Sanford, 1950; Rokeach, 1961), and a recent series of analytic and empirical studies in social power (Cartwright, 1959). It owes much to the long concern with *suggestion* in social psychology, both in its normal forms (e.g. Binet, 1900) and in its clinical manifestations (Charcot, 1881). But it derives, in the first instance, from direct observation of a social fact; the individual who is commanded by a legitimate authority ordinarily obeys. Obedience comes easily and often. It is a ubiquitous and indispensable feature of social life.

Method

Subjects
The subjects were 40 males between the ages of 20 and 50, drawn from New Haven and the surrounding communities. Subjects were obtained by a newspaper advertisement and direct mail solicitation. Those who responded to the appeal believed they were to participate in a study of memory and learning at Yale University. A wide range of occupations is represented in the sample. Typical subjects were postal clerks, high school teachers, salesmen, engineers, and laborers. Subjects ranged in educational level from one who had not finished elementary school, to those who had doctorate and other professional degrees. They were paid $4.50 for their participation in the experiment. However, subjects were told that payment was simply for coming to the laboratory, and that the money was theirs no matter what happened after they arrived. Table 10.1 shows the proportion of age and occupational types assigned to the experimental condition.

Table 10.1 Distribution of age and occupational types in the experiment.

Occupations	20–29 years n	30–39 years n	40–50 years n	Percentage of total (occupations)
Workers, skilled and unskilled	4	5	6	37.5
Sales, business and white-collar	3	6	7	40.0
Professional	1	5	3	22.5
Percentage of total (age)	20	40	40	

Note. Total $N = 40$.

Personnel and locale
The experiment was conducted on the grounds of Yale University in the elegant interaction laboratory. (This detail is relevant to the perceived legitimacy of the experiment. In a further variation, the experiment was dissociated from the university, with consequences for performance.) The role of experimenter was played by a 31-year-old high school teacher of biology. His manner was impassive, and his appearance somewhat stern throughout the experiment. He was dressed in a gray technician's coat. The victim was played by a 47-year-old accountant, trained for the role; he was of Irish-American stock, whom most observers found mild-mannered and likable.

Procedure

One naive subject and one victim (an accomplice) performed in each experiment. A pretext had to be devised that would justify the administration of electric shock by the naive subject. This was effectively accomplished by the cover story. After a general introduction on the presumed relation between punishment and learning, subjects were told:

But actually, we know very little about the effect of punishment on learning, because almost no truly scientific studies have been made of it in human beings.

For instance, we don't know how much punishment is best for learning — and we don't know how much difference it makes as to who is giving the punishment, whether an adult learns best from a youngster or an older person than himself — or many things of that sort.

So in this study we are bringing together a number of adults of different occupations and ages. And we're asking some of them to be teachers and some of them to be learners.

We want to find out just what effect different people have on each other as teachers and learners, and also what effect punishment will have on learning in this situation.

Therefore, I'm going to ask one of you to be the teacher here tonight and the other one to be the learner.

Does either of you have a preference?

Subjects then drew slips of paper from a hat to determine who would be the teacher and who would be the learner in the experiment. The drawing was rigged so that the naive subject was always the teacher and the accomplice was always the learner. (Both slips contained the word 'Teacher'.) Immediately after the drawing, the teacher and learner were taken to an adjacent room and the learner was strapped into an 'electric chair' apparatus.

The experimenter explained that the straps were to prevent excessive movement while the learner was being shocked. The effect was to make it impossible for him to escape from the situation. An electrode was attached to the learner's wrist, and electrode paste was applied 'to avoid blisters and burns'. Subjects were told that the electrode was attached to the shock generator in the adjoining room.

In order to improve credibility the experimenter declared, in response to a question by the learner: 'Although the shocks can be extremely painful, they cause no permanent tissue damage.'

Learning task

The lesson administered by the subject was a paired-associate learning task. The subject read a series of word pairs to the learner, and then read the first word of the pair along with four terms. The learner was to indicate which of the four terms had originally been paired with the first word. He communicated his answer by pressing one of four switches in front of him, which in turn lit up one of four numbered quadrants in an answer-box located atop the shock generator.

Shock generator

The instrument panel consists of 30 lever switches set in a horizontal line. Each switch is clearly labeled with a voltage designation that ranges from 15 to 450 volts. There is a 15-volt increment from one switch to the next going from left to right. In addition, the following verbal designations are clearly indicated for groups of four switches going from left to right: Slight Shock, Moderate Shock, Strong Shock, Very Strong Shock, Intense Shock, Extreme Intensity Shock, Danger: Severe Shock. (Two switches after this last designation are simply marked XXX.)

Upon depressing a switch: A pilot light corresponding to each switch is illuminated in bright red; an electric buzzing is heard; an electric blue light, labeled 'voltage energizer', flashes; the dial on the voltage meter swings to the right; various delay clicks are sounded.

The upper left-hand corner of the generator is labeled Shock Generator, Type ZLB, Dyson Instrument Company, Waltham, Mass. Output 15 volts–450 volts.

Details of the instrument were carefully handled to insure an appearance of authenticity. The panel was engraved by precision industrial engravers, and all components were of high quality. No subject in the experiment suspected that the instrument was merely a simulated shock generator.*

Sample shock

Each naive subject is given a sample shock on the shock generator, prior to beginning his run as teacher. This shock is always 45 volts, and is applied by pressing the third switch of the generator. The shock is applied to the wrist of the naive subject, and has its source in a 45-volt battery wired into the generator. This further convinces the subject of the authenticity of the generator.

Shock instructions

The subject is told to administer a shock to the learner each time he gives a wrong response. Moreover – and this is the key command – the subject is instructed to 'move one level higher on the shock generator each time the learner flashes a wrong answer'. He is also instructed to announce the voltage level before administering a shock. This serves to

---

*A related technique, making use of a shock generator, was reported by Buss (1961) for the study of aggression in the laboratory. Despite the considerable similarity of technical detail in the experimental procedures, both investigators proceeded in ignorance of the other's work. Milgram provided plans and photographs of his shock generator, experimental procedure, and first results in a report to the National Science Foundation in January 1961. This report received only limited circulation. Buss reported his procedure 6 months later, but to a wider audience. Subsequently, technical information and reports were exchanged. [. . .]

continually remind subjects of the increasing intensity of shocks administered to the learner.

Preliminary and regular run

Pretests revealed that the procedure of reading words and administering shocks requires some practice before it can be handled smoothly. Therefore, immediately preceding the regular run, the teacher is given a preliminary series of 10 words to read to the learner. There are 3 neutral words in the practice series (i.e. words that the learner answers correctly), so that shocks are administered for 7 of the words, with the maximum shock at 105 volts (moderate shock). Almost all subjects master the procedure by the time the preliminary run is over.

Subjects are then presented with a second list, and are told that the procedure is the same as for the first list; the experimenter adds, however:

When you get to the bottom of the list, repeat it over again and continue giving shocks, until the learner has learned all the pairs correctly.

The experimenter instructs the subject to

start from 15 volts and increase the shock level one step each time the learner gives a wrong answer.

Feedback from the victim

In all conditions the learner gives a predetermined set of responses to the word pair test, based on a schedule of approximately three wrong answers to one correct answer. In the present experimental condition no vocal response or other sign of protest is heard from the learner until Shock Level 300 is reached. When the 300-volt shock is administered, the learner pounds on the wall of the room in which he is bound to the electric chair. The pounding can be heard by the subject. From this point on, the learner's answers no longer appear on the four-way panel.

At this juncture, subjects ordinarily turn to the experimenter for guidance. The experimenter instructs the subject to treat the absence of a response as a wrong answer, and to shock the subject according to the usual schedule. He advices the subjects to allow 5-10 seconds before considering no response as a wrong answer, and to increase the shock level one step each time the learner fails to respond correctly. The learner's pounding is repeated after the 315-volt shock is administered; afterwards he is not heard from, nor do his answers reappear on the four-way signal box.

Experimenter feedback

At various points in the experiment the subject may turn to the experimenter for advice on whether he should continue to administer shocks. Or he may indicate that he does not wish to go on. It was important to standardize the experimenter's responses to these inquiries and reactions.

If the subject indicated his unwillingness to go on, the experimenter responded with a sequence of 'prods' using as many as necessary to bring the subject into line.

Prod 1: *Please continue.* or *Please go on.*
Prod 2: *The experiment requires that you continue.*
Prod 3: *It is absolutely essential that you continue.*
Prod 4: *You have no other choice, you* must *go on.*

The prods were always made in sequence: Only if Prod 1 had been unsuccessful, could Prod 2 be used. If the subject refused to obey the experimenter after Prod 4, the experiment was terminated. The experimenter's tone of voice was at all times firm, but not impolite. The sequence was begun anew on each occasion that the subject balked or showed reluctance to follow orders.

Special prods. If the subject asked if the learner was liable to suffer permanent physical injury, the experimenter said:

Although the shocks may be painful, there is no permanent tissue damage, so please go on. [*Followed by Prods 2, 3, and 4 if necessary.*]

If the subject said that the learner did not want to go on, the experimenter replied:

Whether the learner likes it or not, you must go on until he has learned all the word pairs correctly. So please go on. [*Followed by Prods 2, 3, and 4 if necessary.*]

Dependent measures

The primary dependent measure for any subject is the maximum shock he administers before he refuses to go any further. In principle this may vary from 0 (for a subject who refuses to administer even the first shock) to 30 (for a subject who administers the highest shock on the generator). A subject who breaks off the experiment at any point prior to administering the thirtieth shock level is termed a *defiant* subject. One who complies with experimental commands fully, and proceeds to administer all shock levels commanded, is termed an *obedient* subject.

Further records

With few exceptions, experimental sessions were recorded on magnetic tape. Occasional photographs were taken through one-way mirrors. Notes were kept on any unusual behaviour occurring during the course of the experiments. On occasion, additional observers were directed to write objective descriptions of the subjects' behaviour. The latency and duration of shocks were measured by accurate timing devices.

Interview and dehoax
Following the experiment, subjects were interviewed; open-ended questions, projective measures, and attitude scales were employed. After the interview procedures were undertaken to assure that the subject would leave the laboratory in a state of well-being. A friendly reconciliation was arranged between the subject and the victim, and an effort was made to reduce any tensions that arose as a result of the experiment.

Results

Preliminary notions
Before giving an account of the experimental results, it is instructive to consider how persons predict others will perform when commanded to administer powerful shocks to another person. Fourteen Yale seniors, all psychology majors, were provided with a detailed description of the experimental situation. They were asked to reflect carefully on it, and to predict the behaviour of 100 hypothetical subjects. More specifically, they were instructed to plot the distribution of obedience of '100 Americans of diverse occupations, and ranging in age from 20 to 50 years', who were placed in the experimental situation.

There was considerable agreement among the respondents on the expected behavior of hypothetical subjects. All respondents predicted that only an insignificant minority would go through to the end of the shock series. (The estimates ranged from 0 to 3 per cent; i.e. the most 'pessimistic' members of the class predicted that of 100 persons, 3 would continue through to the most potent shock available on the shock generator – 450 volts.) The class mean was 1.2 per cent. The question was also posed informally to colleagues of the author, and the most general feeling was that few if any subjects would go beyond the designation Very Strong Shock.

Result of experiment I
Subjects accept situation   With few exceptions subjects were convinced of the reality of the experimental situation, that they were administering shocks to another person, and the most potent shocks were extremely painful. In the post-experimental interview subjects were asked: 'How painful to the learner were the last few shocks that you administered to him?' Subjects were instructed to indicate their answers on a printed 14-point scale ranging from 'Not at all painful' to 'Extremely painful'. The modal response was 14 (Extremely painful) with the mean at 13.42.

Signs of extreme tension   Many subjects showed signs of nervousness in the experimental situation, and especially upon administering the more powerful shocks. In a large number of cases the degree of tension reached extremes that are rarely seen in sociopsychological laboratory studies. Subjects were observed to sweat, tremble, stutter, bite their lips, groan, and dig their finger-nails into their flesh. These were characteristic rather than exceptional responses to the experiment.

One sign of tension was the regular occurrence of nervous laughing fits. Fourteen of the 40 subjects showed definite signs of nervous laughter and smiling. The laughter seemed entirely out of place, even bizarre. Full-blown, uncontrollable seizures were observed for 3 subjects. On one occasion we observed a seizure so violently convulsive that it was necessary to call a halt to the experiment. The subject, a

Table 10.2 Distribution of breakoff points.

Verbal designation and voltage indication	Number of subjects for whom this was maximum shock
Slight shock	
15	0
30	0
45	0
60	0
Moderate shock	
75	0
90	0
105	0
120	0
Strong shock	
135	0
150	0
165	0
180	0
Very strong shock	
195	0
210	0
225	0
240	0
Intense shock	
255	0
270	0
285	0
300	5
Extreme intensity shock	
315	4
330	2
345	1
360	1
Danger: severe shock	
375	1
390	0
405	0
420	0
XXX	
435	0
450	26

46-year-old encyclopedia salesman, was seriously embarrassed by his untoward and uncontrollable behavior. In the post-experimental interviews subjects took pains to point out that they were not sadistic types, and that the laughter did not mean they enjoyed shocking the victim.

Distribution of scores It had been conjectured that persons would not, in general, agree to administer shocks beyond the level designated as Very Strong Shock. The distribution of maximum shocks for this experiment is shown in Table 10.2. The obtained distribution of scores deviates radically from the prediction.

Upon command of the experimenter, each of the 40 subjects went beyond the expected breakoff point. No subject stopped prior to administering Shock Level 20. (At this level – 300 volts – the victim kicks on the wall and no longer provides answers to the teacher's multiple-choice questions.)

Of the 40 subjects, 5 refused to obey the experimental commands beyond the 300-volt level. Four more subjects administered one further shock, and then refused to go on. Two broke off at the 330 volt level, and 1 each at 345, 360, and 375 volts. Thus a total of 14 subjects defied the experimenter. It is instructive to reprint their remarks at the point of defiance, as transcribed from the tape recordings:

[0124] *I think he's trying to communicate, he's knocking . . . Well it's not fair to shock the guy . . . these are terrific volts. I don't think that is very humane. . . . Oh, I can't go on with this; no, this isn't right. It's a hell of an experiment. The guy is suffering in there. No I don't want to go on. This is crazy. [Subject refused to administer more shocks.]*

[0123] *He's banging in there. I'm gonna chicken out. I'd like to continue, but I can't do that to a man. . . . I'm sorry I can't do that to a man. I'll hurt his heart. You take your check. . . . No really, I couldn't do it.*

These subjects were frequently in a highly agitated and even angered state. Sometimes, verbal protest was at a minimum, and the subject simply got up from his chair in front of the shock generator, and indicated that he wished to leave the laboratory.

Of the 40 subjects, 26 obeyed the orders of the experimenter to the end, proceeding to punish the victim until they reached the most potent shock available on the shock generator. At that point, the experimenter called a halt to the session. (The maximum shock is labeled 450 volts, and is two steps beyond the designation: Danger: Severe Shock.) Although obedient subjects continued to administer shocks, they often did so under extreme stress. Some expressed reluctance to administer shocks beyond the 300-volt level, and displayed fears similar to those who defied the experimenter; yet they obeyed.

After the maximum shocks had been delivered, and the experimenter called a halt to the proceedings, many obedient subjects heaved sighs of relief, mopped their brows, rubbed their fingers over their eyes, or nervously fumbled cigarettes. Some shook their heads, apparently in regret. Some subjects had remained calm throughout the experiment, and displayed only minimal signs of tension from beginning to end.

Discussion

The experiment yielded two findings that were surprising. The first finding concerns the sheer strength of obedient tendencies manifested in this situation. Subjects have learned from childhood that it is a fundamental breach of moral conduct to hurt another person against his will. Yet, 26 subjects abandon this tenet in following the instruction of an authority who has no special powers to enforce his commands. To disobey would bring no material loss to the subject; no punishment would ensue. It is clear from the remarks and outward behavior of many participants that in punishing the victim they are often acting against their own values. Subjects often expressed deep disapproval of shocking a man in the face of his objections, and others denounced it as stupid and senseless. Yet the majority complied with the experimental commands. This outcome was surprising from two perspectives: first, from the standpoint of predictions made in the questionnaire described earlier. (Here, however, it is possible that the remoteness of the respondents from the actual situation, and the difficulty of conveying to them the concrete details of the experiment, could account for the serious underestimation of obedience.)

But the results were also unexpected to persons who observed the experiment in progress, through one-way mirrors. Observers often uttered expressions of disbelief upon seeing a subject administer more powerful shocks to the victim. These persons had a full acquaintance with the details of the situation, and yet systematically underestimated the amount of obedience that subjects would display.

The second unanticipated effect was the extraordinary tension generated by the procedures. One might suppose that a subject would simply break off or continue as his conscience dictated. Yet, this is very far from what happened. There were striking reactions of tension and emotional strain. One observer related:

I observed a mature and initially poised businessman enter the laboratory smiling and confident. Within 20 minutes he was reduced to a twitching, stuttering wreck, who was rapidly approaching a point of nervous collapse. He constantly pulled on his earlobe, and twisted his hands. At one point he pushed his fist into his forehead and muttered: 'Oh God, let's stop it.' And yet he continued to respond to every word of the experimenter, and obeyed to the end.

Any understanding of the phenomenon of obedience must rest on an analysis of the particular conditions, in which it occurs. The following features of the experiment go some distance in explaining the high amount of obedience observed in the situation.

1. The experiment is sponsored by and takes place on the grounds of an institution of unimpeachable reputation, Yale University. It may be reasonably presumed that the personnel are competent and reputable. The importance of this background authority is now being studied by conducting a series of experiments outside of New Haven, and without any visible ties to the university.

2. The experiment is, on the face of it, designed to attain a worthy purpose – advancement of knowledge about learning and memory. Obedience occurs not as an end in itself, but as an instrumental element in a situation that the subject construes as significant, and meaningful. He may not be able to see its full significance, but he may properly assume that the experimenter does.

3. The subject perceives that the victim has voluntarily submitted to the authority system of the experimenter. He is not (at first) an unwilling captive impressed for involuntary service. He has taken the trouble to come to the laboratory presumably to aid the experimental research. That he later becomes an involuntary subject does not alter the fact that, initially, he consented to participate without qualification. Thus he has in some degree incurred an obligation toward the experimenter.

4. The subject, too, has entered the experiment voluntarily, and perceives himself under obligation to aid the experimenter. He has made a commitment, and to disrupt the experiment is a repudiation of this initial promise of aid.

5. Certain features of the procedure strengthen the subject's sense of obligation to the experimenter. For one, he has been paid for coming to the laboratory. In part this is canceled out by the experimenter's statement that:

> *Of course, as in all experiments, the money is yours simply for coming to the laboratory. From this point on, no matter what happens, the money is yours.* *

6. From the subject's standpoint, the fact that he is the teacher and the other man the learner is purely a chance consequence (it is determined by drawing lots) and he, the subject, ran the same risk as the other man in being assigned the role of learner. Since the assignment of positions in the experiment was achieved by fair means, the learner is deprived of any basis of complaint on this count. (A similar situation obtains in Army units, in which – in the absence of volunteers – a particularly dangerous mission may be assigned by drawing lots, and the unlucky soldier is expected to bear his misfortune with sportsmanship.)

7. There is, at best, ambiguity with regard to the prerogatives of a

---

*Forty-three subjects, undergraduates, at Yale University, were run in the experiment without payment. The results are very similar to those obtained with paid subjects.

psychologist and the corresponding rights of his subject. There is a vagueness of expectation concerning what a psychologist may require of his subject, and when he is overstepping acceptable limits. Moreover, the experiment occurs in a closed setting, and thus provides no opportunity for the subject to remove these ambiguities by discussion with others. There are few standards that seem directly applicable to the situation, which is a novel one for most subjects.

8. The subjects are assured that the shocks administered to the subject are 'painful but not dangerous'. Thus they assume that the discomfort caused the victim is momentary, while the scientific gains resulting from the experiment are enduring.

9. Through Shock Level 20 the victim continues to provide answers on the signal box. The subject may construe this as a sign that the victim is still willing to 'play the game'. It is only after Shock Level 20 that the victim repudiates the rules completely, refusing to answer further.

These features help to explain the high amount of obedience obtained in this experiment. Many of the arguments raised need not remain matters of speculation, but can be reduced to testable propositions to be confirmed or disproved by further experiments.†The following features of the experiment concern the nature of the conflict which the subject faces.

10. The subject is placed in a position in which he must respond to the competing demands of two persons: the experimenter and the victim. The conflict must be resolved by meeting the demands of one or the other; satisfaction of the victim and the experimenter are mutually exclusive. Moreover, the resolution must take the form of a highly visible action, that of continuing to shock the victim or breaking off the experiment. Thus the subject is forced into a public conflict that does not permit any completely satisfactory solution.

11. While the demands of the experimenter carry the weight of scientific authority, the demands of the victim spring from his personal experience of pain and suffering. The two claims need not be regarded as equally pressing and legitimate. The experimenter seeks an abstract scientific datum; the victim cries out for relief from physical suffering caused by the subject's actions.

12. The experiment gives the subject little time for reflection. The conflict comes on rapidly. It is only minutes after the subject has been seated before the shock generator that the victim begins his protests. Moreover, the subject perceives that he has gone through but two-thirds of the shock levels at the time the subject's first protests are heard. Thus he understands that the conflict will have a persistent aspect to it, and may well become more intense as increasingly more powerful shocks are required. The rapidity with which the conflict

---

†A series of recently completed experiments employing the obedience paradigm is reported in Milgram (1965).

descends on the subject, and his realization that it is predictably recurrent may well be sources of tension to him.

13. At a more general level, the conflict stems from the opposition of two deeply ingrained behavior dispositions: first, the disposition not to harm other people, and second, the tendency to obey those whom we perceive to be legitimate authorities.

References

Adorno, T., Frenkel-Brunswik, E., Levinson, D. J., and Sanford, R. N. (1950) *The Authoritarian Personality*. New York: Harper.

Arendt, H. (1958) 'What was authority?', in C. J. Friedrich (ed.), *Authority*. Cambridge: Harvard U.P., pp. 81–112.

Binet, A. (1900) *La suggestibilité*. Paris: Schleicher.

Buss, A. H. (1961) *The Psychology of Aggression*. New York: Wiley.

Cartwright, S. (ed.) (1959) *Studies in Social Power*. Ann Arbor: University of Michigan, Institute for Social Research.

Charcot, J. M. (1881) *Oeuvres complètes*. Paris: Bureaux du Progrès Médical.

Frank, J. D. (1944) 'Experimental studies of personal pressure and resistance', *Journal of General Psychology*, **30**, 23–64.

Friedrich, C. J. (ed.) (1958) *Authority*. Cambridge: Harvard U.P.

Milgram, S. (1961) 'Dynamics of obedience'. Washington, D.C.: National Science Foundation, 25 Jan. (mimeo).

Milgram, S. (1965) 'Some conditions of obedience and disobedience to authority', *Human Relations*, **18**, 57–76.

Rokeach, M. (1961) 'Authority, authoritarianism, and conformity', in I. A. Berg and B. M. Bass (eds), *Conformity and Deviation*. New York: Harper, pp. 230–57.

Snow, C. P. (1961) 'Either-or', *Progressive*, Feb., 24.

Weber, M. (1947) *The Theory of Social and Economic Organization*. Oxford: Oxford U.P.

11

Reactions to Milgram's 'Behavioural study of obedience'

D. Baumrind

... Most experimental conditions do not cause the subjects pain or indignity, and are sufficiently interesting or challenging to present no problem of an ethical nature to the experimenter. But where the experimental conditions expose the subject to loss of dignity, or offer him nothing of value, then the experimenter is obliged to consider the reasons why the subject volunteered and to reward him accordingly.

The subject's public motives for volunteering include having an enjoyable or stimulating experience, acquiring knowledge, doing the experimenter a favor which may some day be reciprocated, and making a contribution to science. These motives can be taken into account rather easily by the experimenter who is willing to spend a few minutes with the subject afterwards to thank him for his participation, answer his questions, reassure him that he did well, and chat with him a bit. Most volunteers also have less manifest, but equally legitimate, motives. A subject may be seeking an opportunity to have contact with, be noticed by, and perhaps confide in a person with psychological training. The dependent attitude of most subjects toward the experimenter is an artifact of the experimental situation as well as an expression of some subjects' personal and need systems at the time they volunteer.

The dependent, obedient attitude assumed by most subjects in the experimental setting is appropriate to that situation. The 'game' is defined by the experimenter and he makes the rules. By volunteering, the subject agrees implicitly to assume a posture of trust and obedience. While the experimental conditions leave him exposed, the subject has the right to assume that his security and self-esteem will be protected.

There are other professional situations in which one member – the patient or client – expects help and protection from the other – the physician or psychologist. But the interpersonal relationship between experimenter and subject additionally has unique features which are

From L. S. Wrightman and J. C. Bingham (eds) *Contemporary Issues in Social Psychology,* Monterey: Brooks/Cole, 2nd edn, 1973, Article 18, pp. 182–5. This article is extracted from 'Some thoughts on ethics of research'. After reading: Milgram's *'Behavioral study of obedience; American Psychologist,* **19** (1964), 421–3.

likely to provoke initial anxiety in the subject. The laboratory is unfamiliar as a setting and the rules of behavior ambiguous compared to a clinician's office. Because of the anxiety and passivity generated by the setting, the subject is more prone to behave in an obedient, suggestible manner in the laboratory than elsewhere. Therefore, the laboratory is not the place to study degree of obedience or suggestibility, as a function of a particular experimental condition, since the base line for these phenomena as found in the laboratory is probably much higher than in most other settings. Thus experiments in which the relationship to the experimenter as an authority is used as an independent condition are imperfectly designed for the same reason that they are prone to injure the subjects involved. They disregard the special quality of trust and obedience with which the subject appropriately regards the experimenter.

Other phenomena which present ethical decisions, unlike those mentioned above, *can* be reproduced successfully in the laboratory. Failure experience, conformity to peer judgment, and isolation are among such phenomena. In these cases we can expect the experimenter to take whatever measures are necessary to prevent the subject from leaving the laboratory more humiliated, insecure, alienated, or hostile than when he arrived. To guarantee that an especially sensitive subject leaves a stressful experimental experience in the proper state sometimes requires special clinical training. But usually an attitude of compassion, respect, gratitude, and common sense will suffice, and no amount of clinical training will substitute. The subject has the right to expect that the psychologist with whom he is interacting has some concern for his welfare and the personal attributes and professional skill to express his goodwill effectively.

Unfortunately, the subject is not always treated with the respect he deserves. It has become more commonplace in sociopsychological laboratory studies to manipulate, embarrass, and discomfort subjects. At times the insult to the subject's sensibilities extends to the journal reader when the results are reported. Milgram's (1963) study is a case in point. The following is Milgram's abstract of his experiment:

This article describes a procedure for the study of destructive obedience in the laboratory. It consists of ordering a naive S to administer increasingly more severe punishment to a victim in the context of a learning experiment. Punishment is administered by means of a shock generator with 30 graded switches ranging from Slight Shock to Danger: Severe Shock. The victim is a confederate of E. The primary dependent variable is the maximum shock the S is willing to administer before he refuses to continue further. 26 Ss obeyed the experimental commands fully, and administered the highest shock on the generator. 14 Ss broke off the experiment at some point after the victim protested and refused to provide further answers. The procedure created extreme levels of nervous tension in some Ss. Profuse sweating, trembling, and stuttering were typical expressions of this emotional disturbance. One unexpected sign of tension – yet to be be explained – was the regular occurrence of nervous laughter, which in some Ss developed into uncontrollable seizures. The variety of interesting behavioral dynamics observed in the experiment, the reality of the situation for the S, and the possibility of parametric variation within the framework of the procedure, point to the fruitfulness of further study.

The detached, objective manner in which Milgram reports the emotional disturbance suffered by his subject contrasts sharply with his graphic account of that disturbance. Following are two other quotes describing the effects on his subjects of the experimental conditions:

I observed a mature and initially poised businessman enter the laboratory smiling and confident. Within 20 minutes he was reduced to a twitching, stuttering wreck, who was rapidly approaching a point of nervous collapse. He constantly pulled on his earlobe, and twisted his hands. At one point he pushed his fist into his forehead and muttered : 'Oh, God, let's stop it.' And yet he continued to respond to every word of the experimenter, and obeyed to the end (Reading 10, p. 234).

In a larger number of cases the degree of tension reached extremes that are rarely seen in sociopsychologcal laboratory studies. Subjects were observed to sweat, tremble, stutter, bite their lips, groan and dig their fingernails into their flesh. These were characteristic rather than exceptional responses to the experiment.

One sign of tension was the regular occurrence of nervous laughing fits. Fourteen of the 40 subjects showed signs of nervous laughter and smiling. The laughter seemed entirely out of place, even bizarre. Full-blown, uncontrollable seizures were observed for 3 subjects. On one occasion we observed a seizure so violently convulsive that it was necessary to call a halt to the experiment . . . (Reading 10, p. 232).

Milgram does state that,

After the interview, procedures were undertaken to assure that the subject would leave the laboratory in a state of well-being. A friendly reconciliation was arranged between the subject and the victim, and an effort was made to reduce any tensions that arose as a result of the experiment (Reading 10, p. 231).

It would be interesting to know what sort of procedures could dissipate the type of emotional disturbance just described. In view of the effects on subjects, traumatic to a degree which Milgram himself considers nearly unprecedented in sociopsychological experiments, his casual assurance that these tensions were dissipated before the subject left the laboratory is unconvincing.

What could be the rational basis for such a posture of indifference? Perhaps Milgram supplies the answer himself when he partially explains the subject's destructive obedience as follows: 'Thus they assume that the discomfort caused the victim is momentary, while the scientific gains resulting from the experiment are enduring (p. 236).' Indeed such a rationale might suffice to justify the means used to achieve his end if that end were of inestimable value to humanity or were not itself transformed by the means by which it was attained.

The behavioral psychologist is not in as good a position to objectify his faith in the significance of his work as medical colleagues at points of breakthrough. His experimental situations are not sufficiently accurate models of real-life experience; his sampling techniques are seldom of a scope which would justify the meaning with which he would like to endow his results; and these results are hard to reproduce by colleagues with opposing theoretical views. Unlike the Sabin vaccine, for example, the concrete benefit to humanity of his particular piece of work, no matter how competently handled, cannot justify the risk that real harm will be done to the subject. I am not speaking of physical discomfort, inconvenience, or experimental deception per se, but of permanent harm, however slight. I do regard the emotional disturbance described by Milgram as potentially harmful because it could easily affect an alteration in the subject's self-image or ability to trust adult authorities in the future. It is potentially harmful to a subject to commit, in the course of an experiment, acts which he himself considers unworthy, particularly when he has been entrapped into committing such acts by an individual he has reason to trust. The subject's personal responsibility for his actions is not erased because the experimenter reveals to him the means which he used to stimulate these actions. The subject realizes that he would have hurt the victim if the current were on. The realization that he also made a fool of himself by accepting the experimental set results in additional loss of self-esteem. Moreover, the subject finds it difficult to express his anger outwardly after the experimenter in a self-acceptant but friendly manner reveals the hoax.

A fairly intense corrective interpersonal experience is indicated wherein the subject admits and accepts his responsibility for his own actions, and at the same time gives vent to his hurt and anger at being fooled. Perhaps an experience as distressing as the one described by Milgram can be integrated by the subject, provided that careful thought is given to the matter. The propriety of such experimentation is still in question even if such a reparational experience were forthcoming. Without it I would expect a naive, sensitive subject to remain deeply hurt and anxious for some time, and a sophisticated, cynical subject to become even more alienated and distrustful.

In addition the experimental procedure used by Milgram does not appear suited to the objectives of the study because it does not take into account the special quality of the set which the subject has in the experimental situation. Milgram, is concerned with a very important problem namely, the social consequences of destructive obedience. He says,

Gas chambers were built, death camps were guarded, daily quotas of corpses were produced with the same efficiency as the manufacture of appliances. These inhumane policies may have originated in the mind of a single person, but they could only be carried out on a massive scale if a very large number of persons obeyed orders (p. 224).

But the parallel between authority-subordinate relationships in Hitler's Germany and in Milgram's laboratory is unclear. In the former situation the SS man or member of the German Officer Corps, when obeying orders to slaughter, had no reason to think of his superior officer as benignly disposed towards himself or their victims. The victims were perceived as subhuman and not worthy of consideration. The subordinate officer was an agent in a great cause. He did not need to feel guilt or conflict because within his frame of reference he was acting rightly.

It is obvious from Milgram's own descriptions that most of his subjects were concerned about their victims and did trust the experimenter, and that their distressful conflict was generated in part by the consequences of these two disparate but appropriate attitudes. Their distress may have resulted from shock at what the experimenter was doing to them as well as from what they thought they were doing to their victims. In any case there is not a convincing parallel between the phenomena studied by Milgram and destructive obedience as that concept would apply to the subordinate-authority relationship demonstrated in Hitler Germany. If the experiments were conducted 'outside of New Haven and without any visible ties to the university', I would still question their validity on similar although not identical grounds. In addition, I would question the representativeness of a sample of subjects who would voluntarily participate within a non-institutional setting.

In summary, the experimental objectives of the psychologist are seldom incompatible with the subject's ongoing state of well-being, provided that the experimenter is willing to take the subject's motives and interests into consideration when planning his methods and correctives. Section 4b in *Ethical Standards of Psychologists* (APA, undated) reads in part:

Only when a problem is significant and can be investigated in no other way, is the psychologist justified in exposing human subjects to emotional stress or other possible harm. In conducting such research, the psychologist must seriously consider the possibility of harmful aftereffects, and should be prepared to remove them as soon as permitted by the design of the experiment. Where the danger of serious aftereffects exists, research should be conducted only when the subjects or their responsible agents are fully informed on this possibility and volunteer nevertheless (p 12).

From the subject's point of view procedures which involve loss of dignity, self-esteem, and trust in national authority are probably most harmful in the long run and require the most thoughtfully planned reparations, if engaged in at all. The public image of psychology as a profession is highly related to our own actions, and some of these actions are changeworthy. It is important that as research psychologists we protect our ethical sensibilities rather than adapt our personal standards to include as appropriate the kind of indignities to which Milgram's subjects were exposed. I would not like to see experiments such as Milgram's proceed unless the subjects were fully informed of the dangers of serious aftereffects and his correctives were clearly shown to be effective in restoring their state of well-being.

References

American Psychological Association (undated) *Ethical Standards of Psychologists: A Summary of Ethical Principles,* Washington, D.C.: APA.

Milgram, S. (1963) 'Behavioral study of obedience', *Journal of Abnormal and Social Psychology,* **67,** 371–8.

12

Sampling minority populations

B. M. Hedges

Introduction to Reading 12

Hedges' article is concerned with obtaining probability samples of minorities.

By 'probability' we imply that the survey researcher wishes at some point in the analysis to draw conclusions about the population (all the minority group members) from the evidence of the sample. 'Minority' means any social category – e.g. Jamaicans, university teachers, homosexuals, motorcyclists – which is substantially less than half of the general population of an area such as England and Wales or Great Britain: The word 'minority' does not carry here the spurious pejorative connotations which contemporary usage has given it.

As Hedges points out, the size of the minority under investigation is one important factor in the cost of obtaining an adequate sample. There are other factors to do with the nature of the minority which bear upon both the cost of obtaining a sample of sufficient size and its adequacy in terms of representativeness. One such factor which should be borne in mind is the extent to which a minority is 'hidden'; the extent to which its members conceal their minority characteristics from public knowledge. Hedges does not deal with this question because his assumption is that once contacted a member of a minority category will have no more than the average reluctance or enthusiasm to be questioned. Yet his methods can be adapted even to this sort of 'minority', as long as the ethics and techniques of gaining the confidence of respondents are observed as well.

The Rev. Laud Humphries, (Humphries, 1970) an American sociologist, undertook a study of homosexuals who used public lavatories for sexual liaisons ('tea rooms' in American slang, 'cottages' in English). He had first to identify typical tea rooms and then to contact its homosexual users. Although Humphries was not concerned with collecting a probability sample, he was keen that his sample was reasonably representative and was not obviously biased by such means as interviewing only respondents who were willing to give him their addresses on the spot. From Humphries' description of the nature of such contacts, he would have found only an unusual minority of his minority willing to agree to an interview in that context.

This paper is previously unpublished.

Humphries would also have compromised his observational role as voyeur had he revealed his academic interest at that point. What he did, in order to interview as many as possible of the tea-room men he identified, was to note down the licence numbers of their cars and to trace their names and addresses from licence records (in confidence). This is a form of 'locational' sampling in Hedge's terms, although it hardly compares to contacting air-travellers at airports to give another example of locational sampling. Also, of course, Humphries was concerned as much with the dynamics and roles of the 'tea-room trade' as he was with the backgrounds and characteristics of tea-room customers; so he was both participant observer and survey researcher.

The availability of a list or sampling frame of some sort is the usual starting point for drawing a sample. If the list contains only minority group members then sampling problems reduce to questions concerned with the coverage provided by the list, e.g. who is likely to be missed from the list, will that affect the representativeness of the sample? If, however, a list covers a population in which the minority is scattered, then some method of 'screening' the list to identify the minority is required. Hedges discussed 'screening' thoroughly, with respect to techniques and efficiency (and therefore costs).

A research problem which frequently arises is one in which no lists, or very inadequate ones, are obtainable. Hedges suggests area sampling as a way round this problem, but as he points out, much depends on *how* the minority is physically distributed. Where a minority is evenly distributed throughout a city or other geographically defined area, the need to sample small areas first, and then screen a large number of households to find members of the minority can be inefficient and therefore expensive. We can be thankful, as researchers, that many minorities are physically concentrated in cities thus making the sampling task easier. Even so, one must keep Hedges' point in mind that though a minority is concentrated, many of its members may be found outside the concentration and these individuals must also have an equal chance of appearing in the sample.

Although the social patterns of residence in Britain are such that ethnic minorities tend to live in particular districts one cannot always rely on this fact to draw samples through area sampling. The researcher must be prepared to be eclectic and inventive in his sampling methods. An illustration of this need was research in a West Riding city into the fertility aspirations of Jamaican immigrants to Britain (research carried out by S. R. Goodman). Unfortunately, the Census tabulates 'West Indians' rather than Jamaicans, British Guyanans, Barbadians, etc. and although the Small Area Statistics from the 1961 Census could be used to show the enumeration districts in which West Indians were concentrated, there was no way of distinguishing Jamaicans as such.

Since the research was concerned with Jamaican families, the population was defined as Jamaican women between fifteen and forty-five who had borne at least one child and who were resident in the West Riding city. The research aimed to interview every member of the population in the city.

Though not strictly a *sampling* exercise, exactly the same problems of identification and coverage were presented by this population as if it had been a sample.

The solution adopted was to use a number of sources to identify and enumerate the target population. A start was made with health visitors' lists which contained the precise place of origin of the mother. Other lists used included those of the Local Education Authority, which sometimes contained place of origin sufficiently exactly to identify Jamaicans, and information from headmistresses about their pupils' mothers' country of origin. These last two sources were rather haphazard with regard to (a) completeness, and (b) knowledge of precise country of mother's origin. In addition, only the health visitors' lists contained information about children up to five years of age. Education lists contain information for children from nearly five years to school-leaving age.

Interviews were begun with mothers identified from the lists named above. At the end of each interview the interviewers asked for the names and addresses of other Jamaicans whom the respondent knew in the city. Many new names were gathered in this way and visited to see if they qualified. The researcher also contacted the West Indian community leaders and West Indian clubs, both to introduce himself and to assure the community of his goodwill. In the course of these contacts extra names were obtained.

Towards the end of the interviewing phase of the research, comparison of names gathered from respondents began to show that the new individuals had already been identified. As this pattern became confirmed the conclusion was drawn that the target population had been as fully enumerated as possible. Of course, lone Jamaicans not in touch with their community would be missed, so that the target population could never be fully enumerated. Comparison of the sample in terms of its characteristics of occupation, social class, mental states, age and number of children would normally be carried out against the most up-to-date census figures for the city. This was not possible because of the census tabulation of 'West Indian' rather than of origins by individual islands.

References

Humphries, Laud (1970) *The Tea Room Trade,* Duckworth.

Sample survey work in Britain in the 1950s and early 1960s was characterised by a marked emphasis on obtaining a broad picture of the entire population, or of major segments of it.

In the past decade or so there has been an important change of emphasis. Nationally representative samples of households or of adults, though not uncommon, do not dominate the scene to the extent that they previously did. Far more projects than formerly are undertaken among minority groups within the population.

Considerable problems have as a result been posed for research design, and not only because of the high cost of searching for small minorities in a large population. It is the purpose of this reading to explore these problems and discuss possible solutions, with the aid of a variety of examples. We shall take minority population surveys to be primarily those designed to obtain a sufficient sample of members of the minority group for its characteristics to be analysed; such surveys need to be distinguished from those designed solely to estimate the size of the group.

The problems

The problems of sampling minorities are of several kinds. Probably the most important is economic. It is evident that a sufficiently large general population sample must contain sufficient minority group members. But 'screening' a large general population sample to find minority group members is expensive, and the sample designer must consider whether more economical solutions can be found.

But there is another type of problem. The principal frame for sampling the British population, the Electoral Register, gives reasonably good coverage of the population as a whole, but the small proportion of addresses missing from the Electoral Register may be ones in which the target group is particularly likely to be found (as is the case, in fact, with coloured immigrants). A sampling frame which covers, say 95 per cent of a population might well cover only 50 per cent of a specified small minority – or might even omit it entirely.

A third problem is the absence of good prior information about the minority concerned. In a general population survey there is a great deal of data which will help to design the sample and assess the quality of the results. When surveying a minority the sample designer may not know even its size, let alone its characteristics; he will not easily be able to design an efficient sample, nor will he have any prior information with which to compare his results in order to detect the presence of bias.

The use of lists

The two main approaches to sampling minorities are *the use of lists* and *screening*.

A list of members of the target population is the best basis for sampling, provided it meets certain criteria, notably completeness of coverage, absence of duplication, up-to-dateness of addresses and convenient format and ordering. The problems associated with using lists are well documented in the literature (e.g. Kish, 1965), and will not be discussed at length here. For many minority populations no list at all is available. Where one does exist it may well have important shortcomings in respect of one or more of the criteria referred to above. Incompleteness is perhaps the most common problem, often because the list is out of date; or because the purpose for which it was compiled did not require comprehensive coverage; or because the process of compilation was not sufficiently thorough. Omissions are particularly likely to occur when the people whom the list is intended to cover must themselves take action to appear on it.

Some practical examples will illustrate the diversity of the problems that occur, and will demonstrate that it is sometimes possible to compile lists that do not initially exist in complete and accessible form.

Very often the statement defining the group to be surveyed immediately suggests the likelihood of a list being available in a form suitable for sampling. This is particularly true of small groups with a coherent identity; for example, surveys have been carried out among Members of Parliament, and little thought is needed to see that a list of MPs must be publicly available. There have, similarly, been surveys of the elected members of local authorities (e.g. Field, 1975). A recent survey was conducted among the officials of major trade unions (Stowell, 1978): here too, we would expect a list to exist, though it might be less easily accessible. A somewhat less extreme example is provided by certain professions with a numerous membership, such as doctors and solicitors. Because of the requirements of their calling, their existence must be recorded (otherwise they are not allowed to practice). Usable lists may not be readily accessible, however, and in particular they are likely not to be entirely up-to-date. Doctors, for example, may be recorded at hospitals from which they have now moved on, and they may not readily be traceable. This is a salutary reminder that it is not enough to know that a person exists: there also needs to be a way to contacting him reasonably economically.

An interesting solution to the problem of out-of-date addresses was employed in a survey of social science graduates of certain years at certain universities (Westoby *et al.,* 1976). Some of their graduation years preceded the survey by as much as fifteen years, and the only available addresses were those applying at graduation. It was thought likely that *some* of the graduates would still be at the same addresses, or could be readily traced through them, but not enough to reduce possible biases to safe magnitudes. Accordingly, with each questionnaire mailed to these last known addresses went lists of fellow-graduates of the same place and year, with a request for up-to-date addresses, if known, for any on the list. By this means, capitalising on the fact that there is a tendency for graduates to keep in touch with at least some of their former fellow-students, a much improved address list was compiled and a higher response rate thus achieved. A similar procedure was adopted in the survey described by Kelsall *et al.* (1972).

A list of members of another professional group, hospital nurses, was known to exist piecemeal: it was held by individual hospital management committees (HMCs), but not centrally. The compilation of a central list would have been an enormous task. The solution to this sampling problem was to select the sample in two stages. First a sample of HMCs was selected; then, within each, a sample of nurses was selected (Morton-Williams, 1971). Such a design needs care to maintain equal chances of selection for every element in the population: one way to achieve this, as in the survey referred to above, is to select HMCs with equal probability and take a uniform proportion of nurses within all the selected HMCs. But if the necessary data are available in advance it may be more efficient to let the selection probabilities of HMCs vary in proportion to the number of nurses they have. An appropriate sampling fraction is then used to select nurses from the lists provided by the selected HMCs in such a way that all nurses in the survey population have equal chances of selection.

In 1976, when a survey of motorcyclists was begun (Courtenay, 1978), there were over a million motorcyclists, and it was not unthinkable that a sample of them could have been found by 'screening' a large general population sample. But this would have been very expensive, and two alternatives were accordingly considered. The first was to follow up people who had already been identified as motorcyclists in a recent large transport survey. It was soon established that the number of these was insufficient for the purpose, but in any case there were certain objections to such a proceeding. Chief among these was the time interval: both surveys involved fieldwork systematically spread over a year, and although they overlapped in time the gap between the identification of a motorcyclist on the transport survey and his re-interview on the motorcycle survey could have been very long in some instances. There would thus be loss (and possibly a resultant bias) due to people changing addresses. It would also mean that people who had just acquired motorcycles (who might be an important group for the purpose of the second survey, which was concerned with safety) would tend to be under-represented. Another factor was the desirability of avoiding re-interviews in a situation where respondents to the earlier interview had not been asked whether they would mind being approached again. The suggestion is not infrequently made that samples of minorities should be obtained from large surveys conducted for other purposes, but similar objections usually apply. It is neccessary to accumulate several successive repetitions of a regular survey, such as the General Household Survey, in order to provide enough members of the minority group, the time-interval objection is likely to have particular force unless the follow-up interviews can be similarly phased, a procedure that on other grounds may not be desirable. The third scheme considered, and finally adopted, for the motorcycle survey, was the use of lists. There was no list of motorcyclists as such, but a list of *motorcycles* was available from vehicle licence records. The use of such a sampling frame, however, involved acceptance of the risk of bias due to the omission of unlicensed vehicles. A motorcyclist's chance of selection is also proportionate to the number of registered motorcycles he has, but this can, if appropriate, be dealt with by weighting after obtaining this information from him.

The sample design was complicated by the fact that vehicle licenses were in the process of transfer from local taxation offices to the Driver and Vehicle Licensing Centre at Swansea. A systematic procedure was being adopted of transferring them in order of suffix letter (denoting year of registration), so that at any one office some of the original records would have gone to Swansea and others not. It was therefore necessary to divide the population of motorcycle registrations into two strata, those at Swansea and those still at local offices. The first (and much larger) stratum was readily sampled from the computer file; the second stratum was sampled by a procedure analogous to that used to sample nurses – a sample of local offices was first selected, and registrations were then sampled within them.

The use of a list of motorcycles as a substitute for one of motorcyclists is a fairly obvious one. A less obvious substitute was employed in a survey of people moving out of the London borough of Southwark (Fernando and Hedges, 1976). Migration is a very important issue, especially for London, and it is necessary to find some way of surveying movers of various kinds. People who move into (or within) an area can be surveyed by screening a general population sample within that area, but movers out usually cannot be found by screening a general sample of the population outside the area, because they will form far too small a proportion of it for this to be practical.

Following them up from their previous address is the principal alternative. But how are they to be identified and traced? There is no easy way. The Southwark survey found an interesting substitute for a list of movers, namely a list of electricity account terminations in a four-month period. This list was supplied by the local Electricity Board. Forward addresses were available for most (about three-quarters) of these, and a sample of those who had moved to addresses outside the borough was interviewed. The limitations of this method are worth noting. If an individual (or group) moved out of a household that stayed at the address he would be missed. So would tenants paying for electricity to a landlord who had the account with the Board. Also missed would be those with no ascertainable new address: in this particular survey these were discarded at the time of sample selection, but contact with the Post Office (or, possibly, neighbours) might have produced addresses and thus reduced their number.

As is usual, especially when unfamiliar sampling methods have been used, an attempt was made to find data with which the survey results could be compared in order to assess whether the limitations of the method had led to substantial biases. The best source found was the 1971 Census, but close comparisons were not possible for a variety of reasons. It was tentatively concluded that the method had produced a not unexpected upward socio-economic bias, but in other respects it seemed to have been reasonably satisfactory.

This was a case where a list, admittedly with deficiencies, was perhaps unexpectedly found to be available. Sometimes the reverse is found: a group for which lists might be expected to exist cannot in the event be sampled by this convenient method. In 1977 a survey was begun of users of legal services (Wood, 1978). Now since solicitors, the principal providers of legal services directly to the public, know who their clients are, it might be expected that a solution could be found along the lines of the nurses' sampling via HMCs: legal service users via solicitors. This solution was considered, but was abandoned (in favour of a general population screening) for the following reasons. First, it was unlikely that access to the records of a properly representative sample of solicitors could be obtained. Both practical and ethical considerations would be likely to lead many to refuse their cooperation. Second, even had access been obtained there would have been large technical and practical problems to overcome. These will not be discussed at length here, but as an illustrative example the problem of compiling lists of users from solicitors' records may be considered. Solicitors are likely to have files on each case, but will not necessarily have comprehensive files on each client. If a sample of cases is taken, clients with more legal business will be overrepresented in the sample: the compilation of a client list eliminating such duplication is thus likely to be a necessary first step. But duplication between solicitors would be harder to eliminate. A client who had had work done by more than one solicitor also has thereby a greater chance of inclusion, and there is no ready means of dealing with this. In spite of its superficial similarity, this sampling problem is *not* closely analogous to that exemplified by the hospital nurses' survey.

The reference to ethical considerations in the foregoing paragraph prompts the general reflection that by the nature of many minorities, lists – where they exist – are quite likely to be confidential: for example, people in receipt of welfare benefits, or on low incomes, or attending a family planning clinic.

Screening

If the sample designer does not find, or cannot get access to, a suitable list, or cannot compile one, he is likely to be obliged to consider some form of population screening: that is to say, taking a general population sample sufficiently large to contain an adequate number of members of the minority group. It is evident that if the minority group is small, the general population sample will have to be correspondingly large. Suppose, for instance, that the minority forms 1 per cent of the population, and that 500 members of it are required. Then the screening sample would need to number 50,000. Nevertheless, screening methods have been successfully employed even in extreme cases such as this, although their most frequent application is to larger minorities forming more than just 1 or 2 per cent of the total.

The critical nature of the size of the percentage is readily illustrated by Table 12.1 which shows the size of screening sample needed to get 500 members of the specified minority group under various assumptions about the incidence of that group. The incidence of the minority group may not be known in advance with any precision. It may well be necessary, therefore, to employ a design of a sequential kind. If, for instance, a part of the screening work is done first, it may be used to make the required estimate of the minority group's incidence, and thus to enable a decision to be taken about the number of further screening interviews needed. It is essential in such designs that the first part of the screening should itself constitute a properly representative sample.

Table 12.1

Incidence (%)	Size of screening sample required
1	50,000
2	25,000
3	16,666
4	12,500
5	10,000
10	5,000

Non-response is a problem in all survey work, but it can be particularly troublesome in sampling small minority groups by screening methods. This is because the number of non-respondents in the screening sample is large relative to the number of minority group members. Suppose that a screening sample of 5,000 is selected; that 4,000 respond; that 400 of these are minority group members. The response rate at the screening stage among the survey population as a whole is 80 per cent: but what is the response rate among the minority group itself? If it is assumed to be the same, 80 per cent, then there must be 500 minority group members altogether, from 400 of whom a response has been obtained. But this 500 is an estimate based on a rather uncertain assumption: it is possible – though not very likely – that there are as few as 400 or as many as 1,400 in all, so that the response rate among the minority could be as high as 100 per cent or as low as 29 per cent. This uncertainty about the response rate makes it more difficult to gauge the likelihood of bias being present in the survey results.

Screening by personal interview

It is clearly essential to use screening methods that obtain a high level of response. This can be achieved by personal interview screening, but only if the screening interview is simple. How simple it will be depends largely on the way the minority group is defined: we must clearly have enough information to establish whether or not the person or household contacted is or is not a member of the minority group.

It is sometimes tempting, however, to add futher items of information to the screening interview in order to permit additional sophistication in the sample design. Consider, for example, a survey, initiated in late 1977, for which the defined target population was certain ethnic groups living in poor housing (Field, 1978). It is not entirely easy to define either an ethnic group or poor housing, so the screening operation already involved a sufficiently stiff task. However, it was further suggested that because of the importance of socio-economic group to the survey's objectives, the screening should record this too: it would then be possible to take differing proportions of the various socio-economic groups for a full interview. To establish socio-economic groups requires a substantial number of questions about occupation; these are asked on many surveys, but usually at the end of the interview, not at the beginning. It was thus possible that the addition of socio-economic questions might cause the response rate at screening to fall, and the improvement to the sample design permitted by this extra information had to be carefully weighed against the potential loss.

Where the definition of the minority involves multiple characteristics, care taken about the ordering of the questions can reduce the total workload. Suppose, for example, that in the case mentioned above, a much higher proportion of those approached will be in poor housing than will be members of the specified ethnic groups. It is in that case better, if other things are equal, to ask the ethnic questions first, to save wasting a lot of time on establishing the housing conditions of people who will then prove to be ineligible on ethnic grounds.

Screening procedures cannot necessarily be expected to identify the required minority group with complete precision, even when the questioning is brief and specific. For example, Woolf (1971) noted a tendency for some persons near the boundaries of a specified age group to mis-state their ages. The solution adopted was to extend the boundaries of the screened age range, thus bringing in those who formed part of the original target but would, wrongly, have been missed. Those who really were outside the original target range were included at the screening but were eliminated at the subsequent full interview.

This example illustrates a general point. Screening error can arise either from 'false negatives' (elements that should be included, but are missed) or from 'false positives' (elements that should not be included, but are). The first category presents the more serious problem, since it may introduce a bias; the second, provided that it is possible subsequently to eliminate the false positives, merely involves wasted effort. If accurate classification cannot be relied on, it is better to err on the side of false positives.

The amount of screening can sometimes be reduced by using a household-based approach in place of an individual one. The Compensation Survey was designed to examine the circumstances of those who had suffered a variety of mishaps such as industrial accidents. In principle a sample of individuals could have been selected, contacted and screened. It was thought that a screening sample of 30,000 or more would be needed. The approach that was in fact adopted was to sample 15,000 *households,* which contained rather more than 30,000 adult individuals. At most households it was possible, by speaking to one of the household members, to find out whether *any* of the household members were eligible for interview. Thus only 15,000 contacts were needed to find the required number of eligible persons, instead of 30,000 contacts that would have been required by the alternative method.

The economy offered depends on whether the screening can be, so to speak, at 'second-hand' with *any* member of the household, as it was in this case. If everyone in the household has to be interviewed separately to establish membership of the minority group, there will be less saving relative to approaches to a sample of individuals selected independently. But if one person can tell the interviewer whether the others are members of the minority group or not, the savings can be considerable. They may be partially off-set, however, by the likelihood of intra-household correlation, which tends to diminish the statistical efficiency of this type of design.

An extension of the idea of identifying minority population membership through third parties is found in 'multiplicity sampling' (Nathan, 1976). But applications of this technique have been confined to making estimates of the size of certain minority populations, and it does not appear to have been used for obtaining samples of such populations.

Screening by postal methods
Screening need not necessarily involve personal interviews: postal screening is an alternative that has been successfully employed (Cartwright, 1964; Parker, 1978), but response rates on postal surveys are very variable and it is necessary to do a careful pilot test to ensure that rates of response are going to be acceptably high. There are other difficulties with postal screening. One is that if a minority is being sought there may be some bias in the response, members of the target group being more likely to reply than others. In one sense this is all to the good, but it may mislead the researcher about the true size of the minority group within the population. Although making an estimate of the size of the group is usually not his principal aim, this is a useful piece of information about which an unbiased estimate is clearly to be preferred. In postal surveys response is likely to be more dependent on interest in the subject than in interview surveys, and a biased response may occur *within* the minority group, with a higher level of response

from the more interested. A further complication may be caused by well meaning recipients of postal questionnaires passing them on to friends whom they believe would be more interested, thus undermining the basis of the sampling: Scott (1961), in a general paper on postal surveys, discusses response by persons other than the addressee. Some minority groups are particularly difficult to screen postally, for example, Asian immigrant populations, where language barriers may impede response. Furthermore, the deficiencies in the coverage of such groups by the Electoral Register, a convenient frame, are also more easily coped with in a personal interview screen than in a postal screen.

However, postal methods offer one advantage which, important in any survey, is especially so in one that involves large numbers of contacts to elicit simple information prior to a full interview. That advantage is low unit cost. Postal methods are thus well worth consideration in screening for minorities, and various methods can be used to minimise the potential problems referred to above: for example, a subsample of non-respondents may be personally contacted in an attempt to establish whether or not they belong to the minority group. Leach (1975) describes a postal screening of young West Indians in which personal calls were used in support of a basically postal approach. An account of another postal screening exercise is given by Milne (1977).

Area sampling

In Britain, area sampling is not used nearly as widely as it is in the United States. In both countries most national samples will begin with the selection of a sample of areas, but whereas in Britain the sampling of individuals or households within those areas will usually be based on a publicly available frame (most commonly the Electoral Register), United States' practice is to compile a list of dwellings within the area (which may, for example, be a city block); the list of dwellings can then be screened either *in toto* or on a sample basis.

It is principally in sampling minorities that area sampling procedures have a useful role in British practice. One situation in which they are valuable is where the minority is defined in precise geographical terms with boundaries that do not coincide with conveniently identifiable portions of the customary frames. An example of this is provided by a survey of railway noise (Fields *et al.,* 1976), which required that interviews be made with people living within a certain distance of a railway line. The boundaries of this corridor were mapped, and a list of the dwellings it contained was compiled. The Electoral Register's arrangement in urban areas is by street within polling district, and although it would have been possible, with the aid of field visits, to identify on it the addresses contained in a specified area, it was considered that the process would be more cumbersome than compiling a fresh list. In rural areas the Electoral Register's arrangement is by alphabetical order of elector names, and the difficulties of relating addresses to a mapped area is much greater; so, of course, is the compilation of an address list.

A second use of area sampling occurs in relation to the use of Census data to identify areas to be surveyed: examples of this are studies of urban deprivation as defined by Census indicators, or of immigrant populations. The smallest areal unit analysed in the British Census is the Enumeration District, which contains on average about 150 addresses. If Enumeration Districts are selected for survey, it may well be more convenient, as it was in the railway noise example above, to compile a list of addresses within each than to map them on to the Electoral Register.

When Census or other available information is used to select districts containing a minority population, attention needs to be paid to the stability of this characteristic over time. Some characteristics are relatively persistent: that is to say if a district has that characteristic at one period (say, at Census time) it will tend also to have it some years later (at the date, say, of a survey). Population density, tenure and socio-economic composition are probably fairly stable characteristics; Osborne (1975) reporting on a study of day-care, suggests that the proportion of households with children under five may be a good deal less stable.

One of the advantages of a freshly compiled list, if it is accurately made, is that it will be complete and thus not suffer from the incomplete coverage that is one of the limitations of the Electoral Register as a sampling frame. But it must be stressed that considerable care is needed in compiling address lists, and enumerators must be provided with detailed instructions. It may be advantageous to equip them with copies of the Electoral Register which they can use where convenient, ticking off addresses as they find them and adding in any unregistered ones they find. The extent to which this will be of practical value will depend on the configuration of streets and buildings in the area.

In screening for minority groups it is often possible to employ large, dense clusters, since only a small proportion will finally prove to be members of the minority group and the *effective* cluster size will not be particularly large. As a rough rule of thumb, about 15 interviews per PSU (primary sampling unit) is often considered suitable for a general population sample: for a minority forming 5 per cent, say, it would thus be reasonable to undertake about 300 screening interviews per PSU, since this would yield an average of 15 effective interviews. However, account must be taken of the likely distribution of the minority group across areas: if it is very uneven, some areas may have unacceptably large clusters of final interviews.

Where large, dense clusters are required, area sampling is often a convenient method, giving enumerators a more compact work-load than conventional frames can provide. However, the Electoral Register can be used – in urban areas at least – to provide reasonably compact clusters. An example of this is provided by the Compensation Survey already referred to, in which the PSUs consisted of addresses contained within blocks of 158 consecutive elector names. These addresses mostly tend to be adjacent, but at the end of each street the Electoral Register moves on to the next street *alphabetically,* which may be in another part of the polling district. However, the fact that polling districts are usually not very large prevents the cluster from becoming unduly fragmented.

In a sample based on Census data and using Enumeration Districts (EDs) as its base, it may happen that the entire ED constitutes a convenient cluster, and all dwellings within it can, after listing, be screened. If the required cluster size is smaller than this, the ED can first be subdivided into segments by mapping, and ED segments can form the PSUs. Alternatively, the ED can remain as the PSU, but a sample of its constituent dwellings, instead of all, is screened.

In any particular case, the decision between area sampling and conventional frames must depend on a variety of factors, including the size of the minority, its distribution, cluster sizes and any geographical restriction imposed by the nature of the survey. If the survey is concerned with a minority that is particularly likely to be omitted from the Electoral Register, the compilation of a fresh address list is an attraction of area sampling, but it should be noted that omissions can at least partly be made good in Electoral Register sampling using the principle of half-open interval sampling described, for example, by Moser and Kalton (1971). Half-open interval sampling was used in the Compensation Survey.

Sampling immigrant minorities

An important application of minority sampling techniques has been concerned with immigrant minorities. Analysis of Census data shows that many immigrant subpopulations are geographically concentrated in a small number of areas. Even though they might form less than 1 per cent, say, of the total population, and thus be uneconomical to screen by means of a general population sample, it is evident that screening would be perfectly practicable if it could be confined to areas in which these groups were concentrated.

Such an approach is permissible, however, only if the degree of concentration is very marked: there are few survey populations other than immigrant groups of which this is true. As Kish (1965) observed there are areas in the USA which are occupied largely or exclusively by rich people, but most rich people nevertheless live scattered elsewhere, and the concentrations are thus of little use for sampling purposes.

The degree of concentration of a population can be expressed in the form of a curve like that given in Fig. 12.1. To plot the curve (known as a 'Lorenz curve') it is necessary first to list districts in descending order of target group membership, see Table 12.2. For simplicity, it is assumed that the populations of all districts are equal; it does not then matter whether we talk about the proportion of the population covered or the proportion of districts covered, since they are equivalent.

Table 12.2

	a Population	b No. in target group	c Cumulative population	%	d Cumulative number in target group	%	e Density percen- tage (d/c)
District 1	150	70	150	2	70	10	47
District 2	150	63	300	4	133	19	44
District 3	150	55	450	6	188	27	42
District 4	150	47	600	8	235	34	39
.	.	.	.		.		.
.	.	.	.		.		.
.	.	.	.		.		.
.	.	.	.		.		.
District 50	150	0	7,500	100	700	100	0
Total for 50 districts	7,500	700	7,500		700		9

It will be obvious that if it were decided to survey only the district with the highest proportion (District 1) only 10 per cent of the target population would be covered, an unacceptably low figure. By going further down the list and taking in more districts, a rapid improvement is made in the proportion of the target group covered. But the price to be paid is the necessarily decreasing density of target group members within these districts: taking the top four, for example, the target group now forms only 235 out of 600 (30%). More screening will thus be needed to obtain each target group interview. The further we go down the list, the lower this percentage (the density percentage) will become.

The point at which it is decided to draw the line is thus a compromise. The incidence percentage must be kept reasonably high, yet the survey must take in most if not all of the target population. If it does not, the results may be biased. This is a very real possibility: it is clear, for example, that immigrants living in non-immigrant districts may have different characteristics from those in predominantly immigrant districts, and their exclusion will result in a bias whose acceptability must depend on the aims of the survey. One major survey among immigrants (Smith, 1976) drew the line at the point at which 80 per cent of immigrants were included.

As already noted, the degree of concentration can be shown as a Lorenz curve by plotting the percentage form of columns c and d of the above table against each other. If the minority population is evenly distributed throughout the parent population, the result will be a straight line (a). But if it is concentrated, the result will be a curve somewhere to the right of (a), for example at (b). The shape of the curve is affected not only by the actual facts of the distribution of the

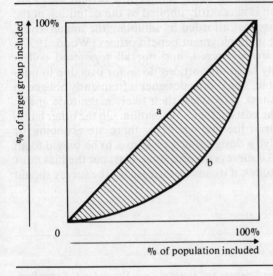

Fig. 12.1

target group but also by the type of district chosen. In general, the smaller the district units the more likely it is that useful patterns of concentration will be found. Most work of this kind in Britain has used Census Enumeration Districts. Also, as will be evident, it is necessary that distributional information be available in advance of the survey. It is no use having a concentrated target population if the extent and location of concentrations is not known. The Census is the only effective source of British Small Area Statistics, and offers either Enumeration Districts or wards, which are very much larger (though in principle intermediate units could be built by aggregating Enumeration Districts). There is virtually no useful information for the polling districts into which wards are subdivided in the Electoral Register.

Locational sampling

While the use of special lists and screening exercises are the most common, they are not the only methods of sampling minorities. The most important class of methods among the remainder is probably locational sampling, in which members of the minority are sampled at a particular location at which, by definition, they are likely to attend. Examples of this have been air travellers, as in the International Passenger Surveys carried by the Social Survey Division of the Office of Population Censuses and Surveys; users of a particular bus service (Smith, 1974); users of sports centres (Prescott-Clarke, 1978); and museum visitors (Wingfield-Digby, 1974). These groups could in principle be sampled by screening, but at uneconomic cost. They are particularly obviously suited to being sampled at certain locations, since use of the location is necessarily implied by the definition of the group. A less direct case was afforded by sampling the unemployed, who were contacted at unemployment benefit offices (Wood, 1977). Not all unemployed are registered, and not all registered collect benefits, but sufficiently large proportions do so for bias due to non-coverage to be acceptable. The survey designer is frequently obliged to accept such biases: his task is to assess their likely magnitude and to balance them against the costs of their elimination. On the other hand, he must be ready to draw the line whenever there are economic or other pressures to evolve a design which he knows to be biased to an unacceptable degree. All surveys involve some bias, but the bias must be kept to small magnitudes: if it cannot, the case for the survey should be re-examined.

References

Cartwright, A. (1964) *Human Relations and Hospital Care,* Routledge & Kegan Paul.

Courtenay, G. (1978) *A Survey of Motorcyclists,* Social and Community Planning Research (SCPR), p. 416.

Fernando, E. and Hedges, B. M. (1976) *Moving out of Southwark,* SCPR, p. 387.

Field, J. (1975) *Gloucestershire: A Survey of Attitudes Among Elected Representatives,* SCPR, p. 366.

– (1978) *Housing Stress Survey* (Methodological report), SCPR, p. 490.

Fields, J. M., Walker, J. G. and Large, J. B. (1976) 'Designing a national sample of railway noise in Great Britain', Proceedings of INTER-NOISE, 1976, Zurich, Switzerland: National Institute of Noise Control Engineering, pp. 203–8.

Kelsall, R., Poole, A. and Kuhn, A. (1972) 'The questionnaire in a sociological research project', *British Journal of Sociology,* **23**, 344–57.

Kish, L. (1965) *Survey Sampling,* New York: Wiley.

Leach, B. (1975) 'Postal screening for a minority group: young West Indians in Leeds', *Urban Studies,* **12**, 285–94.

Milne, A. (1977) 'Response to a postal sift of addresses', OPCS Methodological paper.

Morton-Williams, J. (1971) *Nurses' Attitude Survey,* SCPR, p. 194.

Moser, C. A. and Kalton, G. (1971) *Survey Methods in Social Investigation,* 2nd edn, Heinemann.

Nathan, G. (1976) 'An empirical study of response and sampling error for multiplicity estimates with different counting rules', *Journal of the American Statistical Association,* **71**, No. 357.

Osborne, A. (1975) *The Day Care of Children Under 5 in Westminster,* Westminster City Council, Social Services Dept., Nov.

Parker, S. R. (1978) *Retirement Survey,* OPCS (to be published).

Prescott-Clarke, P. (1978) *Joint Provision: The School Leaver and the Community,* SCPR, p. 431.

Scott, C. (1961) 'Research on mail surveys', *Journal of the Royal Statistical Society,* **A124,** 143–205.

Smith, D. J. (1976) 'The facts of racial disadvantage', Broadsheet No. 560, PEP.

Smith, D. V. L. (1974) *London Transport Minibus Study* (Methodological report), SCPR, p. 255.

Stowell, R. (1978) *Survey of Trade Union Officers* (Methodological report), SCPR, p. 487.

Westoby, A., Webster, D. and Williams, G. (1976) *Social Scientists at Work,* University of Surrey, Guildford: Society for Research into Higher Education.

Wingfield-Digby, P. (1974) *Visitors to Three London Museums,* HMSO.

Wood, D. S. (1977) *The Young Unemployed,* SCPR, p. 458.

– (1978) *Survey of Users of Legal Services,* SCPR, p. 491.

Woolf, M. (1971) *Family Intentions,* HMSO.

Section 4

Data collection and codification

13

An index for designation of Educational Priority Areas

A. Little and C. Mabey

Introduction to Reading 13

The policy objective of the Plowden Report on *Children and their Primary Schools* was the recommendation for Educational Priority Areas. This was to be a compensatory programme directed at *schools* which had a higher than average proportion of low-achieving children. From the findings of the Plowden-commissioned National Survey of Primary School Children, it was expected that schools such as these would be located in poor neighbourhoods where a high number of parents were unskilled, where housing was poor, and where the . . . 'neighbourhood [was one] where the jobs people do and the status they hold owe little to their education [and where] it is natural for children as they grow older to regard school as a brief prelude to work rather than an avenue to future opportunities' (Plowden 1967, reading 1).

Somewhat later, well after the Plowden Report was published (January 1967), its critics recorded their grave doubts about the Plowden strategy as a means of compensating the children from schools in 'EPA' areas. One major criticism by Acland (who re-analysed the Plowden Survey data) was that the schools thought to be poor in the Plowden analysis did not contain all or most of the low-achieving children. Many such children were not in EPA schools. (Acland 1971a, reading 2).

If compensation for educational disadvantage is to be carried out through designated schools and not aimed specifically at the real problem – the low-achieving child, then the policy will be inefficient. Many children in EPA schools do not require extra help (but the EPA policy would give it to them) and many children who do need extra help will not get it, because they are not in EPA schools. As Bynner (1978) writes: 'The Plowden Committee was using a blunderbuss to hit a very specific target, the low achieving child.'

Little and Mabey (of the Inner London Education Authority's Research and Statistics Group) define the aim of the work reported in this article as '. . . an attempt to create an instrument that turned a policy objective into administrative practice'. The policy objective had to be taken as a 'given' as did the reasoning behind the Plowden Committee's recommendation of positive dis-

From A. Shonfield and S. Shaw (eds) *Social Indicators and Social Policy,* London: Heinemann, 1972, Ch. 5, pp. 67–93.

crimination in favour of low-achieving children through the *agency* of EPAs. The failure of EPAs to do the task set for them is a weakness attributable to Plowden and not to Little and Mabey. When the ILEA group tried to operationalise the criteria for classifying schools and their neighbourhoods as EPAs, the limitations of the Plowden policy became apparent to these authors as they note in their article.

Little and Mabey imposed two limitations on their work from the start – their measures to classify schools had to be unobtrusive, and the exercise had to be relatively cheap. Unobtrusive measures in this case meant the use of information already recorded as a matter of routine for other research or for general administrative purposes. In other words, Little and Mabey used secondary sources of data rather than primary sources as the means to meet their requirements to be both unobtrusive and cheap.

also – not much time available

A problem of secondary source material is that one has to rely on information collected by another agency in pursuit of ends different to those of the researchers. Sometimes this proves compatible with the researcher's aim as in the case of the proportion of pupils receiving free school meals, considered as an indicator of the incidence of poverty. The rules for calculating disposable income for a family, and the level of income set as the poverty-line will differ on one indicator (free school meals) compared to another (e.g. Family Income Supplement). But if the one indicator, for which information is readily available, is comparable across schools, because it is administered in the same way, then we should have a reasonable reliable measure of family poverty. The *validity* of the measure will be problematic, simply because what constitutes 'family poverty', is dependent on a datum line which must be arbitrary. Still, good reliability is highly desirable, and 'receipt of free school meals' is valid as a measure on the face of it, although it might distribute the population differently, to FIS for example.

Another problem if one relies on secondary sources only is that the information required has never been collected by another agency because no one saw a use for the material. This is the case with the variable 'size of family' which figures as one aspect of EPAs in Plowden but which was not available to Little and Mabey. The variable could not be obtained from the 1961 Census tabulations to which they had access, nor could a standard and reliable measure of 'size of family' be obtained from the school by the school reports of the Care Committee workers who are all unpaid volunteers. The size of a 'large family' was not defined; some interpreted it as three or more children, some as four or more, and some even six or more children. Furthermore, some workers reported the number of children in a school who came from large families, and some reported the number of large families in a school. The use of these reports would have been unreliable. Low reliability must mean low validity, though not necessarily vice versa.

The use of secondary sources always brings problems for the researcher and often means that some variables have to be omitted from the analysis despite their relevance. Little and Mabey had to leave out the variable of 'incomplete families' which was specifically suggested by the Plowden Report as one associated with EPAs because information was not available.

Secondary source material often means that variables as originally defined cannot be used, again because of lack of information, but substitutes may be found. Substitute variables may be reasonable replacements for the originals if they seem to 'tap' the dimension of concern equally well. A good example of this is Little and Mabey's use of lack of basic housing amenities derived from 1961 Census data, where Plowden had specified sharing a house as an indicator of housing stress. Not to have exclusive use of an inside W.C. or bath, for example, is an indicator of housing stress in its own right and, in any event, more likely to be the case where a house has been inadequately subdivided among more than one family. This variable is a reasonable substitution for the Plowden one of 'shared houses', particularly since it is clear from the context that Plowden means what is now better known as 'housing stress', which can take several manifestations and therefore for which several indicators could be used.

More dubious is the substitution of a proportion of immigrant children, which was used as an indicator in Little and Mabey's Index, for the Plowden definition of one aspect of EPAs – a high population of children unable to speak English. Not all immigrant children have poor spoken English. Some Africans, some upper-class Indians, and most East African Asians have English as either their first tongue or at least a fluent second language. Moreover, some children whose parents were born in the New Commonwealth but who were themselves born in England may well have the normal command of English appropriate to their social class. In short, 'immigrant' does not necessarily mean speaking poor English. The use of immigrants as a measure will show an inflated estimate of the number whose English is poor.

If the ratio of good English speakers to poor ones is constant for immigrants throughout school catchment areas then there is no problem, since it is the *relative* comparison of schools, in order to rank them in terms of deprivation, which counts not the absolute number of immigrants. We do not know if this is the case, though in principle, an estimate of the proportion of all immigrants coming from areas where English is spoken in the home could be made by inspecting the Census data where country of origin of parents is tabulated.

Little and Mabey may well have improved upon Plowden by taking proportion of immigrants as a measure since this indicator will be highly correlated with other aspects of EPAs – with poor housing, unskilled occupations, and poor school facilities. The problem, as Little and Mabey define it, is to prevent this particular measure from 'swamping' the other measures in an index.

An index is an aggregate measure made up by combining several measures into one. If this were not done, the result of ranking schools would be as many rank-orders as there are measures. With many rank-orders, the problem becomes one of deciding which rank-order has priority, since the rankings will be different to some degree or other. This difficulty is overcome by 'adding' measures beforehand so as to leave a single index value for each school. But this exercise immediately faces the same problem as comparing several rank-orders – what orders of priorities do we set on the group of measures? In the language of Little and Mabey, how are the measures to be weighted? Without clear weightings from the Plowden Report (which simply lists the dimensions of EPAs – for which Little and Mabey selected indicators) it is difficult to give differential weightings. In other words, it would be illegitimate for Little and Mabey to argue that pupil turnover (for example) had more effect as a variable influencing low achievement than does overcrowding in pupils' homes (as another example) because they had no good evidence from Plowden to justify it. Their decision, then, could only be that the measures should contribute to the index equally. To achieve equal weightings required modification to the immigrant measure. The variance of this measure was higher than any other indicator and so could 'swamp' the index if not checked. The effect of transforming the scores by each indicator, as shown in paragraphs (a) and (b) page 281 is to equalise the variances of each indicator and so make them contribute equally to the average index.

Lastly, you will see that as Little and Mabey carried out their translation of Plowden's policy objective into an administrative tool two government circulars to Local Education Authorities were issued which made the Department of Education and Science's own interpretation of EPA criteria. Since Little and Mabey's aims were administrative, their own choice of criteria to operationalise the concept of EPAs was, rightly, overridden by the government's own choice. It was the DES, after all, who allocated the extra resources.

References and further reading

J. Bynner, *DE 304 Research Methods in Education and the Social Sciences,* block I, part 2, The Open University, 1978.

A. N. Oppenheim *Questionnaire Design and Attitude Measurement,* London: Heinemann, 1966.

A. Shonfield and S. Shaw *Social Indicators and Social Policy,* London: Heinemann 1972.

R. L. Thorndike and E. P. Hagen *Measurement and Evaluation in Psychology and Education,* New York: Wiley, 1969.

In January 1967, the Central Advisory Committee for Education under the chairmanship of Lady Plowden published its report on *Children and their Primary Schools.*[1] The aspect which particularly distinguished the report and which has probably received most attention since was the concept of educational priority areas. The concept and problems of deprived, primarily urban areas was not, of course, a new one. It was probably most effectively highlighted in recent years in the Milner Holland report on housing in London.[2] What, however, was new in the Plowden Report's concept was that the Committee defined these areas as those 'where educational handicaps are reinforced by social handicaps' and recommended positive educational discrimination in favour of such areas. The other distinguishing feature of the report was that it stated that *'objective criteria* for the selection of educational priority schools and areas will be needed to identify those schools which need special help and to determine how much assistance should be given by the Government'.

Against this background the Inner London Education Authority (ILEA) decided to develop an index by which schools or areas best answering the Plowden definition of 'education priority' could be identified. This paper is an account of the work which was done by the ILEA research and statistics group and the practical problems involved. The work reported here was undertaken over the period 1967–69. Since then there have been various changes within the ILEA; for example, the School Inquiry Service and Care Committee referred to have been reorganized into a new Educational Welfare Service.

Requirements for an index of EPAs

The problems involved in such an exercise are, as the Report acknowledged, threefold:

(a) The criteria selected must identify those areas 'where educational handicaps are reinforced by social handicaps', i.e. there is a problem in arriving at agreed *criteria.*

(b) Measures of the criteria must be relevant, quantifiable, standardized and fairly readily available, i.e. there is a problem of *measurement.*

(c) Some method of combining all measures into a single factor needs to be devised, i.e. a problem of *scaling* or *weighing* the different items in the index.

Pilot study, Spring 1967

With these conditions in mind a pilot study was begun in February 1967. It was decided initially that the Research Group should rely only on information which could be collected independently of the schools; there were to be no special surveys involving the teachers of children. It should be remembered that at this stage there had been no government statement about implementation of any of the recommendations of the Plowden Report so that the exercise was seen as primarily a domestic one to enable the ILEA, if it wished, to rank its primary schools on a scale of relative deprivation.

1. Areas   For the pilot study, it was decided to select two areas in London as dissimilar as possible containing a reasonable number of primary schools. The two areas chosen were part of Islington (the electoral division of South-West) and part of Greenwich (the former metropolitan borough). The first area contained 24 primary schools, the second 23; the total population of these schools was 12,412.

2. Criteria chosen   At this initial stage, there was relatively little discussion about what criteria should be adopted; the chief object was to discover the practical problems of developing an index; how difficult and, for example, time consuming it was to assemble data on social and educational factors. The criteria, therefore, listed in the Plowden Report were accepted as ones for which measures should be found. These were:

(a) Occupation.
(b) Size of families.
(c) Supplements in cash or kind from the State.
(d) Overcrowding and sharing of houses.
(e) Poor attendance and truancy.
(f) Proportions of retarded, disturbed or handicapped pupils.
(g) Incomplete families.
(h) Children unable to speak English.

In addition to these, it was thought that two other criteria should be considered. These were (i) high pupil turnover, the Plowden Report itself spoke of the problems of schools with 'admission registers whose pages of new names with so many rapid crossings out told their own story of the migratory population', and (ii) high teacher turnover, possibly the end product of a school in a deprived area which has difficulty in attracting and retaining teachers.

3. Measures Taken   The sources of information available were:

(a) Routine returns submitted to the Research and Statistics Group by schools.
(b) Records from the schools kept at the 10 divisional offices both by administrative and School Care and School Inquiry Officers.
(c) Census 1961 with all information on Inner London stored on tape by the smallest area, the enumeration district, and some information already tabulated by e.d.

As can be seen from the two chief sources of information, data were recorded by individual schools. Partly for this reason and partly because a primary objective was to rank schools it was decided to collect information for schools rather than areas.

A. Definition of catchment area of schools
At the start it was known that for at least two of the criteria no information would be available in ILEA records and, therefore, the Census would have to be used. The problem, then, was how to relate Census data to a school's population. In the ILEA there is no zoning, no fixed catchment area, and parental choice operates freely. The actual catchment area, however, can be plotted from the home addresses of all children attending a particular school. Theoretically, it should have been possible to plot the addresses of the 12,000 children in the pilot study and from these to establish the real area from which each of

the 47 schools recruited its children. It would have been possible to identify the enumeration district in which each child lived, sum the information for the districts involved, weighing each by the number of children there. Such an exercise for even 12,000 children was formidable but to envisage eventually doing it for all primary school children, about ¼ million, was rejected as impractical. Home addresses were collected for all children in the pilot study and the method finally adopted was to measure the distance travelled to school. This was done for 10 schools in each of the two areas using the home addresses of all children on roll during the previous academic year 1965–66 (current records were in constant use for other purposes). Of these 20, 4 were Roman Catholic, 5 were Church of England and 11 were County schools. The results on distance travelled to school showed, as expected, little difference between County and Church of England schools, but a great difference between them and Roman Catholic schools. The majority of children attending County and Church of England schools travelled under ¼ mile to school; this distance accounted for over four-fifths of the children in 10 schools, approximately two-thirds in 5 schools and just under that for the remaining school. In Roman Catholic schools, however, in order to account for similar proportions, a distance of ½ mile had to be taken; this accounted for approximately two-thirds. Thus, for the purposes of using Census data a school's catchment area was defined as the enumeration districts which fell wholly or partly within ¼ mile radius of the school, if it was a county or Church of England school, and ½ mile radius if a Roman Catholic school.

There are clearly a number of weaknesses in this method. First, only a very small sample of schools was taken and they might be unrepresentative of some if not all schools. Further, the two areas selected might not have provided an adequate cross-section. Second, even if the assumption (that about two-thirds to four-fifths of the population will live within ¼ mile of the school) were correct, it might be that the remaining one-third or one-fifth live in areas with very different characteristics. This seems unlikely, but it could lead to minor distortions. Another problem (which has in fact subsequently been noted) is the school in which the majority of whose population live within ¼ mile radius but that area is fairly heterogeneous in socio-graphic terms and the school's population lives in a distinctive part of that area. For example, in one school four-fifths of the children lived within ¼ mile radius of the school but nearly all in overcrowded, sub-standard Victorian tenement dwellings. The ¼ mile area, however, also contained some good quality, low density housing, into which middle-class families are moving and some council flats. Thus, on measures such as overcrowding, lack of housing amenities, and social class, the school's population is not a cross-section of the immediate neighbourhood of the school. This is the only school known in this extreme position and it is probably not that common (a ¼ mile radius is in fact a very small area). However, it must be accepted that the definition is crude and takes no account of the different recruitment of schools with overlapping catchment areas.

B. Measures for individual criteria

(a) Occupation Using the catchment area, as defined above, information on occupations was derived from the 1961 Census. For each school the distribution of socio-economic groupings was found and the final measure adopted was that suggested in the Plowden Report: the proportion of semi-skilled and unskilled manual workers.

(b) Size of families The Plowden Report pointed out the research evidence on the correlations between large families and low scores on attainment and ability tests. From the Greater London Council (GLC) printouts of Census data, no information on family size could be derived and as it was hoped that data from the 1966 Census would shortly be available it was decided not to ask for special tabulations. It was thought also that a school-based source would provide the relevant information. The Care Committee workers for their annual reports in 1966 were asked specifically to report on the 'number of cases of acute poverty known to them' and in their reports gave details on incomplete families and family size. Care Committee workers are voluntary, unpaid workers assigned to one or more schools to carry out certain social work duties. They were in origin appointed to provide meals for necessitous children and still their main duty is to ensure that children whose family has a low income receive free school meals and also other help, such as uniform grants. They are recruited by the full-time paid School Care Organizers who train them. The annual reports for 1966 by these workers were examined in detail for one of the two areas. From these, it was clear that there were a number of problems in attempting to use this as a standard measure. First, there was the problem referred to in the general annual report – 'voluntary workers always prefer to do the work rather than to write detailed reports about it' – i.e. some workers had not provided information on the subject. Reports had not been submitted for 3 of the schools either because they had no worker or for some other reason. Secondly, as with all voluntary workers, there is a great difference in their calibre and experience. Some may be former social workers and have been attached to a particular school for a long period and spend a considerable time on the work. At the other extreme, some may be virtually untrained, inexperienced, possibly newly appointed to a school and unable to give much time to the work. Thus, the report for one school may be a complete and accurate record, but for another a gross underestimation; there is difficulty, therefore, in accepting these reports as standard information. Furthermore, when the actual details were examined other problems arose. Some workers had reported the number of *children* in a particular school who were members of large

families, while others reported the number of large *families* they knew of or had had contact with in the school. It was clear from the records that some workers had only recorded large families with low incomes and except with an exceptional worker, it is unlikely that the voluntary worker would know of other cases, since they are primarily concerned with children from poor families. In some cases where one worker was responsible for two schools (usually the Junior and the Infant, either on the same site or very close) figures were given for both schools together.

Finally, there was no generally accepted definition of a 'large' family: some did not define the term, one worker described it as containing 3 or more children, another as containing 4 or more and a third as containing 6 or more. This source was, therefore, rejected as not providing standard and accurate measurement of children in large families.

(c) Supplements in cash or kind from the state   The Plowden Report suggested as measures of this either the proportions of children receiving free meals or the proportions of children in families receiving supplementary benefit from the Ministry of Social Security. Another measure of this might have been the annual Care Committee Workers' reports, but this was rejected for the sorts of reasons described above in *(b)*. To have obtained information from the Ministry about named families, supposing that they had made this available, would have involved considerable effort in relating information about families to children in particular schools. On the other hand, information on free school meals is regularly, routinely provided by the schools to the Research Group. The measure taken was the proportion of children in the school receiving free meals as recorded in September 1966. The limitation to this measure is that it does not necessarily measure all those eligible to receive free meals; some parents through pride or ignorance will not claim the entitlement for their child. It is difficult to determine how good a measure of poverty this one is; certainly receipt of free meals depends on a number of factors and people. In London, the usual practice appears to be the following:

The Headmaster (and in some cases, the initiative must come from the class teacher) recommends to the Care Committee Worker that a child should receive free meals. The voluntary worker visits the family and completes a fairly detailed form on family income and expenditure, on the number of dependants, which is then signed by the child's guardian. From this, the Care Worker can assess the child's eligibility. There is certain room for discretion and, in an emergency, the Headteacher can act on his own authority. However, receipt of free meals is dependent either on the parents' knowing their rights and insisting on them or on the teachers and Care Committee Workers approaching families whom they think are likely to to be eligible.

(d) Overcrowding and sharing of houses Two measures of this were collected from the Census. First, the proportion of households living at a density of more than $1\frac{1}{2}$ persons per room (ppr), i.e. the generally accepted technical definition of overcrowding was calculated. Second, the proportion of households sharing a dwelling was established. This last measure was thought to be a highly unsatisfactory index of housing stress because of the technical definition of a 'dwelling', i.e. a self-contained unit with its own front door. Thus, for example, an eighteenth-century London house with possibly ten or more rooms is often a dwelling shared by two households, possibly with only a few people and in many cases no housing stress is involved. As a useful indicator of housing stress in London, this criterion was rejected. Another measure was easily available from the GLC printout of Census 1961 and this was used: the proportion of households lacking one or more of the 4 basic amenities, i.e. exclusive use of inside lavatory, bathroom, hot and cold water and stove and sink.

(e) Poor attendance and truancy 'Poor attendance and truancy, are a pointer to home conditions and to what Burt long ago singled out as a determinant of school progress, the efficiency of the mother', so states the Plowden Report. No information was available on truancy but two measures of poor attendance were collected, one from a routine return, the other from School Inquiry Officers' records of children's attendance. Every year schools complete a card giving the average attendance in the school during the second week in May. From this, the percentage absenteeism for each school for that week can be established. The second source was the individual attendance slips completed each week by class teachers and passed to the School Inquiry Officers. As the current ones were in constant use the previous year's (1965–66) were examined. From these could be obtained the percentage absence/attendance of each child at each school. It was decided to define children as poor attenders if they had made less than 80 per cent of their possible attendances. Clearly, this was a fairly arbitrary measure, the reason for selecting it was that the National Child Development Study 1958 cohort, in their follow-up of the children at 7 found a fairly short cut-off at this point; only 9 per cent of children having more than 20 per cent absences. It was felt that there were a number of criticisms of both the criteria and the measures. First, attendance officers were agreed that truancy was not a serious problem in the primary school; furthermore no measure of truancy as distinct from absenteeism was possible. Poor attendance was thought to be a dubious criterion. In the primary school, attendance is often affected by childhood illnesses. Further, it was felt that poor attendance was not so much a measure of the 'efficiency of the mother' as the anxiety of the mother-children, particular at primary age, being kept at home when they are not really ill. In contrast some children, particularly those from poor homes, are sent to school when they are ill because there is

no adult at home during the day to look after them. The second measure used is better than the first, but as already pointed out, it is a fairly arbitrary one. A practical disadvantage was the time taken to calculate it, particularly when trying to maintain a high level of accuracy. The first measure was even more unsatisfactory in that it only showed the proportion of children absent in a given week and not the percentage of children with poor attendance; an epidemic in a school in that week could give the school a high figure of absenteeism.

(f) Proportions of retarded, disturbed or handicapped pupils   This criterion involves three separate (although possibly closely related) groups and it was decided initially to attempt to establish separate measures of each. The only source available for a measure of *retarded pupils* was the routine transfer procedure for 11+ pupils. At that time, two measures of attainment, in English and Mathematics, and one measure of ability, verbal reasoning, was obtained. The proportion of children in the school with low attainment scores could be taken as a measure of retarded pupils.

The only generally available source for a measure of *disturbed children* was the records of the Problem Case Conferences (PCCs) which are arranged by the Divisional School Care Organizers. This procedure was established in 1965 and is held monthly in each division to discuss children with problems, mainly behavioural ones. Referral of a child's case for discussion may be made by the school, the school doctor, a private doctor, the Health Visitor, School Care Committee Worker or, if the child is attending a clinic, workers from that clinic. The records for the years 1964–65 and 1965–66 were examined in both areas and the number of children discussed per school (a) during the two years; (b) during 1965–66, was counted and expressed as a percentage of the roll (any child discussed at more than one Conference was counted once only). This measure has three important weaknesses. First, referral of a child depends on the regard the referee, usually the school, has (since most referrals are made by the headteacher), for the PCC; if he thinks it is a useless service, then few referrals will be made. Secondly, referral appears to be conditioned by the extent of and pressure on remedial facilities available in the area. In the Greenwich area, for example, there was no Child Guidance Unit at that time and the School Care Organizer thought that this fact deterred schools from referring to the PCC children whom they considered needed treatment at a Child Guidance Unit. Further, as all these specialist remedial services are limited, it seemed that most schools only referred a few children. This is linked with the third weakness. Referral is almost certainly dependent on the norms of the school, or of whomever refers, as there is no commonly accepted definition of a disturbed child. This means that what is 'disturbed' in one school may be the norm in another. To some extent these objections were borne out in the figures collected. Some schools thought by local workers to contain a number of disturbed children had fewer referrals than some schools thought to have relatively few problems. Relatively few referrals were made: the range throughout both areas was for 1965–66 from 0 per cent (9 schools) to 6.3 per cent. For practical reasons, therefore, as well as theoretical ones, this did not seem a very good measure, since it did not provide much 'spread' among schools and at this stage one of the objectives was to develop measures which would discriminate between schools.

There was no readily available source to give a measure of *handicapped children*. Information could have been collected from the individual medical records kept at each school on physically handicapped children. These record for each child details of his medical health usually at the age of 7. There were two problems in using this source. First, the research worker had no medical experience and the work would have involved making decisions and categorizing medical information. Second, the use of these records would have involved visiting each school, a very time-consuming task; or asking the schools for information – a method ruled out from the beginning. Another source of information was supplied by the Senior Social Worker in the Public Health Department of one of the areas. This was a list called the 'handicapped register', which included information on children with physical handicaps. Not included were children with serious handicaps who were awaiting places in Special Schools, but only those with slight handicaps who needed attention. There were a number of problems, it appeared, in using this register. First, there is the problem of whether the schools inform the Borough department regularly of their 'handicapped children'. Secondly, there was the problem mentioned above of little differentiation between the schools. The average was 1.4 per cent, the lowest 0 per cent and the highest 4.6 per cent. It was decided that this was not a particularly useful measure.

From the outset there had been some argument about what interpretation should be given to the term 'handicapped'; the Plowden Report itself does not clarify this. A different and possibly equally important measure is the proportion of children handicapped because of low ability. A measure of this was readily available in the routine transfer procedure mentioned earlier. From this was derived the proportion of children of low ability as measured at 11+. Again, a number of criticisms can be made of this measure. First, it only deals with one kind of handicap. Second, the measure is not entirely objective. The child's final placing may differ from his score in the test if his teacher thinks from his experience it is not an accurate assessment. It was thought that there was probably little regrading according to teachers' assessment since the resulting distribution for all ILEA children was not very dissimilar from what would be expected if:

(a) London children have similar standards to those nationally (the National Foundation for Educational Research (NFER) standardized the test used each year on a national sample); and
(b) if teachers record the test placing of a child as a result of the test.

(g) Incomplete families   Once again no school-based information existed centrally. It was thought that the 1966 annual reports of the voluntary School Care Committee Workers might be used. Unfortunately, all the limitations listed above under *(b)* (except of course that of the definition of a 'large family) applied to this measure. This source was discarded, therefore, as being not sufficiently complete, accurate or standard to provide a useful measure.

(h) Ability to speak English   'Children unable to speak English need much attention if they are to find their feet in England.' Measures of this criterion were readily available since both the ILEA and the Department of Education and Science (DES) collect statistics by school annually on immigrant children with language difficulties. The definitions in fact are different and the DES for the first three years in which it collected statistics on this has used a different definition each time. The DES definition in January 1967 was of immigrant 'pupils whose standards of English, whether written or spoken, are so far below those of local non-immigrant children as to demand special tuition', and the ILEA definition was (immigrant) 'children unable to follow a normal school curriculum with profit to themselves'. Two criticisms can be made against either of these definitions providing a useful measure. First, the measure involves a subjective assessment and not only that but, over all ILEA primary schools, 900 different subjective assessments. Second, as a result of the information provided schools with large numbers of non-English-speaking immigrants receive additional off-quota teachers. There is, therefore, a direct incentive to schools to record large numbers, although some schools probably were still unaware of the use made of this return. Furthermore, there is in London particularly a special problem with West Indian children many of whom speak a dialect of English. Are they to be recorded in a limited English category? It seems clear from analysis of the returns that schools interpret this differently. Some schools recorded no West Indian children as requiring special tuition, while others often in the same neighbourhood, recorded a fair number. It was thought that neither of these returns with the definitions used provided a good measure. In addition, there was serious criticism of the criterion itself. It is not only by language that many immigrant children are handicapped, but also often by limited previous education and by having come from a different country and culture. It was thought, therefore, that a much more realistic criterion would be that of the proportion of immigrant children in a school which could be measured using either of the sources referred to above, preferably the Department of Education and Science's return in January 1967.

(i) Pupil turnover This criterion was included since many London schools experience very high pupil mobility. It was argued that children who change schools frequently are handicapped educationally and that even 'stable' children in a school of high child mobility may be affected adversely. The only source which it was thought could provide the required information was one designed for other purposes. These were the School Inquiry Officers' attendance slips (referred to above for the absentee measure). In theory, each child is assigned a slip on which his attendances are marked each week by his class teacher and even if he leaves the school the slip is retained. From these slips the number of children who had either entered or left the school during the course of the academic year, 1965–66, was established and this was expressed as a proportion of the school population. (Children starting school for the first time at 4+ or 5 and entering mid-year were excluded.) If a child both entered and left during the year he was only counted once. Thus a measure was established of the proportion of children who had spent an incomplete year in the school. The only serious limitation to the measure was thought to be the completeness of the records; it was thought that in some cases, the slips of children who had left schools had not been retained.

(j) Teacher turnover This criterion was included for the same sorts of reasons as the previous one. It was thought that children in schools with high teacher turnover were probably educationally handicapped, and certainly it provides problems for the headteacher and administration. This criterion has been criticized on the grounds that some schools in very deprived areas which have a dedicated and stable staff are being 'penalized' in terms of their qualifying as a 'Plowden' school.[3] This criticism seems to result from a confusion of what the concept of Educational Priority Areas involves. In our interpretation of the Plowden concept focus was placed on the *needs* of children and schools and not on the *merits*. A school with high turnover almost certainly needs more help than a school with a stable teaching force, if all other factors are equal and, therefore, it is useful to include this as a criterion. The records of teachers kept at divisional offices were examined and a number of different measures were collected. It was decided only to include full-time teachers since the Plowden report in its Survey had concentrated on them and also it was thought that what was important to the primary-aged child was the class teacher and, in most cases, class teachers are full-time teachers. The date of appointment of full-time teachers then teaching in the school was established. From this were derived measures of the median length of service teachers at each school, the proportion of teachers with less than 2, 3 or 4 years' service in that school. Another source used was to look at resignations of full-time teachers from each school over a period and express that as the rate of turnover in the school. This was considered a good measure, but unfortunately it was thought that the records were not complete.

(k) *Other Criteria*   In addition to the criteria described above, there were others which it was thought should be included in any index of Educational Priority Areas. These fell into two main groups. The first were those describing home or environmental deprivation or handicaps. The most important was parental attitudes and interest in education, shown in the analysis in the Plowden Report as of crucial importance. Other criteria suggested were criminal parents or delinquent areas and mental illness of parents. With all these, the problem was of measurement; without special surveys no measures could be devised. The second main group concerned the physical conditions in the school. These are in no way suggested in the Report itself as items which should be included in an index but there was discussion on whether factors like pupil-teacher ratios, age of school buildings, provision of amentities, etc. should be included. With these, there was no problem of measurement since existing central records contained information. After discussion, however, it was decided not to use these criteria, the main argument being that the Plowden concept was not about existing provision in the schools, but about the educational and social handicaps faced by the children; factors like pupil-teacher ratios, it was argued, should be examined when it came to implementing recommendations.

General study 1967

As a result of the pilot study described above, it was decided to attempt to collect data for all ILEA primary schools. It was decided to limit the exercise to those factors outlined above, which it was felt were:

(a) satisfactory criteria;
(b) for which adequate measures were readily available.

On this basis absenteeism or truancy and children unable to speak English were rejected as poor criteria and size of families, incomplete families and proportions of disturbed or physically handicapped pupils were rejected since only inadequate measures were available. Further, it was decided to wait until the 1966 Census material became available within the ILEA.

During this general exercise, the DES issued on 24 August 1967 their circular 11/67. This provided for £16 million to be made available for school building in Educational Priority Areas and invited Local Education Authorities to submit proposals. This general exercise, therefore, changed from being a somewhat academic, domestic project to being an exercise to provide information to support claims by the ILEA. This had a number of important effects. First, it became necessary to include the criteria referred to in the circular as well as those listed in the Plowden Report. This stated that the Secretary of State will attach particular attention to:

(a) evidence that children in a district are suffering from multiple deprivations because of the combination of several disadvantages in their environment. As examples of these, it listed the following factors: overcrowding of houses, family sizes above the average, high incidence of supplements in cash or kind from the State, high incidence of truancy or poor attendance, a rapid turnover of teachers or difficulty in attracting them to the district.

(b) The general quality of the physical environment. A concentration of crowded, old, sub-standard and badly maintained houses is the most obvious and generally accepted sign of the sort of district which the Plowden Committee had in mind. Further, in submitting proposals, authorities were asked to 'include such statistical evidence as may be readily available'.

A second effect of the circular was to attempt to select, wherever possible measures which would provide national comparability so that the claim for any ILEA school could be put against a national standard. Thirdly, time became an important factor. Proposals had to be submitted by 6 November and they had to include initial building proposals.

1. Criteria

The criteria included for this exercise were:

(a) Occupation.
(b) Supplements in cash from the State.
(c) Overcrowding of houses.
(d) Lack of basic housing amenities.
(e) Poor attendance.
(f) Proportions of handicapped pupils.
(g) Immigrant children.
(h) Teacher turnover.
(i) Pupil turnover.

From this list, it can be seen that the criteria of poor attendance was included because specifically asked for in the circular, although the research group had originally thought it not a meaningful index.

2. Measures and sources

(a) Occupation The measure taken was the proportion of occupied males in unskilled or semi-skilled jobs (Registrar-General's socio-economic groups 7, 10, 11, 15, 16, 17). The source used was Census 1961, unfortunately, since data from Census 1966 were still unavailable. Catchment areas were defined as described for the pilot study.

(b) Supplements in cash from the State The measure taken was the percentage of children in the school receiving free meals as recorded on the annual return in September 1966. This return is the basis of information supplied by Local Education Authorities each year to the Department of Education and Science, so that this measure provides national comparability.

(c) Overcrowding of houses The measure adopted was that described above: the percentage of households living at a density of more than 1½ ppr. Once again the source was Census 1961 so that, although outdated, standard national comparisons could be made.

(d) Lack of basic housing amenities This measure was included in the second main category described in the Circular 11/67. The measure was the percentage of households lacking one or more of the 4 basic amenities. The source was Census 1961.

(e) Poor attendance As it had not been originally intended to include this criterion in the general exercise, the better measure described in the pilot study had to be rejected because of the time factor. Instead, the annual return in May 1967 was used and poor attendance measured as the average absence during the sample week. As far as was known, there would be no comparable data from other authorities.

(f) Proportions of handicapped pupils As discussed above, there were many problems in obtaining an adequate measure. The one adopted, therefore, was the percentage of children of low ability at the 11+ transfer stage in 1967. Low ability was defined as those placed into the bottom two of seven groups which should contain 25 per cent of the children. As the NFER standardized the test for the ILEA on a national sample, national comparability was available.

(g) Immigrant children This was measured as the proportion of immigrant children as recorded on the annual Department of Education and Science return in January 1967.

(h) Teacher turnover The measure adopted was the proportion of full-time teachers in school in July 1967 who had taught there for less than three academic years. In many ways this was not a satisfactory measure, but it had no practical disadvantages (as would a measure of resignation from a school over a period) and also it provided national comparability. In the National Survey reported in Vol. II of the Plowden Report, figures were given of staff movement over a three-year period. The only differences between these two measures were that the ILEA measure was retrospective (it measured those in school with less than three years' experience) and measured in 1967, whereas the National Survey measure followed up the teachers in school in 1961 through to 1964.

(i) Pupil Turnover The measure and source for this was that described in the pilot study, i.e. the percentage of pupils in a school who spent an incomplete year there. Unfortunately, the 1965–66 records had to be used and no national comparisons could be made except for a crude approximation using the 1961 Census Mobility Tables.

3. *Scaling*

Having collected the measures, the problem arose of how to combine them into a single index for each school. The Plowden Report itself evaded the question. The basic problem is of course, what weight should be given to each factor since almost certainly all are not equal. Complicating this is the fact that possibly important criteria have been omitted; the most obvious omission is probably that of parental attitudes, while the criteria of incomplete and large families were omitted because of inadequate measures. Because of the limited time, the decision was made to construct an index giving equal weight to each of the items. There were three stages in the development of the final index:

(a) Initially it was intended to express the school's score on each of the criteria listed above as a percentage of the national average score, then sum these percentages, and rank schools on the basis of this total score. This exercise was completed, but found unsatisfactory because the contribution of a single criterion to the total score depended upon the range of observations and the variation between these and the national average. For one criterion, in particular, this gave distorted results, namely immigrants: the national average percentage of pupils who are immigrants (DES definition) is 2.5 per cent, the ILEA average is 15.8 per cent and certain schools have 65 per cent. Therefore, using the method of scoring outlined a school with 25 per cent immigrants would score 1,000, one with 50 per cent 2,000. Such a score on this criterion alone would mean that the school would rank as an EPA school. Finally, certain help is already provided for schools with a high proportion of immigrants, and therefore, it would be unwise to overweight this criterion.

(b) Therefore, it was decided to revise the scoring method to ensure that each criterion contributed equally to the total score. This can be done by ranking each set of observations so that the lowest score is 0 and the highest 100. The formula for this is the following:

$$\frac{(\text{Observation} - \text{lowest score})}{(\text{Highest} - \text{lowest score})} \text{ multiplied by } 100$$

By definition the lowest will score 0 [i.e. lowest − lowest =] and the highest 100.

(c) The difficulty about the method outlined above is that extreme observations at both ends may distort the scores of other schools on a particular criterion. In an attempt to overcome this problem, the range of observations for each criterion was taken to be plus or minus 2 standard deviations from the mean. Thus, all schools with an observation more than 2 standard deviations would score 100 and all schools with an observation of less than 2 standard deviations would score 0.

Final scores, Y, were obtained in this way:

$$Y = \begin{cases} \dfrac{x-(\bar{x}-2s)}{4s} \times 100 & \text{if } \bar{x}-2s < x < \bar{x}+2s \\[2ex] 0 & \text{if } x < \bar{x}-2s \\[1ex] 100 & \text{if } \bar{x} < \bar{x}+2s \end{cases}$$

where x is the original score for a school,

$\bar{x}$ is the mean for all ILEA schools,

s is the standard deviation of the original scores.

Improvements to general study, Spring 1968

After the general exercise had been completed two important improvements were needed. One was the technical point of improving the data, in particular for area-based data a recalculation using Census 1966. Further, it was thought better measures of pupil and teacher turnover and attendance could be developed if the schools rather than existing central records were used. The more important problem, however, was to improve the scaling of the different items. It was decided to attempt a number of statistical analyses to try to determine the inter-relationship of the different variables and their relative weight. Three analyses were planned: simple correlations, regression and component analysis.

Administrative Memorandum 6/68

Once again the technical exercise was overtaken by events. In March 1968 the Department of Education and Science published a Memorandum which stated that an additional £75 would be paid to teachers serving in schools 'recognized by the Secretary of State as being of exceptional difficulty following recommendations by Local Education Authorities'. This Memorandum was followed by a letter to all Local Eduation Authorities specifying the criteria to be used together with forms on which applications were to be made.

The index was the same as the one described above with the following exceptions. 1966 Census data were available and used. Unfortunately, for the first GLC printout produced, it was not possible to obtain a composite measure of housing stress; instead a single measure was used, that of the percentage of households without an inside lavatory. The decision to use this measure of housing stress rather than, for example, access to bathroom was clearly an arbitrary and, it was hoped, temporary one. From the 1966 data it was possible to obtain a crude index of large families. The measure used was the percentage of children living in households containing 6 or more people. This was based on the increasingly common definition of a large family as one containing 4 or more children and also on the assumption that in most cases, if the household was a family unit it could contain more or less than 2 adults. Information on pupil turnover was updated and improved as schools were asked to record the number of pupils who spent an incomplete year in their school in 1966–67. Unfortunately, the results were not received soon enough to be used for the application for the £75 allowances. This second index, then, was made up of 10 items, each given equal weighing as described earlier.

Practical results

Table 13.1 shows what picture emerged of those schools which figured at the 'top' of the Index constructed, that is the most disadvantaged London schools according to the criteria used. In Table 13.1 are the percentage observations for the 1st, 50th, 100th, and 150th schools in the Index; the final Index consisted of approximately 600 schools since, where infant and junior schools existed on the same site, they were treated as one unit. Also shown are national percentages, that is the average for England and Wales, with information drawn from the same source as that used in the Index except where stated otherwise.

Table 13.1 Percentages for each criterion.

	Criteria*									
School	1	2	3	4	5	6	7	8	9	10
1st	47.8	43.4	15.9	35.6	29.5	14.7	68.1	75.0	83.3	55.5
50th	42.1	39.1	10.7	30.4	34.3	12.3	53.0	65.0	71.4	39.1
100th	39.3	36.6	9.1	26.2	13.5	10.8	35.0	49.4	66.7	28.5
150th	32.7	33.2	5.4	22.2	11.4	9.5	21.8	38.9	57.1	23.5
E+W average	31.9†	26.7†	1.2	19.8	5.1	NA‡	2.5	25.0	35.6§	9.6†

*Criteria: 1 Social class composition; 2 Family size; 3 Overcrowding; 4 Housing stress; 5 Cash supplements; 6 Absenteeism; 7 Immigrants; 8 Retarded handicapped pupils; 9 Teacher turnover; 10 Pupil turnover.

†. National figures abstracted from Census 1961 as 1966 figures not available.
‡. National data not available.
§. Not strictly comparable; figures used for England + Wales abstracted from Plowden Report.

The measures and sources used are those given in the General Study 1967, section 2 above (pages 279–80). This means that in the school figuring first on the Index nearly half of the employed men in the immediate area were in semi-skilled or unskilled jobs, half of the children in the area were in large families, one-eighth of the households in the area were technically overcrowded and over one-third of them without inside lavatories. In school nearly one-third of the children received free school dinners, an average of one-seventh of the children were absent in a selected week, two-thirds of the children were immigrants, three-quarters of the children were placed in the lowest quarter on an ability test, over half of them had had an incomplete year in the school and 4 out of 5 teachers in the school had been there for less than 3 years.

Looking at the 150th school and comparing it with the 'national average', there are only small differences in social class, family size and housing stress. However, more than twice the national average receive free dinners; instead of one immigrant pupil for every 40 children it is one for every 5. The incidence of teacher turnover is 50 per cent above the national average and pupil turnover more than twice the national average. Finally, instead of a class of 40 having 10 pupils of low ability and performance, this school will have 16. For schools like this one the problem is not so much the area (housing stress, overcrowding, class composition) but much more the social pathologies that are reflected within the school (high rates of teacher turnover, large number of backward pupils).

Problems of a weighted index

As stated earlier it was our intention to produce an index of items weighted according to their importance in contributing to an Educational Priority Area. To this end certain statistical analyses were planned. Before examining these, it is worth reiterating that for each school only ten items of information were collected and as made clear above both the criteria and measures used are open to criticism.

The decision to include only one measure of each of the ten criteria was taken specifically so that there should be no over-weighting of any individual item. With the exception, therefore, of the two housing factors, there is virtually no overlapping in the criteria used. This is worth remembering when considering the statistical results.

Initially, correlation coefficients between the criteria measures were worked out for the ILEA as a whole, for County and Voluntary Schools separately and for each of the 10 administrative divisions: with two exceptions the divisions are equivalent in geographical area to a London borough, the exceptions being division 1 which comprises Hammersmith and Kensington and Chelsea and division 2 covering Camden and Westminster. The 10 measures used were:

Variables

1	Occupation	6	Immigrants
2	Lack of inside w/c	7	Teacher turnover
3	Overcrowding	8	Pupil turnover
4	Free meals	9	Absenteeism
5	Handicapped children	10	Large families

There was relatively little difference in the correlations between those using 1966 and those using 1961 data. The only real difference to emerge was the higher correlation between overcrowding and free meals on the 1966 data (0.306 as compared with 0.192), and the lower correlation between overcrowding and immigrants on the 1966 data (0.437:0.543), suggesting perhaps that in the five-year period there had been a change in the economic and racial characteristics of people in overcrowded conditions. Further, there is the considerable difference, with nearly all variables, in the correlation coefficients of housing stress as between the 1961 measure and the 1966 measure.

The correlations were in general rather low. There is, of course, no objective dividing line between 'high' and 'low' correlations and as this exercise involved population rather than sample data, all correlations were statistically significant. However, from other research evidence (e.g. Moser and Scott's *British Towns*[4] one might have expected slightly higher correlations).

Given these relatively low correlations, it is not surprising that when the component analysis was carried out, it was not possible to extract principal components accounting for a large proportion of the total variance.

It was found that the first component accounted for 25.2 per cent of the variance over all ILEA, with a range of 23.2 per cent to 38.4 per cent between divisions. The first four components accounted for 61.8 per cent of the variance over the Authority with a range between divisions of 60.9 per cent to 71.6 per cent.

Looking at the principal components themselves it was found that there was a marked similarity across divisions. In nearly all cases variables 1, 3, 4, 5 and 6 had heavy weightings although occasionally there were other variables with similar loadings; subsequent components did not seem to follow any particular pattern between divisions with different variables having high weightings in each division.

From the viewpoint of ranking schools on the principal components, this analysis was highly unsatisfactory. It would, of course, have been possible to rank on the first component about which there was very much similarity across divisions but as this only accounted for 25 per cent of the total variance, this would not have been a satisfactory method. Why this analysis would have been so unfruitful is debatable. Partly, of course, there is the fact that certain key variables may have been omitted. Secondly, the validity of the inclusion of certain variables is perhaps arguable; in particular, teacher turnover has been much criticized as a criterion. Thirdly, the measurement of certain factors, e.g. large families and poor attendance, was very crude. Fourthly, there is the question of the applicability of area-data, i.e. Census information, to a school base. Furthermore, there is the fact that other component analyses have involved more variables often closely related. For example, Moser and Scott[4] included a number of measures of occupation, of housing conditions, etc. For whatever reasons, however, it was decided that the results of the analysis did not warrant weighting and ranking according to loadings of the principal component. In default, therefore, of better evidence it was decided to use equal weighting of all 10 items.

Validity and usefulness of the exercise

It is easier to describe the usefulness of the exercise, and the uses to which it was put, than to evaluate the validity. As mentioned earlier all ILEA primary schools were ranked according to their final score on the final Index adopted, i.e. on the 10 items enumerated each with equal weighting. This Index has been used both within the ILEA and in negotiations with the DES as the basis of the allocation of additional resources. Clearly, as had usually happened in the past, local officers could have been asked for their recommendations as to which schools needed help. In each division there is a local office headed by a Divisional Officer, a senior, experienced administrative officer, and the local office is in close, almost daily contact, with the schools. In addition, within the Authority's own Inspectorate two inspectors are assigned to each division and each is responsible for the regular inspection of half of the schools. The problems, of course, in using the recommendations of the Divisional Officers are District Inspectors (DOs and DIs) are that (*a*) recommendations would be subjective, coming from a number of different officers; and (*b*) should relative weight be given for example, to the recommendations for Bethnal Green as against North Kensington? The Index, although imperfect, overcame these two problems.

The question of validity is more difficult to deal with. There are two sorts of criticisms to which it needs to be subjected: the subjective reactions of those with intimate local knowledge, and the objective technical criticisms. Throughout this paper the limitations of the criteria and measures have been described. Finally, there was the problem of the scaling, or weighting of the 10 items. In essence this revolves around the problems of *defining* an EPA; the Plowden Report merely *described* the sort of factors likely to be present in an EPA. It seemed to us that an EPA could be defined in two distinct ways. One definition proposed was that what the Plowden Committee was concerned with was the limiting conditions which affected a child in an EPA, and so retarded his educational development. Thus it was argued what should be considered was the difference between the child's innate ability and his educational attainment and that handicaps should be weighted in an index according to the extent to which they contributed to this difference. Alternatively, it was argued that this was too narrow a definition and that an EPA is simply an area where certain restricting or limiting factors are present. But how do you determine which are the factors and what weight should be applied to each? The component analysis as described above gave no sound justification for applying a weighting factor to the different items and hence the decision to use equal weighting. Clearly, the decision was arbitrary and as such is open to criticism. One point worth noting in passing is the degree of relationship between the two Indices; the first was produced for the claim for the building money, the second for the teacher allowances. The differences between the two concerned four of the factors, as six were measured in exactly the same way using the same data. The different items were those based on Census information. On the first Index Census 1961 was used for measures of occupation, overcrowding and lack of basic housing amenities. On the second index the 1966 10 per cent Sample Census was used to give measures of occupation, overcrowding (the same measures were used); lack of inside w.c. (a different measure); and an estimate of large families (a new criterion and thus a new measure). The rank correlation was worked out from the rankings of each of the 900 schools on each Index, $r = 0.95$. This does not mean that for certain schools their rank position was not substantially different on the two Indices but this was uncommon. As the coefficient suggests most schools' rankings were very similar.

On the completion of the second Index (the one using Census 1966 data) a copy of the rankings of the first quartile, i.e. the most deprived schools, was circulated within the Authority to the Deputy Education Officer (DEO), the heads of all Branches, Divisional Officers, the Senior Educational Psychologist, the Staff Inspectors for Primary Education and the District Inspectors. It was suggested that claims should be made for those schools listed for the £75 teacher allowance. Detailed comments were received and subsequently a meeting to discuss this list was called by the DEO at which these people or their representatives were present. It is difficult to summarize briefly the comments, but it is probably true to say that there were two main types of reaction. Negatively, it is worth mentioning that there was no general outcry that this method had produced a wildly improbable list of schools, and, in general, there was substantial agreement about those schools at the 'top' of the list. One sort of reaction was in terms of comparability: if school 'a' is to be included, then school 'b' should also receive help. In some cases the argument for this was that two or more schools served the same area, were not noticeably different, and, very practically, how could such a decision be justified locally? The other type of reaction was in terms of a different priority for certain schools; that school 'x' should rank higher than school 'y'. In many, not all, cases when these criticisms were pursued it transpired that the local officers concerned used different criteria from those adopted in the exercise. It is worth mentioning that of the 152 schools listed the inclusion or ranking was queried in respect of 18 and an additional 45 were thought to merit inclusion on the grounds of comparability with those already listed.

As a result of the discussion which was held two decisions were made. First that the Index should be used substantially as it stood for the purposes of allocating additional resources. Secondly, to the list of 152 schools to be submitted to the DES for the teachers' additional £75 allowance seven alterations were made; the rank position was raised for three schools on the grounds that their infant departments had much higher scores than their junior counterparts and that the 'problem' would shortly reach the junior school. Three schools were excluded. One school due to be opened in six months was included on the grounds that it was in a neighbourhood in which all the other schools figured as highly disadvantaged.

A considerable amount of further analysis was undertaken in respect of those schools whose ranking was in any way queried. An hypothesis put forward to explain anomalies between the Index and the DO/DI expectations was the importance of 'tone-related criteria'. Tone-related criteria were defined as pupil and teacher turnover and poor attendance, i.e. those factors which the 'tone' of a school might influence. The thesis put forward was that these schools, which DOs/DIs ranked higher than the Index, would have high scores on other factors but low scores on tone-related criteria and thus a lower final ranking than local officers would have expected knowing the backgrounds of the children in the schools. This thesis, or rather the suggestion that tone-related criteria should be weighted differently is, of course, related to the earlier argument on the inclusion of teacher turnover as a criterion: 'Why should schools who manage to retain their staff be penalized?' Tone-related criteria are intrinsically merit criteria and it was decided originally that they should be included equally with the other criteria. The exercise, however, was carried out but with no clear pattern emerging for the schools examined. In some schools the average scores on tone-related criteria were markedly lower than on the other criteria, but the reverse was true for other schools. In all the scores of 75 schools were examined (for this exercise, departments on the same site were examined separately); for 40 of these the average scores on tone-related criteria were within 10 points of the average score on non-tone-related criteria (in 20 schools higher and in 20 lower); of the remaining schools 24 schools had average scores on tone-related criteria more than 10 points lower than the non-tone-related criteria while the reverse was true for the remaining 13 schools. The only conclusion we could draw from this exercise was that the evidence was so conflicting that, even if one had a prior reason for thinking some differentiation should be made for schools with high tone-related scores, one would not be justified in accepting the hypothesis of tone-related criteria.

Examination was also centred on those schools considered by local judgment to recruit from the same sort of area as other schools whose final ranking was in some cases much higher. As explained earlier the Census data were used for an area of $\frac{1}{4}$ mile radius of the school and it was agreed that 2 schools ½ mile apart might have different scores because of Census differences even though they recruited from much the same area; i.e. catchment areas overlapped. The scores for a large number of schools were examined but in all cases the Census data were very similar, differences being in the school variables.

Subsequently, since additional resources have been allocated critic- isms have come from individual schools or school managers. The majority of these have stressed factors present in the school which were not included in the criteria used for the Index. One school thought that four additional criteria should have been included: incomplete families (recommended in the Plowden Report itself), sick parents, criminality of parents/area, and restricted code of children. Another school argued the problems posed by 'the native and Irish immigrant population with its high proportions of criminals, prosti- tutes and mentally unstable parents'. Clearly, these are criticisms about the criteria used which it must be reiterated were accepted both by the ILEA and by the representatives of the teachers' organizations, who were consulted on this, as the best available. In summary, one can only add that there was substantial agreement about the exercise both in the planning stage and then as regards the practical results.

In conclusion certain final points can be made. It is the logic of this Index that is important, not its detail: in other words attempting to designate areas of special concern by objective, reproducible criteria and measures which are agreed prior to the designation. In addition, the reason for giving equal weighting to these factors was not because we thought that a weighted index would not be more useful, it was simply because there is no theoretical or empirical justification for a differential weighting scheme. A further issue previously mentioned is relevant in this context: would any system of weighting (either intui- tively defended or empirically evolved) be satisfactory either for one local area or for the whole country? Put another way, are the same criteria satisfactory for the variety of local conditions that add up to the United Kingdom? We cannot give a definite answer to these questions: the only assertion we would make is that the attempt to obtain general agreement is worthwhile, and initially this should concentrate upon outlining relevant criteria, and after that developing adequate meas- ures. The Index described above is an example of what might be done; it is the first step in rational resource allocation but not a final answer.

Essentially the Index was an attempt to create an instrument that turned a policy objective into administrative practice. Its main limita- tions stem from the following:

lack of either clarity or specificity in the policy objectives;
lack of empirical-theoretical support for the policy objectives;
lack of precision in criteria for determining policy;
lack of adequate measures of agreed criteria.

In a sense they are limitations that stem from ignorance about the meaning and cause of multiple deprivation and lack of available data about the distribution of deprived areas. A final point is worth making about the Index as an administrative tool; it was designed to help with determining both the volume of 'need' in a large authority and the distribution of extra resources designed to help Educational Priority Areas. It was not designed as a means of evaluating the effectiveness of any help that was to be given. Possibly it might enable a comparison to be made between degree of deprivation and amount of resources mobilized, but its very nature does not permit any measurement of impact of resources allocated. To do this another, and different, index would be necessary (although some of the 'tone' criteria might be common). The reason for this is that the Plowden Report recommended the use of the education system as a means of funnelling resources to disadvantaged areas to compensate children for these disadvantages. The Plowden strategy did not recommend operating on the socio-economic causes of deprivation, merely using the school as a means of compensating for these deprivations.

References

1. Department of Education and Science, *Children and their Primary Schools: A Report of the Central Advisory Council for Education (England)*, (Chairman: Lady Plowden, JP), London: HMSO, reprinted 1969.
2. Ministry of Housing and Local Government, *Report of the Committee on Housing in Greater London* (Chairman: Sir Milner Holland, CBE, QC), London: HMSO, 1965.
3. Article printed in *The Times*, 3 Mar. 1968.
4. C. A. Moser and W. Scott, *British Towns*, London: Oliver and Boyd, 1961.

14

Pupils' expectations for their teachers

R. Nash

Introduction to Reading 14

Nash reports his research from what appears (from internal evidence) to be a study of a class in an Edinburgh secondary school.

He used two methods of data collection in a complementary fashion. The first was a form of the Kelly Repertory Grid, the second was observation of the class in action with a number of different teachers.

The two methods of data collection used in this research differ in the degree of 'structuring' which they impose when they are used to collect data. In the variant of the Kelly Grid technique which Nash used, the class pupils were first asked to sort their teachers into two groups; those which the pupil felt he or she 'got on with', and those which he or she felt they 'didn't get on with'. So far, the data are highly structured. The stimuli (the general term for what the researcher does in order to obtain a response from the subject) are fixed rather than variable according to the subject; furthermore, the data which the subject 'supplies' is categorised into only two groups. That is, responses are not open-ended but fixed.

From this point on, the Kelly Grid technique (and the adaptation of it used by Nash) becomes relatively unstructured in form. The comparison of teachers who belong to the two groups is *elicited* from the pupil in a naturalistic, non-directive conversation, of which Nash gives us an example in his appendix to the paper. Thus the constructs (or we could say 'concepts') which the pupil uses to evaluate teachers are the ones which he or she used in everyday speech. They are not drawn from a language imposed in advance by the researcher, who may bias his results by prematurely structuring them. In terms of the pupils' expectations of teachers – the subject of the article – bias could be introduced by a researcher who provides a list of teacher-qualities with which the pupil is expected to agree or disagree. Attitude surveys use just this sort of 'structuring' of stimuli and of possible responses. The survey researcher should have carried out a number of *pilot* (or exploratory) interviews before designing the questionnaire. Part of the purpose of the pilot survey is to elicit the natural perceptions and evaluations of subjects so as to yield the range of attitudes actually held by the population before the main

From *Research in Education*, No. 12, Nov. 1974, pp. 47–61.

survey proceeds to find out the incidence and correlates of attitudes held in the population. Even with good piloting, the researcher may find that some subjects simply 'do not see' their world in the way in which the structured questionnaire allows him to see it. By eliciting responses in an unstructured interview, this misclassification of responses (a form of bias) is avoided. Nash does not give us sufficient information in his article for us to judge whether the bipolar constructs for pupils' expectations of teachers are a fair representation of the *common* view. He does lay stress in his theoretical introduction to the paper on the interactionist perspective in sociology; a theory which sees the social group as enforcing shared views on its members, so we should not be surprised if the pupils show a marked agreement in the attributes of a 'good' teacher. He does, however, use another method of data collection in order to check the extent to which verbal attitudes correspond to actual behaviour. Here he employs sustained observation of the class being taught by a number of teachers.

This sort of observation is very unstructured; there are no stimuli in the sense of something which the researcher does in order to get a response. On the contrary, Nash relies on the natural interaction of the classroom to furnish him with data. The evaluation of teachers by pupils is implicit in their classroom behaviour, including such matters as whether they become unruly or not and how they talk to teachers. Nash uses here, as in the ethnographic method generally, his interpretation of the significance of the various interchanges he observes. His observations are structured to some degree by knowing what he is looking for, what is significant in the classroom, and what is not. This structuring of the range of potential observations is supplied by the constructs which he has previously elicited, and from the categorisation of teachers which the pupils have made. Though I call it 'structure', it is a very loose form of structure compared to something like the Flanders System of Interaction Analysis which has a complete list of codes to cover every piece of interaction in a group, even though the codes are very abstract. Structured observation means standardised stimuli, and standardised response categories. By this definition, Nash's classroom observation is relatively unstructured.

References and further reading

D. Bannister and J. M. M. Mair, *The Evaluation of Personal Constructs,* London: Academic Press, 1968.

J. Bynner, 'Data collection procedures – the nature of data', in *DE304 Research Methods in Education and the Social Sciences,* Block IV, Part 1; The Open University, 1978.

A. N. Oppenheim, *Questionnaire Design and Attitude Measurement,* London: Heinemann, 1966.

During the last few years research in education has become concerned with the problem of 'expectancies', the idea that teachers' beliefs about pupils may act as self-fulfilling prophecies. Rosenthal and Jacobson (1968) described how children mentioned to their teachers as 'spurters' showed greater gains in measured IQ than a control group. Although this pioneer study was seriously criticised by Thorndike (1968) and Snow (1969), the results were startling enough to promote further research. Recently, Pidgeon (1970) and Barker-Lunn (1970) have both reported findings which, though by no means conclusive, do suggest that this phenomenon may be important. However, almost all research so far has been based on indirect survey methods rather than on direct observation. Its empirical nature has also meant that relevant theoretical frameworks have been ignored; moreover, researchers have paid no attention to the obvious reciprocal hypothesis that the expectations pupils have for teachers may be an important influence on their behaviour. Although there have been investigations of the qualities pupils like to see in their teachers, the analysis has rarely been carried beyond the level of simple description. Taylor (1962), for example, analysed children's essays on the 'Good Teacher' and formed a scale to measure the favourable qualities most often mentioned. The composite scale was composed of the following traits: helpful, fair, patient, firm, encouraging and friendly. Similar conclusions were reached by Evans (1962), who summed up previous research in this area rather neatly:

Children like teachers who are kind, friendly, cheerful, patient, helpful, fair, have a sense of humour, show an understanding of children's problems, allow plenty of pupil activity and at the same time maintain order. They dislike teachers who use sarcasm, are domineering and have favourites, who punish to secure discipline, fail to provide for the needs of individual pupils and have disagreeable personality peculiarities.

One may think these findings unremarkable; it would be more than odd if they were not the case. But they became more interesting when it is understood that these findings are not merely a description of children's likes and dislikes about teachers, but are a formulation of the rules of conduct which they lay down for them. Morrison and MacIntyre (1969) are the first (within the mainstream tradition of British educational research) to realise that these attitudes and expectations become norms. They write:

One expectation of teachers which appears to be shared by many British pupils is that among their primary functions are those of policeman and judge in the classroom. . . . A teacher entering this sort of situation who behaves as if these were not important functions, but as if his task were simply to instruct or as if he will be accepted as a friend, counsellor and stimulator of ideas, is not likely to be perceived as he perceives himself. He will rather be categorized by pupils as 'soft' and incompetent, and be given little respect.

Although only lately come to the consciousness of the empirically minded this idea is a commonplace of interaction psychology. For example, the way in which children's expectations for their teachers become normative has been specifically discussed by Geer (1971). She argues that the class transforms what the teacher says and does into rules for him to follow: rules which he must not change and which he must apply to all pupils. Following Becker (1952) and Geer (1971) in thinking of the classroom as a setting for social action, Nash (1973) has shown that within every classroom there is a high consensus of opinion among the teachers and pupils about the relative abilities of the members of the class. It is suggested that these findings support the interactionist theory that children are continually engaged in forming a self-concept and in developing consistent patterns of behaviour appropriate to this self-concept. The firmer these patterns of behaviour become the more unshakeable the perceptual models of them held by others will be, and the more power their expectations will have in confirming the actor's behaviour.

This interactionist model enables us to go beyond the mere collection of children's views on the behaviour of their teachers and begin to analyse their status as determinants of teacher action. We need to study the 'taken for granted' rules children formulate for their teachers. One way in which members' rules tend to become normative has been discussed by Waller and Hill (1951). They suggest that regular patterns of behaviour will be perceived as rule-bound because innovations by either actor upset the other's expectations and thus prompt him to correct the deviation from the expected norm. Garfinkel's (1967) argument that members' commonsense knowledge of the facts of social life act as a self-fulfilling prophecy in that the features of society are produced by members' compliance with each others' background expectancies, has also contributed to our understanding of this problem. Elements of Garfinkel's ethnomethodology may be applied to the statements children make about their teachers' actions. We are interested in making accountable the everyday descriptions children give of their teachers' behaviour. Schutz (1967) reminds us that the logic of the everyday thinking we are here studying will be inconsistent, incoherent, and only partially clear. Nevertheless, it has for members the appearance of a sufficient coherence, clarity and consistency to provide a reasonable chance of understanding and of being understood.

Method

In this study a fairly structured technique for holding conversations with children was adopted. The procedure employed was a modification of the traditional elicitation routine designed by Kelly (1955) for use with his repertory grid technique. Each child in a class of thirty-four 12-year-olds in their first term at secondary school was seen individually, and presented with a set of cards each bearing the name of one of his teachers. He was asked to sort the cards into two sets, (i) teachers he 'got on with', and (ii) teachers he did not 'get on with'. This done, one card from each set was shown to the child and he was asked to explain in what ways those teachers behaved differently. Ideally, the child may say, for example, 'Well, Mrs X [whom he 'gets on with'] and Mrs Y [whom he does not 'get on with'] are different because Mrs X helps you more. Mrs Y just walks up and down.' Thus the bi-polar construct, *Behaves helpfully – Behaves unhelpfully* would be obtained. The procedure was repeated until the child had finished what he had to say. He was not in any way asked to force his thoughts into a clear and consistent set of bi-polar constructs. Rather he was encouraged to enlarge on the teachers' behaviour and to discuss and compare them as he liked. The aim was to use the elicitation procedure as an aid to keep the conversation focused on the characteristics of his teachers. In this it was very successful. The conversations were tape-recorded and later transcribed. The transcript of one conversation is presented as an Appendix.

Analysis

On analysis six common constructs were found. Very often seemingly identical constructs appeared to be given different labels by different children. This is inevitable, but it does seem fair to regard many differently expressed constructs as being essentially the same. It is a matter of fine judgement to decide whether some of the bracketed alternatives given below are true alternatives or whether they are, in fact, descriptions of different aspects of teacher behaviour. The six constructs were:

1. *Keeps order–Unable to keep order*
   (Strict–Soft)
   (Punishes you–Doesn't punish you)
2. *Teaches you–Doesn't teach you*
   (Keeps you busy—Doesn't keep you busy)
   (Lets you get on–Just talks)
3. *Explains–Doesn't explain*
   (Helps you–Doesn't help you)
   (Can be understood– Can't be understood)
4. *Interesting–Boring*
   (Good–Dull)
   (Unusual–Ordinary)
5. *Fair–Unfair*
   (No favourites–Has favourites)
   (Consistent–Inconsistent)
   (Fair–Picks on people)
6. *Friendly–Unfriendly*
   (Nice/Kind–Unkind)
   (Talks gently–Shouts)
   (Has a laugh–Gets on at you)

These constructs show clearly that the pupils' view of what is appropriate teacher behaviour and what is not is well developed. The discussion below illustrates with representative comments how children use these constructs in their conversations about teachers. It is interesting that both Geer (1971) and Morrison and MacIntyre (1969) give as examples of the normative nature of children's rules those they formulate about the teacher's disciplinary function. The children in this study also were certain that the teacher had an obligation to keep order. The following comments from different children are representative:

Keeps order–Unable to keep order
Mrs K keeps the class in order but Mrs A just lets them speak and doesn't keep them in order like Mrs K –she gives them the belt if they misbehave. Mrs A just sends them out of the room.
I don't like her that much because, well, she should be stricter. And she says please be quiet –and I like Mrs K better –she gives you a good laugh sometimes. Mrs K is stricter – because, say we're reading a book like Patrick Kentigern, *as we're reading now, if we talk she'll say, 'Right, put your books away', and you're enjoying yourself and she has to put the books away and you're doing English – which not many people like doing.*
Mrs A is not strict enough. Mrs K, she makes you work – she gives you reading and all this kind of thing. Mrs A just lets you do anything you really want and she isn't strict enough – well, she'll tell you to be quiet and you don't be quiet and she'll tell you to be quiet again – but if it was Mrs K she wouldn't let you do that – well, Mrs A is soft. She just says, 'I'll give you one more warning.' I think there's a lot of noise because she doesn't belt them.
Instead of giving people the belt Mrs A says, 'Stand up' or something – 'Who's speaking?' or something like that. And if there's anybody speaking they don't get the belt.

The children were here voicing the opinions of almost the entire class. Everyone was generally agreed that teachers should be able to keep order. Pupils who were well behaved considered that the teacher should keep the noisy ones quiet so that they could work in peace. This is no more than one would expect. However, somewhat less obviously, the noisy children also believed that teachers should keep them quiet. These children commonly blamed the teacher for being 'soft' and thus failing to keep them under control. Clearly, as Morrison amd MacIntyre (1969) say, the teacher who thinks he can opt out of this particular requirement of the job, or believes he can relegate it to an unimportant part of his role, is likely to be quickly disillusioned. Without the checks they expect the class will soon become so rowdy that only wholesale repression will suffice to quieten them, a repression, incidentally, for which the teacher will gain no respect. The pupils will simply believe that he should have been more strict in the first place.

After getting his discipline right the teacher is expected by the pupils to teach. Most pupils of this age appear to have a fairly coherent idea of what real teaching is. Comments from seven boys and girls will illustrate this conception:

Teaches you—Doesn't teach you

Mrs K – she gives us stories, and Mrs X, she makes us write a lot. She does teach you more.
Well, with her you learn things. About plants and science.
Mrs K she give you good work and that and Mrs L and Mr B and Mr M give you good maths to get on with – well, so you can get on with instead of just sitting about.
Well, she's all right but she doesn't give us enough work to do really. She just gives you stories and that and – well, you're not learning anything and it's – you just have to sit back and you get bored.
She's good. She teaches us about copper sulphate and you learn a lot.
Mrs L always gives you things to do and sometimes – well, you do learn things from Mrs L.
Well, I like woodwork. He teaches you how to make boats and all things you would need.

Clearly the teacher is expected to teach well-defined and specific subjects. These children tend not to regard discussion as real work; they don't think it demands an essential part of the teacher's skills and they feel they learn little from it. This suggests that the teacher who attempts to encourage discussion, and strives to break down the barriers between subjects, needs to be careful to give the impression that she is still 'learning' them 'things'.

The next set of extracts show the high value placed on the teacher who explains the work carefully. This is clearly another part of the teacher's task he is not expected to shirk.

Explains things—Doesn't explain things

Say you got stuck on a certain sum – he explains it out in detail to you but with Mr G, I think he'd say, 'Well, it's simple. Work it out for yourself.'
Mr D shows you if you get it wrong and – tells you what to do. So does Mr M. But he [Mr B] just tells you to open the page and go on with it. Don't tell you much.
She just tells us about Greece and we have to write about it and take dictation and you just ask what she said and she'll say, 'Just work it out for yourselves and think.'
Mr M just gives you more attention than Mr B does – well, if you – you just need to ask him something and he'll tell you, but you – Mr B – he comes along and says 'What do you think?' and every sum, you have to try to figure it out for yourself, but Mr M gives you more attention than Mr B does.

Well, she [Mrs K] describes things more better than Mrs L and she explains what to do; and Mrs L just gives it to you, and I'd rather have Mrs K.

With Mr M he explains things first on the board – where Mr B gives you things out of books and he canna explain same as Mr M does on the board. A lot of people get stuck with Mr B but Mr M when you do it – well, he helps you learn.

Evidently, children do expect to be helped and to have difficulties explained to them. Specifically, they expect the teacher to be patient and not to shrug off his teaching responsibilities by telling them to work things out for themselves when they ask for help. The children feel that the teacher is employed to *teach*. If he does not they will think the worse of him for it.

A further important demand pupils make of their teachers is that they should not bore them. The extracts from six children are representative of this feeling:

Interesting–Boring

This one takes you out to places. Out into the playground and she takes you up Arthur's Seat and down to Inch Burn. And Mrs A keeps you to work all the time – and reading.

Well, sometimes, say, well – she gives us an exercise and we've done it and we've got to wait until the rest catch up. I just like to get on with some work.

She doesn't give us enough interesting work. Mrs K she does give us stories out of the book – and it doesn't make any sense.

Well, everybody – you ken, they stand there and nobody listens because they don't really like French. She should give you different things because you do the same things as last week.

It's awful boring with Mrs A – Well, in – she stops reading the story and that and she's telling you and you don't really want to listen and you start talking.

Mrs A she can't get you interested in it but Mrs K she can get you interested more.

These quotations show that pupils appreciate the teacher who can make his lessons flow and knows how to put the subject across in a way that makes sense. They do not like the teacher who continually interrupts the lesson to put what often appear as disruptive questions. Lessons which are disturbed and difficult to understand are perceived as boring. General quotations suggest that the pupils' perception of a teacher as boring and uninteresting does alter their behaviour. And because the pupils' behaviour changes, so does that of the teacher. If a teacher's lessons are always the same the pupils become bored; therefore they talk or mess about, the teacher interrupts the flow of the lesson to quieten them, her exhortations prove ineffectual, the pupils perceive her as 'soft', and so on.

Though it is important to be strict it is just as important to be fair.
The following are representative extracts:

Fair–Unfair

*Mrs E, she's too strict – Say you're in a group and somebody talks she'd
most likely give the whole group the belt, and she'd shout, and one
person talking she'd give the whole class lines.*

*Well, for the slightest thing you're getting into trouble. One time some-
body said something funny and everybody started laughing and then she
just took everybody she saw laughing and just gave them the belt and I
dinna think that was all that fair. And Mrs K – I dunnon – she only
punishes you when there is a reason – a good reason.*

*If you do anything in Mr M's room he'll give you a proper row but he
won't give you the belt first time. But Mrs E she gives you the belt for
almost everything.*

*Well, Mrs K's fair and that. Sometimes it is interesting. She gives you
time to talk and that.*

*Well, Mrs E I dinna like her much. She seems to be the same as the other
teachers, kinda – some of them seem to be all right, fair and that. But
other teachers – Mrs J, if everybody in the other class is making a noise,
well, she'll look at me and she'll give me the blame while everyone else is
doing it too.*

*I like Mr M because he talks to you gently all the time, and Mr G, he
laughs with you and then he gives you a row for laughing at him.*

Obviously there are certain rules of behaviour that pupils expect
from the teacher. He should give you a second chance or a fair warning.
But then he should be strict. He should allow a certain amount of quiet
talking, particularly towards the end of the period when most people
have finished their work. He should not insist on complete silence
throughout the entire lesson. He should not joke and then punish
children for laughing. He should not pick on pupils or have favourites.
These are standards that the teacher is required to live up to. The
novice teacher, for example, can easily fall foul of these expectations.
He may give too many warnings or not take action until it is too late.
The action he does take may then be perceived as over-severe; a panic
six strokes of the belt to the whole of the back row instead of one stroke
to the responsible boy in the corner. Inexperience at spotting culprits is
not considered an excuse for indiscriminate punishment. Nor is it
thought fair to punish one offender unless all the others are equally
punished. These are hard conditions for the novice teacher, especially
if he thinks that ignoring initial instances of misbehaviour is a good way
of deterring further instances. It is not.

Friendliness is something of a bonus. Children seem not to *expect* it;
but they are grateful when they receive it. The extracts which follow
are representative of the behaviour of teachers children perceived as
friendly:

Friendly–Unfriendly

I like her. She gives you a laugh sometimes.
Mrs K's nice – Well, she sort of – I think she likes children really.
Well, I like Mrs K because, well, you ken, she talks to you – just like Mr W does – she doesn't give you the belt for anything.
Mrs J, yes, I like her, because, well, all the people I like, you ken, they talk to you, and then – well, you can understand them. And it's like my Mum you can understand her, but sometimes with my Dad you can't because he gets on at you all the time. And that's what I like about Mrs K. He's quite a nice teacher. He sort of likes you, I think. He doesn't shout and bawl all the time. And he gives you work to do.
Mrs K never shouts and Mrs E is always shouting. The least little movement and she's always shouting and telling you to be quiet. I don't think she likes teaching and children.

The teacher most liked by the children is the one who is quiet and friendly. The one who can talk easily with them and share the occasional joke. Many children of this age do become easily upset and made nervous by the shouting which they hear not only from the over-strict domineering teacher, but also from many novice teachers. And though it can reasonably be argued that it is the children's exploitation of the new teacher's inexperience which provokes his loud reaction, the pupils, as we have seen, blame him.

Discussion

One may conclude that the expectations the children create for their teachers are very powerful. It certainly seems that they have a considerable influence on the behaviour of the teacher. It is clear that the teachers the children did not 'get on with' were those who did not keep the rules. With some teachers the misunderstanding was particularly tragic. Several times I have observed liberally minded teachers who cared deeply for their pupils but who, because they would not follow the recognised ways of getting control of the class, were unable to gain even minimum co-operation from them. Because these teachers were felt to have broken the rules they were considered fair game and were teased unmercifully. It does seem difficult for the liberally minded teacher in a conventionally run school to avoid being constructed by his pupils as 'soft'. Most such teachers are forced, after a very short time, to begin to punish children severely, and to be more formal and distant in their relations with them.

One way to see how much easier the teacher makes her task by acting in line with the expectations of her pupils is to show how two different teachers react to a 'trying on' process by children of the same class. Mrs C and Mrs A are both young women, fairly new to teaching, and they taught English to the class I studied. Their effectiveness with this class was very different.

Mrs C was quiet and effective in her management of discipline. To the best of my knowledge she never used the belt. The following incident, taken from field notes made at the time, was the most serious challenge she experienced:

All reading. Silence. Nothing to write about for minutes. Heads down. A little restlessness from Alec and George. 'What's the matter, boys?' This settles it. 'Why are you talking? Have you finished?' 'Yes', says Alec. 'Well, you'd better read on.' Silence for about two minutes. 'You're still talking. Stand out there.' To Alec. 'Take the book with you.' 'I've finished.' Mrs C looks at him. 'Carry on where you left off. Right down in the corner.' She speaks very quietly. Alec walks over to the corner. The class look unaffected. They are all concentrating on their reading. Everything is very still.

Alec was a bright boy with a rather strong tendency to make a fuss when he became bored or thought the teacher 'soft'. He went too far with the abrupt 'I've finished', but Mrs C refused to rise, which might have given him support from the class, and Alec was left in the corner. The effectiveness of Mrs C's response lies in her ability to spot immediately the implied threat to her maintenance of discipline in Alec's response. The moment seemed very important and the notes may be glossed at this point. Most members of the class were aware of the interaction between Mrs C and Alec, and they perceived it as a confrontation. The behaviour they expect of a teacher is to recognise and deal with such a challenge. Mrs C shows that she perceives Alec's behaviour as the class perceive it, as a threat, and demonstrates the effectiveness of her control by her quiet insistence on isolating him in the corner as a punishment. The class take in this meaning. To them it is another indication that Mrs C 'knows the ropes'. She cannot be 'messed about'.

Mrs A's response to a similar 'trying on' by the class is very different. It was quite clear that Mrs A very much disliked resorting to corporal punishment or even punishment of any kind. Her approach to teaching was fundamentally progressive but it was difficult for her to translate her ideas into practice. Mrs A wanted her pupils to internalise the value system she held. She wanted them to work because they were interested in what they were doing and to be quiet from a realisation that noise disturbs their classmates. Mrs A often made this philosophy explicit. 'Class, I do not like these bad manners. When anybody is reading or speaking we will have quietness then they'll do the same for you.' The class clearly didn't believe this and they perhaps knew themselves better than Mrs A did. Because of this attitude Mrs A allowed a freedom of comment unprecedented in this school and habitually ignored remarks obviously meant to challenge her authority. The following field note extract provides a good example:

Teacher reads the poem. Emily and the other girls near her call for another poem. 'We want Rats, *Miss. Page 63.' 'Wait a minute,' says the teacher, 'Do you think* My Sister *is as good as* My Father?'*William calls out, 'Don't know – never met your father.' Teacher ignores this. But she gives up the attempt to ask questions.*

This was the usual fate of Mrs A's attempt to question the class. The boys especially were so disruptive that Mrs A would quickly move on to written work which could be more closely supervised. Because Mrs A refused to act as the class expected a teacher to act, in that she declined to check provocative comments and neither defined nor enforced clear limits to the pupils' behaviour, they soon became almost completely out of hand. The following notes adequately demonstrate this:

Alec and William are chattering and dancing up and down on their seats. Mrs A calls out the names of pupils who are not present. She dusts the board. William chats to Irene. Alec is messing about. Great noise. Irene, William, Alec and Rosemary chatter together. 'Edzel, you are not doing very well this afternoon.' William is moved to the other side of the room. 'Wasn't me talking', he says. 'You've been talking on and off all afternoon.' 'Wasn't me', he says again. 'Get over there and don't answer back.' He goes. Mrs A quietens the class a little. 'You know what this is?' she asks holding up her belt. Mrs A wants to do a lesson on Blishen's The school that I'd like. *There is a great noise. 'You must be quiet or you won't get anything interesting to do. You'll just get boring work.' The lesson proceeds for ten minutes. Mrs A calls for attention. Listen. 'Listen!' It is impossible to hear. Mrs A gives up. 'If there are any more comments you'll just get dictation.' George and Judi call out. Jim is giggling. Someone (William?) is making a noise like a cuckoo. 'If there are any more of those noises I'll pick out the people and even if it isn't the right ones, I'll belt them. And you'll get dictation.' This doesn't quieten them. People call 'Unfair' and 'Wasn't me' and so on. Alec, Kathleen and Helen chant 'Dic-dic-tation corporation.' Mrs A is getting pretty flustered and starts to write up names on the board. She writes up Eileen's name. William is still hooting from time to time. Mrs A is definitely getting very cross. She catches Hamish (!) hooting. Kathleen yells, 'Belt him, Miss. Belt him good'. Uproar again.*

Mrs A never really succeeded in quietening the class at all during that lesson. Admittedly this was one of the class's bad days but episodes like this were very frequent in Mrs A's lessons. Her ineffectual threats were treated with open contempt by most of the children. Her determination to control William achieved results for only a few minutes because the same firmness was not applied to the rest of the class. It should also be noted that when the situation got really out of hand even timid and inoffensive children like Hamish would join in. It hardly needs to be emphasised that these were the very ones to be caught. Kathleen clamours joyously for him to be belted because she is delighted to see a 'good' child in trouble.

It would be wrong to assume from this account that Mrs A was an ineffective teacher. Most people would agree that faced with this class the style she adopted was unsuitable, but this is not to say that with other classes or perhaps in other schools her methods and philosophy would not be more helpful. But even Mrs A herself would not deny, I think, that this class gave her a hard time. I suggest that the fundamental reason for this was Mrs A's insistence on teaching, or trying to teach, in a style which was quite out with the experience and expectations of her pupils.

It is because the classroom is rarely seen as a setting for social action that many novice teachers have such difficulties. Most of the so-called practical training in discipline offered to teachers has no more scientific status than a tip for the Derby. Trainee teachers are told variously to, 'project the voice', 'make your lessons interesting', 'isolate the rowdy ones', 'clamp down on the first day' and so on. More to the point would be to teach student teachers to learn the members' rules. The 'trying on' process described so well by Waller (1932) and Geer (1971) and in several 'non-fiction novels' by school teachers, for example, Blishen (1955), has a vital importance. It means, 'Do you know the rules?' 'Are you prepared to follow them?' If the teacher doesn't or won't, then in a very real sense he isn't a proper teacher. Therefore, there is no need to listen to him or try to learn from him; he has no bona fides. There is a dilemma for teachers who know the rules but don't like them. Many 'progressive' teachers do not believe it should be part of their role to check the class for noise; they feel the children should regulate their own behaviour in this respect. Unfortunately, it may take a long time to establish the new idea as the norm. It is a matter of renegotiating the contract between teacher and pupils. A new class is not a clean slate passively waiting for the teacher to inscribe his will on it. It is an ongoing social system with very definite expectations about appropriate teacher behaviour. If these are not confirmed the pupils will protest and the renegotiated patterns of behaviour may not prove to be just what the teacher intended.

The six distinct characteristics I have suggested children expect from their teachers are a powerful agent working against change in the classroom. Changes, initiated by a group of teachers who are in the majority in the school probably can overcome the existing expectations and create new ones. But the lone teacher, seeking to innovate in a traditional school, is likely to fail uncomfortably.

One other point needs to be mentioned. Many of these expectations pupils have implicitly recognise a passive conception of their role. For example, the children think they should be kept in order. They do not believe they should be given the opportunity to control their own behaviour. Again they say that they should be 'taught things'. They don't demand to be given the opportunity to find things out for themselves. In some ways this seems to be particularly disturbing. The conception of teacher behaviour they consider correct is one that considerably restricts their own autonomy and their range of purposeful action. If the experience of school does generate such limiting self-definitions it is surely not wholly achieving its aims.

Appendix

The following is a transcript of a structured conversation with one of the boys aged 12 in this class. William sorted out a set of cards each bearing the name of one of his teachers into two groups; (i) a group he 'gets on with', and (ii) a group he doesn't 'get on with'.

Roy Nash. These are in order?

William. That's first.

R.N. That's first.

W. And that's the last.

R.N. Um. Fantastic. Let's write them all down to begin with. The ones you get on with. Mr G, Mr H, Mr C, Miss E, Mrs I, Mrs K, and Mr B. Right. So let's take these as people you get on with pretty well. OK? Would that be fair enough to say that.

W. Yes.

R.N. OK. Well, what I want you to do – What can you tell me about the differences between these two teachers? [Hand cards of Mr G and Mrs A.] Do you see any differences in them?

W. Yes. She hardly talks to us and she [Mrs A] dinna come up to your desk and say, 'How are you getting on?' and that. Mr G comes round and looks at your paintings and like Mrs L, here, she comes round to see your experiments – Mr G, he has fun with you, no other teacher more or less has fun with you.

R.N. Yes, what do you mean, fun, William?

W. Well, he comes up to you and talks with you. He says, 'What would happen if you lived in these days?' and all this. And, 'What would you be like if you had no clothes on?'

R.N. Does he? That's the sort of joke he has with you, is it?

W. Yes, he takes the micky as we say. Takes a lot of fun.

R.N. So it's fun being in his classes?

W. Yes.

R.N. What about these? [Hand cards of Mrs L and Mrs E.] You were saying something about Mrs L coming and looking at your experiments.

W. If you call her she comes, she says, 'Wait a minute', and then she comes up. She doesn't – like Mrs E says – she doesn't say – 'That's good writing', or 'OK, that's a good one, how about focusing it up?' or something like that. Or doing something else to it. Mrs E doesn't do that. She just tells you to do something and you've got to do it.

R.N. Great. What about these teachers? [Hand cards of Mr C and Mr D.]

W. Well, he [Mr C] only checks you a few times and he has a good laugh with you. And he helps you paint, if you're not a good drawer he draws a picture and you paint it.

R.N. Right, who else is there? You've got Mr H. What does he teach?

W. Music.

R.N. Ah, yes.

W. He's pretty good. If you want, say you want such and such a song he'll play it for you and that. He's good.

R.N. Fine. Now what about these? [Hands cards of Mrs A and Mrs E.]

W. Oh, she [Mrs E] – you just – er – ask for a loan of a pencil and she comes out and you get three of the belt for that, for absolutely asking, for a pencil.

R.N. No other teacher's like that?

W. No other teacher's like that.

R.N. Why do you think she's like that?

W. Don't know, it's just – she does that.

R.N. OK. How do you get on with Mrs A. What's she like?

W. Oh, I get on pretty well with her.

R.N. And Mrs J, here, how do you get on with Mrs J?

W. Well, I sometimes get on with her and I sometimes don't.

R.N. Do these two teachers [Mrs A and Mrs J] have any differences? Or anything in common?

W. Well, they're both about the same – like Mrs J might be – no writing at all one day and then maybe you're slogging away at writing the – another day. Mrs A, she keeps you like that as well, sometimes she just has fun with you, tells you poems and that, but sometimes she might get strict and give us writing and that – she's sometimes strict.

R.N. You say she's sometimes strict?

W. Yes, sometimes.

R.N. Very often?

W. Not very often – but sometimes.

R.N. Let's see if we can see any differences between Mrs K and Mrs A. What did you say the differences between them were?

W. Mrs K is stricter.

R.N. What do you mean stricter? What does she do?

W. Because, say we're reading a book like *Patrick Kentigern,* as we're doing now, if we talk she'll say, 'Right, put the books away', and you've got to put the books away and you're enjoying yourself and she has to put the books away and you're doing English – which not many people like doing. Mrs A doesn't do that. If you start talking she tells you to be quiet or gives you stricter work or something.

R.N. But very often people are not quiet whatever the work is in her class.

W. I think she should give you lines or the belt or if you're naughty or that or anything like that they should take you out at the end of the period and should give you about four of the belt maybe that would quieten them down – or maybe send you to Mr T. Because he's got a very good belt.

R.N. Fine. Are there any differences between people that we haven't mentioned?

W. No – some things are – it's really good. Art and History are good, so's Music. They're all interesting subjects.

R.N. Are they interesting in themselves or are they interesting because of the people who teach them?

W. In themselves I suppose. Because History is about the clothes and you get this thing printed into your book – it's a sort of ink thing – and you colour it in and he hardly checks you and if you're quiet he gives you more stuff and it's more fun if you're quiet.

R.N. Yes . . .

W. Mr G's only got to say, 'Be quiet', and you're quiet because it's that interesting a subject.

R.N. Um. We haven't mentioned Mrs F?

W. It's not really interesting. There [Mrs E and Mrs W] they don't like me very much.

R.N. How can you tell that? I'm not saying they don't, but what makes you think that?

W. Well, last week, for instance, we got lines instead of Library because of me and John, we just walked into the class whispering and we sat down and we got our books and that and she [Mrs E] said, 'Oh, it's no use taking your books out because you are going to do lines', and ever since then she's been checking us. We went into the classroom today and she said, 'Remember, no talking', to me and John. She'll do that next week probably if I come in with John. 'Remember, no talking.'

R.N. OK. Fine. We've done that all right. Thanks.

References

Barker-Lunn, J. C. (1970) *Streaming in the Primary School.* Slough: National Foundation for Educational Research.

Becker, H. S. (1952) 'Social class variations in the teacher-pupil relationship', *Journal of Educational Sociology,* **25,** 8.

Blishen, E. (1955) *Roaring Boys.* London: Panther.

Evans, K. M. (1962) *Sociometry and Education.* London: Routledge & Kegan Paul.

Garfinkel, H. (1967) *Studies in Ethnomethodology.* New Jersey: Prentice-Hall.

Geer, B. (1971) 'Teaching', in B. R. Cosin *et al.* (ed.), *School and Society: A Sociological Reader.* London: Routledge & Kegan Paul.

Kelly, G. A. (1955) *The Psychology of Personal Constructs.* New York: Norton.

Mead, G. H. (1934) *Mind, Self and Society,* ed. C. W. Morris. Chicago: University of Chicago Press.

Morrison, A. and MacIntyre, D. (1969) *Teachers and Teaching.* Harmondsworth: Penguin.

Nash, R. (1973) *Classrooms Observed.* London: Routledge & Kegan Paul.

Pidgeon, D. A. (1970) *Expectation and Pupil Performance*. Slough: National Foundation for Educational Research.

Rosenthal, R. and Jacobson, L. (1968) *Pygmalion in the Classroom*. New York: Holt, Rinehart and Winston.

Schutz, A. (1967) *The Phenomenology of the Social World*, trans. G. Walsh. Evanston: Northwestern University.

Snow, R. (1969) 'Review of *Pygmalion in the Classroom* by Rosenthal and Jacobson', *Contemporary Psychology*, **14**, 197–9.

Taylor, P. H. (1962) 'Children's evaluations of the characteristics of a good teacher', *British Journal of Educational Psychology*, **32**, 258–66.

Thorndike, R. L. (1968) 'Review of *Pygmalion in the Classroom* by Rosenthal and Jacobson', *AERA Journal*, **5**, No. 4, 708–11.

Waller, W. (1932/65) *The Sociology of Teaching*. New York: Wiley.

Waller, W. and Hill, R. (1951) *The Family*, New York: Dryden Press.

Data analysis

15

The fate of idealism in medical school

H. S. Becker and B. Geer

Introduction to Reading 15

Becker and Geer were part of a research group at the University of Chicago in the 1950s who conducted a study of the *socialisation* of medical students. The article in this reader is a report on one aspect of the study. (The full report is in Becker *et al.*, 1961.) Socialisation is a process frequently studied by sociologists and psychologists. The first studies in socialisation were undertaken by anthropologists who wanted to know how children in simple societies became fully fledged, conforming, and knowledgeable members of their own cultures. Modern societies are more complex than those which anthropologists have studied, and the socialisation of individuals takes many forms: into the family, a social class, the school, the peer group, and in occupation.

Individuals are socialised into cultures, into the wider culture of their society and into the specific subcultures of their families, their occupations, their social classes, etc. Culture consists of patterns of belief (how we see the world), of sentiment (how we are taught to value some goals and not others), and of forms of behaviour. These cultural patterns do not exist as written charters, they are both explicit and implicit, or official and unofficial. They are, if you like, mysteries reserved for the initiated, and occupations which are strange to us can be just as alien as another culture – in fact they are other cultures.

How does the sociologist study the world of an alien occupation? From the outside, by means of formal interviews or by becoming as far as possible, a participating member of the occupational group? The danger of being a non-participating observer is shown by Becker and Geer's reference to the reports in psychological research which show medical students scoring higher each year on a test of 'cynicism' and lower on 'idealism'.

As Becker and Geer show, cynicism and idealism are not fixed personality characteristics of the medical student, gradually acquired as the student moves through the years of his medical training. Rather, the development of a cynical or realistic conception of the doctor's role is dependent on the context in which it is expressed. Cynical expressions depend partly on whether the student is speaking or acting as a member of the group of his fellow-students

From *American Sociological Review*, **23** (Feb. 1958), 50–6.

or as an individual relatively free from the pressure to conform to the group's norms. Idealism does not disappear, piece by piece as the student progresses, but changes from the layman's version held by the freshman to the more qualified idealism of the socialised doctor.

By using the method of participant observation, the balance between cynicism and idealism and the contexts in which they are expressed need to be discovered in a way which formal interviews or attitude tests cannot do. As do the causes of cynicism in medical students. If one simply knows only that a sample of medical students scores low on a test of cynicism in their first year, and progressively higher as their training advances, the processes in the medical school which produce these changes must remain a black box in which we can only know what goes in and what comes out, not how the transformation takes place. The method of participant observation opens up the black box for us and transforms the concepts of cynicism/idealism into something more subtle and further removed from the essentially lay idea of the 'tough, hardened, unfeeling doctor'.

As Becker (1956/57, p. 199) writes in a related paper on his research methods:

Probably most commonly, individuals feel both ways [i.e. cynical and idealistic – ed.] about the values of their groups at the same time; or one way in some situations, the other way in others. In which of these moods are they likely to respond to the interviewer seeking sociological information? Or to turn attention to the interviewer himself: which of these is he looking for in the people he talks to? Which kind of response is he concerned with eliciting?

Becker notes that when he first began participant observation of the medical students he was sensitised to the development of cynicism and his field notes accordingly show how the student group develops a realistic or cynical attitude to medical school as a strategy for coping with stresses of examinations. When Becker reviewed his field notes during the study he found frequent implicitly idealistic comments from some of the medical students which he had missed on first analysis. The observer's initial perspective, as Becker (1956/57, p. 200) notes, creates the problem 'that he will either misinterpret idealism sincerely presented to him or, by his manner of questioning, fashion a role for himself in the interview that encourages cynicism whilst discouraging idealism'.

Becker and Geer's article (and Becker's related article) can be read as an illustration of 'progressive focusing' in ethnographic research. Starting from the layman's conception of the hardened, unfeeling doctor they looked to the social interaction in the medical school to explain the transition from idealism to cynicism. But their initial research problem changes as their familiarity with the field improves. Now they look not for the movement from the pole of idealism to the pole of cynicism, but to the coexistence of both perspectives in the same subject. Admittedly, these perspectives do not equally coexist, some subjects will exemplify one pole rather than the other, but the central analytical interpretation of the authors is that the students can manifest cynicism in one context, and idealism in another. The students can balance in some way what appear as contradictory perceptions. The balancing act is achieved by expressing beliefs in a way which is dependent on the context in which views are elicited. The art of the sociological analyst is to be able to go behind the rhetoric of the actors, for 'every conversation has its own balance of revelation and concealment of thoughts and intentions: only under very unusual circumstances is talk so completely expository that every word can be taken at its face value' (Benney and Hughes, 1956/57). As in ethnographic research in general, the analysis of their data is a continuous process and not a phase of research which occurs after the research has been designed, the data collected, and before writing up the report. Continuous analysis means that the rhetoric of the early natural interviews or conversations must be initially dissected by the observer before he can decide how to proceed to deeper layers of rhetoric. Becker's account of his discovery of implicit idealism in his field notes which he had at first missed is an example of analysis and reanalysis followed by more data collection until the processes are 'understood'. The fundamentals of ethnographic research are the repeated sequences of discovery, reinterpretation of data, and the collection of new data in order to refine the understanding of the social processes being studied.

The authors cite George Orwell's essay on 'How the poor die' as an example of the layman's view of the cynical doctor. This view is one of the sensitising concepts which first guided their research. Orwell makes an ideal layman, more lucid and more penetrating than the great majority of the public but still someone who sees the doctor as a patient would. In 1929 Orwell entered the pauper's ward of a Parisian hospital:

During my first hour in the Hospital X, I had had a whole series of different and contradictory treatments, but this was misleading for in general you got very little treatment at all, either good or bad, unless you were ill in some interesting or instructive way . . . the tall, solemn, black bearded doctor made his rounds with an interne and a troop of students following at his heels, but there were about sixty of us in the ward and it was evident that he had other wards to attend to as well. There were many beds past which he walked day after day, sometimes followed by imploring cries. On the other hand if you had some disease with which students wanted to familiarise themselves you got plenty of attention of a kind. . . . About a dozen beds away from me was numéro 57 . . . – a cirrhosis of the liver case. Everyone in the ward knew him by sight because he was sometimes the subject of a medical lecture. On two afternoons a week the tall, grave doctor would lecture in the ward to a party of students and on more than one occasion old numéro 57 was wheeled on a sort of trolley into the middle of the ward, where the doctor would roll back his nightshirt, dilate with his fingers a huge flabby protuberance on the man's belly – the diseased liver I suppose – and explain solemnly that this was a disease attributable to alcoholism. . . . As usual he neither spoke to his patient nor gave him a smile, a nod or any kind of recognition. While he talked, very grave and upright, he would hold the wasted body beneath his two hands, sometimes giving it a gentle roll to and fro, in just the attitude of a woman handling a rolling pin. Not that old numéro 57 minded this kind of thing obviously he was an old hospital inmate, a regular exhibit at lectures, his liver long since marked down for a bottle in some pathological museum. Utterly uninterested in what was said about him, he would lie with his colourless eyes gazing at nothing, while the doctor showed him off like a piece of antique china. (Orwell and Angus 1970.)

Shortly afterwards, Orwell records, numéro 57 died.

Clear-sighted and observant as Orwell was, his is still a view from outside the medical world. Through Becker's sharing of the students' life at medical school and through his learning of their strange culture, we learn, too, how medical students come to see patients as specimens, interesting for the possibilities they present as illustrations of medical diagnoses. What appeared to Orwell as heartless indifference to the plight of numéro 57, could be the professional detachment taught to those French medical students of the 1920s in the same way as the implicit rules of Becker and Geer's American medical school socialised their students into their professional culture.

References

Becker, H. S. (1956/57) 'Interviewing medical students', *American Journal of Sociology*, **62**, 199–201.

Becker, H. S., Geer, B., Hughes, E. C. and Strauss, A. L. (1961) *Boys in White: Student culture in medical school.* Univ. Chicago Press.

Benney, M. and Hughes, E. C. (1956/57) 'Of sociology and the interview', *American Journal of Sociology*, **62**, 137–44.

Orwell, S. and Angus, I. (1970) 'How the poor die', in *The Collected Essays, Journalism and Letters of George Orwell*, Vol. 4, Penguin, p. 261.

It makes some difference in a man's performance of his work whether he believes wholeheartedly in what he is doing or feels that in important respects it is a fraud, whether he feels convinced that it is a good thing or believes that it is not really of much use after all. The distinction we are making is the one people have in mind when they refer, for example, to their calling as a 'noble profession' on the one hand or a 'racket' on the other. In the one case they idealistically proclaim that their work is all that it claims on the surface to be; in the other they cynically concede that it is first and foremost a way of making a living and that its surface pretensions are just that and nothing more. Presumably, different modes of behaviour are associated with these perspectives when wholeheartedly embraced. The cynic cuts corners with a feeling of inevitability while the idealist goes down fighting. *The Blackboard Jungle* and *Not as a Stranger* are only the most recent in a long tradition of fictional portrayals of the importance of this aspect of a man's adjustment to his work.

Professional schools often receive a major share of the blame for producing this kind of cynicism – and none more than the medical school. The idealistic young freshman changes into a tough, hardened, unfeeling doctor; or so the popular view has it. Teachers of medicine sometimes rephrase the distinction between the clinical and pre-clinical years into one between the 'cynical' and 'pre-cynical' years. Psychological research supports this view, presenting attitude surveys which show medical students year by year scoring lower on 'idealism' and higher on 'cynicism'.[1] Typically, this cynicism is seen as developing in response to the shattering of ideals consequent on coming face-to-face with the realities of professional practice.

In this paper, we attempt to describe the kind of idealism that characterizes the medical freshmen and to trace both the development of cynicism and the vicissitudes of that idealism in the course of the four years of medical training. Our main themes are that though they develop cynical feelings in specific situations directly associated with their medical school experience, the medical students never lose their original idealism about the practice of medicine; that the growth of both cynicism and idealism are not simple developments, but are instead complex transformations; and that the very notions 'idealism' and 'cynicism' need further analysis, and must be seen as situational in their expressions rather than as stable traits possessed by individuals in greater or lesser degree. Finally, we see the greater portion of these feelings as being collective rather than individual phenomena.

Our discussion is based on a study we [. . .] conducted at a state medical school,[2] in which we [. . .] carried on participant observation with students of all four years in all of the courses and clinical work to which they are exposed. We joined the students in their activities in school and after school and watched them at work in labs, on the hospital wards, and in the clinic. Often spending as much as a month with a small group of from five to fifteen students assigned to a particular activity, we came to know them well and were able to gather information in informal interviews and by overhearing the ordinary daily conversation of the group. In the course of our observation and interviewing we have gathered much information on the subject of idealism. Of necessity, we shall have to present the very briefest statement of our findings with little or no supporting evidence. The problem of idealism is, of course, many-faceted and complex and we have dealt with it in a simplified way, describing only some of its grosser features.[3]

The freshmen

The medical students enter school with what we may think of as the idealistic notion, implicit in lay culture, that the practice of medicine is a wonderful thing and that they are going to devote their lives to service to mankind. They believe that medicine is made up of a great body of well-established facts that they will be taught from the first day on and that these facts will be of immediate practical use to them as physicians. They enter school expecting to work industriously and expecting that if they work hard enough they will be able to master this body of fact and thus become good doctors.

In several ways the first year of medical school does not live up to their expectations. They are disillusioned when they find they will not be near patients at all, that the first year will be just like another year of college. In fact, some feel that it is not even as good as college because their work in certain areas is not as thorough as courses in the same fields in undergraduate school. They come to think that their courses (with the exception of anatomy) are not worth much because, in the first place, the faculty (being Ph.D.s) know nothing about the practice of medicine, and, in the second place, the subject matter itself is irrelevant, or as the the students say, 'ancient history'.

The freshmen are further disillusioned when the faculty tells them in a variety of ways that there is more to medicine than they can possibly learn. They realize it may be impossible for them to learn all they need to know in order to practice medicine properly. Their disillusionment becomes more profound when they discover that this statement of the faculty is literally true.[4] Experience in trying to master the details of the anatomy of the extremities convinces them that they cannot do so in the time they have. Their expectation of hard work is not disappointed; they put in an eight-hour day of classes and laboratories, and study four or five hours a night and most of the weekend as well.

Some of the students, the brightest, continue to attempt to learn it all, but succeed only in getting more and more worried about their work. The majority decide that, since they can't learn it all, they must select from among all the facts presented to them those they will attempt to learn. There are two ways of making this selection. On the one hand, the student may decide on the basis of his own uninformed notions about the nature of medical practice that many facts are not important, since they relate to things which seldom come up in the actual practice of medicine; therefore, he reasons, it is useless to learn them. On the other hand, the student can decide that the important thing is to pass his examinations and, therefore, that the important facts are those which are likely to be asked in an examination; he uses this as a basis for selecting both facts to memorize and courses for intensive study. For example, the work in physiology is dismissed on both of these grounds, being considered neither relevant to the facts of medical life nor important in terms of the amount of time the faculty devotes to it and the number of examinations in the subject.

A student may use either or both of these bases of selection at the beginning of the year, before many tests have been given. But after a few tests have been taken, the student makes 'what the faculty wants' the chief basis of his selection of what to learn, for he now has a better idea of what this is and also has become aware that it is possible to fail examinations and that he therefore must learn the expectations of the faculty if he wishes to stay in school. The fact that one group of students, that with the highest prestige in the class, took this view early and did well on examinations was decisive in swinging the whole class around to this position. The students were equally influenced to become 'test-wise' by the fact that, although they had all been in the upper range in their colleges, the class average on the first examination was frighteningly low.

In becoming test-wise, the students begin to develop systems for discovering the faculty wishes and learning them. These systems are both methods for studying their texts and short-cuts that can be taken in laboratory work. For instance, they begin to select facts for memorization by looking over the files of old examinations maintained in each of the medical fraternity houses. They share tip-offs from the lectures and offhand remarks of the faculty as to what will be on the examinations. In anatomy, they agree not to bother to dissect out subcutaneous nerves, reasoning that it is both difficult and time consuming and the information can be secured from books with less effort. The interaction involved in the development of such systems and short-cuts helps to create a social group of a class which had previously been only an aggregation of smaller and less organized groups.

In this medical school, the students learn in this way to distinguish between the activities of the first year and their original view that everything that happens to them in medical school will be important. Thus they become cynical about the value of their activities in the first year. They feel that the real thing – learning which will help them to help mankind – has been postponed, perhaps until the second year, or perhaps even farther, at which time they will be able again to act on idealistic premises. They believe that what they do in their later years in school under supervision will be about the same thing they will do, as physicians, on their own; the first year had disappointed this expectation.

There is one matter, however, about which the students are not disappointed during the first year: the so-called trauma of dealing with the cadaver. But this experience, rather than producing cynicism, reinforces the student's attachment to his idealistic view of medicine by making him feel that he is experiencing at least some of the necessary unpleasantness of the doctor's. Such difficulties, however, do not loom as large for the student as those of solving the problem of just what the faculty wants.

On this and other points, a working consensus develops in the new consolidated group about the interpretation of their experience in medical school and its norms of conduct. This consensus, which we call *student culture,* focuses their attention almost completely on their day-to-day activities in school and obscures or sidetracks their earlier idealistic preoccupations. Cynicism, griping, and minor cheating become endemic, but the cynicism is specific to the educational situation, to the first year, and to only parts of it. Thus the students keep their cynicism separate from their idealistic feelings and by postponement protect their belief that medicine is a wonderful thing, that their school is a fine one, and that they will become good doctors.

Later years

The sophomore year does not differ greatly from the freshman year. Both the work load and anxiety over examinations probably increase. Though they begin some medical activities, as in their attendance at autopsies and particularly in their introductory course in physical diagnosis, most of what they do continues to repeat the pattern of the college science curriculum. Their attention still centers on the problem of getting through school by doing well in examinations.

During the third and fourth, or clinical years, teaching takes a new form. In place of lectures and laboratories, the students' work now consists of the study of actual patients admitted to the hospital or seen in the clinic. Each patient who enters the hospital is assigned to a student who interviews him about his illnesses, past and present, and performs a physical examination. He writes this up for the patient's chart, and appends the diagnosis and the treatment that he would use were he allowed actually to treat the patient. During conferences with faculty physicians, often held at the patient's bedside, the student is quizzed about items of his report and called upon to defend them or to explain their significance. Most of the teaching in the clinical years is of this order.

Contact with patients brings a new set of circumstances with which the student must deal. He no longer feels the great pressure created by tests, for he is told by the faculty, and this is confirmed by his daily experience, that examinations are now less important. His problems now become those of coping with a steady stream of patients in a way that will please the staff man under whom he is working, and of handling what is sometimes a tremendous load of clinical work so as to allow himself time for studying diseases and treatments that interest him and for play and family life.

The students earlier have expected that once they reach the clinical years they will be able to realize their idealistic ambitions to help people and to learn those things immediately useful in aiding people who are ill. But they find themselves working to understand cases as medical problems rather than working to help the sick and memorizing the relevant available facts so that these can be produced immediately for a questioning staff man. When they make ward rounds with a faculty member they are likely to be quizzed about any of the seemingly countless facts possibly related to the condition of the patient for whom they are 'caring'.

Observers speak of the cynicism that overtakes the student and the lack of concern for his patients as human beings. This change does take place, but it is not produced solely by 'the anxiety brought about by the presence of death and suffering'.[5] The student becomes preoccupied with the technical aspects of the cases with which he deals because the faculty requires him to do so. He is questioned about so many technical details that he must spend most of his time learning them.

The frustrations created by his position in the teaching hospital further divert the student from idealistic concerns. He finds himself low man in a hierarchy based on clinical experience, so that he is allowed very little of the medical responsibility he would like to assume. Because of his lack of experience, he cannot write orders, and he receives permission to perform medical and surgical procedures (if at all) at a rate he considers far too slow. He usually must content himself with 'mere' vicarious participation in the drama of danger, life, and death that he sees as the core of medical practice. The student culture accents these difficulties so that events (and especially those involving patients) are interpreted and reacted to as they push him toward or hold him back from further participation in this drama. He does not think in terms the layman might use.

As a result of the increasingly technical emphasis of his thinking the student appears cynical to the non-medical outsider, though from his own point of view he is simply seeing what is 'really important'. Instead of reacting with the layman's horror and sympathy for the patient to the sight of a cancerous organ that has been surgically removed, the student is more likely to regret that he was not allowed to close the incision at the completion of the operation, and to rue the hours that he must spend searching in the fatty flesh for the lymph nodes that will reveal how far the disease has spread. As in other lines of work, he drops lay attitudes for those more relevant to the way the event affects someone in his position.

This is not to say that the students lose their original idealism. When issues of idealism are openly raised in a situation they define as appropriate, they respond as they might have when they were freshmen. But the influence of the student culture is such that questions which might bring forth this idealism are not brought up. Students are often assigned patients for examination and follow-up whose conditions might be expected to provoke idealistic crises. Students discuss such patients, however, with reference to the problems they create for the *student*. Patients with terminal diseases who are a long time dying, and patients with chronic disease who show little change from week to week, are more likely to be viewed as creating extra work without extra compensation in knowledge or the opportunity to practice new skills than as examples of illness which raise questions about euthanasia. Such cases require the student to spend time every day checking on progress which he feels will probably not take place and to write long 'progress' notes in the patient's chart although little progress has occurred.

This apparent cynicism is a collective matter. Group activities are built around this kind of workaday perspective, constraining the students in two ways. First, they do not openly express the lay idealistic notions they may hold, for their culture does not sanction such expression; second, they are less likely to have thoughts of this deviant kind when they are engaged in group activity. The collective nature of this 'cynicism' is indicated by the fact that students become more openly idealistic whenever they are removed from the influence of student culture – when they are alone with a sociologist as they near the finish of school and sense the approaching end of student life, for example, or when they are isolated from their classmates and therefore are less influenced by this culture.[6]

They still feel, as advanced students, though much less so than before, that school is irrelevant to actual medical practice. Many of their tasks, like running laboratory tests on patients newly admitted to the hospital or examining surgical specimens in the pathology laboratory, seem to them to have nothing to do with their visions of their future activity as doctors. As in their freshman year, they believe that perhaps they must obtain the knowledge they will need in spite of the school. They still conceive of medicine as a huge body of proven facts, but no longer believe that they will ever be able to master it all. They now say that they are going to try to apply the solution of the practicing M.D. to their own dilemma: learn a few things that they are interested in very well and know enough about other things to pass examinations while in school and, later on in practice, to know to which specialist to send difficult patients.

Their original medical idealism reasserts itself as the end of school approaches. Seniors show more interest than students in earlier years in serious ethical dilemmas of the kind they expect to face in practice. They have become aware of ethical problems laymen often see as crucial for the physician – whether it is right to keep patients with fatal diseases alive as long as possible, or what should be done if an influential patient demands an abortion – and worry about them. As they near graduation and student culture begins to break down as the soon-to-be doctors are about to go their separate ways, these questions are more and more openly discussed.

While in school, they have added to their earlier idealism a new and peculiarly professional idealism. Even though they know that few doctors live up to the standards they have been taught, they intend always to examine their patients thoroughly and to give treatment based on firm diagnosis rather than merely to relieve symptoms. This expansion and transformation of idealism appear most explicitly in their consideration of alternative careers, concerning both specialization and the kind of arrangements to be made for setting up practice. Many of their hypothetical choices aim at making it possible for them to be the kind of doctors their original idealism pictured. Many seniors consider speciality training so that they will be able to work in a limited field in which it will be more nearly possible to know all there is to know, thus avoiding the necessity of dealing in a more ignorant way with the wider range of problems general practice would present. In the same manner, they think of schemes to establish partnerships or other arrangements making it easier to avoid a work load which would prevent them from giving each patient the thorough examination and care they now see as ideal.

In other words, as school comes to an end, the cynicism specific to the school situation also comes to an end and their original and more general idealism about medicine comes to the fore again, though within a framework of more realistic alternatives. Their idealism is now more informed although no less selfless.

Discussion

We have used the words 'idealism' and 'cynicism' loosely in our description of the changeable state of mind of the medical student, playing on ambiguities we can now attempt to clear up. Retaining a core of common meaning, the dictionary definition, in our reference to the person's belief in the worth of his activity and the claims made for it, we have seen that this is not a generalised trait of the students we studied but rather an attitude which varies greatly, depending on the particular activity the worth of which is questioned and the situation in which the attitude is expressed.

This variability of the idealistic attitude suggests that in such an element of personal perspective in sociological analysis one should not treat it as homogeneous but should make a determined search for subtypes which may arise under different conditions and have differing consequences. Such subtypes persumably can be constructed along many dimensions. There might, for instance, be consistent variations in the medical students' idealism through the four years of school that are related to their social class backgrounds. We have stressed in this report the subtypes that can be constructed according to variations in the object of the idealistic attitude and variations in the audience the person has in mind when he adopts the attitude. The medical students can be viewed as both idealistic and cynical, depending on whether one has in mind their view of their school activities or the future they envision for themselves as doctors. Further, they might take one or another of these positions depending on whether their implied audience is made up of other students, their instructors, or the lay public.

A final complication arises because cynicism and idealism are not merely attributes of the actor, but are as dependent on the person doing the attributing as they are on the qualities of the individual to whom they are attributed.[7] Though the student may see his own disregard of the unique personal troubles of a particular patient as proper scientific objectivity, the layman may view this objectivity as heartless cynicism.[8]

Having made these analytic distinctions, we can now summarize the transformations of these characteristics as we have seen them occurring among medical students. Some of the students' determined idealism at the outset is reaction against the lay notion, of which they are uncomfortably aware, that doctors are money-hungry cynics; they counter this with an idealism of similar lay origin stressing the doctor's devotion to service. But this idealism soon meets a setback, as students find that it will not be relevant for a while, since medical school has, it seems, little relation to the practice of medicine, as they see it. As it has not been refuted, but only shown to be temporarily beside the point, the students 'agree' to set this idealism aside in favor of a realistic approach to the problem of getting through school. This approach, which we have labeled as the cynicism specific to the school experience, serves as protection for the earlier grandiose feelings about medicine by postponing their exposure to reality to a distant future. As that future approaches near the end of the four years and its possible mistreatment of their ideals moves closer, the students again worry about maintaining their integrity, this time in actual medical practice. They use some of the knowledge they have gained to plan careers which, it is hoped, can best bring their ideals to realization.

We can put this in propositional form by saying that when a man's ideals are challenged by outsiders and then further strained by reality, he may salvage them by postponing their application to a future time when conditions are expected to be more propitious.

Notes and References

1. Leonard D. Eron, 'Effect of medical education on medical students', *Journal of Medical Education,* **10** (Oct. 1955), 559–66.
2. The University of Kansas Medical School.
3. Renee Fox has shown how complex one aspect of this whole subject is in her analysis of the way medical students at Cornell become aware of and adjust to both their own failure to master all available knowledge and the gaps in current knowledge in many fields. See her 'Training for uncertainty', in Robert K. Merton, George G. Reader, and Patricia L. Kendall (eds), *The Student Physician: Introductory Studies in the Sociology of Medical Education,* Cambridge: Harvard U.P., 1957, pp. 207–41.
4. Compare Fox's description of student reaction to this problem at Cornell (*op. cit.,* pp. 209–21).
5. Dana L. Farnsworth, 'Some observations on the attitudes and motivations of the Harvard medical student', *Harvard Medical Alumni Bulletin,* Jan. 1956, 34.
6. See the discussion in Howard S. Becker, 'Interviewing medical students', *American Journal of Sociology,* **63** (Sept. 1956), 99–201.
7. See Philip Selznick's related discussion of fanaticism in *TVA and the Grass Roots,* Berkeley: University of California Press, 1953, pp. 205–13.
8. George Orwell gives the layman's side in his essay, 'How the poor die', in *Shooting an Elephant and Other Essays,* London: Secker and Warburg, 1950, pp. 18–32.

16

National wealth and infant mortality
D. M. Smith

Introduction to Reading 16

The Smith reading presents data as an illustration of a significant pattern. He does not seek to interpret the *meaning* of the relationship between level of economic development (as measured in Gross National Product *per capita*) and rate of infant mortality in twenty-five European countries, but to find the best relationship between the variables.

Note that his data includes countries covering a wide range of economic development in 1965; from Albania and Portugal to Sweden and Switzerland. The meaning of the pattern which he demonstrates so clearly is discussed in the preface to Castle's and McKinlay's paper which follows this one as a reading. Do not, however, assume that level of economic development is *the* cause of infant mortality rates. You can see from his straight-line regression in Fig. 16.1 [and even from the better regression curve in Fig. 16.3] that the points of the regression diagram are scattered about the line. This means that there are other causes of differences in infant mortality rates besides level of economic development. For if level of economic development were the only cause, then the points would lie on the regression line. Or in other words, the correlation coefficient could be 1, and not −0.85 as it is in the case of his line of best fit — the curvilinear regression line. With these qualifications in mind, it is still true that the simple, straight-line regression in Fig. 16.1 is a reasonable fit to the relationship between the two variables. The fit is improved still further by plotting a curved regression line. Smith does this by taking the logarithms of the level of economic development (his independent variable) which is the simplest way of fitting a curved regression line rather than a straight one.

Remember that even a clear-cut statistical relationship between two variables is not an adequate explanation which relates the independent variable (level of economic development) to the dependent variable (infant mortality per 1,000 live births). An adequate explanation must come from a model or theory which shows the mechanisms in social scientific language which connect the independent variable to the dependent variable. You may be tempted to supply the model and the mechanisms by common-sense reason-

From D. M. Smith, *Patterns in Human Geography,* Newton Abbot: David and Charles, 1975, pp. 264–70.

ing of the form 'if a country is wealthy there will be more to spend on preventive medicine and hospital care for babies and mothers-to-be so that we can expect fewer deaths in young children'. This is certainly plausible and partly true, but it cannot be the whole explanation. For a start there are unexplained differences between countries; why does Ireland (infant mortality of 25, GNP of $1,000) fall below the regression line in Fig. 16.3, as do some other countries?

If the 'normal' relationship between the two variables holds, then Ireland should have a higher rate of infant mortality than it does. What is it about Irish maternity services which produces results better than its economic development would lead us to believe? This oddity in the Irish position impels us to ask questions about the access to medical treatment which its population has. Perhaps the poor are more heavily subsidised in medical care than other countries with comparable wealth. If so, we should need to know something about Irish domestic politics and its social structure. Thus, a simple causal interpretation of correlation, even a strong one, such as Smith shows can be dangerous without a clear conception of how economic and social processes work to translate *per capita* wealth into welfare benefits, such as low infant mortality.

The detection of clear-cut patterns in data is only the first step in framing an explanation of phenomena such as variations in the rates of infant mortality.

It is the first phase of the analysis of quantitative data and should lead on to the testing of specific hypothesis drawn from a model which is an attempt at explaining the variations in infant mortality in a sample of countries.

The [. . .] example is concerned with the relationship between infant mortality and level of economic development in 25 European nations. Infant deaths (Y) are expressed per 1,000 live births and economic development (X) is measured by GNP per capita (Table 16.1). As X increases Y decreases quite regularly, the linear correlation coefficient (r) being -0.804.

Regression analysis gives the following equation for the linear relationship between the two variables:

$$Y = 63.4 - 0.23X$$

The line is plotted in Fig. 16.1 sloping down to the right because the relationship is negative, and a fairly close fit to the scatter of dots is revealed. The residuals are mapped in Fig. 16.2. The pattern fails to show any obvious spatial regularity or geographical grouping which might suggest additional causal factors. Tests of association between positive or negative residuals and the dichotomous variables of communist or non-communist government, above or below average number of doctors per capita and above or below average protein in national diet also failed to reveal anything of significance (chi-square tests at $p = 0.05$).

Table 16.1 Data for correlation and regression analysis of infant mortality and level of economic development in Europe.

| Nation | Infant deaths /1,000 live births | GNP per capita ($US × 10) | | Nation | Infant deaths /1,000 live births | GNP per capita ($US × 10) | |
	Y	X	log X		Y	X	log X
Albania	87	36	1.56	Italy	36	110	2.04
Austria	28	128	2.11	Luxembourg	24	197	2.29
Belgium	24	180	2.26	Netherlands	14	155	2.19
Bulgaria	31	82	1.91	Norway	16	189	2.28
Czechoslovakia	25	156	2.19	Poland	42	97	1.99
Denmark	19	212	2.33	Portugal	65	40	1.60
Finland	18	179	2.24	Rumania	44	77	1.89
France	22	192	2.28	Spain	37	56	1.75
Germany (East)	24	126	2.10	Sweden	13	254	2.40
Germany (West)	24	190	2.28	Switzerland	18	233	2.37
Greece	34	68	1.83	UK	20	181	2.25
Hungary	39	109	2.04	Yugoslavia	71	45	1.65
Ireland	25	98	1.99				

(*Source: World Handbook of Political and Social Indicators*, 2nd edn., Yale U.P. 1972 (figures *c.* 1965).)

On the basis of all this we might conclude the analysis, satisfied that an interesting empirical relationship had been established and that there was little further to be learned. However, an examination of the graph (Fig. 16.1) suggests that the linear trend identified may not be the most accurate description, for some pattern can be discerned in the residuals. The regression equation under-predicts infant mortality at the lower and upper ends of the GNP scale and over-predicts in the middle. Thus a *curvilinear* relationship is suggested, for infant mortality falls rapidly at first as GNP increases but tends to even off around 20 when the richer nations are reached.

Curvilinear correlation and regression analysis can be attempted by any appropriate transformation of either of the variables. In this case an effective method is to convert the data on GNP per capita into logarithms (Table 16.1). Putting $\log X$ instead of X into the formula for the correlation coefficient produces the result $r = -0.853$, and an explained variance (r^2) or 0.728 compared with 0.646 from the linear relationship. The regression equation can also be reworked using the $\log X$ values, to give:

$$Y = 157.8 - 60.6 \log X$$

Calculating the estimates of Y from this expression and plotting them on a graph now produces a curve (Fig. 16.3) which is a better fit to the data than the line in Fig. 16.1. The curve can itself be transformed into a line simply by replacing the horizontal scale of actual GNP values by

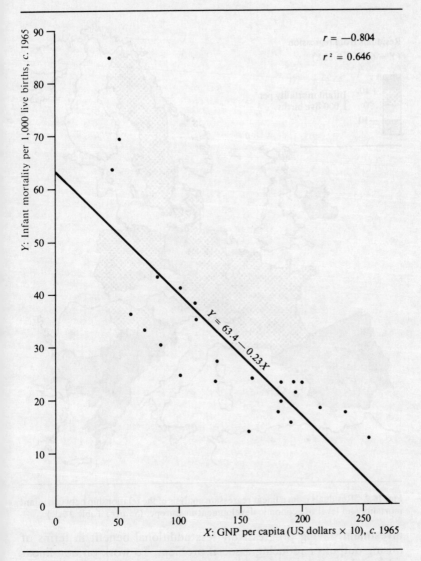

Fig. 16.1 The linear relationship between infant mortality and level of economic development (GNP per capita) in Europe. (*Source*: Table 16.1.)

their logs (Fig. 16.4). The relationship depicted is thus log-linear, or very nearly so.

This example emphasizes the importance of the nature of the relationship when correlation and regression analysis is used. Many 'input–output' relationships within a society or economy are similar to that between GNP and infant mortality, with increasing wealth or

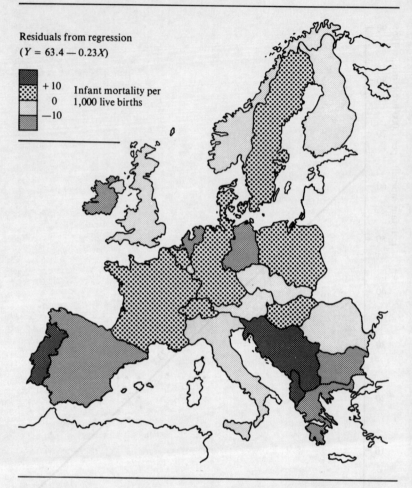

Residuals from regression
($Y = 63.4 - 0.23X$)

+ 10   Infant mortality per
0   1,000 live births
−10

Fig. 16.2 Residuals from a linear regression analysis of the relationship between infant mortality and level of economic development in Europe. (*Source*: Table 16.1.)

investment having progressively less additional benefit in terms of raising output or reducing a social problem. To work on non-linear relationships without an appropriate transformation thus risks misinterpretation of the process involved as well as underestimating the strength of the association and predicting less accurately than might otherwise be possible. An initial examination of a plot of the data can help to avoid this.

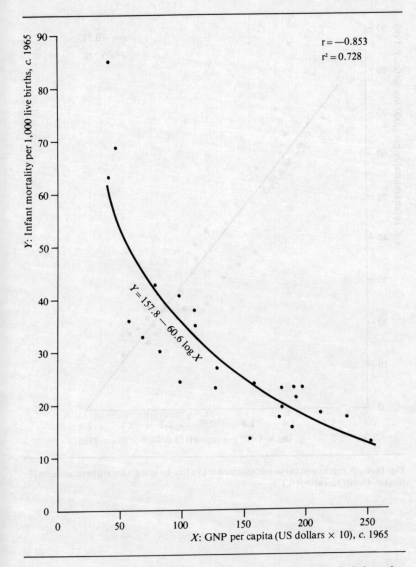

Fig. 16.3 A curvilinear regression analysis achieved by transforming the independent variable into logarithms. (*Source*: Table 16.1.)

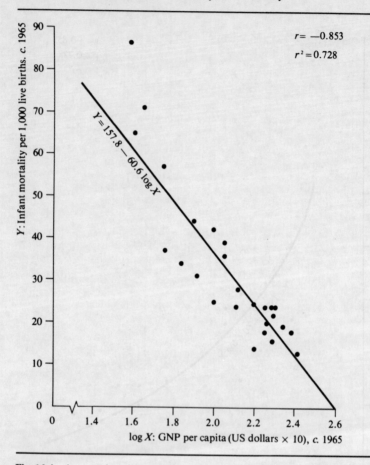

Fig. 16.4 A regression curve transformed into a line by using a logarithmic scale on the *X*-axis. (*Source*: Table 16.1.)

17

The importance of politics: an analysis of the public welfare commitment in advanced democratic states

F. Castles and R. D. McKinlay

Introduction to Reading 17

Castles' and McKinlay's article is an attack on one aspect of an influential and wide-ranging theory of the logic and consequences of social change in advanced societies. Really, we are not dealing with one theory but with a number of related theories in politics and sociology. These theories are usually known collectively as the Theory of the Convergence of Advanced Industrial Societies.

According to this theory, industrialisation imposes its logic on the social, political, and cultural institutions of advanced societies, so as to bring about a convergence to common patterns. In sociology, social stratification and family structure are the two social institutions most commonly studied as examples of convergence (Goldthorpe 1964). The evidence for similar patterns of class stratification mainly comes from research into how samples of respondents in different industrial countries rank a number of key occupations. There is a striking similarity in the relative prestige given to professional occupations on the one hand, and to unskilled manual occupations on the other. This holds true across a wide range of societies, both those which are communist or socialist, and those which are capitalist to some degree. The similarity holds, be it noted, in *advanced* industrial countries. If the similarity is evidence for the alikeness of advanced societies, the logic of their (supposed) convergence from different starting points to the same end is conjectured to be the way in which industrialism demands the same sort of skills wherever it appears. These skills will be scarce or abundant depending on their nature, and therefore the relative prestige of these scarce or abundant skills is going to be much the same in any advanced society.

You will note how the logic of industrialism is brought into this argument as an 'extra'. It is quite possible that the observed higher prestige of professional occupations is due to the shared high status in European countries which has always been given to the learned professions, even before industrialisation made any great impact. It may be that advanced societies, as far as social stratification is concerned, are not converging from different starting points to a common end but were always similar, at least in this respect. The same 'fact'

This paper was previously unpublished.

could be interpreted in two ways unless one has a historical knowledge of the societies concerned, so as to make the choice.

In politics, the spread of social democracy in the form of 'welfarism' is taken as another sign of convergence to a common pattern. Quite how growing wealth (as measured by GDP *per capita* or otherwise) causes a higher level of welfare benefits is never adequately spelt out. The advocates of the theory have been content to assert the connection and to produce empirical evidence which seems to support it.

For convergence theory to be convincing as an explanation of the social and political patterns of advanced industrial countries two requirements must be met. Firstly, an explanation for the convergence of *particular* institutions must be fully worked out. Secondly, the empirical evidence must support hypotheses which are validly deduced from the theory of the convergence of advanced societies and they must do so without ambiguity in the interpretation of the results.

A fully worked out explanation demands that a social effect (such as the predominance of the nuclear family) is explained by other social patterns, such as the higher geographical mobility demanded by industrial economies. A full explanation sets out the mechanisms of *how* industrial societies might produce similar social patterns. A weak or statistical explanation (which is not a true explanation at all) simply shows the correlation between an indicator of advanced industrialisation (e.g. GDP *per capita*) and a social or political effect (e.g. infant mortality per 1,000 live births). Now, if this correlation is 1 or unity, we might be satisfied since the 'explanation' is complete in one sense; advanced industrial countries always have nuclear family patterns we could say. What sort of mechanism translates wealth into low infant mortality may be interesting to know, but it is not strictly necessary since the relationship always holds and we can operate with it and predict results with it. Only if the correlations are less than 1 do we need to spell out the mechanisms linking advanced industrialisation to low infant mortality or to nuclear family patterns (for example).

But the correlations are not unity, Castles and McKinlay report that only 15 per cent of the variance in infant mortality is 'explained' by differences in GPD *per capita*. It follows then, that other causes also produce differences in the rates of infant mortality in the group of advanced countries for which the authors had data. The authors suggest that the way in which welfare benefits are distributed is one cause of the differences in the rates of infant mortality. The distribution of welfare benefits is a political matter; countries with equal GPDs per head will distribute welfare benefits differently, according to their political structures and ideologies. If this were not the case, equal GDP *per capita* would always lead to the same, or close to the same, rates of infant mortality.

Now that we have a theory (Castles' and McKinlay's amalgamated model) which allows for multiple causes of social and political effects, we can discover how the causes are arranged – i.e. which cause precedes which, and how the several causes are 'weighted' – i.e. which are the stronger causes and which are the weaker? The results of the 'weighting' of causes may be seen in the authors' Table 17.5, from their multiple-regression analysis using several independent variables. In Table 17.5 they compare the importance of each of their political variables to the economic one of *per capita* wealth (measured by GDP) in accounting for differences in general welfare. As they point out in note 20, the gap between the richest of the poor countries and the poorest of the rich countries is about $3,000 per head. Three of their six political dichotomies or alternatives require bigger increments in GDP *per capita* to equalise welfare benefits than the gap between the group of rich countries and the group of poor countries.

So politics does matter. Political variables are independent causes of differences in the distribution of welfare benefits, along with the variable of *per capita* wealth. Moreover, political variables are important causes of differences in levels of welfare benefits, not simply minor factors.

The empirical evidence presented in this paper does not support one of the theories of the convergence of industrial societies. To the contrary it asserts an independent and large effect due to differences in political structures and beliefs. How then did the convergence theory gain the major hold that it has? I would suggest two reasons for the tenacity of the theory, one from the history of social thought and the other from statistical error.

1. A strong impetus was given to theories of convergence by the writings of classical sociologists in the period at the turn of the nineteenth and early twentieth centuries. In particular I suggest that the works of Emile Durkheim (1893) in France, Max Weber (1925) in Germany, and the German-Italian sociologist Roberto Michels (1911) were very influential in this area. Weber's work on the increasing bureaucratisation of political and industrial organisations in developed countries suggested that bureaucrats would resemble each other more in their aims than they would obey the orders of their political masters or the owners of capital. Durkheim's work on the problems of social integration in mass society, which he equated with industrial society, suggested that the occupation which a man followed would become his main cultural bond to society and that family, or regional ties would weaken to the gain of the new industrial occupations. Michels exploded the myth of democracy, the common political doctrine of advanced societies, by predicting that any supposedly democratic organisation (whether the state or a political party) would necessarily be run by an oligarchy. It is no accident that all three writers were continental Europeans, responding to the rapid industrial and social change which northern Italy (after Italian unification), Germany (after Bismarck), and France (from the Second Empire) had experienced within the memory of each of the writers. Naturally, as industrialism transformed their societies, it was the similarities between their countries and others undergoing that same transformation which they saw most clearly.

A writer who drew on these sources but who was more 'popular' and therefore more widely read may be claimed as the immediate origin of the convergence theory. This is the American James Burnham. Burnham is an apostate Marxist who in his book, *'The Managerial Revolution'* (Burnham 1941) adds Marxist categories and thought to the contributions of Michels, Weber, and Durkheim. Burnham added to these doctrines the essentially

Marxist ideas of (a) the primacy of economic forces in determining the social and political superstructure of societies, and (b) the convergence of advanced societies to a common form – which in Marx takes the shape of monopoly capitalism.

Burnham, still Marxist enough to see the 'inevitable' end of capitalism becomes a heretic when he predicts its replacement not with socialism but by 'managerialism' – domination by the new managerial class. This class comprises the industrial managers, the administrative bureaucrats and high officials of the state. This new class does not *own* the means of production or administration, it *controls* them.

Burnham argues that Marxism is wrong in predicting that the masses can take power but partly right in predicting the growth of monopoly capitalism and of imperialist super-states. He amends Marxism with the idea of a new class – 'the managers'. All advanced societies, he argues, follow the same path in creating the conditions for this new class to arise and dominate through industrialisation which leads to centralisation and to large organisations. Domination by the managerial class is real but hidden from the masses. However, the slogans of democracy and social justice still obtain but are essentially empty. But the forms of social justice are still observed, particularly in the shape of social security and welfare benefits. The old ideology of *laissez-faire* capitalism with its doctrines of individualism, self-help, and minimum state intervention, is dead or dying, and the new managerial ideology of 'welfarism' and 'social justice' is replacing it.

Although Burnham's predictions derived from his theory have been falsified in many instances, his theory is still influential and his contribution to the convergence theory should be clear enough from the outline of his thinking given above. His influence has been mainly in political thought, but also to a lesser extent in sociology (Dahrendorf's theory of class conflict in industrial society, for example; Dahrendorf 1959). In short, the political convergence of advanced societies is due to their common domination, ideologically and politically, by the managerial élite, whose rise to power is produced by industrialisation which leads to large bureaucratic organisations in industry, the state, and in administration generally.

2. The second explanation for the hold which convergence theory seems to have on social scientists is an empirical one – the evidence seems to support it. Castles and McKinlay argue, in note 20, that their findings are in marked contrast to those of Wilensky and Cutright who both found empirical support for aspects of the convergence thesis. Can these differences in the evidence be explained?

Wilensky and Cutright both commit an error in deducing hypotheses to be tested from convergence theory. The theory proposes that *advanced* societies are growing more alike in their institutional structure. But Wilensky and Cutright include in their sample of countries which they investigate both advanced and relatively undeveloped societies. Wealth *per capita* is, as Castles and McKinlay show, one cause of the differences between societies in the distribution of welfare benefits, but only *one* of several causes. If the variable of wealth *per capita* is allowed to range widely, from $1,000 *per capita* or less to $7,000 *per capita* or more, then statistically the variable is going to obscure differences *between advanced* democratic countries. If you recall the regression line and scatter diagram in Smith between infant mortality rates and wealth *per capita*, you will notice that the relationship is not perfect by any means. You can see this by inspecting the residuals (the difference between the true position of the country and what the regression line supposes it to be) in the graph. Smith maximises the possible relationship between two variables by taking a wide range of countries, including such poorly developed economies as Albania, Bulgaria, Greece, Spain, and Yugoslavia. What is it that is being investigated in the convergence theory – the variance (or differences) *within* the group of advanced democratic countries or the variances *between* the group of low-income countries and the group of high-income, advanced countries? To demonstrate that wealthy countries spend more per head on welfare than poor countries is banal, even if the 'more' is expressed in terms of the *proportion* of GDP spent on welfare. With GDP below a certain point, which we need not define, the efficiency of the tax system is so poor and the relative cost of basic government services is so high that there is no financial surplus available to be distributed as welfare so that political options such as how much to redistribute in welfare are not available.

This is a statistical error which Wilensky *et al.,* have committed. It is furthermore an error in deduction, because the convergence theory requires that *advanced* democratic societies are similar in social patterns, such as welfare spending. To lump together both underdeveloped and developed countries is not a fair test of the theory.

Smith is not setting out to test the convergence theory but his results show how Wilensky and Cutright could have got the results which they did, in contrast to Castles' and McKinlay's findings.

References

Burnham, J. (1941) *The Managerial Revolution,* originally published in New York. Eng. edn, London: Penguin Books, 1962.

Dahrendorf, R. (1959) *Class and Class Conflict in Industrial Society,* originally published in German, 1957. Eng. trans. by the author, London: Routledge & Kegan Paul, 1959.

Durkheim, E. (1893) *The Division of Labour in Society,* originally published in French, Paris. Eng. trans. by George Simpson, New York: The Free Press of Glencoe, 1947.

Goldthorpe, J. H. (1964) 'The development of industrial society' *Sociological Review Monograph* **8,** Keele: University of Keele.

Michels, R. (1911) *Political Parties,* originally published in German, Leipzig. Eng. trans. New York: The Free Press, 1949.

Weber, M. (1925) *Wirtschaft und Gesellschaft,* originally published in German, Tubingen. Eng. trans. by A. M. Henderson and T. Parsons as *The Theory of Social and Economic Organisation,* New York: The Free Press, 1964.

Introduction

There has been a pronounced tendency in recent research for political scientists to be so concerned with explaining political behaviour in terms of social and cultural patterns and processes of economic development that the political mechanism has progressively emerged as a 'black box' automatically transforming social forces into authoritative decisions. Politics is not considered to have major consequences, partly because the discipline has been increasingly disinclined to see consequences as its province, but more crucially, because the intellectual apparatus of explanation that has been adapted is sufficiently deterministic to leave nothing for politics to explain. In short, politics has come to appear as irrelevant.[1]

The propensity to de-emphasize the significance of politics has been particularly prevalent in the field of policy studies. The recent cross-national policy studies have been able to draw upon a more enduring and well-established convergence theory of industrial society.

The convergence argument is basically that as societies adopt a progressively more industrial infrastructure, certain determinate processes are set in motion which make them more and more alike. Technology and economic development have their own inherent logic which has a levelling and convergent impact on diverse social structures, cultural traditions and political systems. Thus, Goldthorpe in a critical review of the literature on the development of industrial societies points out:

These factors (modern technology and an advanced economy) which make for uniformity in industrial societies are seen as largely overriding other factors which make for possible diversity, such as different national cultures or different political systems. Thus, the overall pattern of development which is suggested is one in which, once countries enter into the advanced stages of industrialization, they tend to become increasingly comparable in their major institutional arrangements and in their social systems generally. In brief a convergent pattern of development is hypothesized.[2]

This theory of industrial society makes quite clear the importance of the controlling role of the administrative apparatus in the emergent industrial society, while simultaneously suggesting the relative unimportance of differences in political structures and ideas.[3] Thus, seemingly, the new society has room for the state, but not for politics.

The end-of-ideology thesis is but another variation on the same theme. Political ideas no longer matter because:

The political problems of the industrial revolution have been solved: the workers have achieved industrial and political citizenship; the conservatives have accepted the welfare state; and the democratic left has recognized that an increase in overall state power carried with it more dangers to freedom than solutions to economic problems. The very triumph of democratic social revolution in the West ends domestic politics for those intellectuals who must have ideologies and utopias to motivate them to political action.[4]

While this formulation of the end of ideology thesis by Lipset has been much criticized for its conservative bias, its essential diagnosis of the cessation of ideological struggle in the industrialized nations of the West is accepted by those who, like Marcuse, see the working-class movement becoming ever more deradicalized through the 'Collusion of Business and Labour within the Strong State'.[5]

Naturally enough, the general acceptance of an inevitable logic of industrialism has mitigated against research into the possible impact of variations in political activity on the nature of policy outcomes in advanced democratic states. The assumption has generally been 'that the policy dilemmas facing decision-makers of public consumption expenditure are quite similar in all nations, regardless of system', and that, consequently, 'it should not be too surprising that the decisions are roughly similar'.[6]

Some more recent cross-national studies provide further corroboration for the general convergence thesis. Thus, Wilensky points out:

. . . the primacy of economic level and its demographic and bureaucratic correlates is support for a convergence hypothesis; economic growth makes countries with contrasting cultural and political traditions more alike in their strategy for constructing the floor below which no one sinks.[7]

Cutright has also shown that the variance in social security coverage and level of benefits could be explained by the level of energy consumption (his measure of economic development), and that the degree of political representativeness of a nation had very little impact on social security programmes.[8] Dye, in summarising a number of studies, concludes:

Thus most comparative cross-national policy studies indicate that health and welfare policies, regardless of political systems, are closely associated with levels of economic development.[9]

The apparent irrelevance of the influence of political factors on policy outputs now seems tantamount to conventional wisdom. While we do not wish to reject this conventional wisdom entirely, it is our contention that it has seriously underestimated the significance of politics in shaping social reality. Much research in the field of policy studies, in our opinion, has been guilty of emphasizing the processes whereby political activity is shaped to the neglect of the impact of politics on social life. What is required is a reassessment of the role of political activity as one among a number of crucial factors determining the nature and conduct of human affairs.[10] The basic objective of this paper is to make such a reassessment. We do so by examining public welfare outcomes in advanced democratic states. At least as far as this area of policy studies is concerned, we shall show that political structure and ideology are of vital consequence. Thus, contrary to conventional wisdom, politics does matter.

Research design

The population of this study consists of advanced democratic states. For our purposes, such states may be operationally defined as those which have a continuous history of universal suffrage, majority government, free elections for at least twenty years (since 1958), and a level of GNP *per capita* (in 1974) in excess of $2,000.[11]

Our primary objective is to try to explain the different levels of commitment to public welfare in these advanced democratic states. More precisely, we are concerned to analyse the relative utility of two rival models for explaining the variations in public welfare commitments.

We use four measures of public welfare as our dependent variables.

1. Total public educational expenditure as a percentage of gross domestic product.[12]
2. Total general government transfer payments as a percentage of gross domestic product – such as pensions, unemployment benefits, and social security.[13]
3. Infant mortality per 1,000 live births – this gives a measure of the diffusion of public health benefits.[14]
4. Welfare index – this general index is constructed by standardizing the variables of education, transfer payments and infant mortality, and adding them.[15]

Our analysis proceeds in three stages. In the first, we test the capacity of a 'politics is irrelevant' model to explain the variations in public welfare commitments in advanced democratic states; in the second stage, we test a 'politics matters' model; and in the third stage, we combine the two models and test this amalgamated model. The independent variable in the 'politics is irrelevant' model is *per capita* gross domestic product, which we use as the measure of the level of economic development. The dependent variables are the four measures of public welfare. From this simple model we derive two hypotheses:

Hypothesis 1:   The commitment to public welfare increases with the level of economic development.

Hypothesis 2:   The variation in countries' commitment to public welfare reduces with increases in economic development.

The rationale for each of these hypotheses derives unequivocally from the convergence theory of industrial society. If economic growth and technology are the overriding factors making for uniformity in industrialized societies, then we would expect hypothesis 1 to hold. Furthermore, we should also expect uniformity to be greater at higher levels of economic development, hence hypothesis 2.

We can test the first hypothesis by simply regressing each of the four welfare indicators into *per capita* gross domestic product. If we are to accept this hypothesis, then we need to find significant regression equations.

In order to test the second hypothesis, we need initially to rank the population of advanced democratic states in terms of *per capita* gross domestic product and divide them into two groups, the higher and lower income categories. We then calculate the variance of each of the welfare variables in the higher and lower income categories. We may then use the *F* test for equality of variance. If we are to be able to accept the second hypothesis, we would need to find that the variance in the welfare indicators is greater in the lower income category.

In the second stage of the analysis, we evaluate the utility of a 'politics matters' model. Instead of modelling variations in public welfare in terms of economic development, we attempt to model welfare using a set of political variables. Three political variables are used:

1. Type of political structure – we measure the formal distribution of power embodied in constitutional procedures in a dichotomous or dummy variable of unitary or federal structure.
2. Type of political leadership – we use Lijphart's distinction between competitive and coalescent leadership styles, which again constitutes a dummy variable.[16]
3. Dominant political ideology – we again use a dichotomous or dummy variable to measure the presence or absence of an ideological dominance of the Right in terms of whether a secular or religious party of the Right was in office for more than half the period, 1950–74.[17]

From the 'politics matters' model we can derive three hypotheses by relating the four dependent welfare variables to each of the three independent political variables:

Hypothesis 3: Federal states will be characterized by lower levels of welfare state provision than unitary states.

Hypothesis 4: States with competitive leadership styles will have lower levels of welfare state provision than those with coalescent styles.

Hypothesis 5: States, characterized by dominance of parties of the Right, will have lower levels of welfare than where this is not the case.

The rationale for hypothesis 3 derives from the different policy potential of federal and unitary structures. The crucial difference between federal and unitary states lies not so much in the devolution of power to local territorial units (all democratic states have some form of local government), but rather in the existence within federal states of institutional guarantees that the division of powers will not be arbitrarily changed without the consent of territorial subunits. For a variety of reasons, federal states impose serious constraints on policy outcomes which involve a major alteration in the distribution of scarce values. First, federal states tend to have greater inbuilt stipulated majority requirements than unitary states, which are expressly devised to make structural change extremely difficult. Second, the various structures and procedures which are inherent in federal systems – state governments, legislative chambers representing state interests at the national level, and constitutional courts – create a proliferation of political levers which can be used to defeat proposals for policy changes. Third, the restricted political competence of the central government makes it impossible for a truly national policy to emerge in these areas where states have independent powers.

The rationale for hypothesis 4 stems from the different nature of the utilization of power in systems with competitive and coalescent leadership styles. A coalescent leadership exists when leaders of opposing groups perceive that there are advantages to be derived from mutual accommodation and can create formal or informal coalitions to achieve that goal. In contrast, opposing élites are competitive when their only goal is to maximize the advantage of their own constituents at the expense of others. Thus, coalescent leadership is premised on a variable-sum conception of power, in which common advantages are a major determinant of policy-making; competitive leadership is premised on a zero-sum conception of power in which advantages are only to be won at the expense of others. To the degree that such leadership attitudes are general attributes of given types of political system, this will have important implications for policies designed to implement welfare-state objectives. Greater welfare is generally advocated in order to enhance the common advantage of the vast mass of the population, and necessarily involves certain groups foregoing advantages in order to promote the common good. Where leadership is competitive, those groups which stand to lose by greater welfare provision will resist such social reforms more strenuously than is likely to be the case where a coalescent leadership's most important consideration is the common advantage.

The rationale for hypothesis 5 starts from the proposition that the political ideologies espoused by political parties are likely to be reflected in the policies they adopt when in office. In general, the Left is associated with a set of political beliefs which favour greater economic and social equality, see welfare-state reforms as a crucial element in achieving social justice, and regard state interference as a means of procuring these goals. The Right is associated with opposition to such beliefs, generally premised on the arguments that carried too far they must be detrimental to individual freedom and destructive of social harmony. Moreover, these differences in the nature of political beliefs are firmly grounded in the material interests (i.e. class and occupational interests) of different groups within a society. The rationale for hypothesis 5 is the perfectly simple and old-fashioned notion that parties, whose programmes are less favourably inclined to welfare-state provision and a substantial proportion of whose voters may lose from the redistribution of resources effected by such provision, are less likely to implement welfare policies than parties for which this is not the case.

The test procedures for hypotheses 3, 4, and 5 are identical. In each case the political variable is dichotomized and the hypothesis asserts that the level of public welfare provision is higher in one category (for example, unitary systems). The appropriate test statistic is of course the one-tailed t test. We can achieve exactly the same result and at the same time provide a measure of the level of explained variation by using a simply, dummy-variable regression.[18] Consequently, we shall regress each of the welfare variables on to each of the political variables.

In the third and final stage of the analysis, we combine the 'politics is irrelevant' and the 'politics matters' models. In this combined model the dependent variable is the composite welfare index and the independent variables are *per capita* gross domestic product and the three political variables. The hypothesis derived from this model states:

Hypothesis 6: The level of public welfare commitment in advanced democratic states is a positive function of economic development, a unitary political structure, the absence of an ideological dominance of the Right, and coalescent political leadership.

The rationale for this hypothesis is simply an amalgam of the preceding individual rationales. The test procedure is to make a multiple regression of the composite welfare variable on to the economic and political variables. We will already know by this stage of the analysis which of the two basic models is the more useful in isolation. By using the combined, additive model, we may examine whether we can better explain levels of public welfare commitment using both economic and political variables.

Findings

Stage 1: The 'politics is irrelevant' model

We can find virtually no support for the first hypothesis. The regressions of three of the welfare variables – education, transfer payments, and the general welfare index – on to *per capita* gross domestic product do not produce significant regression equations. The regression for infant mortality does produce a significant result (at the 0.05 level), but the level of explained variation is low (15 per cent).[19] We are obliged to conclude, therefore, that the level of commitment to public welfare in advanced democratic states is unrelated to economic development.[20]

We can also find no support for the second hypothesis. The variance in transfer payments and infant mortality is lower in the higher income group of countries, but the variance in education and in the composite welfare index is greater in the higher income group (see Table 17.1). None of the differences, however, is significant.

Table 17.1 Variance in public welfare indicators in the higher and lower income categories of advanced democratic states.

	Variance in the higher income group	Variance in the lower income group
Educational expenditure	2.25	0.92
Transfer payments	18.57	33.75
Infant mortality	14.75	22.46
General welfare	5.13	4.35

Since we can find no support for either hypothesis, we must conclude that the 'politics is irrelevant' model cannot provide an adequate explanation of the behaviour of public welfare in advanced democratic states. Applied to the commitment to public welfare in these countries, the convergence theory in isolation is invalid.[21]

Stage 2: The 'politics matters' model

There is strong support for our third hypothesis. Though political structure appears to have no significant impact on levels of educational

Table 17.2 Mean levels of public welfare indicators by political structure.

Political structure	Public welfare indicators			
	Educational expenditure	Transfer payments	Infant mortality	General welfare
Unitary systems	6.02	17.46	13.43	0.77
Federal systems	5.60	12.65	17.98	−1.68
	(NS)*	(21)*	(25)*	(30)*
	(NS)†	(05)†	(01)†	(01)†

*This is the R^2 derived from the simple dummy variable regression.
†This is the significance level for the one-tailed t test.

expenditure, unitary systems have significantly higher levels of transfer payment, general welfare, and significantly lower levels of infant mortality (see Table 17.2).

There is also strong support for the fourth hypothesis. Although leadership style has no significant impact on the level of transfer

Table 17.3 Mean levels of public welfare indicators by political leadership style.

Leadership styles	Public welfare indicators			
	Educational expenditure	Transfer payments	Infant mortality	General welfare
Coalescent	6.10	17.16	13.25	0.97
Competitive	5.28	14.26	16.68	−1.35
	(20)*	(NS)*	(17)*	(30)*
	(05)†	(NS)†	(05)†	(01)†

*This is the R^2 derived from the simple dummy variable regression.
†This is the significance level for the one-tailed t test.

payments, countries with coalescent leadership styles have significantly higher levels of educational expenditure, general welfare, and significantly lower levels of infant mortality (see Table 17.3).

There is even stronger confirmation for the fifth hypothesis. States characterised by an ideological dominance of the Right, have significantly lower levels of performance on each of the four public welfare attributes (see Table 17.4).

Table 17.4 Mean levels of public welfare indicators by dominant political ideology.

Dominant ideology	Public welfare indicators			
	Educational expenditure	Transfer payments	Infant mortality	General welfare
Absence dominant Right	6.58	17.70	13.05	1.17
Presence dominant Right	5.22	13.98	16.55	−1.31
	(30)*	(15)*	(18)*	(37)*
	(01)†	(05)†	(05)†	(01)†

*This is the R^2 derived from the simple dummy variable regression.
†This is the significance level for the one-tailed t test.

The simple regressions, though not producing particularly high levels of explained variation, indicate unequivocally that the commitment to public welfare in advanced democratic states is influenced by political considerations.

We can generally improve the level of explained variation by regressing each of the welfare variables on to all of the political variables, i.e. by using multiple rather than simple regression. The sole exception is educational expenditure. The multiple regression in this case shows that we cannot improve on the simple regression of educational expenditure on ideology alone.[22] In the case of transfer payments, we find that both type of political structure and ideology appear as significant influences (with the type of political structure being the more important influence), and the level of explained variation increases to 29 per cent.[23] In the case of infant mortality, type of political structure and type of political leadership appear as significant influences (with type of political structure once again being the more important influence), and the level of explained variation increases to 39 per cent.[24] The most impressive result appears in the case of the general welfare index, where, with ideology and type of political structure as significant influences, the level of explained variation increases to 53 per cent.[25]

Though we are still somewhat removed from a complete explanation of the commitment to public welfare, it is quite clear that our second basic model makes a useful contribution to such an explanation. Thus, the answer to the question of whether politics is relevant for an understanding of the public welfare commitment in advanced democratic states is unequivocally that politics does matter.

Stage 3: The combined model

We have shown beyond reasonable doubt that there is substantial support for the 'politics matters' position and little support for the 'politics is irrelevant' position. We can still inquire, however, whether economic development has any impact once we have taken account of political differences.

To answer this question we need to make a multiple regression of the general welfare index on to the three political variables and *per capita* gross domestic product. This regression produces a very satisfactory level of explained variation (64 per cent), indicating thereby that hypothesis 6 is our strongest hypothesis. The significant estimators are types of political structure, ideology, and *per capita* gross domestic product. The successful equation is:

$$W = 1.63 - 1.43I - 2.79S + 0.000601G$$

Where W is the general welfare index;
  I is the type of ideology (ideological dominance of the Right is scored 1 and no such dominance is scored 0);
  S is the type of political structure (federal systems are scored 1 and unitary systems are scored 0);
  G is *per capita* gross domestic product.

We can see from this equation that if we hold constant ideology and *per capita* gross domestic product, unitary systems will have higher levels of public welfare than federal ones – in fact the difference is 2.79. Also, holding constant type of political structure and *per capita* gross domestic product, states without a dominant Right have higher levels of public welfare than those where there is such a dominant ideology – in fact the difference is 1.43. Finally, holding a constant type of political structure and ideology, countries with higher levels of economic development will have higher levels of public welfare – a differential in gross domestic product *per capita* of $1,000 between two countries will result in a differential in general welfare of 0.601.

At any one level of *per capita* gross domestic product, since the gap between the unitary and federal systems is greater than that between the non-right and right-wing systems, we will always find the hierarchy: unitary non-right followed by unitary Right, followed by federal non-right, followed by federal Right. However, we can see from Fig.17.1 that this hierarchy can be upset once we allow per capita gross domes-

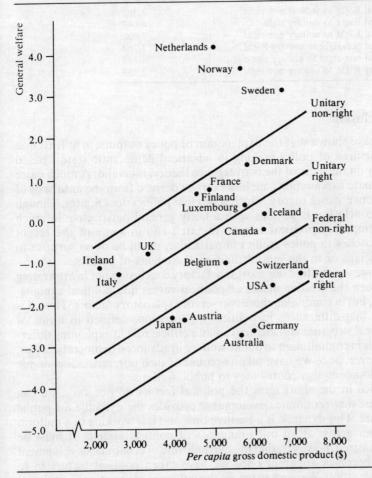

Fig. 17.1 General welfare by political organization and *per capita* gross domestic product.

tic product to vary (for example, a federal right-wing system can have a higher level of general welfare than a federal non-right system). We can see from Table 17.5, however, that there has to be a pronounced difference in *per capita* gross domestic product before any one type of political system attains the same level of commitment to public welfare as a country with a type of political system which is higher up the hierarchy.

Table 17.5 Size of *per capita* gross domestic product differential required to equalize general welfare differentials between different types of political organization.

Types of political organization	*Per capita* GDP
Federal Right to federal non-right	2,383
Federal Right to unitary right	4,647
Federal Right to unitary non-right	7,030
Federal non-right to unitary Right	2,264
Federal non-right to unitary non-right	4,647
Unitary Right to unitary non-right	2,383

Conclusion

We have shown that the explanation of policy outputs, in at least one major area of policy-making in advanced democratic states, based solely on the logic of the convergence theory, is invalid. A much more adequate explanation can, however, be derived from the antithesis of the convergence theory, which states that politics does matter. Though this conclusion is at odds with a fairly general perspective in much contemporary political science research and in some of the recent approaches to policy studies in particular, it will be of no surprise to politicians or to the more 'traditional' students of politics.

However, we find our most satisfactory conclusion not in arbitrating between the relative merits of political versus non-political explanations, but in combining these two sets of explanatory factors. Thus, it is clear that differences in political organization, defined in terms of political structure and ideology, play a critical role in explaining differentials in commitment to public welfare in advanced democratic states. However, once we have taken account of such differences, economic development also contributes to public welfare.

Since in the short term the political factors do not vary, we can suggest that economic development provides the dynamic for public welfare. This dynamic is a positive one, and it is working in a uniform manner across all of our four types of political system. It must be emphasized, however, that the dynamic role of economic development only becomes apparent once we have taken political factors in to consideration. Were we to ignore the influence of variations in political organization on public welfare commitment, we would even be unable to identify the dynamic role of economic development.

Thus, while economic development does encourage higher levels of public welfare within advanced democratic states, the dynamic of economic development is manifested only within quite pronounced differentials in public welfare provision, which are dictated by political considerations. Although economic development can erode differentials in public welfare among the different types of political organization found in advanced democratic states, the differences in levels of economic development in those countries have to be quite pronounced before the basic differentials, set by variations in political organization, are undermined.

In the context of the public welfare commitment in advanced democratic states, therefore, politics is both relevant and irrelevant. However, not only is politics more relevant than irrelevant, but also its irrelevance is only manifested once its relevance has been taken into account.

In short, politics does matter.

Notes and References

1. For a general discussion of this point, see G. D. Paige, 'The rediscovery of politics', in P. G. Lewis *et al.* (eds.), *The Practice of Comparative Politics,* London: Longman, 1978.
2. J. H. Goldthorpe, 'The development of industrial society', *Sociological Review Monograph,* **8** (1964), 97–8.
3. Such arguments are to be found for example in: J. K. Galbraith, *The New Industrial State,* London: Hamish Hamilton, 1967, and C. Kerr *et al., Industrialism and Industrial Man,* Cambridge, Mass.: Harvard U.P., 1960.
4. S. M. Lipset, *Political Man,* London: Heinemann, 1960, p. 406. Though the end of ideology school is principally associated with writers such as Lipset and Bell, it was anticipated in the mid-1950s by a commentator on the Swedish political scene. See, H. Tingsten, 'Stability and vitality in Swedish democracy', *Political Quarterly,* **26** (1955). For a more recent statement that ideological conflicts, which had motivated the party struggle, are dead or dying, see: R. M. Christenson *et al., Ideologies and Modern Politics,* London: Nelson, 1971.
5. H. Marcuse, *One Dimensional Man,* London: Routledge & Kegan Paul, 1964, p. 11.
6. F. L. Pryor, *Public Expenditures in Communist and Capitalist Nations,* Homewood: Richard D. Irvin, 1968, p. 310. For a rather different explanation, which none the less ends up with a similar conclusion, see F. Parkin, *Class Inequality and Political Order,* London: MacGibbon and Kee, 1971.
7. H. Wilensky, *The Welfare State and Equality,* Berkeley: University of California Press, 1975, pp. 27–8.
8. P. Cutright, 'Political structure, economic development, and national security programs', *American Journal of Sociology,* **70** (1965).
9. T. R. Dye, *Policy Analysis,* Alabama: University of Alabama Press, 1976, p. 51.
10. For some attempts at such a reassessment, see for example: A. J. Heidenheimer *et al., Comparative Public Policy,* London: Macmillan, 1976; A. King, 'Ideas, institutions, and the policies of governments: a comparative analysis', *British Journal of Political Science,* **3** (1973); B. G. Peters *et al.,* 'Types of democratic systems and types of public policy', *Comparative Politics,* **9** (1977).
11. The countries making up the population are: Australia, Austria, Belgium, Canada, Denmark, Finland, France, Germany, Iceland, Ireland, Israel, Italy, Japan, Luxembourg, The Netherlands, New Zealand, Norway, Sweden, Switzerland, United Kingdom, United States. We have been obliged to exclude Israel because of missing data. New Zealand is excluded from part of the analysis (transfer payments and general welfare) for the same reason.

12. The data points for all the variables, unless stated otherwise, is 1974 or the last year of available data closest to 1974. The data for educational expenditure is taken from *UNESCO Statistical Yearbook 1975*, (1976), Paris.

13. The data for transfer payments is taken from *OECD Economic Surveys* (1977), Paris.

14. The data for infant mortality is taken from *OECD Economic Surveys* (1977), Paris. Infant mortality operationalizes a slightly different feature of public welfare than education and transfer payments. While the former profiles impact, the latter two profile commitments to welfare. We use infant mortality to measure public health, as it is impossible to obtain comparable health expenditure figures. We choose infant mortality rather than the number of doctors, a common measure of health standards, because it is in our opinion a more valid measure of public health. The variable of number of doctors includes doctors employed in both the public and private sectors, and therefore confounds public and private aspects of welfare. Infant mortality also reflects private aspects of welfare, but to a lesser degree. If access to public health facilities is low, even though the number of doctors may be high, then infant mortality will be high. In other words, infant mortality is a better measure of the diffusion of public health benefits. This argument is supported by an examination of the correlation between infant mortality and the number of doctors, which is a highly significant one of 0.56. (The superficial moral of this story may be that if you have a sick infant, do not send it to the doctor.) The explanation, of course, derives from socialized medicine. Several advanced, democratic states have relatively high numbers of doctors, but in the absence of socialized medicine access to these doctors is severely restricted. Hence we can find relatively high levels of infant mortality, despite a relatively high number of doctors.

15. Since the direction of infant mortality is opposite to education and transfer payments (i.e. high infant mortality indicates low welfare), we have standardized the reciprocal of infant mortality.

16. A. Lijphart, 'Typologies of democratic systems', *Comparative Political Studies*, 1 (1968). Lijphart in fact uses two criteria of distinction: that between homogeneous and fragmented political cultures, and between coalescent and competitive leadership behaviour. This leads to four types of democratic system, which Lijphart describes as 'centripetal' (homogeneous and competitive), 'centrifugal' (fragmented and competitive), 'consociational' (fragmented and coalescent), and 'depoliticized' (homogeneous and coalescent). We omit the classification based on political culture, as taken in isolation it points to the social mechanisms by which conflict can be reconciled within groups, but ignores the political mechanisms which may exist to reconcile differences between groups. Lijphart himself in attempting to explain political stability accords priority to the leadership distinction. For an attempt to investigate the policy consequences of each of the four types of political system, see Peters *et al.*, 'Types of democratic system and types of public policy'.

17. All attempts to compare countries along an ideological dimension involve complex operational problems. Here we shall not try to place nations on a common ideological spectrum, but simply locate countries according to whether the major parliamentary party of the Right has been in office for more than a stipulated period. We concede that such a measure is crude and only taps one aspect of cross-national ideological differences, but would suggest that it does at least avoid many of the insuperable difficulties that are inherent in the attempt to locate nation-specific beliefs on a single cross-national spectrum. We require that parties of the Right be in office for more than half the stipulated period in order that they can have had a significant impact on policy. If the party of the Right was in office in coalition with other parties, we require that the party of the Right must hold more parliamentary seats than the other parties combined. In the case of Christian Democratic parties, a distinction is made between countries in which a secular party of the Right has consistently polled more than 10 per cent of the pole and those in which they have not. In the former (Belgium, Luxembourg, and The Netherlands), the secular party is classified as the party of the Right, and in the latter (Austria, Germany, Italy, and Switzerland), the Christian Democratic Party is so classified.

18. In a dummy variable regression of the form: $y = a + bx$, the a term corresponds to the mean of one group, and the term $a + b$ corresponds to the mean of the other group. Consequently, the test of significance for the b term is exactly analogous to a test of the difference of means ($m_1 - m_2 = (a + b) - a = b$). The test of the significance of the b is analogous to a two-tailed t test, and so we divide the significance value by two to get the one-tailed test.

19. These results are from simple linear regressions. It could be argued by convergence theorists that with increasing economic growth there will be a change in the marginal utility of public and private goods. This could lead either to a relative reduction in the level of welfare (i.e. welfare would continue to increase with economic development but at a slower rate) or an absolute reduction in welfare (i.e. welfare would continue to increase with economic development but after a certain point begin to decline). In both cases welfare is a function of economic development, but we would be hypothesizing respectively logarithmic and quadratic relationships between welfare and economic development instead of the linear relationship. We have tested for these relationships, but the logarithmic and quadratic regressions still yield insignificant results.

20. These results are in marked contrast to the findings of Cutright and Wilensky. The superficial explanation for the divergence lies in the composition of the population. While we use only high-income countries, Cutright and Wilensky combine both high- and low-income countries. In so doing, they perpetrate, in our opinion, a major methodological mistake. The problem derives from the huge gap in *per capita* incomes between the high- and low-income countries. This gap results in a major discontinuity in the distributions of *per capita* GDP. The distribution of countries along the variable of *per capita* GDP is in fact bimodal. The majority of low-income countries, ranging in *per capita* GDP from $100 to $1,000, are separated by a huge gap from the majority of high-income countries, ranging in *per capita* GDP from $4,000 to $7,000. The problem in regressing any variable on to *per capita* GDP for a population, containing both high- and low-income countries, is essentially a variant of the outlier problem. We are dealing in this situation basically with two groups of outliers. Essentially all that Wilensky and Cutright have discovered is that public welfare is higher in the high-income countries. Given that there is a difference, then it is very easy to find a significant regression equation, because the huge gap in *per capita* GDP between the high- and low-income countries cancels out any variation that may exist in each of these two groups. We would be quite happy to accept the conclusions of Wilensky and Cutright if in addition to finding a difference in welfare between the high- and low-income countries, they had also shown a systematic relationship between welfare and *per capita* GDP in each of these distrinct populations. However, as our results demonstrate very clearly such a relationship does not hold in the population of high-income countries.

21. One possible salvation of the convergence theory still remains in the argument that a relationship between welfare and economic development in the high-income countries would not be expected. Thus, it could be argued that, since convergence has by and large already taken place, the most salient characteristic of the variance in welfare among the advanced democratic states is that it is extremely small. Any remaining variance is likely to be due to idiosyncratic features rather than levels of economic development. Since convergence theorists have never argued that societies are becoming identical, this is a perfectly plausible and consistent position. This argument hinges on the claim that the variance in welfare among the advanced states is very small. This, however, is not the case. The coefficients of variation of education, infant mortality, and transfer payments are respectively 0.21, 0.29, and 0.31. These coefficients are unequivocally not small. (Put another way less precise way, variations in levels of education of 4.1 to 7.8, in infant mortality of 9.6 to 22.6, and in transfer payments from 9.1 to 22.6 can hardly be construed as extremely small.) Thus, even this final salvation for the convergence theory is invalid.

22. The R^2 remains at 30. Leadership style, which in simple terms does have a significant relationship with education, does not enter into the equation because of its relatively high correlation (0.70) with ideology. Thus, the aspects of education which can be explained by leadership are contained within the aspects explained by ideology. (The relatively high correlation between ideology and leadership style is no great surprise. It will be recalled that the rationales for each of these variables, which were developed in the research design, were tolerably similar.)

23. Since both of the independent variables are measured on the same scale, we can use the regression coefficients to gain a precise indication of the relative importance of each variable. The regression coefficients for political structure and ideology are respectively 4.04 and 2.72.

24. The regression coefficients for political structure and political leadership are 4.32 and 3.17. The reason for the failure of ideology to appear, even though it has a significant simple relationship with infant mortality, is once again due to its correlation with leadership style (see note 22).

25. The regression coefficients for ideology and political structure are 2.02 and 1.88, respectively.

Index